Computer Models for Facial Beauty Analysis

David Zhang · Fangmei Chen
Yong Xu

Computer Models for Facial Beauty Analysis

David Zhang
The Hong Kong Polytechnic University
Hung Hom
Hong Kong

Yong Xu
Harbin Institute of Technology
Shenzhen
China

Fangmei Chen
Tsinghua University
Shenzhen
China

ISBN 978-3-319-81323-3 ISBN 978-3-319-32598-9 (eBook)
DOI 10.1007/978-3-319-32598-9

Softcover reprint of the hardcover 1st edition 2016

Printed on acid-free paper

This Springer imprint is published by Springer Nature
The registered company is Springer International Publishing AG Switzerland

Preface

The human face plays an important role in daily life. Pursuing beauty, especially facial beauty, is the nature of human beings. As the demand for esthetic surgery has increased tremendously over the past few years, an understanding of beauty is becoming utmost important for medical settings.

The physical beauty of faces affects many social outcomes, such as mate choices and hiring decisions. Facial beauty analysis is an emerging topic. The study of facial beauty has attracted efforts of researchers from diverse fields. However, most existing works focus on verifying the relevance between predefined characteristics and facial beauty, and they are far from adequate for developing application systems. Recently, computational facial analysis has been developed rapidly and is successfully used in applications of face verification, expression recognition, age estimation, etc. Besides a couple of methods, algorithms and schemes in general computational facial analysis communities can be applied to facial beauty analysis. Many new ideas, specialized methods and research paths have been proposed in this field. Of course, there have been sufficient new research outputs on facial beauty analysis and it is meaningful to summarize them including the newest research advance, technical means, experimental analysis, and results as well as possible applications of them.

This book is based on our research work and has the following background: previous studies on facial beauty analysis have drawbacks. Though experimental evaluation based on large-scale databases is very important for demonstrating the performance of beauty analysis methods and schemes, it seems that some of previous studies lack sufficient experiments and definitely convincing experimental results. In addition, though various studies including ideas, methods, and schemes on facial beauty are available, there are no very comprehensive comparison and testing under a fair and benchmark condition. In addition, almost all previous studies did not provide practical facial beauty analysis systems.

One of main focuses of this book is on computer models for facial beauty analysis. Moreover, our goal is to make more objective and quantitative analysis of facial beauty. As a result, all studies are based on the well-defined metric, quantitative algorithms, and procedures. Compared to most of previous works, our studies lay much emphasis on data-driven research as well as evidence—and seriously experimentally tested—based facial beauty analysis. Large-scale database-based and repeatable experiments are another characteristic of our studies. Main aspects of our novel studies include the proposed new hypotheses, computationally efficient mathematical models and algorithms, and serious experimental evaluation. Moreover, all putative rules on facial beauty perception used in previous and our studies are fairly tested with biometric techniques and large databases. In the book, detailed descriptions on methods, schemes, and procedures of our studies allow readers to grasp well and easily apply them.

This book explores the secrets of facial beauty with a computational perspective and also provides the following techniques that are used in our facial beauty analysis: face image processing, facial landmark extraction, face representation, face image warping, and soft biometrics. Since the facial beauty is measurable, and there have been a long period of facial beauty studies, the book first introduces previous works including hypotheses, definitions, evidences, and experiments. Then the book turns into a systematic introduction to our studies, including the idea, hypotheses, scientific means, computational results, and conclusions. The comparison between previous and our studies is also included. Finally, we present a facial beauty analysis system designed by our research team and make a prospect for future work.

The book is organized into five main parts. Part I briefly introduces the basic concepts and some typical facial beauty analysis methods. Part II presents some useful features and face models on facial beauty study. Moreover, feature selection and fusion methods related to our study are also presented in this part. In Part III, some hypotheses based on facial beauty perception methods are described. Some computational models of facial beauty analysis are defined in Part IV. The final part shows an online facial beautification simulation system and makes a conclusion for the book.

This book will be beneficial to researchers, professionals, and postgraduate students working in the fields of computer vision, pattern recognition, biometrics, multimedia, etc. The book will also be very useful for interdisciplinary researchers.

December 2015

David Zhang
Fangmei Chen
Yong Xu

Acknowledgments

We would like to express our special gratitude to Dr. Zhaotian Zhang and Dr. Ke Liu in National Natural Science Foundation of China (NSFC) for their help and support. Sincere thanks should go to both Dr. Lei Zhang and Dr. Mingming Sun for their useful contribution to some chapters in this book. We would also like to express our gratitude to Mr. Xihua Xiao for his system design. Moreover, we would like to thank Mr. Jie Wen for his editing work.

Contents

Part I
Introduction

Chapter 1
Overview

The physical beauty of faces affects many social outcomes. The secrets of facial beauty have attracted the attention of researchers from many fields. Recently, computer-based facial beauty analysis has become an emerging research topic, which has many potential applications. This chapter reviews the history of facial beauty research, discusses the key problems and challenges in computer-based facial beauty analysis, and introduces the databases used in the following chapters. After reading this chapter, people will have some shallow ideas on computer-based facial beauty analysis.

1.1 Background

Human faces play an important role in our social life, from which we can obtain many kinds of information, such as identity, gender, race, age, emotions, health, personality, and attractiveness. In recent years, as the performances of computers and digital cameras have significantly improved, computer-based facial image analysis has attracted extensive attention. The most investigated research topic is face recognition, which has been successfully used in entrance control, homeland security, and computer security (Li and Jain 2011). However, research on computer-based facial beauty analysis is still in its infancy. There are many problems waiting for us to explore (Gunes 2011; Laurentini and Bottino 2014).

Different from the attributes of identity, expression, and age, the study of facial beauty not only involves faces, which are aesthetic objects, but also concerns humans which are aesthetic subjects. Therefore, it is an interdisciplinary problem. Different disciplines have different aims and scopes. Psychology emphasizes the human part. For example, how facial attractiveness affects employment and mate choices (Walster et al. 1966; Dion 1972; Sala et al. 2013; Huh et al. 2014), and the agreement of facial beauty judgments between individuals or different cultural groups (Cunningham et al. 1995; Langlois et al. 2000; Honekopp 2006).

D. Zhang et al., *Computer Models for Facial Beauty Analysis*,
DOI 10.1007/978-3-319-32598-9_1

Evolutionary biology aims to interpret the rules of facial beauty perception from the evolutionary perspective (Penton-Voak 2011; Little et al. 2011; Rhodes 2006). Aesthetic plastic surgery aims to find rules for surgery planning and preview of results (Farkas et al. 1985; Wang et al. 1997; Choe et al. 2004). Neuroscience researchers are interested in physiological reactions of brains during the process of facial beauty perception (Martín-Loeches et al. 2014). Computer scientists attempt to discover the rule of facial beauty perception from data, build computational models of facial beauty, and develop application systems (Leyvand et al. 2008; Gray et al. 2010). Facial beauty perception involves complicated mental activities, which may change with different times and cultures. However, for a specific time and culture, it is found that people use similar criteria in their judgments of facial beauty. Humanity disciplines study facial beauty perception from historical and cultural perspective, whereas engineering disciplines focus on the consistency and regularities of facial beauty perception. The findings of studies from different fields are complimentary and deepen our understanding of facial beauty perception.

Computer-based facial beauty study aims to discover the rules of facial beauty from data using techniques such as image processing, statistical analysis, and machine learning, and develop application systems based on the discovered rules. One may have concern of whether there are some shared rules or if facial beauty is just in the eye of the beholder. At the individual level, different persons may have different opinions about the attractiveness of some specific faces. However, at the population level, there are obvious trends of facial beauty preferences. Many psychological studies show that although some individual differences exist, strong agreement is found between facial beauty judgments of people even from different races and cultural backgrounds (Martin 1964; Udry 1965; Cunningham et al. 1995; Langlois et al. 2000). Hence, the rules obtained from one subset of people are also applicable to others. This is the rationale of data-driven facial beauty analysis and guarantees the usability of the findings.

In the past 20 years, the Internet has developed very fast, and has supplied a large number of facial images, especially those of beautiful celebrities. Collecting enough facial images with diversified attractiveness is essential in database construction. At the same time, some related topics on facial image analysis have been extensively studied, such as face recognition and facial expression analysis. The methods that are successfully used in these topics can be helpful for facial beauty analysis. For example, facial landmark localization, facial feature extraction, and pattern recognition algorithms are important modules in all image-based facial analysis tasks.

Computer-based facial beauty analysis has many potential applications. Some typical applications are as follows:

- Plastic aesthetic surgery and cosmetic industries. The pursuit of beauty is part of human nature and has been since ancient times. In modern society, with the development of plastic surgery techniques, more and more people are willing to spend money on aesthetic surgery and cosmetics to obtain more beautiful faces, which are beneficial for finding jobs and partners. According to the statistical report of the American Society for Aesthetic Plastic Surgery (American Society for Aesthetic Plastic Surgery 2013), Americans spent more than 120 million dollars on aesthetic plastic surgery. As a country with a large population, the demand of China is in second place, just following the United States. Also, cosmetics are daily consumer goods for most young women. The rules learned from data are valuable for surgery and makeup planning. Moreover, the preview of different plans can be generated by utilizing image synthesis techniques, which make it convenient for users to compare and make choices.

- Social networks. For example, an online dating website often requires users to upload their images, especially facial images. Facial beauty is an important factor for first impressions, which affects the users' decision. If the website can automatically know the attractiveness of facial images and add the beauty score to their recommender system, then the satisfaction of users could be further improved.
- Image editing applications. Digital cameras and smartphones are popular in daily life. It has become a fashion to share images with friends via social networks. Many people would like to beautify captured photos before uploading. The well-known Photoshop software developed by Adobe is a powerful image editing tool. However, it requires professional skills and practical experience. Recently, a number of mobile Apps have sprung up and achieved commercial success. However, to the best of our knowledge, existing products still have many limitations. For example, most of the Apps require manual operations, and the beautification results are not always satisfactory. Automatic and intelligent face beautification methods would make a great improvement in the usability and performance of these Apps.

Moreover, computer-based facial beauty analysis can also be applied to animation design and arts.

1.2 History of Facial Beauty Research

Although computer-based facial beauty analysis is a new member in pattern recognition society, research on facial beauty is not new. It began in ancient times and has lasted to today. The history of facial beauty study can be divided into several stages, from the ideal ratios proposed by ancient artists to the measurement-based rules used in aesthetic plastic surgery and from the hypotheses proposed by modern psychologists to data-driven facial beauty modeling emerging in the computer science society. The following sections give an overview of each stage.

1.2.1 Early Exploration of Facial Beauty

The exploration of human physical beauty dates back 4000 years. In order to create beautiful and harmonious works, artists in ancient Egypt defined a series of ratio rules of the human body. Sculptors of ancient Greece and ancient Rome followed the Egyptian rules. For example, the sculptor Polycleitus (450-420 BC) indicated that the length of face is 1/10 of the body height, and the length of the head is 1/8 of the body height (Atiyeh and Hayek 2008). Artists during the Renaissance developed more detailed ratio rules, which are called neoclassical rules. The Golden ratio ($\Phi = 1.618$) was also believed to underlie beautiful faces. In ancient China, there were also rules defined in ratios, e.g., the vertical thirds and horizontal fifths rule. Faces that conformed to the defined rules were considered to be harmonious and beautiful.

Early explorations of facial beauty tried to find some numerical descriptions, mostly in the form of ratio rules. Some of the rules are still applied in modern arts and aesthetic surgery. However, restricted by the time, district, and measuring techniques, those rules have some limitations. First, they have limited precision. Most of ratios are defined in the form of simple numbers or fractions, e.g., 1, 1/3, and 1/5, according to subjective observations and preferences. Although these ratios can be used as references during artistic creation, they are often not consistent with the true values measured on real faces (Chen and Zhang 2014). Second, the rules are not complete. Only vertical and horizontal ratios are concerned, which can only describe the size and position of facial organs. The shape of facial organs and skin texture, which are also important factors of facial beauty, are ignored.

1.2.2 Facial Beauty Study in Psychology

In 1960s, two important findings facilitated the study of facial beauty in the psychological field. In 1964, Martin found that people from different backgrounds have similar judgments of facial beauty (Martin 1964). Walster et al. (1966) found that facial attractiveness significantly affected dating behavior. After that, more researchers joined facial beauty study and published thousands of papers. Table 1.1 lists the problems concerned in psychology and the progress of the solutions. It can be seen that most of the problems focus on social and historical factors in facial beauty perception. For example, social factors include context (e.g., heterosexual/homosexual Feingold 1988, self-assessment Feingold 1992), age (e.g., young adults Perrett et al. 1994, infants Slater et al. 1998, elderly persons Mathes et al. 1985), atypical forms of facial preference (e.g., prosopagnosia), social consequences of facial beauty (e.g., marriage Walster et al. 1966, income Sala et al. 2013; Huh et al. 2014, and treatment Dion 1972). Historical factors include how the trends of individual's and population's facial beauty preferences change with time. Another category of research is trying to find the internal cause of facial preference.

Table 1.1 Current state of knowledge on facial beauty

Problem	State of knowledge
Facial beauty assessment in various contexts	
• Reproductive context (dating, mating, marriage)	★★★★
• Same-sex persons	★★★☆
• Self-assessment	★★★☆
• Social context	★★☆☆
• A context suggesting kinship	★★☆☆
Age of judges and assessed persons	
• Young adults	★★★★
• Infants	★★★☆
• Children, adolescents	★★☆☆
• Elderly persons	★☆☆☆
Determinants of facial beauty	
• Averageness, symmetry, masculinity, frontal and profile view	★★★☆
• Scalp and facial hair, color of skin and hair, skin condition, expression	★★☆☆
• Eyes color, semi-profile view	★★☆☆
• Relative importance of determinants	★★☆☆
Inter-population variation of preferences	
• Populations exposed to Western culture	★★☆☆
• Populations not exposed to Western culture	★☆☆☆
Determinants of facial beauty	
• Biological quality	★★★☆
• Personality, experience	★★☆☆
• Ecological factors	★★☆☆
• Intellectual competence and education level	★★☆☆
Intra-population variation of preferences over time	★★☆☆
Intra-individual variation of preferences over time	★☆☆☆
Determinants of intra-individual variation of preferences	
• Menstrual cycle	★★★☆
• Other factors	★☆☆☆
Atypical forms of facial preferences	★☆☆☆
Physiological explanations	
• Of facial beauty	★★★☆
• Of facial preferences	★★☆☆
Ontogenetic explanations	
• Of facial beauty	★★☆☆
• Of facial preferences	★★☆☆
• Heritability of facial beauty and facial preferences	★☆☆☆
Phylogenetic explanations	★☆☆☆
Functional explanations	★★☆☆

(continued)

Table 1.1 (continued)

Problem	State of knowledge
Social consequences of facial beauty	
• Short-term	★★★★
• Long-term	★☆☆☆
Biological consequences of facial beauty	★★☆☆

★★★★—quite good, ★★★☆—moderate, ★★☆☆—poor, ★☆☆☆—very poor

For example, some researchers tried to find physiological explanations of facial preference, using fMRI to track brain activities during facial beauty perception (Martín-Loeches et al. 2014) or analyzing the effects of hormone levels on facial preference (Welling et al. 2008). Some researchers tried to find functional explanations and considered that facial preference reflects a kind of evolutionary adaption (Little et al. 2011). Another branch of study focuses on faces, e.g., finding general patterns of facial beauty. The averageness, symmetry, and sexual dimorphism hypotheses have been proposed and extensively investigated.

As shown in Table 1.1, although very many problems have been proposed, only a few of them have been well investigated, whereas most of them still have not been solved. The study of facial beauty from social, historical, and physiological perspectives has many difficulties. For example, it needs 60 years to study the trend of one person's facial beauty preference (from 10 years old to 70 years old). Researchers need to explore remote and isolated districts when studying the differences of two culture-isolated populations in facial beauty preference, which requires a long period and ample financial support. Based on image synthesis techniques, the study of facial beauty patterns has become more convenient and developed fast. However, the patterns are limited to several hypotheses, which are hard to use to solve practical problems in real-life applications.

1.2.3 Facial Beauty Study in Aesthetic Surgery

The patterns of facial beauty are also studied in the aesthetic plastic surgery field. Similar to the early explorations, the rules of facial beauty are also defined in ratio form. However, anthropometry is applied, and the rules are more objective and accurate than the traditional rules. Farkas et al. (1985) measured the neoclassical rules on 153 faces of American Caucasians and found that most of the neoclassical rules were not consistent with the measured values. Wang et al. (1997) measured 206 Chinese faces and compared the results with those of Farkas, finding that the nosewing of Chinese is wider than that of Caucasians and the mouth width of Chinese is smaller than that of Caucasians. Choe et al. (2004) measured 72 Korean faces and found they were not consistent with the neoclassical rules. The golden ratio rules were also tested with measurements on real faces. The results showed that in most cases, the golden ratio is outside the normal range of the defined ratios. Fan et al. (2012) generated a synthesized face with the most golden ratios, which only obtained a low beauty score in their rating experiment.

The above works show that the neoclassical rules and golden ratios are not accurate, but the idea of using ratios to describe facial geometry has been accepted. Ratios corrected according to real faces are used to help diagnosis and guide surgery planning. Nevertheless, it is still not clear that with so many ratio rules which ones/combinations are more important. In practice, the experience of surgeons plays a more important role, and the ratio rules only serve as a reference.

1.2.4 Facial Beauty Study in Computer Science

The rapid development of computer science has not only changed people's way of life but has also promoted research in many other disciplines. Computer science also facilitates the study of facial beauty. Computer-based facial beauty study is divided into four stages.

In the first stage (1990–2000), the published works on facial beauty study were dominated by psychology and aesthetic surgery fields. Computers were used to generate stimuli images or measure ratio values. Some problems were raised but unsolved, e.g., finding a relative and complete feature set for facial beauty analysis and comparing the discriminative power of different kinds of features, which provides the motivation of computer-based facial beauty analysis. At the same time, the Internet and computer-based information processing techniques were developing very fast. Many effective algorithms in image processing and machine learning fields were proposed and successfully applied, which laid the foundation for computer-based facial beauty analysis.

The second stage (2001–2007) focused on automatic facial beauty prediction based on ratio features. It was a transitional stage. On one hand, the ratio features were selected according to the traditional rules. On the other hand, the idea of data-driven facial beauty modeling was proposed, and machine learning algorithms were applied for facial beauty analysis. First, a data set of facial images were prepared, and the beauty scores of the faces were collected by rating experiments (Schmid et al. 2008; Eisenthal et al. 2006; Whitehill and Movellan 2008; Kagian et al. 2006; Gunes and Piccardi 2006). Second, the selected ratio features were extracted based on the facial images (Schmid et al. 2008; Gunes and Piccardi 2006). Third, a computational model of facial beauty was built by supervised learning methods (Schmid et al. 2008; Eisenthal et al. 2006;), such as linear regression (Duda et al. 2000) and support vector regression (SVM) (Vapnik 1995). The performance of the model was evaluated by the Pearson correlation between the predicted beauty scores and human-rated beauty scores. The limitations of the research in this stage were: (1) the data sets used for building models were of small-scale (91–452). (2) Only ratio features were used for building facial beauty prediction models. However, other features, such as the shape of facial organs and skin conditions, are also important factors of facial beauty. Hence, the models built in this stage had limited performances.

In the third stage (2008–2009), computer-based facial beauty study was further developed and had more applications. Some successful image processing methods were employed to facilitate the automation of facial beauty analysis. The Viola-Jones (Viola and Jones 2001) method was used for face detection, active shape models (ASMs) (Cootes et al. 1995) was used for facial landmark localization, and the Multilevel Free-Form Deformation (MFFD) (Ojala et al. 2002) algorithm was used for facial deformation. The models learned from data were used to guide facial geometry beautification, which is an application of the facial beauty models. In this stage, the experiments were still based on databases of small size, and the study still only focused on geometric features.

The fourth stage is from 2010 to today. Computer-based facial beauty analysis has the following tendency. First, the size of the facial image data sets are significantly increased, and the sources of the images are various, including those collected from the web (Gray et al. 2010) and videos (Leyvand et al. 2008). Second, in addition to geometric features, local descriptors that work well in facial recognition are also used to build facial beauty models, e.g., the Gabor filter response (Liu and Wechsler 2002) and Local Binary Patterns (LBP) (Ojala et al. 1996). Third, up-to-date machine learning algorithms are applied to facial beauty modeling, e.g., the convolutional neural network (Gray et al. 2010), cost-sensitive ordinal regression (Yan 2014), and deep learning (Gan et al. 2014), which is very popular. It can be seen that with the development of the relative research topics, the methods for facial beauty modeling become more diversified. However, compared to face recognition and expression recognition, facial beauty modeling is still in its infancy. Many specific problems are waiting for solutions.

1.3 Key Problems and Difficulties

In computer-based facial beauty analysis, beauty is considered as a kind of information, such as identity, age, and expression. The progress of the related research topics can promote facial beauty study. However, the latter also has its particular problems. This section discusses the key problems and challenges of computer-based facial beauty analysis.

1.3.1 Key Problems

- Deepen the understanding of facial beauty perception. A series of hypotheses of facial beauty perception have been proposed in the psychology field. To verify these hypotheses, perception experiments are often carried out using stimuli generated by image warping techniques and the contents of the hypotheses.

However, existing works have the following limitations. First, the calculation of face shapes is not normalized, so it is affected by translation, scale, and rotation variations. Second, the stimuli in existing perception experiments are based on only a small number of faces. Experiments based on a large database would give more convincing results. Moreover, using image processing and machine learning methods, new rules can be found from data, which can advance our understanding of facial beauty perception.

- More accurate facial beauty prediction. The core of this problem is to build a model that maps facial biometrics to a facial beauty score. Until now, there has been no public database for facial beauty study. Therefore, existing works are all based on private databases, and a comparison of different methods is lacking. New features and machine learning methods are worth trying. How to select effective facial features to build the model and how to combine different types of features to further improve the model are still waiting for an answer.
- Face beautification. It is a typical application of the learned facial beauty rules and models. Existing works only focus on facial geometry beautification. Obviously, facial texture also plays an important role in facial beauty. How should the learned knowledge be used to beautify facial texture? As every hypothesis and model can derive a beautification method, which one achieves better beautification results? Can we get further improved results by combining different methods? The above questions are very interesting and require more experiments and investigations.
- Develop application systems. One advantage of computer-based facial beauty analysis is the convenience of developing application systems with the learned knowledge. According to different application scenarios, the software should contain the corresponding functions. The architecture design of the software and the optimization of each functions deserve further research.

1.3.2 Difficulties

Based on the current research background, computer-based facial beauty analysis has the following challenges:

- Computer-based facial beauty analysis is a new research topic that has few research resources. The number of published works on this topic is small. There is neither a unified research framework nor recognized problems. Existing works focus on scattered aspects of facial beauty analysis, and there are few comparisons of different methods.
- There is no public database for facial beauty study. A dataset for facial beauty study is required to have sufficient variability in attractiveness. As far as we know, none of the existing open face databases were designed considering this requirement. There are few extremely beautiful faces in existing databases, and the faces often come from limited ethnic groups. In addition, human-rated

beauty scores of the faces are required. To build such a database, we need to first collect facial images from various sources, and ask a number of persons to make judgments on the attractiveness of these faces. It is time consuming and requires funding (to pay for the rating experiments).

- The goal of facial beauty analysis is different from other facial analysis tasks, such as face recognition, age estimation, and facial expression recognition, which aim to increase the recognition rate or decrease the mean squares error. When building facial beauty models, prediction accuracy is only one aim. The interpretability and practicability of the models are also important and need more investigations.
- In facial beauty study, perception experiments have to be often carried out, which require a lot of labor and time consumption. This is one constraint of facial beauty study.

1.4 Databases

In this book, two databases are used, which are gradually collected with our research progress.

The first database includes 929 female facial images and 1384 male facial images, which are captured in a constraint environment. All the faces are frontal with neutral expressions. Because the faces are from Shanghai, China, this database is called the SH_Face. Figure 1.1 shows some examples of this database. This database does not have human-rated beauty scores.

The second database includes 799 female facial images collected from various sources. There are 390 celebrity facial images of Miss Universe, Miss World, movie stars, and super models collected via Google and 409 common facial images collected from a website (http://faceresearch.org), Flicker, and other face databases (e.g., XM2VTS Messer et al. 1999, FERET Phillips et al. 2000, etc.). All facial images are confined to be frontal with near-neutral expressions (neutral and gentle smile are allowed) and have adequate resolution. The size of the collected images is normalized to 480 × 600. As shown in Fig. 1.2, the facial images have large variations in illumination, sharpness, and tone. Human rating is the usual approach to measure facial beauty. Conventionally used measurement scales are 5-point,

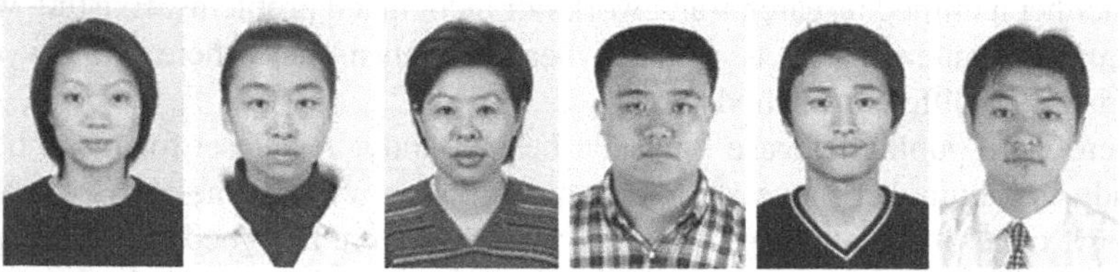

Fig. 1.1 Examples of SH_Face database

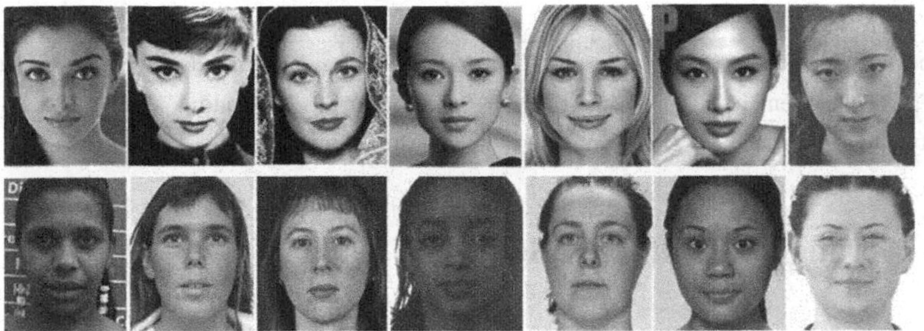

Fig. 1.2 Examples of Beauty_DB database

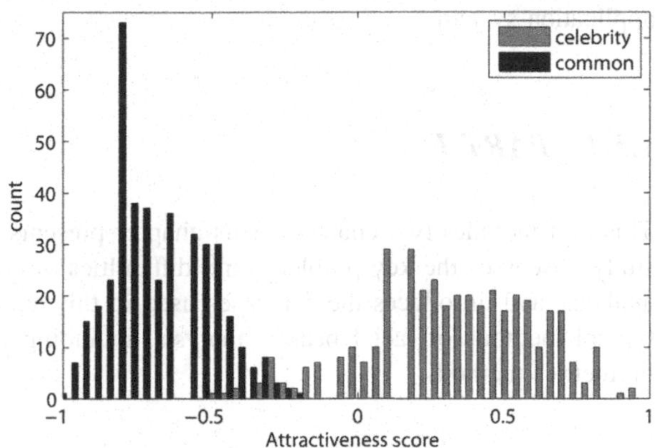

Fig. 1.3 Histogram of beauty scores of the celebrity and common faces in the Beauty_DB database

7-point, and 10-point scales. However, according to our experience, people find it more difficult and time consuming to rate with more points of scale. In order to release the burden of raters, we use a 3-point integer scale: –1 (unattractive), 0 (common), and 1 (very attractive). An interactive tool for image rating was developed, which displayed facial images in random order. The raters were asked to first scan through the entire dataset to obtain a general notion of the relative attractiveness of the images and then proceed to the actual rating stage. A rater could look at a picture for as long as he or she liked and then score it. In total, 25 volunteers attended the rating procedure, most in their 20 s. On average, each person spent 40 min to rate 799 images. The attractiveness score of a facial image is the mean of its ratings across all raters. Figure 1.3 presents the histogram of the attractiveness scores of the facial images in our dataset. It can be seen that most of the celebrity facial images achieved higher attractiveness scores than the common ones. Table 1.2 gives a summary of the two databases.

Table 1.2 Database summary

Database	Gender (number)	Race	Rating scale	No. of raters
SH_Face	Female (729) + Male (1343)	Chinese	No rating	–
Beauty_DB	Female (799)	Multi-race	3-scale	25

1.5 Arrangement of This Book

In this book, we summarize our work on facial beauty analysis. Its fourteen chapters are in five parts, covering verification of traditional rules and hypotheses, new hypothesis on facial beauty perception, face image processing and feature extraction, facial beauty modelling, face beautification, and presentation of the designed application system.

1.5.1 PART I

This part includes two chapters. This chapter presents the history of facial beauty study, discusses the key problems and difficulties of computer-based facial beauty analysis, and introduces the databases used in this book. Chapter 2 introduces the typical methods of facial beauty analysis, including ratio rules, hypothesis, and biometrics methods.

1.5.2 PART II

This part is about facial images and features for facial beauty analysis. Chapter 3 proposes an optimized landmark model which can well represent facial geometry. Chapter 4 investigates the shape principle component features and compares them with the averageness and symmetry features based on the hypotheses. Chapter 5 examines the putative ratio rules of facial beauty, selects the most discriminative ones and makes corrections of their ideal values. Chapter 6 proposes combining block-LBP and geometric features for facial beauty prediction. Chapter 7 compares multiple types of features and investigates the optimal fusion strategy for facial beauty modeling.

1.5.3 PART III

This part focuses on the hypotheses on facial beauty perception. Chapter 8 examines the averageness hypothesis on a large database. Chapter 9 proposes a new hypothesis:

the weighted averageness (WA) hypothesis. Both perception experiments and facial beauty models agree with this hypothesis. The corollary of the WA hypothesis derives a convex hull based face beautification method.

1.5.4 PART IV

This part focuses on some dedicated data-driven facial beauty modeling methods and model selection. Chapter 10 proposes an evolutionary cost-sensitive extreme learning machine for facial beauty analysis. To emphasize the interpretability and usefulness of facial models, Chap. 11 proposes a causal effect criterion for model evaluation. Chapter 12 proposes a framework of data-driven facial beauty modeling and its three applications.

1.5.5 PART V

In Chap. 13, we present our online and offline facial beauty analysis system, which integrates facial image processing, facial beauty prediction, and face beautification functions.

At the end of this book, a brief book review and future work are presented in Chap. 14.

The main body of this book can be presented in Fig. 1.4. From this figure, we easily see that connections of different parts of the book. PART I provides an outline of the book. Following PART I, PART II presents the base of facial beauty analysis i.e. features for facial beauty analysis. Then PART III describes hypotheses based facial beauty perception. Data-driven facial beauty modeling methods shown in PART IV analyzes facial beauty from a general viewpoint. It is easy to know these methods are able to obtain facial beauty from raw facial images, though in our

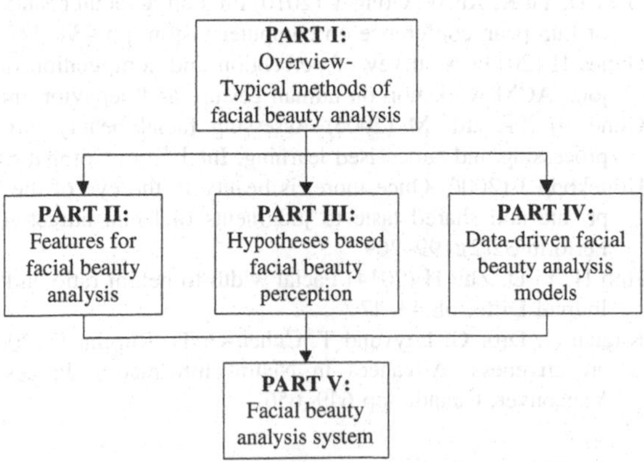

Fig. 1.4 Illustration of the main body of this book

book they can also work with extracted facial features. PART V introduces our implemented facial beauty analysis system which not only allows a number of methods in the book to be illustrated but also is interesting and useful.

References

American society for aesthetic plastic surgery [EB/OL] (2014) Statistics 2013. http://www.surgery.org/sites/default/files/Stats2013_3.pdf

Atiyeh BS, Hayek SN (2008) Numeric expression of aesthetics and beauty. Aesthetic Plast Surg 32 (2):209–216

Chen F, Zhang D (2014) Evaluation of the putative ratio rules for facial beauty indexing. In: Proceedings of international conference on medical biometrics, pp 181–188

Choe KS, Sclafani AP, Litner JA, Yu GP, Romo T III (2004) The Korean American woman's face anthropometric measurements and quantitative analysis of facial aesthetics. Arch Facial Plast Surg 6(4):244–252

Cootes TF, Taylor CJ, Cooper DH, Graham J (1995) Active shape models-their training and application. Comput Vis Image Underst 61(1):38–59

Cunningham MR, Roberts AR, Barbee AP, Druen PB, Wu CH (1995) Their ideas of beauty are, on the whole, the same as ours": Consistency and variability in the cross-cultural perception of female physical attractiveness. J Pers Soc Psychol 68(2):261–279

Dion KK (1972) Physical attractiveness and evaluation of children's transgressions. J Pers Soc Psychol 24(2):207–213

Duda RO, Hart PE, Stork DG (2000) Pattern classification. Wiley Interscience

Eisenthal Y, Dror G, Ruppin E (2006) Facial attractiveness: beauty and the machine. Neural Comput 18(1):119–142

Fan J, Chau KP, Wan X, Zhai L, Lau E (2012) Prediction of facial attractiveness from facial proportions. Pattern Recogn 45(6):2326–2334

Farkas LG, Hreczko TA, Kolar JC, Munro IR (1985) Vertical and horizontal proportions of the face in young adult North American Caucasians: revision of neoclassical canons. Plast Reconstr Surg 75(3):328–337

Feingold A (1988) Matching for attractiveness in romantic partners and same-sex friends: a meta-analysis and theoretical critique. Psychol Bull 104:226–235

Feingold A (1992) Good-looking people are not what we think. Psychol Bull 111:304–341

Gan J, Li L, Zhai Y, Liu Y (2014) Deep self-taught learning for facial beauty prediction. Neurocomputing 144:295–303

Gray D, Yu K, Xu W, Gong Y (2010) Predicting facial beauty without landmarks. In: Proceedings of European conference on computer vision, pp 434–447

Gunes H (2011) A survey of perception and computation of human beauty. In: Proceedings of joint ACM workshop on human gesture and behavior understanding, pp 19–24

Gunes H, Piccardi M (2006) Assessing facial beauty through proportion analysis by image processing and supervised learning. Int J Hum Comput Stud 64(12):1184–1199

Honekopp J (2006) Once more: is beauty in the eye of the beholder? Relative contributions of private and shared taste to judgments of facial attractiveness. J Exp Psychol Hum Percept Perform 32(2):199–209

Huh H, Yi D, Zhu H (2014) Facial width-to-height ratio and celebrity endorsements. Personality Individ Differ 68:43–47

Kagian A, Dror G, Leyvand T, Cohen-Or D, Ruppin E (2006) A humanlike predictor of facial attractiveness. Advances in Neural Information Processing Systems (NIPS). MIT Press, Vancouver, Canada, pp 649–656

Langlois JH, Kalakanis L, Rubenstein AJ, Larson A, Hallam M, Smoot M (2000) Maxims or myths of beauty? A meta-analytic and theoretical review. Psychol Bull 126(3):390–423
Laurentini A, Bottino A (2014) Computer analysis of face beauty: a survey. Comput Vis Image Underst 125:184–199
Leyvand T, Cohen-Or D, Dror G, Lischinski D (2008) Data-driven enhancement of facial attractiveness. ACM Trans Graph 27(3):Article 38
Li SZ, Jain AK (2011) Handbook of face recognition, 2nd edn. Springer
Little AC, Jones BC, DeBruine LM (2011) Facial attractiveness: evolutionary based research. Philos Trans Royal Soc B 366(1571):1638–1659
Liu C, Wechsler H (2002) Gabor feature based classification using the enhanced fisher linear discriminant model for face recognition. IEEE Trans Image Process 11(4):467–476
Martin JG (1964) Racial ethnocentrism and judgment of beauty. J Soc Psychol 63(1):59–63
Martín-Loeches M, Hernández-Tamames JA, Martín A, Urrutia M (2014) Beauty and ugliness in the bodies and faces of others: an fMRI study of person esthetic judgement. Neuroscience 277:486–497
Mathes EW, Brennan SM, Haugen PM, Rice HB (1985) Ratings of physical attractiveness as a function of age. J Soc Psychol 125:157–168
Messer K, Matas J, Kittler J, Luettin J, Maitre G (1999) XM2VTSDB: The extended m2vts database. In: Proceedings of International conference on audio and video-based biometric person authentication, pp 72–77
Ojala T, Pietikäinen M, Harwood D (1996) A comparative study of texture measures with classification based on featured distributions. Pattern Recogn 29:51–59
Ojala T, Pietikainen M, Maenpaa T (2002) Multiresolution gray-scale and rotation invariant texture classification with local binary patterns. IEEE Trans Pattern Anal Mach Intell 24:971–987
Penton-Voak I (2011) In retreat from nature? Successes and concerns in Darwinian approaches to facial attractiveness. J Evol Psychol 9(2):173–193
Perrett DI, May KA, Yoshikawa S (1994) Facial shape and judgements of female attractiveness. Nature 368(6468):239–242
Phillips PJ, Moon H, Rizvi SA, Rauss PJ (2000) The FERET evaluation methodology for face-recognition algorithms. IEEE Trans Pattern Anal Mach Intell 22(10):1090–1104
Rhodes G (2006) The evolutionary psychology of facial beauty. Annu Rev Psychol 57:199–226
Sala E, Terraneo M, Lucchini M, Knies G (2013) Exploring the impact of male and female facial attractiveness on occupational prestige. Res Soc Stratification Mobility 31:69–81
Schmid K, Marx D, Samal A (2008) Computation of a face attractiveness index based onneoclassical canons, symmetry, and golden ratios. Pattern Recogn 41(8):2710–2717
Slater A, Von der Schulenburg C, Brown E, Badenoch M, Butterworth G, Parsons S, Samuels C (1998) newborn infants prefer attractive faces. Infant Behav Dev 21(2):345–354
Udry JR (1965) Structural correlates of feminine beauty preferences in Britain and the United States: A comparison. Sociol Soc Res 49:330–342
Vapnik V (1995) The nature of statistical learning theory. Springer
Viola P, Jones M (2001) Rapid object detection using a boosted cascade of simple features. In: Proceedings of IEEE conference on computer vision and pattern recognition, pp 511–518
Walster E, Aronson V, Abrahams D, Rottman L (1966) Importance of physical attractiveness in dating behavior. J Pers Soc Psychol 4(5):508–516
Wang D, Qian G, Zhang M, Farkas LG (1997) Differences in horizontal, neoclassical facial canons in Chinese (Han) and North American Caucasian populations. Aesthetic Plast Surg 21:265–269
Welling LLM, Jones BC, DeBruine LM, Smith FG, Feinberg DR, Little AC, Al-Dujaili EAS (2008) Men report stronger attraction to feminity in women's faces when their testosterone levels are high. Horm Behav 54(5):703–708
Whitehill J, Movellan JR (2008) Personalized facial attractiveness prediction. In: Proceedings of IEEE international conference on automatic face and gesture recognition, pp 1–7
Yan H (2014) Cost-sensitive ordinal regression for fully automatic facial beauty assessment. Neurocomputing 129:334–342

Chapter 2
Typical Facial Beauty Analysis

As an interdisciplinary research topic facial beauty can be investigated understood from many aspects. An important issue is to determine features closely associated with facial beauty. In this book after introducing conventional features for facial beauty analysis we also present typical facial beauty analysis methods. The literature shows that researchers favor different methods. Some researchers believe that facial beauty underlies in the golden ratio. Some are interested in the averageness symmetry hypotheses. Recently biometrics techniques are also utilized for facial beauty analysis. This chapter gives a review of the typical facial beauty analysis methods discusses the advantages limitations of them. After reading this chapter people can have preliminary knowledge on features methods for facial beauty analysis. With this knowledge people will easily understand the following chapters.

2.1 Introduction

The secret of facial beauty has attracted the attention of artists and researchers for a long time. In ancient time, some sculptors and painters believed that the golden ratio is underlying beautiful faces. In ancient China, the vertical thirds and horizontal fifths rule was proposed. Since 1990s, the study of facial beauty perception has been popular in the psychology field. Some influential hypotheses, such as the averageness hypothesis, have been proposed and numerous studies have been reported and published. Facial beauty study has attracted the attention of computer scientists since 2000. Biometric techniques have been used for facial beauty modeling and developing real-life application systems.

D. Zhang et al., *Computer Models for Facial Beauty Analysis*,
DOI 10.1007/978-3-319-32598-9_2

2.2 Golden Ratio Rules

The golden ratio (1.618), also called the divine proportion, can be seen in art, architecture, fashion, birds, insects, and flowers, etc. and has been believed to underlie the human body since the renaissance. Leonardo Da Vinci's drawing, Human Figure in a circle, is a great example of illustrating the golden ratio of the human body, see Fig. 2.1. The famous painting Mona Lisa also embodies the golden ratio, as shown in Fig. 2.2. The golden ratio is also believed to underlie beautiful faces. Marquardt proposed an 'ideal' face template based on the golden ratio, which is called the Phi mask, as shown in Fig. 2.3. It is exciting to set up a universal standard for facial beauty. However, many measurement-based studies showed that the golden ratio is not related with facial beauty, i.e., most beautiful faces do not conform to the golden ratio rules (Kiekens et al. 2008; Holland 2008; Peron et al. 2012). Also, in many cases the golden ratio exceeds the normal range of facial ratios. Fan et al. (2012) generated a 3D synthesized face model that conformed to as many golden ratio as possible, but only obtained a below average ratings in their perception experiment.

The golden ratio rules are an idealized description of facial beauty. Although they are not accurate, the idea of using ratios to understand facial beauty has been accepted. The ideal values of the ratios can be corrected according to the measurements on the target population. The corrected ratios still serve as references in today's aesthetic surgery plans. Moreover, the ratios are also taken as features for facial beauty modeling and automatic facial beauty prediction.

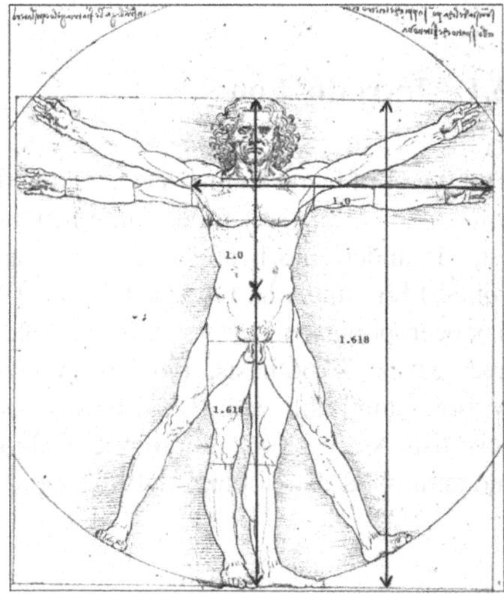

Fig. 2.1 Human figure in a *circle*, illustrating divine proportion (by Leonardo Da Vinci)

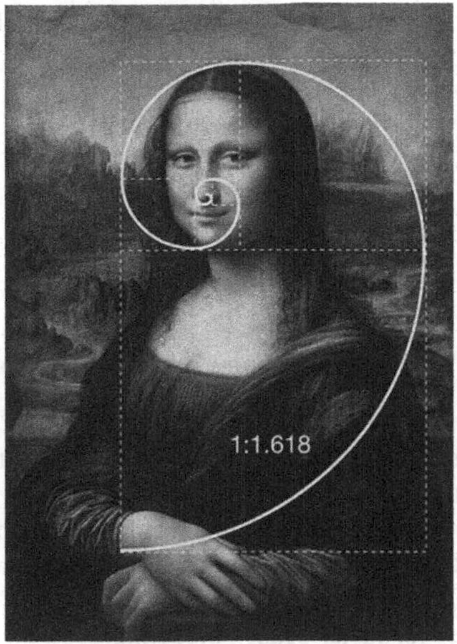

Fig. 2.2 Mona Lisa (by Leonardo Da Vinci)

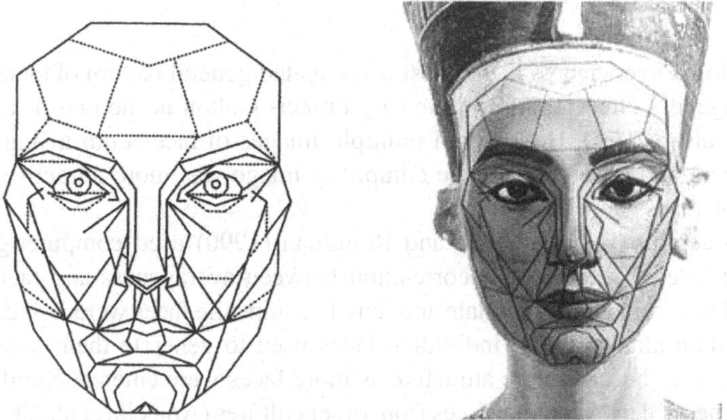

Fig. 2.3 *Left* Marquardt's Phi mask (beauty analysis, Inc. http://www.beautyanalysis.com/). *Right* Egyptian queen Neferneferuaten Nefertiti (1370–1330 BC)

2.3 Vertical Thirds and Horizontal Fifths

The vertical thirds and horizontal fifths rules were proposed in ancient China. As shown in Fig. 2.4, the vertical thirds rules divide the length of the face into three parts of equal length: from hairline to eyebrow, from eyebrow to nasal floor, and from nasal floor to chin. The horizontal rules divide the width of the face into five

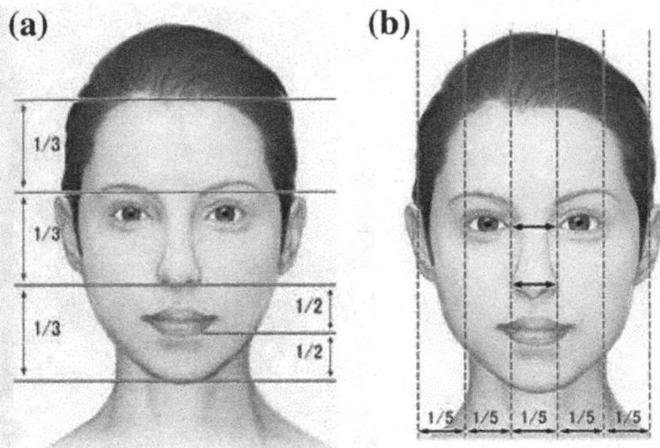

Fig. 2.4 Sketch of *vertical thirds* and *horizontal fifth rule*. **a** Vertical thirds. **b** Horizontal fifths

parts of equal width, i.e., the width of one eye. Faces that conform to these rules are considered to be beautiful.

Similar to golden ratio rules, limited to the measuring techniques in ancient time, the vertical thirds and horizontal fifths rules are not accurate enough. Beautiful faces do not often conform to these rules. However, the ratios defined in these rules can be taken as features for facial beauty modeling.

2.4 Averageness Hypothesis

In psychology, averageness is the most investigated general pattern of facial beauty. The averageness effect was first found by Francis Galton at the end of nineteenth century (Galton 1878). He overlaid multiple images of faces onto a single photographic plate and observed that the composite image was more attractive than the component faces.

Over a century later, Langlois and Roggman (1990) used computer-generated composite faces to examine the correlation between averageness and facial attractiveness. They found that both male and female composite faces were judged as more attractive than almost all the individual faces used to generate them, and that the composite faces became more attractive as more faces were entered. Similar results were obtained when examining faces from other cultures (Apicella et al. 2007). These studies suggested that averageness is positively correlated with facial attractiveness. Figure 2.5 shows four individual facial images and a computer-generated average face.

Studies on babies reveal that the preference of facial averageness is biological rather than cultural. New-born infants will gaze longer at attractive faces than at unattractive ones (Langlois et al. 1991; Slater et al. 1998; Kramer et al. 1995), and infants respond to average faces in the same way as they respond to attractive faces (Strauss 1979; Rubenstein et al. 1999). Moreover, the ability to extract the average from a set of realistic facial images operates from an early age, and it is almost instinctive.

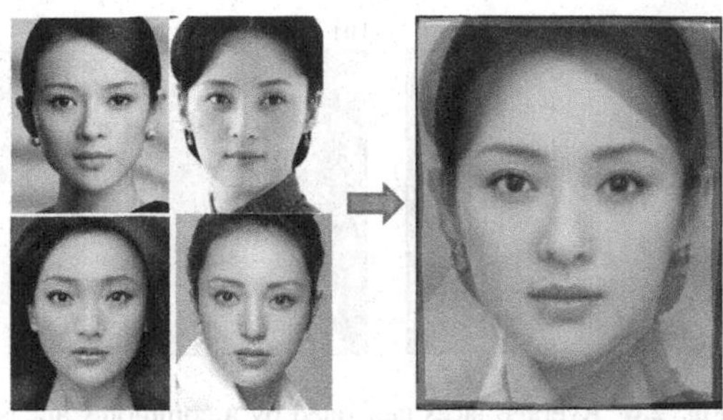

Fig. 2.5 Four individual face images and the computer-generated average face

Many researchers interpret the preference for facial averageness from the evolutionary perspective. Thornhill and Gangestad (1993) argued that average faces may be preferred to less-average faces because owners of average faces possess a more diverse set of genes, which may result in less common proteins to which pathogens are poorly adapted. Parasites are generally best adapted to proteins that are common in the host population, and hence, parasites are adapted to the genes that code for the production of these proteins. Another evolutionary theory for the preference of averageness in faces is that extreme genotypes are more likely to be homozygous for deleterious alleles. Rhodes et al. (2001b) showed that facial averageness is positively related to medical health as measured from actual medical records in both men and women. Facial averageness can then be potentially associated with both direct benefits in terms of associating with healthy, parasite- and/or disease-free partners and indirect benefits of heterozygous genes that can be passed onto offspring.

Despite these findings, the averageness hypothesis has to face many doubts and challenges. One challenge is that the attractiveness of average composite faces may be due to other factors co-varying with the averaging operation such as smoothed skin texture and the improved symmetry of the average composite faces (Alley and Cunningham 1991). In order to investigate the effect of individual factors on facial beauty, some researchers separately manipulated the averageness of shape and texture (O'Toole et al. 1999; Rhodes et al. 2001a). In their experiments, it was reported that individual faces warped into average face shapes were rated as more attractive than the original, and that decreasing averageness by moving the faces away from average face shapes decreased attractiveness. The results show that skin smoothness is not the only determinant of the attractiveness of average faces. Some researchers dissociated symmetry and averageness in facial beauty perception experiments and showed that symmetry positively contributes to facial beauty, but it cannot solely explain the attractiveness of average faces. Another challenge is whether all attractive faces satisfy the averageness hypothesis. Perrett et al. (1994) found that both men and women considered that a face averaged from a set of attractive faces was more appealing than one averaged from a wide range of women's faces, which implies that attractive faces have other types. Figure 2.6 shows the composite faces generated by common and attractive Caucasian and Asian, which agrees with Perrett's finding. Hence, average faces are attractive.

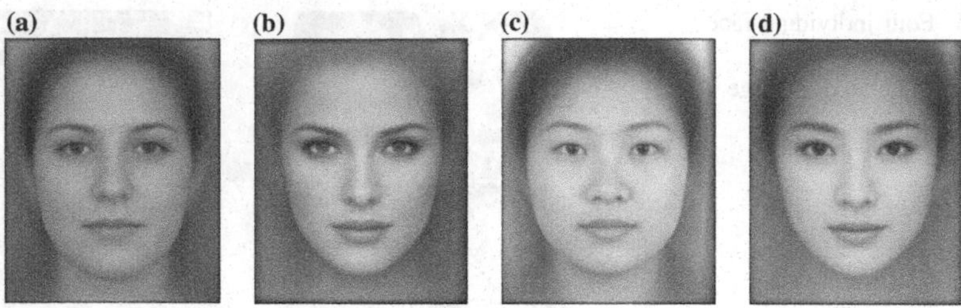

Fig. 2.6 Average faces generated by **a** common Caucasians; **b** attractive Caucasians; **c** common Asians; **d** attractive Asians

However, these results do not mean that all attractive faces are average, or that average faces are optimally attractive (Rhodes 2006).

To summarize, averageness is positively correlated with facial beauty, but it is not the only determinant. Average faces are attractive but not optimally attractive. Facial beauty perception is complex. Although the averageness hypothesis is influential and has some evolutionary explanations, it is still very limited in defining facial beauty.

2.5 Facial Symmetry and Beauty Perception

Facial symmetry is another well investigated trait of facial beauty. From an evolutionary perspective, symmetry may act as a marker of phenotypic and genetic quality and is preferred during mate selection in a variety of species (Perrett et al. 1999). Fluctuating asymmetries (FAs) are nondirectional (random) deviations from perfect symmetry in bilaterally paired traits. In nonhuman animals, FA in body traits reflects developmental instability, and increase with inbreeding, homozygosity, parasite load, poor nutrition, and pollution (Moller and Swaddle 1997; Parsons 1990; Polak 2003). In humans, body FAs increases with inbreeding, premature birth, psychosis, and mental retardation (Livshits and Kobylianski 1991). If similar relationships exist for facial FAs, then they could signal mate quality.

The methodology of symmetry hypothesis research is similar to that of the averageness hypothesis. Symmetric facial images are generated using image processing techniques, which serve as a group of stimuli, and the corresponding original facial images serve as the other group of stimuli. Participants are asked to compare and select the more attractive one between a pair of stimuli. The conclusion, i.e., whether symmetry positively correlates with facial beauty, is made according to the statistical analysis of the experimental results. However, conclusions on the symmetry hypothesis are controversial. Some studies suggested that normal faces with fluctuating asymmetries, FAs, are preferred to perfectly symmetric versions (Kowner 1996; Langlois et al. 1994; Samuels et al. 1994; Swaddle and Cuthill 1995), whereas some studies found that perfectly symmetric faces were more attractive than the original slightly asymmetric faces (Perrett et al. 1999; Rhodes et al. 2001a). Another point of view is that even though symmetry is positively correlated with facial beauty, it is not the major determinant factor (Scheib et al. 1999), i.e., symmetric faces are not necessarily attractive.

Although the amount of effect of symmetry on facial attractiveness is still unclear, symmetry has been widely used as an additional feature in facial attractiveness calculation and modeling (Eisenthal et al. 2006; Schmid et al. 2008). The quantification of facial asymmetry based on 2D and 3D images has been investigated (Berlin et al. 2014; Berssenbrugge et al. 2014). For 2D images, horizontal distances from a vertical reference line (median sagittal plane), vertical distances from a horizontal reference line, and the horizontal direction between centers of bilateral points are used to measure facial asymmetry. The proper selection and identification of reference points is crucial. For highest accuracy, a sufficient number of evenly distributed and reproducible reference points should be used. If 3D point clouds are available, the point cloud representing the face is firstly mirrored at an initial plane which approximately corresponds to the median sagittal plane of the face. Subsequently, the mirrored copy is matched (registered) to the original version of the face using the Iterative Closest Point (ICP) algorithm (Besl and McKay 1992). The third step of the procedure consists in estimating a median sagittal plane. These three steps are repeated several times. The matching process is then repeated with the remaining surface parts. The best-fit plane of the last iteration is the desired estimate of the median sagittal symmetry plane. Local asymmetries are obtained as the distances between the original cloud and its repeatedly mirrored and registered copy.

2.6 Facial Beauty Analysis by Biometrics Technology

In computer science society, beauty is treated as a characteristic of a human face, such as identity, age, and expression, and biometrics techniques have been used for facial beauty analysis. A typical facial beauty analysis system contains four modules, as shown in Fig. 2.7.

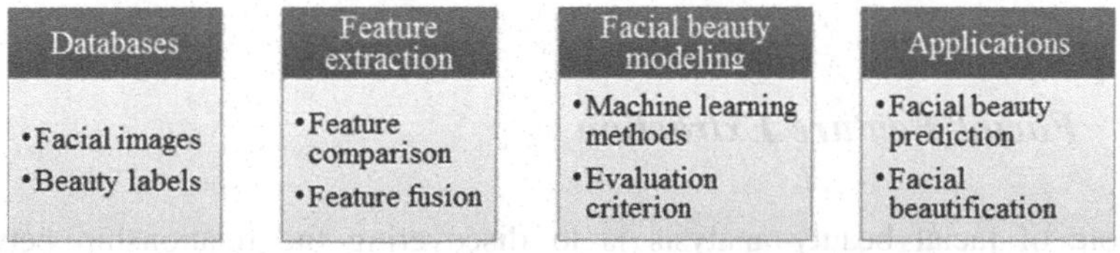

Fig. 2.7 Main modules of a typical facial beauty analysis system

The main issues in biometrics based facial beauty analysis include:

1. Build databases for facial beauty analysis and applications.
2. Decide which facial features work well for facial beauty analysis.
3. Build computational models that are able to map the facial features to a facial beauty score.
4. Develop applications using the results of facial beauty analysis.

The following subsections review the recent developments of the above issues and introduce the corresponding contents in the following chapters of this book.

2.6.1 Databases Used in Existing Works

To the best of our knowledge, there has been no public database established for facial beauty study. Most of the databases used in existing works were collected by the authors. A database for facial beauty study requires two types of data: facial images and their corresponding beauty scores. The facial images can be obtained from three sources: (1) Frontal portraits captured by a photographer. These images are often captured in a controlled environment with similar illumination conditions and image qualities. However, the number of images is limited, and very beautiful faces are scarce. (2) Facial images collected from the Internet, which can provide not only plenty of facial images but also those of well-known beautiful faces. A major challenge is related to the large variability and low quality (i.e., different resolutions, orientations, illuminations and expressions) of the images collected. (3) Synthesized facial images. The advantage is that data generation can be controlled, but these images are unrealistic. The beauty score of the collected facial images are usually measured by the average of human ratings. Obtaining human ratings is labor-intensive and time-consuming work. This problem is not obvious for small databases. However, when the size of the database increases, it is difficult to obtain enough human ratings. To solve this problem, researchers often relied on images taken from hotornot.com, a site that allows users to rate, on a 10 point scale, the attractiveness of photos voluntarily submitted by others. Most of databases contain only female images. Table 2.1 is a summary of the databases used in existing works.

2.6.2 Facial Feature Extraction

The core of facial beauty analysis is to discovering the relationship between low-level visual features and high-level perceived attractiveness. Effective features can promote the performance of facial beauty analysis, such as facial beauty assessment and facial beauty manipulation.

Table 2.1 Review of the databases used in existing works

Work	Size	Gender	Rating	Source
Eisenthal et al. (2006)	92	F	7-scale	Captured
Gunes and Piccardi (2006)	215	F	10-scale	Captured
Schmid et al. (2008)	452	F/M	10-scale	Captured
Kagian et al. (2008)	91	F	7-scale	Captured
Whitehill and Movellan (2008)	2000	F/M	4-scale	Internet
Gray et al. (2010)	2056	F	10-scale	Internet
Fan et al. (2012)	545	F	9-scale	Synthesized
Leyvand et al. (2008)	92	F	7-scale	Captured
Melacci et al. (2010)	60	F/M	N/A	Internet

Many types of features have been adopted in existing works. According to the embedded information, the features can be divided into geometric features and appearance features. The ratios suggested by putative rules (e.g., the golden ratio rule, the neoclassical canons, horizontal fifths, and vertical thirds) are typical geometric features, which are often used to assess facial beauty (Gunes and Piccardi 2006; Schmid et al. 2008; Fan et al. 2012). Given a training data set, the authors build computational models using the ratio features as dependent variables. It was found that although ratio based models are capable of reproducing the average human judgment to some extent, only a small subset of ratio features is important for prediction of facial attractiveness (Schmid et al. 2008) and the putative ideal ratio values are not accurate (Fan et al. 2012). Shape is another type of geometric feature, which is represented by the concatenated x- and y-coordinates of a series of facial landmarks (Melacci et al. 2010). The ratio features can be calculated given the shape feature, and hence, the shape feature contains more information than the ratios. In addition, averageness and symmetry are also adopted as supplementary features in facial beauty assessment (Eisenthal et al. 2006; Schmid et al. 2008). Appearance features contains the information of the whole image. Most of them are inspired from face recognition studies, including eigenface, Gabor filter responses (Liu and Wechsler 2002), and local binary patterns (LBP) (Ahonen et al. 2006). According to the characteristics, the features can be divided into holistic features and local features. Shape, eigenface, averageness and symmetry are holistic features, whereas ratios, Gabor filter responses, and LBP are local features.

Researchers also combine multiple types of facial features to build facial beauty models. For example, Eisenthal et al. (2006) and Kagian et al. (2008) combine geometric features, hair color, and skin smoothness into the regression model. Nguyen et al. (2013) concatenated LBP, Gabor filter responses, color moment, shape context, and shape parameters as a feature vector and applied principle component analysis (PCA) (Duda et al. 2000) to reduce the dimensionality.

Although very many handcrafted features have been used in facial beauty analysis, few works compared the discriminative power of different types of features and optimized the feature set. In this book, Chap. 7 focuses on facial feature extraction, comparison, and fusion strategy for facial beauty analysis. Extensive experiments are carried out, new features are tested and compared, and an optimal feature set is obtained.

2.6.3 Modeling Methods

To build a computational model of facial beauty, the general approach is: (1) prepare a training data set, including facial images and their corresponding beauty scores, (2) extract facial features from the facial images, which are supposed to be related to facial beauty, and (3) build a model by supervised learning techniques.

The first two steps were introduced in Sects.2.6.1 and 2.6.2. Given a set of feature vectors and beauty scores, multivariate linear regression (LR) and support vector regression (SVR) (Vapnik 1995) have often been used to learn the beauty model (Eisenthal et al. 2006; Schmid et al. 2008; Kagian et al. 2008; Whitehill and Movellan 2008; Leyvand et al. 2008). The LR method can obtain a beauty model in an explicit form. With radial basis function (RBF) kernels, SVR can model nonlinear structures, but the model cannot be explicitly expressed. LibSVM (Chang and Lin 2011) can be used to train the SVR model, and the parameters can be optimized by grid search. More recently, with the development of the machine learning field, new methods have been proposed for facial beauty modeling. For example, Gray et al. (2014) designed a multi-scale feature model by local filters and down-sampling, which is a form of the convolutional neural network. Gan et al. (2014) applied deep self-taught learning for facial beauty prediction.

Facial beauty models are evaluated by Pearson correlation between machine-predicted beauty scores and human-rated beauty scores. Due to different databases, features, and learning methods used, the reported performances of the models are different, in a range from 0.45 to 0.8. In this book, Chap. 7 optimizes the feature set for facial beauty modeling, which significantly promotes the performance of the model. Except for the Pearson correlation criterion, Chap. 11 proposes a causal effect criterion for model evaluation, which is essential for models used in facial beauty manipulation.

2.6.4 Applications

As presented in Chap. 1, facial beauty analysis has many applications, such as social networks, image editing software, animation design and arts, and plastic aesthetic surgery and cosmetic industries.

Facial beauty assessment and automatic face beautification are the key problems in the real applications. The former is a straight application of facial beauty models. For face beautification, there are two representative works. Leyvand et al. (2008) proposed a SVR-based method to beautify facial geometry, which first trained a beauty model and then modified geometric features to increase the beauty score predicted by the model. Melacci et al. (2010) prepared a set of beautiful faces and proposed beautifying the geometry of a query face by the weighted average of its *k* nearest-neighbors (KNN) in the training set.

Chapters 12 and 13 study facial beauty prediction and face beautification using the learned facial beauty models. By using the optimized feature set, facial beauty prediction accuracy has been significantly improved. By using the Active Appearance Models (AAMs) feature to build the facial beauty model, Chap. 13 realizes facial texture beatification.

2.7 Summary

This chapter surveys typical research methods of facial beauty analysis. First, the studies of golden ratio rules, the averageness hypothesis, and the symmetry hypothesis are reviewed, the main conclusions of these studies are summarized, and the limitations of these methods are discussed. Then, we survey biometric-based facial beauty analysis methods, which contain our key issues: databases, feature extraction, modeling, and applications. Recent progress on these issues is reviewed. Despite the progress, the studies on biometric-based facial beauty analysis are still at a primary stage. A number of issues require further effort. Building a large-scale public database for fair comparison of different methods is necessary. Comprehensive comparison of different types of features, feature selection, and feature fusion strategy needs more research. New machine learning techniques are expected to be applied to the topic of facial beauty analysis. Also, facial geometry beautification, and facial appearance beautification should be more interesting.

References

Ahonen T, Hadid A, Pietikainen M (2006) Face description with local binary patterns: application to face recognition. IEEE Trans Pattern Anal Mach Intell 28(12):2037–2041

Alley TR, Cunningham MR (1991) Averaged faces are attractive, but very attractive faces are not average. Psychol Sci 2:123–125

Apicella CL, Little AC, Marlowe FW (2007) Facial averageness and attractiveness in an isolated population of hunter-gatherers. Perception 36:1813–1820

Berlin NF, Berssenbrügge P, Runte C, Wermker K, Jung S, Kleinheinz J, Dirksen D (2014) Quantification of facial asymmetry by 2D analysis—a comparison of recent approaches. J Cranio-Maxillofacial Surg 42(3):265–271

Berssenbrügge P, Berlin NF, Kebeck G, Runte C, Jung S, Kleinheinz J, Dirksen D (2014) 2D and 3D analysis methods of facial asymmetry in comparison. J Cranio-Maxillofacial Surg 42(6): e327–e334

Besl PJ, McKay ND (1992) A method for registration of 3-D shapes. IEEE Trans Pattern Anal Mach Intell 14:239–256

Chang C C, Lin C J (2011) LIBSVM: A library for support vector machines. ACM Trans Intel Syst Technol, 2:Article 27. Software available at http://www.csie.ntu.edu.tw/~cjlin/libsvm
Duda RO, Hart PE, Stork DG (2000) Pattern classification. Wiley Interscience
Eisenthal Y, Dror G, Ruppin E (2006) Facial attractiveness: beauty and the machine. Neural Comput 18(1):119–142
Fan J, Chau KP, Wan X, Zhai L, Lau E (2012) Prediction of facial attractiveness from facial proportions. Pattern Recogn 45(6):2326–2334
Galton F (1878) Composite portraits, made by combining those of many different persons in a single resultant figure. J Anthropol Inst Great Br Irel 8:132–144
Gan J, Li L, Zhai Y, Liu Y (2014) Deep self-taught learning for facial beauty prediction. Neurocomputing 144:295–303
Gray D, Yu K, Xu W, Gong Y (2010) Predicting facial beauty without landmarks. In: Proceedings of European conference on computer vision, pp 434–447
Gunes H, Piccardi M (2006) Assessing facial beauty through proportion analysis by image processing and supervised learning. Int J Hum Comput Stud 64(12):1184–1199
Holland E (2008) Marquardt's Phi mask: pitfalls of relying on fashion models and the golden ratio to describe a beautiful face. Aesthetic Plast Surg 32(2):200–208
Kagian A, Dror G, Leyvand T, Meilijson I, Cohen-Or D, Ruppin E (2008) A machine learning predictor of facial attractiveness revealing human-like psychophysical biases. Vis Res 48:235–243
Kiekens RM, Kuijpers-Jagtman AM, van 't Hof MA, van 't Hof BE, Maltha JC (2008) Putative golden proportions as predictors of facial esthetics in adolescents. Am J Orthod Dentofac Orthop 134(4):480–483
Kowner R (1996) Facial asymmetry and attractiveness judgment in developmental perspective. J Exp Psychol Hum Percept Perform 22(3):662–674
Kramer S, Zebrowitz LA, San Giovanni JP, Sherak B (1995) Infants' preferences for attractiveness and babyfaceness. Stud Percept Action III:389–392
Langlois JH, Roggman LA (1990) Attractive faces are only average. Psychol Sci 1(2):115–121
Langlois JH, Roggman LA, Musselman L (1994) What is average and what is not average about attractive faces? Psychol Sci 5:214–220
Langlois JH, Ritter JM, Roggman LA, Vaughn LS (1991) Facial diversity and infant preferences for attractive faces. Dev Psychol 27(1):79–84
Leyvand T, Cohen-Or D, Dror G, Lischinski D (2008) Data-driven enhancement of facial attractiveness. ACM Trans Graph 27:Article 38
Liu C, Wechsler H (2002) Gabor feature based classification using the enhanced fisher linear discriminant model for face recognition. IEEE Trans Image Process 11(4):467–476
Livshits G, Kobyliansky E (1991) Fluctuating asymmetry as a possible measure of developmental homeostasis in humans: a review. Hum Biol 63:441–466
Melacci S, Sarti L, Maggini M, Gori M (2010) A template-based approach to automatic face enhancement. Pattern Anal Appl 13(3):289–300
Moller AP, Swaddle JP (1997) Asymmetry, developmental stability and evolution. Oxford University Press, New York
Nguyen T V, Liu S, Ni B, Tan J, Rui Y, Yan S (2013) Towards decrypting attractiveness via multi-modality cues. ACM Trans Multimedia Comput Commun Appl 9(4):Article 28
O'Toole AJ, Price T, Vetter T, Bartlett JC, Blanz V (1999) 3D shape and 2D surface textures of human faces: the role of "averages" in attractiveness and age. Image Vis Comput 18:9–19
Parsons PA (1990) Fluctuating asymmetry: an epigenetic measure of stress. Biol Rev 65(2):131–145
Peron APLM, Morosini IC, Correia KR, Moresca R, Petrelli E (2012) Photometric study of divine proportion and its correlation with facial attractiveness. Dent Press J Orthod 17(2):124–131
Perrett DI, Burt DM, Penton-Voak IS, Lee KJ, Rowland DA, Edwards R (1999) Symmetry and human facial attractiveness. Evol Hum Behav 20(5):295–307
Perrett DI, May KA, Yoshikawa S (1994) Facial shape and judgements of female attractiveness. Nature 368:239–242

Polak M (2003) Developmental instability: causes and consequences. Oxford University Press, New York

Rhodes G (2006) The evolutionary psychology of facial beauty. Annu Rev Psychol 57:199–226

Rhodes G, Yoshikawa S, Clark A, Lee K, McKay R, Akamatsu S (2001a) Attractiveness of facial averageness and symmetry in non-western cultures: in search of biologically based standards of beauty. Perception 30:611–625

Rhodes G, Zebrowitz LA, Clark A, Kalick SM, Hightower A, McKay R (2001b) Do facial averageness and symmetry signal health? Evol Hum Behav 22(1):31–46

Rubenstein AJ, Kalakanis L, Langlois JH (1999) Infant preferences for attractive faces: a cognitive explanation. Dev Psychol 35(3):848–855

Samuels CA, Butterworth G, Roberts T, Graupner L, Hole G (1994) Facial aesthetics-babies prefer attractiveness to symmetry. Perception 23:823–831

Scheib JE, Gangestad SW, Thornhill R (1999) Facial attractiveness, symmetry and cues of good genes. Proc R Soc Lond B Biol Sci 266(1431):1913–1917

Schmid K, Marx D, Samal A (2008) Computation of a face attractiveness index based on neoclassical canons, symmetry, and golden ratios. Pattern Recogn 41(8):2710–2717

Slater AM, Von Der Schulenburg C, Brown E, Badenoch M (1998) Newborn infants prefer attractive faces. Infant Behav Dev 21(2):345–354

Strauss MS (1979) Abstraction of prototypical information by adults and 10-month-old infants. J Exp Psychol Hum Learn Mem 5(6):618–632

Swaddle JP, Cuthill IC (1995) Asymmetry and human facial attractiveness: symmetry may not always be beautiful. Proc R Soc Lond B Biol Sci 261(1360):111–116

Thornhill R, Gangestad SW (1993) Human Facial Beauty. Hum Nat 4(3):237–269

Vapnik V (1995) The Nature of statistical learning theory. Data Min Knowl Disc 1–47

Whitehill J, Movellan J R (2008) Personalized facial attractiveness prediction. In: Proceedings of automatic face and gesture recognition, pp 1–7

Part II
Facial Images and Features

Chapter 3
Facial Landmark Model Design

It is clear that practicable facial beauty analysis should start from extraction of features closely associated with facial beauty. Among all kinds of available features for beauty analysis, facial geometry is one of the most widely used kinds of features for facial beauty analysis. Many researchers have contributed to the study of facial geometry for beauty analysis. Facial landmarks can be used as a compact and effective representation of facial geometry. In this chapter, we present a new landmark model (LM) which divides the landmarks into two categories, namely key points (KPs) and inserted points (IPs). In Sect. 3.1, we briefly introduce the definition of facial landmark and landmark models. Section 3.2 introduces the definition of key point (KP). Section 3.3 presents the iterative IP generation algorithm. In Sect. 3.4, we present the optimized landmark model. Section 3.5 makes comparisons between the optimized LM and other LMs. The chapter is finally concluded in Sect. 3.6. The new landmark model presented in this chapter provides us with an important means to perform feature extraction for beauty analysis in the following chapters.

3.1 Introduction

3.1.1 Landmark

A landmark is a point of correspondence on each object that matches between and within populations. Dryden and Mardia (1998) discriminated landmarks into the following three categories.

- ***Anatomical landmarks***. Points that correspond between organisms in some biologically meaningful way.
- ***Mathematical landmarks***. Points located on an object according to some mathematical or geometrical property, e.g., intersection or extreme points.

D. Zhang et al., *Computer Models for Facial Beauty Analysis*,
DOI 10.1007/978-3-319-32598-9_3

- ***Pseudo-landmarks***. Constructed points on an object either on the outline or between landmarks.

Landmark is a popular method for geometric facial representation. There are several ways to use the landmarks. Landmarks provide the correspondent points for face registration, which is often a preprocessing step in further analysis such as face recognition; well defined landmarks have been used to calculate the length and ratio features, which are important in geometric based facial beauty analysis (Schmid et al. 2008; Eisenthal et al. 2006); landmarks and the texture around them have been used as features for face recognition (Shi et al. 2006), facial expression analysis (Fasel and Luettin 2003), and age estimation (Suo et al. 2010); landmarks have been used to generate facial sketches (Tu and Lien 2010); landmarks serve as the control points in face animation (Zhang et al. 2006, 2011; Schaefer et al. 2006; Liao et al. 2012).

Landmarks have been used for over a century by anthropometrists interested in quantifying cranial variation. A great body of work in craniofacial anthropometry is associated with Farkas who established a database of anthropometric norms (Farkas 1994), which were measured on the base of 47 anatomical landmarks marked on real heads. Computer modeling of faces dates from the 1970s. Farkas's facial measurements have been used in computer graphics to automatically create plausible computer graphic faces. As a result, all existing facial LMs share most of Farkas's landmark points. Moreover, landmarks on facial contours have been added for contour control and description in applications such as facial animation and expression analysis.

Given some manually labeled examples for training, landmarks can be automatically detected based on techniques such as active shape model (ASM) method (Cootes et al. 1995), which increases the accessibility of LMs. Milborrow and Nicolls (2008) shows that the accuracy of landmark detection with the ASM method can be improved by increasing the number of landmarks. However, the time cost also increases linearly with the number of landmarks. Most of the existing LMs, as shown in Fig. 3.1, have moderate number of landmarks, which can be considered as a compromise between the accuracy and time cost.

3.1.2 Landmark Model

The layout of facial landmarks is defined as a landmark model (LM), which takes care of how many landmarks to use to represent facial geometry and where to locate them. During the decades, various LMs have been used for different tasks. For example, several public face databases provide complete sets of landmarks, including the AR database (22 point LM) (Martinez 1998), the BioID database (22 point LM) (BioID Technology Research 2001), the IMM database (58 point LM) (Nordstrom et al. 2004), the XM2VTS database (68 point LM) (Messer et al. 1999), the MUCT database (76 point LM) (Milborrow et al. 2010), and the PUT database

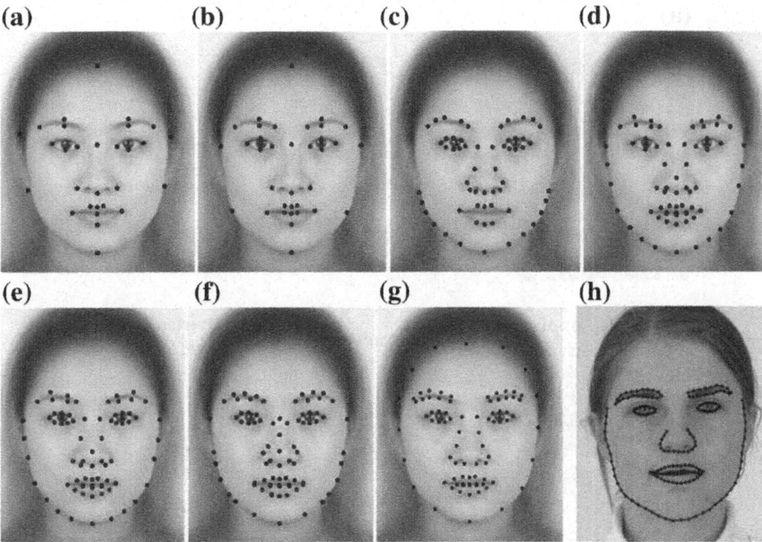

Fig. 3.1 The landmark layout of some typical LMs. **a** 29 point LM. **b** 37 point LM. **c** 58 point LM (IMM database). **d** 68 point LM (XM2VTS database). **e** 76 point LM (MUCT database). **f** 79 point LM. **g** 84 point LM. **h** 194 point LM (PUT database)

(194 point LM) (Kasinski et al. 2008). Except those models, many researchers prefer to use own designed LMs. Schmid et al. (2008) and Eisenthal et al. (2006) used landmarks only to generate length and ratio features such as classical canons and golden ratios, and their models include 29 and 37 landmarks respectively. Leyvand et al. (2008) used a LM with 84 points to control image warping. Seshadri and Savvides (2009) designed a LM with 79 points and claimed it to be competent in dealing with facial expressions. Figure 3.1 shows the landmark layout of some typical LMs.

According to the number of landmarks, the LMs can be classified into three categories: sparse models with less than 50 landmarks; moderate models with 50–100 landmarks; and dense models with more than 100 landmarks. Sparse models contain only the anatomical landmarks, which are often used for face registration or generate predefined length and ratio features. Moderate models add more landmarks on the boundaries and have been used for facial expression analysis (Fasel and Luettin 2003) and face warping (Leyvand et al. 2008). Dense models use equally spaced landmarks to trace the contour and have been used for face caricature generator (Brennan 2007) and face warping (Perret et al. 1994).

To the best of our knowledge, existing LMs are all designed by prior knowledge, such as anatomical landmarks according to anthropometry and contour landmarks with equal intervals. Researchers compare different LMs without reporting why their LMs are better than the other models. There is neither a unified framework for facial LM design nor comparative study of them.

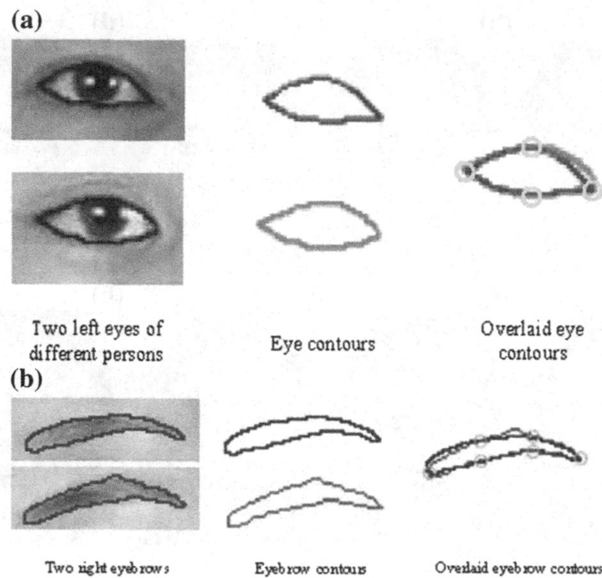

Fig. 3.2 Examples of different shapes with the same landmarks. **a** Eyes. **b** Eyebrows

Although existing LMs are competent for their specific applications, they are not optimized face shape descriptors. Obviously, the sparse models are not able to capture the detailed variations of the shapes of facial regions, such as the shapes of the jaw. Despite being much better than the sparse models, existing moderate models are still not sufficient for delicate shape descriptions. For example, the 68 point LM uses 4 landmarks to represent the shape of an eye. However, the two eyes with the same 4 landmarks may have very different shapes, as shown in Fig. 3.2a, i.e., the shape descriptors and shapes do not exhibit a one-to-one match. Although other moderate models add more landmarks on the eyes, they are not sufficient for describing eyebrow shapes, as shown in Fig. 3.2b. The dense models are capable of delicate shape representation, but they simply sample the boundaries at equal intervals and include too many redundant landmarks.

The existing sparse and moderate models are not sufficient for delicate representation, and the dense models include too many redundant landmarks, which may bring unnecessary computational cost. In this chapter, we present an optimized LM which can delicately represent facial geometry while keeping as few landmarks as possible. Firstly, the optimized LM should take the natural structure of human face into consideration and include as many anatomical and mathematical landmarks as possible. Secondly, the optimized LM is expected to achieve low contour approximation error with as few landmarks as possible.

In this chapter, we divide the landmarks into two categories, namely key point (KP) and inserted point (IP) respectively. KPs include anatomical and mathematical

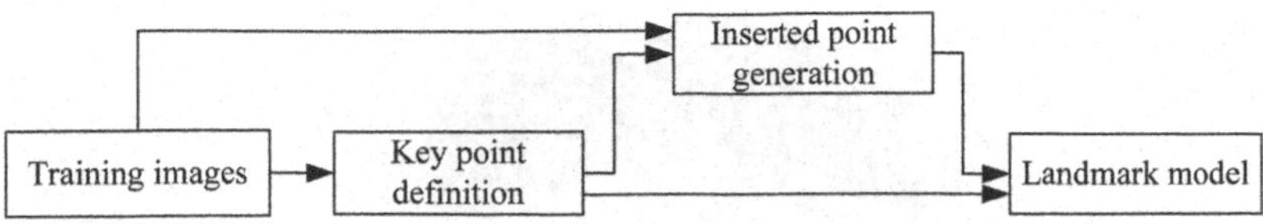

Fig. 3.3 Flowchart of the proposed LM generation method

landmarks. IPs are pseudo-landmarks which help describe the face shape accurately. We use an iterative searching scheme to find a series of optimal positions for IPs until some acceptable error is obtained. Then the optimized LM is built by combining both KPs and IPs. The flowchart of the LM generation is shown in Fig. 3.3.

The optimized LM reserves enough details of facial geometry as well as keeps only necessary landmarks. Hence, it is more desirable in aesthetic facial analysis. Similarly, in face animation applications, a delicate LM could contribute to more natural and vivid results. Besides, different LMs cause difficulties in data and code reusability. Researchers have to pay extra effort in relabeling the facial landmarks when comparing works with different LMs. The proposed method provides a framework to obtain an optimal LM with a given precision, which may encourage standardization of facial LMs.

3.2 Key Point (KP) Definition

KPs include both anatomical landmarks and mathematical landmarks located on the outlines of main facial regions, e.g., mouth corner and chin tip. They are not only the most reliable and easiest to locate but also important for both analysis and manipulation. For KP selection, we take the anthropometry face model (Farkas 1994) into consideration, and take symmetry as a priori. First, a series of horizontal lines ($L_1 - L_6$) passing through different facial regions is introduced, as illustrated in Fig. 3.4. Descriptions of these lines are listed in Table 3.1. The KPs are then defined in the following four fashions:

- *Corner and End Points*, such as eye corner (KP_{24}, KP_{26}, KP_{30}, and KP_{32}), mouth corner (KP_{47} and KP_{51}), eyebrow end points (KP_{18}, KP_{21}, KP_{12}, and KP_{15}), and nose corner points (KP_{37}, KP_{44}, KP_{39}, KP_{42}, KP_{40}, and KP_{41});
- *Extreme Points*, including top and bottom points of the contour in various facial regions (KP_{25}, KP_{27}, KP_{31}, KP_{33} on eyes, $KP_{48\text{–}50}$, $KP_{52\text{–}54}$ on mouth, and KP_6 on face contour), lateral points (KP_{38}, KP_{43} on nose), and central points (KP_{46} on nose tip, and KP_{28}, KP_{34} on pupils);

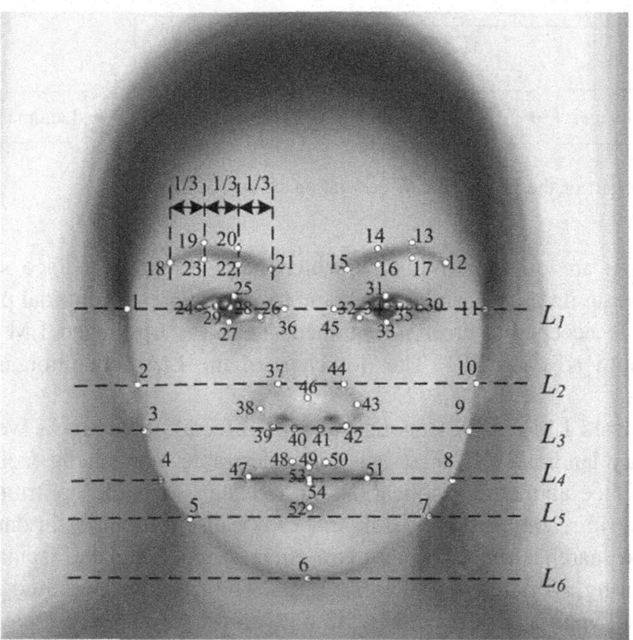

Fig. 3.4 Illustration of *horizontal lines* and KP configuration

Table 3.1 Descriptions of *horizontal lines*

Index	Descriptions
L1	Line at eye level
L2	Line at the level of upper nosal cartilage
L3	Line at the level of the nose base
L4	Line at the level of the mouth
L5	Line through the concave point below the lower lip
L6	Line at the level of the bottom of the chin

- *Intersection Points* of facial region contours and one of the horizontal lines ($KP_{1\text{–}5}$, $KP_{11\text{–}7}$ on face contour, KP_{36}, KP_{45} on nose, and KP_{29}, KP_{35} on eyes); and
- *Trisection Points* of eyebrow contours ($KP_{19\text{–}20}$, $KP_{22\text{–}23}$, $KP_{13\text{–}14}$, and $KP_{16\text{–}17}$).

To summarize, there are totally 54 well defined KPs distributed on different facial regions, i.e., eyebrows, eyes, nose, mouth, and face contour. Detailed descriptions of these KPs are listed in Table 3.2.

Table 3.2 Descriptions of the KPs

Region	Index	Descriptions
Facial contour (Fc)	1, 11	Intersection points of L_1 and Fc
	3, 9	Intersection points of L_2 and Fc
	4, 8	Intersection points of L_3 and Fc
	5, 7	Intersection points of L_4 and Fc
	6	Chin tip
Eyebrow (Eb)	12, 18	Outer end points of Eb
	15, 21	Inner end points of Eb
	19, 20	Trisection points of upper arc of left Eb
	23, 22	Trisection points of upper arc of left Eb
	14, 13	Trisection points of upper arc of right Eb
	16, 17	Trisection points of upper arc of right Eb
Eye	26, 32	Inner eye corner points
	24, 30	Outer eye corner points
	25, 31	Top points of upper eyelid
	27, 33	Bottom points of lower eyelid
	28, 34	Pupils
Nose	29, 35	Intersection points of L_1 and iris contour
	36, 45	Intersection points of *L*1 and nose contour
	37, 44	Intersection points of *L*2 and nose contour
	38, 43	Most lateral points on nosewing
	40, 41	Outer points of the nostril base
	46	Nose tip
Mouth	47, 51	Mouth corner
	49, 52	Top and bottom points of mouth on the midline
	48, 50	Peak points of upper lip
	53	Bottom point of upper lip on the midline
	54	Top point of lower lip on the midline

3.3 Inserted Point (IP) Generation

Important shape differences may also locate between KPs. As illustrated in Fig. 3.5, KPs divide the face outlines into segments of correspondence, e.g., KP_1–KP_6 divide the left part of the face contour into 5 segments. In this way, N_s segments are defined, covering most of the face outline (N_s = 40 in Fig. 3.5). Obviously, some segments, such as those on eyes and jaw, need more points for better description, and we call those points IPs. For each segment, it is important to determine how many IPs to be set and their located regions can be optimized in order to achieve a high precision with as few IPs as possible.

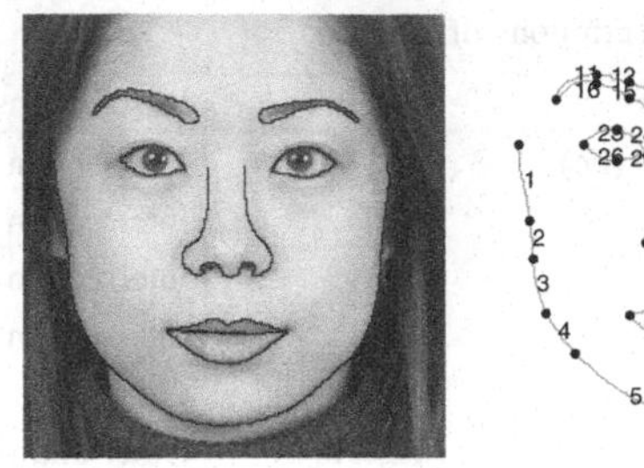

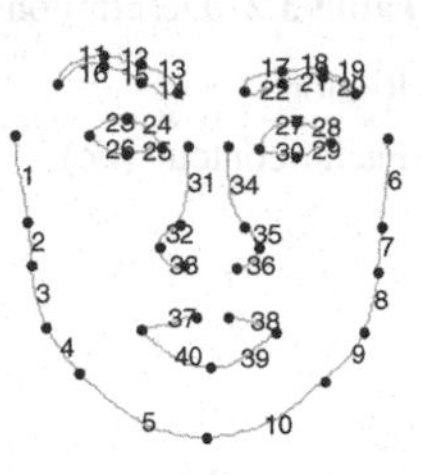

Fig. 3.5 The face outline is divided into 40 segments by KPs

3.3.1 A Quantitative Measure of the Precision of LMs

The approximation error is used to measure the precision of a LM. It is defined as the mean perpendicular distance between a face outline and the approximating polygonal chain connecting the landmarks, i.e.,

$$e = \lambda \frac{1}{N_p} \sum_{p_i \in s} d_{\perp}(p_i, l), \tag{3.1}$$

where λ is inversely proportional to the distance between pupils to make the approximation error independent of the image resolution, p_i represents the point on the face outline s, l represents the polygonal chain, N_p is the number of points on s, and $d_{\perp}$ refers to the perpendicular distance, which is the minimal distance from a point on one object to another object, i.e.,

$$d_{\perp}(p_i, l) = \min_{p_j \in l} \left\| p_i - p_j \right\|. \tag{3.2}$$

For example, Fig. 3.6a shows a manually drawn outline of an eye. If the outline is described by 4 landmarks, as shown in Fig. 3.6b, then the polygonal chain l is the combination of the four line segments (p_1p_2, p_2p_3, p_3p_4, and p_4p_1), and $d_{\perp}(p_i, l)$ is the Euclidean distance from p_i to its foot position on l. In practice, we let λ be 100 divided by the distance between pupils of a given image, which is equivalent to normalize the distance between pupils into 100 pixels.

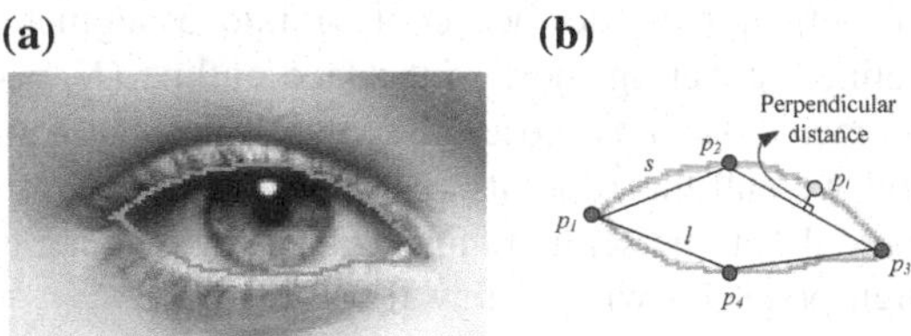

Fig. 3.6 Example to illustrate the definition of approximation error

3.3.2 Iterative Search for Optimal Positions of IPs

Obviously, the precision of a facial LM will increase as more IPs are added. However, the amount of the increase depends on the positions of the IPs. In this section, we introduce an iterative scheme to find the optimal positions for IPs in the manner of greedy search, i.e., selecting the most profitable position for the next IP in each iteration.

There are totally N_s segments $\{s^{(1)}, s^{(2)}, \ldots, s^{(Ns)}\}$ for one face outline s. For each segment $s^{(k)}$, the corresponding line segment passing through its end points, denoted by $l^{(k)}$, is sampled by n points as shown in Fig. 3.7. Lines passing through the sampling points and perpendicular to $l^{(k)}$ intersect with $s^{(k)}$ at $\{p_1, p_2, \ldots, p_n\}$. In this way, each face outline is sampled by $n \times N_s$ points. If they are ordered as $\{p_1, p_2, \ldots, p_n \times N_s\}$, then we can use the index to represent their positions on s, which are also called candidate positions. The precision gain of p_i is defined as

$$\delta_i = e_c - e_{+i}, \tag{3.3}$$

where e_{+i} is the approximation error if p_i is added, and e_c is the approximation error of the LM from the previous iteration step. The optimal inserting position is the one with the largest average precision gain across all training images, i.e.,

$$pos = \arg \max_i \frac{1}{N} \sum_{j=1}^{N} \delta_{ij}, \tag{3.4}$$

where δ_{ij} is the precision gain of position i on image j, and N is the number of training images. This largest average precision gain is denoted as

$$\delta_{max} = \max_i \left(\frac{1}{N} \sum_{j=1}^{N} \delta_{ij}\right). \tag{3.5}$$

If δ_{max} is larger than a threshold ε, pos is considered to be efficient, and corresponding point p_{pos} is added to the point set. Accordingly, one more segment is

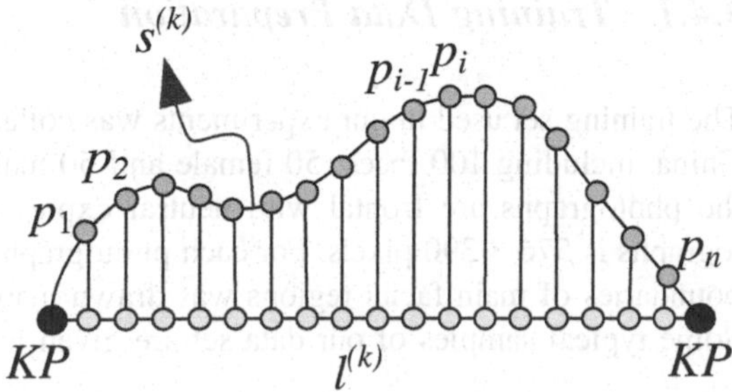

Fig. 3.7 Sample the outline segment $s^{(k)}$ to generate n candidate positions

added because p_{pos} splits one of the segments into two parts. The above process terminates when $\delta_{max} < \varepsilon$. The detailed IP generation process is summarized in Algorithm 3.1. If we take facial symmetry as a priori, two paired positions will be evaluated together by the average of their precision gain. In this case, one pair of IPs will be added to the point set for each iteration.

Algorithm 3.1. IP Generation

Input:

Point set: $P^{(0)} = \{KP_1, KP_2, \ldots, KP_{54}\}$;
Segment set: $S^{(0)} = \{s^{(1)}, s^{(2)}, \ldots, s^{(Ns)}\}$;
Iteration count: $m = 0$;

while $\delta_{max} < \varepsilon$ **do**
  Sample each face outline by $n \times (N_s + m)$ points;
  for $i = 1$ to $n \times (N_s + m)$ **do**
    for $j = 1$ to N **do**
      Calculate the precision gain of p_i on image j using (3.3);
    end for
    Calculate the average precision gain of position i across all training images;
  end for
  $m = m + 1$;
  Find the optimal inserting position using (3.4), then $IP_m = p_{pos}$;
  Add IP_m into point set, e.g.,
  $P^{(m)} = \{KP_1, KP_2, \ldots, KP_{54}, IP_1, IP_2, \ldots, IP_m\}$;
  Split the segment where p_{pos} locates on, and update the segment set, e.g., $S^{(m)} = \{s^{(1)}, s^{(2)}, \ldots, s^{(Ns+m)}\}$;
end while

Output: the added IP series

3.4 The Optimized Landmark Model

3.4.1 Training Data Preparation

The training set used in our experiments was collected from the city of Shanghai in China, including 100 faces (50 female and 50 male photographs respectively). All the photographs are frontal with neutral expression. The resolution of the photographs is 576 × 390 pixels. For each photograph, a face outline which depicts the boundaries of main facial regions was drawn manually with 54 KPs located on it. Some typical samples of our data set are given in Fig. 3.8.

Fig. 3.8 Some typical samples of the data set with face outlines drawn manually

3.4.2 IP Generation and the Optimized LM

Implementing the IP generation algorithm introduced in Sect. 3.3, we obtain a series of optimal positions for IPs. We take symmetry as a priori. The average precision gain of succeeding IP pairs on different facial regions is shown in Fig. 3.9. We can see that only the first several IPs have significant precision gain. Further increasing the number of IPs does not increase the model precision much. By observation, an appropriate threshold is $\varepsilon = 0.01$, because there are obvious gaps between precision gain of the preserved IP pairs and that of the discarded ones for face contour, eye, nose, and mouth. The gap is not so obvious for eyebrow, because the shapes of eyebrows are more diversified and difficult to describe. Hence, the IP generation process terminates when the precision gain is less than 0.01 pixel. The optimized models of the 5 facial regions are shown in Fig. 3.9, and totally 22 pairs of IPs are preserved. Figure 3.10 gives a whole picture of the contribution of the IPs and their effect on the model approximation error. Specifically, the approximation error decreases slowly after the number of IP pairs reaches 22, and the precision gain of the subsequent IP pairs is insignificant.

The optimized LM is a combination of 54 KPs and 44 IPs. A summary of the landmark positions and a list of the detailed position of each IP pair are given in Tables 3.3 and 3.4, respectively. Notice that in Table 3.4, the IP pairs of each facial

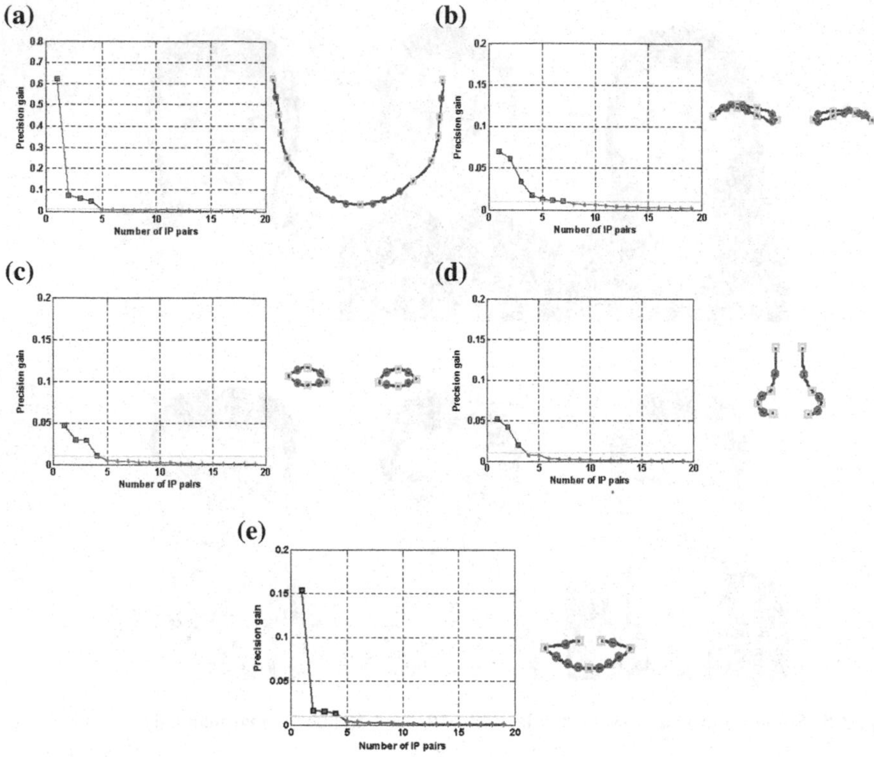

Fig. 3.9 Precision gain of succeeding IP pairs with the selected ones marked in *black squares* and the optimized models of different facial regions ($\varepsilon = 0.01$, KPs are marked with *square*, and IPs are marked with *circle*.) **a** Face contour. **b** Eyebrow. **c** Eye. **d** Nose. **e** Mouth

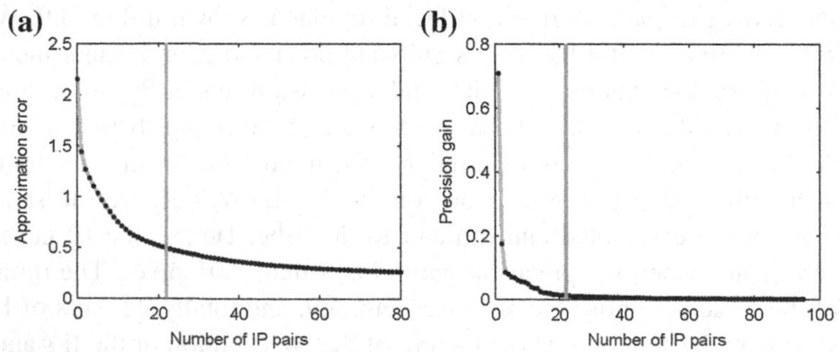

Fig. 3.10 **a** The approximation error with different number of IPs. **b** Precision gain of succeeding IP pairs ($\varepsilon = 0.01$ and the first 22 IP pairs are preserved)

Table 3.3 Summary of the landmark configuration

Region	KP no.	IP no.	Total
Face contour	11	8	19
Eyebrow	12	14	26
Eye	12	8	20
Nose	11	6	17
Mouth	8	8	16
Total	54	44	98

Table 3.4 Positions of the IP pairs

Region	Segment index	Positions
Face contour	5, 10	0.6, 0.4
	5, 10	0.3, 0.7
	5, 10	0.8, 0.2
	1, 6,	0.5, 0.5
Eyebrow	13, 17	0.7, 0.3
	11, 19	0.5, 0.5
	14, 22	0.8, 0.2
	16, 20	0.6, 0.4
	15, 21	0.5, 0.5
	12, 18	0.3, 0.7
Eye	11, 19	0.8, 0.2
	24, 27	0.5, 0.5
	26, 29	0.5, 0.5
	23, 28	0.5, 0.5
	25, 30	0.6, 0.4
Nose	31, 34	0.6, 0.6
	33, 36	0.5, 0.5
	32, 35	0.6, 0.6
Mouth	39, 40	0.4, 0.6
	37, 38	0.6, 0.4
	39, 40	0.7, 0.3
	39, 40	0.2, 0.8

region are ordered by their precision gains. The segment index refers to the segment number in Fig. 3.5. The directions of the segments are defined as either up-down or left-right, i.e., those on eyebrows, eyes, mouth, and jaw are left-right, and others are up-down. The position refers to the IP foot position on the chord along the direction of the corresponding segment. Figure 3.11 illustrates the layout of the proposed LM on a face image. We can see that most of the optimized IPs are located on positions with a large curvature, which is reasonable because high curvature requires more points to describe. Moreover, variances between faces always exist in these high curvature regions.

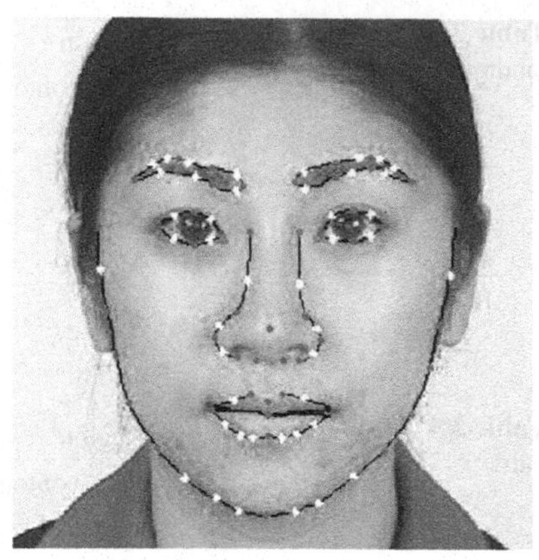

Fig. 3.11 Landmark positions of the optimized LM ("·"—KP and "*"—IP)

3.5 Comparison with Other Landmark Models

In this section, the optimized LM is compared with other LMs under two criteria. The first one is the approximation error defined as (3.1) in Sect. 3.3.1, which measures how precise a LM describes the shapes of facial organs. The second one is landmark detection error defined as the mean Euclidean distance between manually labeled landmarks and automatically detected ones. As mentioned in Sect. 3.1.1, ASM proposed by Cootes et al. (1995) is the most popular landmark detection method. It first trains a point distribution model (PDM) by using a set of labeled examples, then iteratively deforms it to fit to the object in a new image. In this section, we use ASM for landmark detection.

3.5.1 Comparison of Approximation Error

The PUT face database (Kasinski et al. 2008) was used for approximation error comparison. It contains face images of 100 people with the resolution of 1536 × 2048. We randomly selected 50 frontal face images, manually drew their face outlines, and located the landmarks according to different LMs. Then the approximation error of different LMs was calculated. We compared the optimized LM with 37, 68, 84, and 194 point LMs. The 37 point LM represents sparse model, the 68 and 84 point LMs belong to moderate model category, and the 194 LM represents dense model.

Table 3.5 shows that the optimized LM achieves lower approximation error than the 37, 68, and 84 point LMs for all facial regions as well as for the whole model. This is because the IP generation process which is introduced in Sect. 3.3 can better fit facial geometric structure. It achieves this by getting more landmarks where the contour has high curvature and less landmarks when shape of the contour is close to straight line. Although the 194 point LM achieves the lowest approximation error,

Table 3.5 Approximation error of different LMs

Region	37pt	68pt	84pt	194pt	Our model
Face	8.3562	0.7347	1.5076	0.1719	0.5139
Eyebrow	3.5955	1.6417	1.0795	0.2743	0.5042
Eye	0.6212	0.6212	0.1875	0.1299	0.1858
Nose	–	1.4038	1.2375	–	0.6743
Mouth	1.5438	0.3847	0.3847	0.1726	0.3344
Model error	4.9108	0.9868	1.0573	0.1912	0.4632

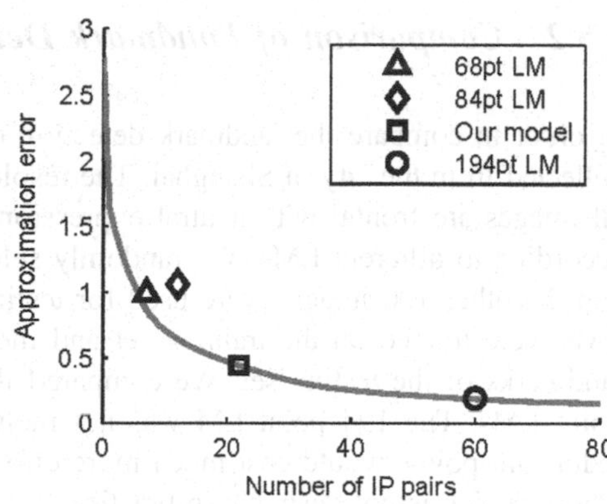

Fig. 3.12 Comparison of different LMs with reference of the approximation error curve of the proposed method

we will show that it is not an efficient design. Actually, there is a tradeoff between approximation error and the number of landmarks. Figure 3.12 shows the approximation error curve with succeeding IP pairs generated by the iterative search method, overlapped with the performance of different LMs. According to the definition of the 68, 84, and 194 point LMs (see Fig. 3.1), except KPs, the 68 point LM has 7 pairs of IPs (3 pairs on face contour, 1 pair on nose, and 3 pairs on mouth); the 84 point LM has 12 pairs of IPs (4 pairs on eyebrow, 4 pairs on eyes, 1 pair on nose, and 3 pairs on mouth); and the 194 point LM has 60 pairs of IPs (15 pairs on face contour, 14 pairs on eyebrow, 16 pairs on eye, 4 pairs on nose, and 11 pairs on mouth). From Fig. 3.12, we can see that the 194 point LM locates on the tail of the curve which is very flat. It means the 194 point LM has redundant landmarks with very small precision gain. We also observe that the approximation errors of the 68 and 84 point LMs are above the curve, which means the IPs generated with the proposed method are more effective. Figure 3.13 plots the approximating polygonal chains of different LMs on an example face. We can see that the 68 point LM has very large error in representing the shapes of eyebrow, eye, and nose. The 84 point LM has significant error in representing face contour and nose shape. The 98 point LM and 194 point LM approximate the contours of all facial regions very well. However, the 98 point LM saves much more landmarks than the 194 point LM.

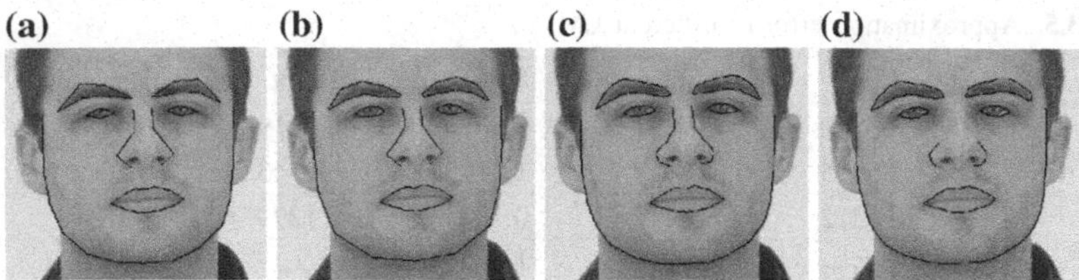

Fig. 3.13 Approximating polygonal chains of different LMs plotted on an example face. **a** 68 point LM. **b** 84 point LM. **c** The proposed 98 point LM. **d** 194 point LM

3.5.2 Comparison of Landmark Detection Error

In order to compare the landmark detection error, another 200 face images were collected from the city of Shanghai. The resolution of the images is 576 × 390 and all images are frontal with neutral expression. Landmarks were manually labeled according to different LMs. We randomly selected 100 images as the training set, and the other 100 images were used for testing. ASMs corresponding to different LMs were trained on the training set and then were used to automatically detect landmarks of the testing set. We compared the 98 point LM with the 68 and 84 point LMs. The 194 point LM was not included because it is not efficient. The redundant points would cost much more efforts when manually labeling the landmarks, which is not desirable in practice.

Figure 3.14 shows the result of this experiment. We can see that the 98 point LM performs better than the 68 and 84 point LMs. The inferior performance of the 84 point LM is due to the larger errors on the face contour, where the landmarks are placed with equal intervals. As it is difficult for human to estimate the intervals precisely, high variability will exist in manual labeling. Different from the 84 point LM, the 68 and 98 point LMs define landmarks on the face contour by taking horizontal levels of other facial organs for reference and obtain better performance.

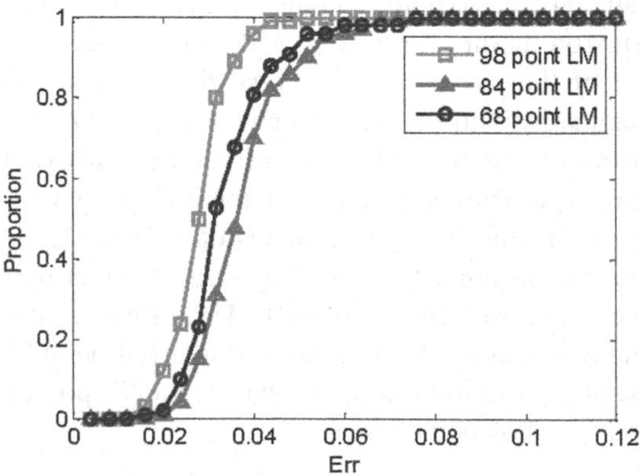

Fig. 3.14 Comparison of landmark detection error obtained using different LMs. The curves are cumulative distributions of the detection errors. The errors have been normalized by dividing the distance between pupils

3.6 Summary

In this chapter, we first introduce the landmark point and landmark model. Then we introduce the definition of the key point and inserted point of the landmark. Then we also present an optimized 98 point facial landmark model for delicate geometric facial representation, which includes 54 KPs and 44 IPs. The experimental results show that the optimized 98 point LM achieves a much lower approximation error than the other existing face LMs with a similar number of landmarks; and the optimized face LM shows its superiority in applications requiring delicate face shape description.

References

BioID Technology Research (2001) The BioID face. http://www.bioid.com

Brennan S (2007) Caricature generator: the dynamic exaggeration of faces by computer. Leonardo 40(4):392–400

Cootes TF, Taylor CJ, Cooper DH, Graham J (1995) Active shape models-their training and application. Comput Vis Image Underst 61(1):38–59

Dryden IL, Mardia KV (1998) Statistical shape analysis. Wiley, West Sussex

Eisenthal Y, Dror G, Ruppin E (2006) Facial attractiveness: beauty and the machine. Neural Comput 18(1):119–142

Farkas LG (1994) Anthropometry of the attractive North American Caucasian face. Anthropometry of the head and face, pp 159–179

Fasel B, Luettin J (2003) Automatic facial: a survey. Pattern Recogn 36(1):259–275

Kasinski A, Florek A, Schmidt A (2008) The PUT face. Image Process Commun 13(3–4):59–64

Leyvand T, Cohen-Or D, Dror G, Lischinski D (2008) Data-driven enhancement of facial attractiveness. ACM Trans Graph 27(3):38

Liao Q, Jin X, Zeng W (2012) Enhancing the symmetry and proportion of 3D face geometry. IEEE Trans Vis Comput Graph 18(10):1704–1716

Martinez AM (1998) The AR face. CVC Technical Report 24

Messer K, Matas J, Luettin J, Maitre G (1999) XM2VTS: The extended M2VTS. In: Proceedings of international conference on audio and video-based biometric person authentication, vol 964, pp 965–966

Milborrow S, Nicolls F (2008) Locating facial features with an extended. In: Proceedings of European conference on computer vision, pp 504–513

Milborrow S, Morkel J, Nicolls F (2010) The MUCT landmarked face. Pattern Recognition Association of South Africa 201

Nordstrom MM, Larsen M, Sierakowski J, Stegmann MB (2004) The IMM face -an annotated dataset of 240 face images. Informatics and Mathematical Modelling: Technical University of Denmark, DTU Informatics, Building 321

Perrett DI, May KA, Yoshikawa S (1994) Facial shape and judgements of attractiveness. Nature 368(6468):239–242

Schaefer S, McPhail T, Warren J (2006) Image deformation using moving least squares. ACM Trans Graph 25(3):533–540

Schmid K, Marx D, Samal A (2008) Computation of a face attractiveness index based on neoclassical canons, symmetry, and golden ratios. Pattern Recogn 41(8):2710–2717

Seshadri K, Savvides M (2009) Robust modified for automatic facial landmark annotation of frontal faces. In: Proceedings of IEEE 3rd international conference on biometrics: theory, applications, and systems, pp 1–8

Shi J, Samal A, Marx D (2006) How effective are landmarks and their geometry for face recognition? Comput Vis Image Underst 102(2):117–133

Suo J, Zhu S, Shan S, Chen X (2010) A compositional and dynamic model for face aging. IEEE Trans Pattern Anal Mach Intell 32(3):385–401

Tu C, Lien J (2010) Automatic location of facial feature points and synthesis of facial sketches using direct combined model. IEEE Trans Cybern Syst Man Cybern Part B 40(4):1158–1169

Zhang Y, Sim T, Tan CL, Sung E (2006) Anatomy-based face reconstruction for animation using multi-layer. J Vis Lang Comput 17(2):126–160

Zhang D, Zhao Q, Chen F (2011) Quantitative analysis of human facial beauty using geometric features. Pattern Recogn 44(4):940–950

Chapter 4
Geometrics Facial Beauty Study

This chapter for facial beauty analysis mainly presents our studies on extraction and normalization of facial geometric features, one important kind of features for facial beauty analysis, as well as model evaluation and statistical analysis of facial beauty. Quantified means used for evaluation of models and hypotheses on facial beauty lead to new and valuable conclusions. For example, the conducted analyses show that male and female faces are generated from two different but overlapping distributions and the mean face shapes of males and females are very similar. This chapter also shows that the multivariate Gaussian model can be used as a benchmark of the landmark model.

The content of this chapter is organized as follows: we briefly introduce facial beauty study in Sect. 4.1. Section 4.2 shows the preliminary work, including data collection, geometric feature extraction and normalization. In Sect. 4.3, we give the statistical analysis and introduce the landmark model evaluation method for facial beauty study. The experimental results and discussion are provided in Sect. 4.4. Finally, we summarize this chapter in Sect. 4.5.

4.1 Introduction

As far as we know, there are several hypotheses and rules of what make a face attractive (Etcoff 1994; Langlois and Roggman 1990; Perrett et al. 1999; Jones and Debruine 2007). For example, faces with the following features are thought to be more attractive: general characteristics like symmetry and averageness, or specific characteristics like high forehead and small nose. However, the published studies have not yet reached consensus on those hypotheses or rules.

In the last few years, computational approaches have been developed, which bring new ways and means to the facial beauty study. For example, morphing and wrapping programs are used to make composite faces or change the appearance of a face, which are further used as stimuli in the experiments (Perrett et al. 1994;

D. Zhang et al., *Computer Models for Facial Beauty Analysis*,
DOI 10.1007/978-3-319-32598-9_4

Pallett et al. 2010; Rhodes et al. 2001; Valenzano et al. 2006). Machine learning techniques such as Support Vector Regression (SVR), kernel regression, and K Nearest Neighbors (KNN) are used for beauty score prediction, virtual plastic surgery and automatic digital face beautification (Leyvand et al. 2008; Davis and Lazebnik 2008; Liu et al. 2009; Whitehill and Movellan 2008; Eisenthal et al. 2006).

Despite the increasing interest and extensive research in this field, the nature of human's aesthetic perception is still not well known. Which rules or models fit better is still in debate. There is no public database or benchmark for the purpose of facial beauty analysis. The databases used in previous studies are not large enough to include adequate attractive faces, due to the fact that beautiful individuals make up a small percentage of the population (Atiyeh and Hayek 2008). Although researchers tried to find some numeric expressions of beauty by extracting geometric related features such as distances or proportions (Wang et al. 1997; Pallett et al. 2010; Schmid et al. 2007), it was not usually possible to generate graphical representations of shape from these features because the geometric relationships among the variables were not preserved (Adams et al. 2004). So in this chapter we mainly present a useful landmark model evaluation method for facial beauty study.

4.2 Preliminary Work

4.2.1 Data Collection

According to earlier studies, beautiful individuals are a small percentage of the population (Atiyeh and Hayek 2008). The features representing a face are high dimensional due to the complexity of human face structures. To study facial beauty, we need a large-scale database which includes enough beautiful faces. Because of the highly non-rigid characteristic and intrinsic 3-D structure of face, automatic geometric feature extraction needs face images of the same pose and expression. The data used in our experiments are frontal photographs with neutral expression collected from Northeast China. The volunteers include 15393 females and 8019 males aged between 20 and 45. Each subject corresponds to one color image with 358×441 pixels in size. A sub-database is constructed by manually selecting more attractive faces. The resulting beauty data set contains 587 female images and 288 male images, which account for 3.7 % of the total images.

4.2.2 Feature Extraction

The attractiveness of a face is affected by a number of factors such as facial skin texture, symmetry, color and shape. To quantify and analyze all factors together is very difficult. Geometric feature plays an important role in facial beauty perception. As it is shown in Fig. 4.1, people will have different attractiveness responses when

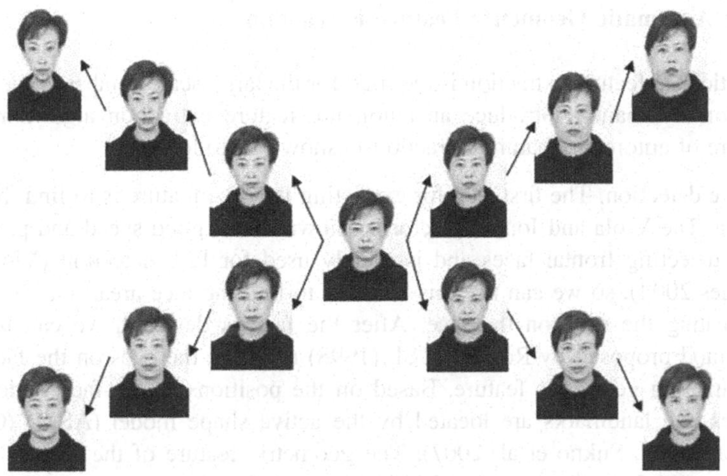

Fig. 4.1 Images with the same texture but different geometric features

changing the geometric features while keeping other factors constant. So it is necessary to learn the effect of geometric feature on the perception of facial beauty.

4.2.2.1 Definition of Geometric Feature

The geometric feature is defined by a set of landmarks on the face (please see Chap. 2 for the detailed introduction of landmarks). Figure 4.2 shows the 68 landmarks of a face. Landmarks are located on the major facial organs, including facial outline, eye-brows, eyes, nose, and mouth. The Cartesian coordinates of the landmarks form a configuration matrix, representing the geometric feature on the face, i.e.,

$$\mathbf{G} = \begin{bmatrix} x_1 & x_2 & \cdots & x_{68} \\ y_1 & y_2 & \cdots & y_{68} \end{bmatrix}^T, \tag{4.1}$$

where 'T' denotes the transpose operator. In this way, the face images are represented by configuration matrices.

Fig. 4.2 Landmarks on the face are used to define its geometric feature

4.2.2.2 Automatic Geometric Feature Extraction

Automatic face feature extraction is required for the large-scale database. So, in this subsection we mainly introduce an automatic feature extraction algorithm. The procedure of automatic feature extraction is shown as follows:

(1) Face detection. The first step for extracting the face feature is to find the face area. The Viola and Jones detector is known for its good speed and precision on detecting frontal faces and is widely used for face detection (Viola and Jones 2004), so we can use this detector to find the face area first.
(2) Locating the eyes on the face. After the face is detected, we can use the method proposed by Rowley et al. (1998) to locate the eyes on the face.
(3) Extracting geometric feature. Based on the positions of the face region and eyes, the landmarks are located by the active shape model (ASM) (Cootes et al. 1995; Sukno et al. 2007). The geometric feature of the face is finally generated from these extracted landmarks.

4.2.3 Geometric Feature Normalization

The feature extraction process converts a face image into a configuration matrix, which contains the shape information of the face. Before statistical analysis, the geometric features need to be normalized by removing the non-shape variations. For 2-D landmarks, the non-shape variations include translation, in-plane rotation and scale. The normalization method presented in this subsection is data driven and carried out once for all, i.e., female and male face shapes are treated together as a whole population. After normalization, the configuration matrices have to be converted into 136-D feature vectors and projected into tangent space. The main step of geometric feature normalization is as follows:

(1) Filtering translation

Translation can be filtered out by moving the center of landmarks to the origin of the coordinate system. It can be achieved by pre-multiplying **G** with a matrix

$$\mathbf{C} = \mathbf{I}_{68} - \frac{1}{68}\mathbf{1}_{68}\mathbf{1}_{68}^{T}. \tag{4.2}$$

Then the centered configuration matrix is obtained using

$$\mathbf{G}_c = \mathbf{CG}. \tag{4.3}$$

(2) Filtering scale

Scale invariance is also desired in shape analysis. The magnitude of a centered configuration matrix is defined as its Euclidean norm

$$\|\mathbf{G}_c\| = \sqrt{trace(\mathbf{G}_c^T \mathbf{G}_c)}. \tag{4.4}$$

Scale can be filtered out by normalizing the configuration matrix, i.e.,

$$\tilde{\mathbf{G}} = \mathbf{G}_c / \|\mathbf{G}_c\|. \tag{4.5}$$

(3) Filtering rotation

In-plane rotation does not change the shape of an object. The pre-shapes need alignment before statistical analysis. The alignment process can be achieved with an iterative scheme shown in Algorithm 4.1.

Algorithm 4.1. Shape Alignment

Step 1: Initialization

Calculate the mean shape and normalize it by

$$\bar{\mathbf{G}}^{(0)} = \frac{1}{n}\sum_{i=1}^{n}(\tilde{\mathbf{G}}_i) \Big/ \left\| \frac{1}{n}\sum_{i=1}^{n}(\tilde{\mathbf{G}}_i) \right\|. \tag{4.6}$$

Rotate the entire shape sample onto the mean shape. The rotation matrix is defined as follows,

$$\mathbf{R}_i^* = \arg\min_{\mathbf{R}} \left\| \beta \tilde{\mathbf{G}}_i \mathbf{R} - \bar{\mathbf{G}}^{(0)} \right\| \quad \beta \in \Re, \tag{4.7}$$

where $\mathbf{R}$ is the 2×2 rotation matrix with one free variable. $\mathbf{R}_i^*$ is given by $\mathbf{R}_i^* = \mathbf{U}\mathbf{V}^T$, where $\tilde{\mathbf{G}}_i^T \bar{\mathbf{G}}^{(t)} = \mathbf{U}\Lambda\mathbf{V}^T$ (Dryden and Mardia 1998). So we get the aligned shape sample

$$\tilde{\mathbf{G}}_i^{(0)} = \tilde{\mathbf{G}}_i \mathbf{R}_i^*. \tag{4.8}$$

Step 2: Mean shape is updated by

$$\bar{\mathbf{G}}^{(t)} = \frac{1}{n}\sum_{i=1}^{n}(\tilde{\mathbf{G}}_i^{(t-1)}) \Big/ \left\| \frac{1}{n}\sum_{i=1}^{n}(\tilde{\mathbf{G}}_i^{(t-1)}) \right\|. \tag{4.9}$$

Step 3: Sample update

$$\mathbf{R}_i^* = \arg\min_{\mathbf{R}} \left\| \beta \tilde{\mathbf{G}}_i^{t-1} \mathbf{R} - \bar{\mathbf{G}}^{(t)} \right\| \quad \beta \in \Re \tag{4.10}$$

$$\tilde{\mathbf{G}}_i^{(t)} = \tilde{\mathbf{G}}_i^{(t-1)} \mathbf{R}_i^*. \tag{4.11}$$

Step 4: Convergence condition

If

$$\left\| \bar{\mathbf{G}}^{(t)} - \bar{\mathbf{G}}^{(t-1)} \right\| < \varepsilon, \tag{4.12}$$

the alignment is completed, or else go to **step 2.**

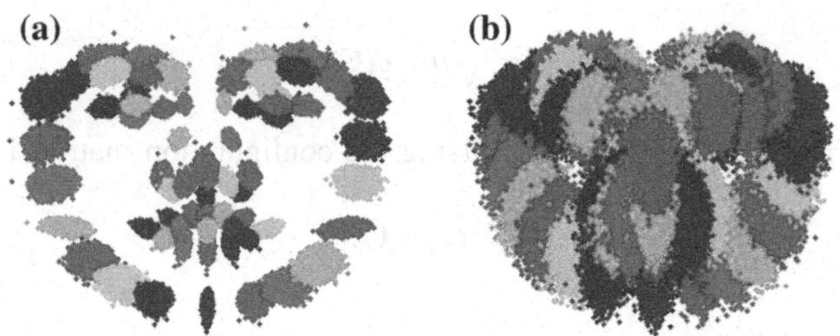

Fig. 4.3 Landmark distributions before and after normalization. **a** Before. **b** After

(4) Projection to tangent space

Tangent space is a linear space and Euclidean distance can be used to measure the difference between shapes. These advantages lead us to do one more step showed below. The configuration matrix can be rewritten in the vector form of

$$\mathbf{g} = \left[G_{1,1}, G_{1,2}, G_{2,1}, G_{2,2}, \ldots, G_{68,1}, G_{68,2}\right]^T. \tag{4.13}$$

The constraint of the tangent space is $(\tilde{\mathbf{g}}_i - \bar{\mathbf{g}}) \cdot \bar{\mathbf{g}} = 0$, where $\bar{\mathbf{g}} = {}^1/_n \sum_{i=1}^{n} \mathbf{g}_i$. When $\|\bar{\mathbf{g}}\| = 1$,

$$\tilde{\mathbf{g}}_i = \frac{\mathbf{g}_i}{\mathbf{g}_i \cdot \bar{\mathbf{g}}}. \tag{4.14}$$

In this way, we project all the geometric feature vectors onto its tangent space. Figure 4.3 shows the scatter plots of landmarks before and after normalization.

4.3 Landmark Model Evaluation Method

4.3.1 Basic Statistical Analysis

One basic statistic we get from the database is mean shape. We are interested in how much difference between female and male mean shapes and whether this difference is statistically significant. So we will analyze the basic statistical in this subsection.

First, the face shapes of the female and male are considered as two groups of independent random samples $X_1, X_2, \ldots, X_{n_1}$ and $Y_1, Y_2, \ldots, Y_{n_2}$ from mean shapes μ_1 and μ_2. To test between

$$H_0 : \mu_1 = \mu_2 \quad versus \quad H_1 : \mu_1 \neq \mu_2.$$

Then carrying out Hotelling's T^2 two sample test (Dryden and Mardia 1998).

The multivariate normal model is proposed in the tangent space, where

$$x_1, x_2, \ldots, x_{n_1} \sim N(\mu_1, \Sigma),$$
$$y_1, y_2, \ldots, y_{n_2} \sim N(\mu_2, \Sigma).$$

The sample means and sample covariance matrices are denoted as $\bar{x}, \bar{y}$ and $\mathbf{S}_x, \mathbf{S}_y$. The Mahalanobis distance squared between $\bar{x}$ and $\bar{y}$ is

$$D^2 = (\bar{x} - \bar{y})^T \mathbf{S}_u^- (\bar{x} - \bar{y}), \tag{4.15}$$

where $\mathbf{S}_u = (n_1 \mathbf{S}_x + n_2 \mathbf{S}_y)/(n_1 + n_2 - 2)$, and $\mathbf{S}_u^-$ is the Moore-Penrose generalized inverse of $\mathbf{S}_u$. The test statistic is

$$F = \frac{n_1 n_2 (n_1 + n_2 - M - 1)}{(n_1 + n_2)(n_1 + n_2 - 2)M} D^2, \tag{4.16}$$

where $M = 68 \times 2 - 4$. It is the dimension of the tangent space, because we have filtered four degrees of freedom, two for translation, one for rotation, and one for scale. The test statistic has $F_{M, n_1 + n_2 - M - 1}$ distribution under H_0. Hence, we reject H_0 for large values of F.

4.3.2 Principal Component Analysis (PCA)

PCA can be used in the tangent space to summarize the main modes of variations in a database, from which we can have an intuitive understanding of the database. Besides, PCA is often applied for dimension reduction, under the criterion of minimum mean square error (MSE) (Liu and Wechsler 2000). We do PCA analysis only on female data and denote them as a sample of random vector X. The covariance of X is defined as

$$\Sigma_X = E\{[X - E(X)][X - E(X)]^T\} = \Phi \Lambda \Phi^T \tag{4.17}$$

with

$$\Phi = [\phi_1, \phi_2, \ldots, \phi_{136}],$$
$$\Lambda = diag\{\lambda_1, \lambda_2, \ldots, \lambda_{136}\},$$

where Φ is the eigenvector matrix, and Λ is the diagonal eigenvalue matrix with diagonal elements in decreasing order.

To visually show the modes of the shape variations, we reconstruct the shape vector along the direction of each PC (principal component). A series of reconstructed shape vectors for PC_i are calculated by

$$X_c^* = E(X) + c\phi_i \tag{4.18}$$

with different c. In this way, we can visually tell what effect each PC has on the variation of shapes. Moreover, we can study the relationship between this variation and the perception of beauty.

In the experiment of this subsection, first 25 PCs are used for dimension reduction i.e., $P = [\phi_1, \phi_2, \ldots, \phi_{25}]$. The correspondent eigenvalues take 95 % of the total energy. Hence, there is almost no information lost in the dimension reduction process

$$Y = P^T X = [Y_1, Y_2, \ldots, Y_{25}]^T. \tag{4.19}$$

4.3.3 Multivariate Gaussian Model

For the high dimensional data, it is extremely difficult to derive accurate non-parametrical density estimation (Liu and Wechsler 2000). In order to simplify the problem, the within class densities are usually modeled as Gaussian distributions. We are interested in distributions of two groups of people, one is the attractive group, and the other is the whole population. For the data after dimension reduction, we define

$$\begin{array}{l} Y_b : \textit{attractive sample} \\ Y : \textit{the whole population} \end{array}, \quad \{Y_b\} \subset \{Y\}.$$

We assume that each element in vector Y follows the Gaussian distribution. Take the first element Y_1 as an example, the Gaussian assumption is an approximate to the real distribution shown in Fig. 4.4, where Fig. 4.4a is the histogram of Y_1 and Fig. 4.4b is its quantile-quantile plot (Thode 2002). If the distribution of Y_1 is Gaussian, the plot will be close to linear. According to Fig. 4.4, the Gaussian assumption is reasonable. Since the covariance matrix of Y is diagonal, the elements of Y are independent of each other. So, we have

$$\begin{array}{l} Y_i \sim N(\mu_i, \sigma_i^2), \quad Y_{bi} \sim N(\mu_{bi}, \sigma_{bi}^2) \\ p(Y) = p(Y_1)p(Y_2)\cdots p(Y_{25}) \end{array} \tag{4.20}$$

$$p(Y_b) = p(Y_{b1})p(Y_{b2})\cdots p(Y_{b25}). \tag{4.21}$$

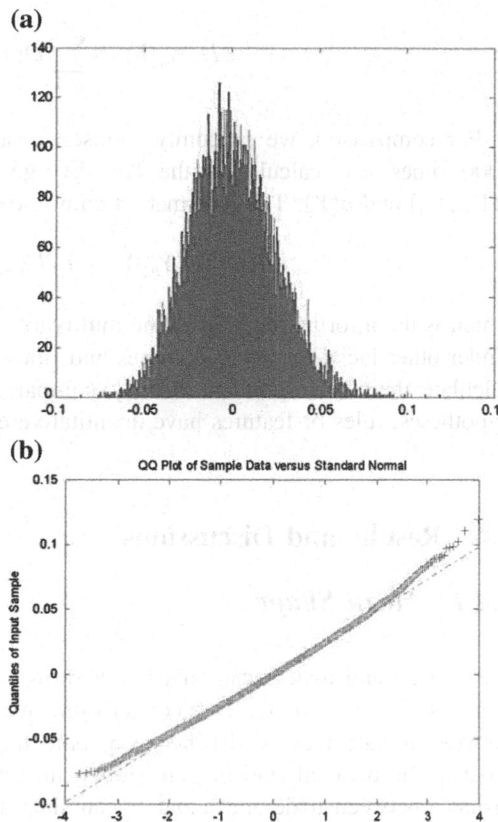

Fig. 4.4 **a** Histogram of Y_1. **b** Quantile-quantile plot of Y_1

4.3.4 Model Evaluation

After $p(Y)$ and $p(Y_b)$ are obtained in previous subsections, we can get the beauty related information brought by people who selected the more attractive images through calculating the difference of them. Kullback-Leibler divergence (KL divergence) is a measure of difference between two probability distributions. For two univariate Gaussian distributions, the KL divergence is defined as

$$\begin{aligned} D(Y_{bi}||Y_i) &= \int_{-\infty}^{\infty} p(Y_{bi})\log\frac{p(Y_{bi})}{p(Y_i)}dy_i \\ &= \frac{(\mu_{bi}-\mu_i)^2}{2\sigma_i^2} + \frac{1}{2}\left(\frac{\sigma_{bi}^2}{\sigma_i^2} - 1 - \ln\frac{\sigma_{bi}^2}{\sigma_i^2}\right). \end{aligned} \tag{4.22}$$

Replacing $p(Y_{bi})$ and $p(Y_i)$ with $p(Y_b)$ and $p(Y)$ given by (4.20) and (4.21), we get the following KL divergence

$$D(Y_b||Y) = \sum_{i=1}^{25} D(Y_{bi}||Y_i). \quad (4.23)$$

For comparison, we randomly choose n_b samples from the whole population 1000 times and calculating the KL divergence between sample distributions $p(Y_{random})$ and $p(Y)$. The information gain is defined as

$$IG = D(Y_b||Y) - E(D(Y_{random}||Y)), \quad (4.24)$$

which is the information gain of the multivariate Gaussian model on the database. Under other facial beauty hypotheses and rules (Schmid et al. 2007), we can also calculate their correspondent *IG*. By comparing the information gain, different hypotheses, rules or features have quantitative evaluations.

4.4 Results and Discussions

4.4.1 Mean Shape

The female and male mean shapes are shown in Fig. 4.5. The distance between them is $d_{\mu_1\mu_2} = 0.0161$. For comparison, we calculate the pairwise distances between female faces (F-F), between male faces (M-M), and between all faces (ALL). The detailed statistics are shown in Table 4.1. The results show that the distance between male and female mean shapes is smaller than any pairwise face shape.

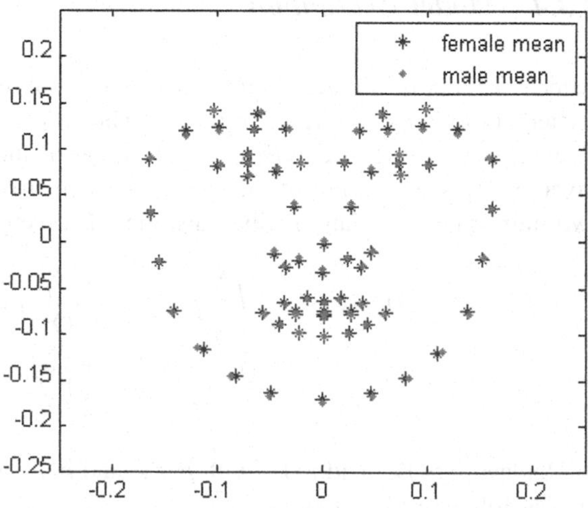

Fig. 4.5 Overlaid female and male mean shapes

Table 4.1 Statistics of pairwise shape distance

Statistics	F-F	M-M	ALL
MAX	0.2284	0.2223	0.2254
MIN	0.0201	0.0208	0.0193
MEAN	0.0717	0.0749	0.0740
STD	0.0165	0.0175	0.0168

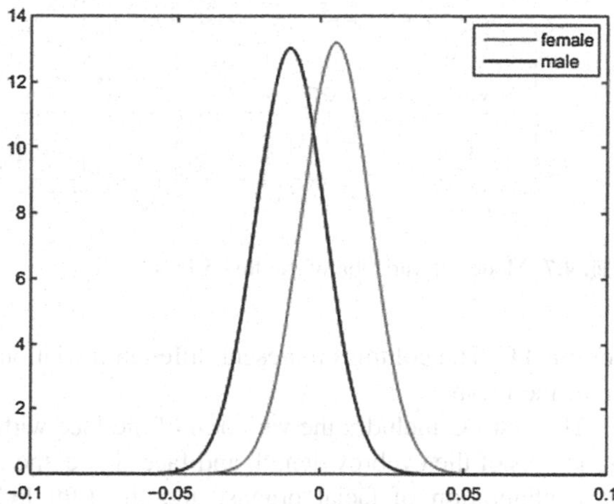

Fig. 4.6 The distributions of α for female and male faces

Now we are interested in whether this distance is caused by chance or statistically significant. We carry out the Hotelling's T^2 two sample test described in Sect. 3.1. The F statistic is calculated in terms of (4.16). We have F=140.85 and the null distribution $F_{123.23279}$. Since $P(F > 1.55) = 0.0001$ and F is much larger than 1.55, they demonstrate that the F statistic has significant difference in female and male shapes.

A projection score can be got by projecting the data onto the direction of $\mu_1 - \mu_2$

$$\alpha = \mathbf{g}^T(\mu_1 - \mu_2)/\|\mu_1 - \mu_2\| \tag{4.25}$$

for each subject. For simplicity, in the experiment, we use the Gaussian model for α, and the distributions for female and male are shown in Fig. 4.6. This result supports the significant difference between female and male mean shapes and gives some hints to sex recognition task.

4.4.2 Main Modes of Variation

The main modes of variations are summarized by applying PCA. Figure 4.7 shows the reconstructed shape vector series along directions of the first 5 PCs, each row

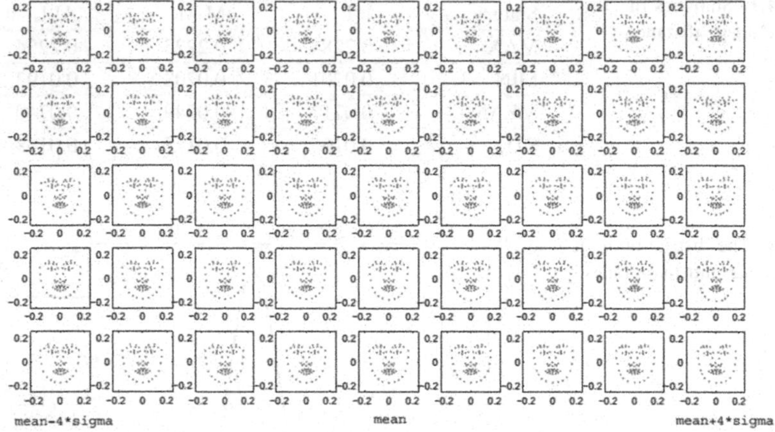

Fig. 4.7 Modes of variation of the first 5 PCs

for one PC. The columns represent different deviations, $[-4\sigma, \ldots, -\sigma, 0, \sigma, \ldots, 4\sigma]$, from the mean.

The first PC includes the variation of the face width, the second PC includes the variations of the eyebrow length and face shape, the third PC includes the variation of configuration of facial organs, and the fifth PC includes slight out-of-plane rotation. As the shape variability is complicated, we can make only coarse descriptions. However, Fig. 4.7 provides visual explanation for beauty studies based on PCA coefficients. For example, the distributions of the first element of Y and Y_b are shown in Fig. 4.8. With reference to the first row in Fig. 4.7, we observe that attractive faces have a tendency to be thinner than the mean face. Results in this part are descriptive. They explain the differences between two groups of faces Y and Y_b visually, which gives some cues for facial beauty perception study.

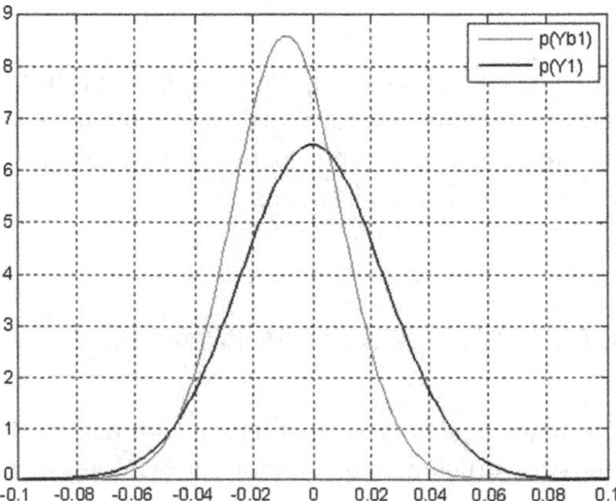

Fig. 4.8 Probability density functions of Y_1 and Y_{b1}

4.4.3 Information Gain

For quantitative study of facial beauty, we calculate the information gain defined by (4.24) under the multivariate Gaussian model, averageness hypothesis, and symmetry hypothesis.

(1) *Multivariate Gaussian model*: the information gain of the multivariate Gaussian model is calculated by (4.22)–(4.24). During the process, we can find that: first, the KL divergence between $p(Y_{random})$ and $p(Y)$ is much smaller than that between $p(Y_b)$ and $p(Y)$. Second, different elements contribute different amount of information. We sort the elements according to their contribution, and show the information gain under different numbers of elements in Fig. 4.9. Some detailed results are listed in Table 4.2.

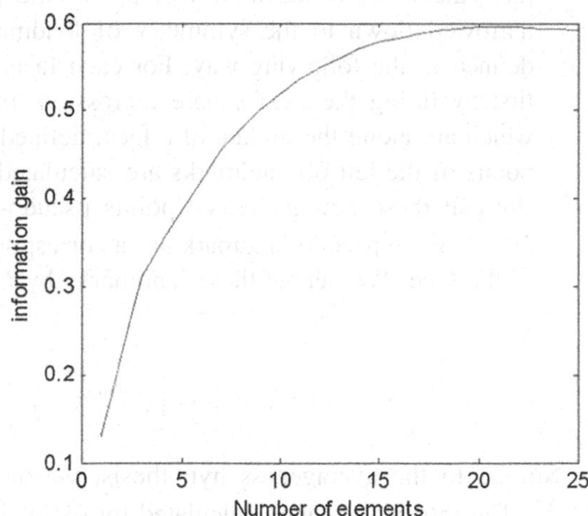

Fig. 4.9 Information gain under different numbers of elements

Table 4.2 Information gain of different methods

Methods	Number of feature dimensions	Information gain
Averageness	1	0.0585
Symmetry	1	0.0046
Multivariate Gaussian model	1	0.1288
	2	0.2210
	3	0.3110
	5	0.3867
	10	0.5191
	25	0.5907

(2) *Averageness hypothesis*: the averageness hypothesis assumes that a beautiful face is a simple one that is close to an average of all faces. The averageness score s_a of subject face shape g can be defined as

$$s_a = -\|g - \bar{g}\|, \tag{4.26}$$

where $\bar{g}$ is the average face shape.

Beautiful group X_b and whole population X have different distributions of s_a. We model them as Gaussian distributions and denote them as $p(s_a^{X_b})$ and $p(s_a^X)$. The information gain can also be calculated by (4.22) and (4.24). The result is shown in Table 4.2.

(3) *Symmetry hypothesis*: the symmetry hypothesis assumes the more symmetric a face, the more beautiful it will be. In the present study, the symmetry is narrowed down to the symmetry of landmarks. The symmetry score s_s is defined in the following way. For each face, the symmetry axis is estimated first by fitting the least square regression line through the eight landmarks, which are along the middle of a face, defined in Fig. 4.2. Then the symmetry points of the left 60 landmarks are calculated in terms of the symmetry axis. We call these new generated points pseudo-landmarks and denote them by L^{pseudo}. Each pseudo-landmark has a corresponding landmark on the same side of the face. We denote these landmarks by L^{cor}, and

$$s_s = -\left\|L^{pseudo} - L^{cor}\right\|. \tag{4.27}$$

Similar to the averageness hypothesis, we have two distributions $p(s_s^{X_b})$ and $p(s_s^X)$. The information gain calculated by (4.24) is shown in Table 4.2.

The results show that averageness hypothesis and symmetry hypothesis reveal much less beauty related information than the multivariate Gaussian model. In the Gaussian model, the information is concentrated in a few elements. Although the multivariate model is not proved to be optimal, it can serve as a benchmark under the information gain criterion.

4.5 Summary

This chapter presents geometric features and a useful evaluation method for facial beauty analysis. The geometric features are normalized and mapped into the tangent space, which is a linear space and the Euclidean distance can be used to measure the shape difference. The statistical analyses show that male and female faces are generated from two different distributions, but these two distributions overlap each other and the two mean face shapes are very similar. PCA is applied to summarize the main modes of face shape variations and perform dimension reduction. Kullback-Leibler divergence between the beautiful group and the whole population is used to measure the beauty related information embodied in the selected features. In this sense, the multivariate Gaussian model performs better than the averageness hypothesis and symmetry hypothesis.

References

Adams DC, Rohlf FJ, Slice DE (2004) Geometric morphometrics: ten years of progress following the 'revolution'. Italian J Zool 71(1):5–16

Atiyeh BS, Hayek SN (2008) Numeric expression of aesthetics and beauty. Aesthetic Plast Surg 32:209–216

Chen F, Zhang D (2010) A benchmark for geometric facial beauty study. Med Biom 21–32

Cootes TF, Taylor CJ, Cooper DH, Graham J (1995) Active shape models-their training and application. Comput Vis Image Underst 61(1):38–59

Davis BC, Lazebnik S (2008) Analysis of human attractiveness using manifold kernel regression. In: Proceedings of IEEE conference on image processing, pp 109–112

Dryden IL, Mardia KV (1998) Statistical shape analysis. Wiley

Eisenthal Y, Dror G, Ruppin E (2006) Facial attractiveness: beauty and the machine. Neural Comput 18:119–142

Etcoff NL (1994) Beauty and the beholder. Nature 368:186–187

Jones BC, Debruine LM (2007) The role of symmetry in attraction to faces. Percept Psychophys 69(8):1273–1277

Langlois JH, Roggman LA (1990) Attractive faces are only average. Psychol Sci 1:115–121

Leyvand T, Cohen-Or D, Dror G, Lischinski D (2008) Data-driven enhancement of facial attractiveness. ACM Siggraph 27(3):38

Liu C, Wechsler H (2000) Robust coding schemes for indexing and retrieval from large face databases. IEEE Trans Image Process 9:132–137

Liu J, Yang X, Xi T, Gu L, Yu Z (2009) A novel method for computer aided plastic surgery prediction. In: Proceedings of IEEE international conference on biomedical engineering and informatics, pp 1–5

Pallett PM, Link S, Lee K (2010) New 'golden' ratios for facial beauty. Vis Res 50(2):149–154

Perrett DI, Burt DM, Penton-Voak IS, Lee KJ, Rowland DA, Edwards R (1999) Symmetry and human facial attractiveness. Evol Hum Behav 20:295–307

Perrett DI, May KA, Yoshikawa S (1994) Facial shape and judgements of female attractiveness. Nature 368:239–242

Rhodes G, Yoshikawa S, Clark A, Lee K, McKay R, Akamatsu S (2001) Attractiveness of facial averageness and symmetry in non-western cultures: In: Search of biologically based standards of beauty. Perception vol 30, pp 611–625

Rowley HA, Baluja S, Kanade T (1998) Neural network-based face detection. IEEE Trans Pattern Anal Mach Intell 20:23–38

Schmid K, Marx D, Samal A (2007) Computation of a face attractiveness index based on neoclassical canons, symmetry and golden ratios. Pattern Recogn 41(8):2710–2717

Sukno FM, Ordas S, Butakoff C, Cruz S, Frangi AF (2007) Active shape models with invariant optimal features: application to facial analysis. IEEE Trans Pattern Anal Mach Intell 29 (7):1105–1117

Thode HC (2002) Testing for normality. Marcel Dekker

Valenzano DR, Mennucci A, Tartarelli G, Cellerino A (2006) Shape analysis of female facial attractiveness. Vis Res 46:1282–1291
Viola P, Jones MJ (2004) Robust real-time face detection. Int J Comput Vis 57(2):137–154
Wang D, Qian G, Zhang M, Leslie GF (1997) Differences in horizontal, neoclassical facial cannons in Chinese (Han) and North American Caucasian populations. Aesthetic Plast Surg 21:265–269
Whitehill J, Movellan JR (2008) Personalized facial attractive prediction. In: Proceedings of IEEE international conference on automatic face and gesture recognition, pp 1–7

Chapter 5
Putative Ratio Rules for Facial Beauty Indexing

Chapters 3 and 4 have shown the significance of geometric features in facial beauty analysis. These two chapters focus on only feature points generated from the landmark model. Ratio associated features are a kind of simple geometric features and their influence on beauty evaluation is easily understood. Since ratio associated features were proposed they had been widely studied in facial beauty analysis. As we know, a number of putative rules were proposed before the computer technique is widespread, so objective analysis on them is necessary. Though previous computer-based facial beauty analysis has studied some of them, the study is still not sufficient. As a result, it is useful to conduct more comprehensive investigation and testing on putative rules for facial beauty analysis.

Averageness and ideal proportions are the most investigated issues in studies on facial beauty. In this chapter, we integrate the findings on these two aspects to identify race invariant ideal facial proportions. We introduce the background of putative ratio rules for facial beauty indexing in Sect. 5.1. Then we present the work of data preparation for testing putative ratio rules, including the average face dataset, facial landmark extraction and putative ratio rules in Sect. 5.2. In Sect. 5.3, we present the multi-national average face clustering method. Section 5.4 assesses the putative ratio rules on both the whole dataset and individual clusters, selects those with high universality, and corrects their ideal values. Section 5.5 tests the corrected rules on both well controlled synthesized faces and beautiful faces in the real world. Finally, we give a summary in Sect. 5.6.

5.1 Introduction

Beauty is easy enough to spot, but tricky to define. The existence of objective and universal criteria of facial beauty has attracted debates among philosophers, psychologists and biologists for centuries (Etcoff 1994; Wolf 1990; Gaut and Lopes 2001).

D. Zhang et al., *Computer Models for Facial Beauty Analysis*,
DOI 10.1007/978-3-319-32598-9_5

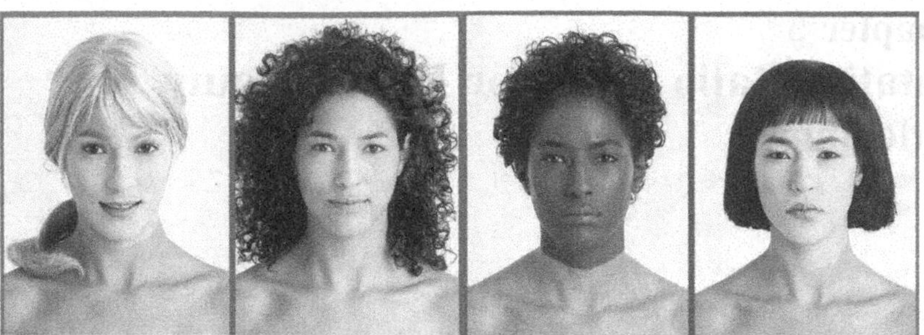

Fig. 5.1 Beautiful faces of different races. This illustration is from New Women Magazine. It is makeup by Paddy Crofton

One popular claim is that 'beauty is in the eye of the beholder', in which the perception of facial beauty stems from personal experience, and cultural background, etc. However, this cannot explain the fact that even two-month-old infants prefer to gaze at faces that adults find attractive. Moreover, there is evidence that shows significant cross-cultural agreement in facial attractiveness rating of faces from different ethnic groups (Perrett et al. 1998). Recently, researchers have also shown that racially and ethnically diverse faces possess similar facial features that are considered desirable and attractive regardless of the racial and cultural background of the perceiver (Jefferson 2004). This is illustrated in Fig. 5.1. At first glance, you will see four beautiful racially diverse women with ideal facial proportions, but actually, they are the same person with makeup and wig. Some attractive traits, which may reflect biological benefits from an evolutionary point of view, may be invariant of culture and time. Such findings encourage us to find objective and universal criteria of facial beauty.

The pursuit of quantitative rules for facial beauty has never stopped. One important category of these rules is defined in the form of ideal ratios, such as neoclassical canons, horizontal fifths and vertical thirds rules and golden ratio (1.618) rule. However, the validity of these putative rules is still in question, and contradictions even exist between different rules. For example, according to the concept of horizontal fifths, the ratio between the face width at eye level and the inter-external canthus distance should be 5/3, while according to the golden ratio, that ratio should be 1.618. Recently, Schmid et al. (2008) found that only a small subset of ratio features is important for prediction of facial attractiveness. For the selected ratio features, the preference of the human raters did not parallel the canons or golden ratios as defined by the putative rules, e.g., female raters preferred the ratio of lip to chin distance with the inter-ocular distance to be less than the golden ratio regardless of the gender of the face. Pallett et al. (2010) and Fan et al. (2012) generated synthesized face images by manipulating a virtual face image to fit and deviate from the rules, and then invited human raters to choose the most attractive one. The results showed that the most preferred face does not correspond with most of the putative ratios, while the face that have neoclassical canons and most possible golden ratios only received a below medium rating. All of these findings reveal that the putative rules are not very precise. So in this chapter, we first introduce the putative rules, and then we present a correction procedure of the putative rules.

5.2 Data Preparation

Langlois and Roggman (1990) showed that composite faces, digitally blended and averaged faces, were regarded as more attractive than most of the faces used to create them. Supportive results have been reported by other researchers, who performed experiments on their own datasets (Komor et al. 2009; Zhang et al. 2011), e.g., Japanese, Chinese and German faces, etc.

In order to find the ratio rules shared by beautiful faces and robust to race variations, we use average faces from 61 countries/regions as the benchmark beautiful faces in this chapter.

5.2.1 *Average Face Dataset*

The averageness hypothesis has aroused the interest of artists and researchers, who have collected face images either by traveling around the world to take photographs or via the Internet, and generated average faces of those from different countries/regions by using a morphing technique. The average face dataset which we used in this chapter has two origins. Some of them were generated by a photographer from South Africa who has travelled around the world, taken pictures of the current inhabitants from different cities. By using morphing software, the photographer can be synthesized into average faces. The other average faces were collected from a website: http://pmsol3.wordpress.com. There are in total, 73 female average faces and 75 male average faces from 61 countries/regions: 23 from Asia, 23 from Europe, 5 from Africa, 2 from Australia, and 8 from the Americas. Table 5.1 lists the detailed information of the countries/regions contained in the dataset. All of the average faces are frontal views with neutral expressions, as shown in the examples in Fig. 5.2.

5.2.2 *Landmark Extraction*

Facial landmarks can be used as a compact and effective representation of facial geometry. As discussed in Chap. 3, the 98 point landmarks have good performance in describing the face. So in this chapter, we also use landmarks with 98 points to analyze the quantitative rules for facial beauty. Figure 5.3 shows a face with 98 landmarks, which are distributed on the major facial organs, including facial outline, eyebrows, eyes, nose and mouth. As in many face images, the hairline is obscured, so that it is difficult to locate the landmarks. Hence, we have omitted these landmarks in this chapter.

Table 5.1 Countries or regions contained in the average face dataset

Index	Region	Index	Region
1	China	31	Russian
2	Hong Kong	32	Ukraine
3	Taiwan	33	Latvia
4	Tibetan	34	Romania
5	Japan	35	Finland
6	South Korea	36	Sweden
7	Philippines	37	Poland
8	Mongolia	38	Czech
9	Burma	39	Austria
10	Thailand	40	Hungary
11	Cambodia	41	Croatia
12	Vietnam	42	Serbia
13	India	43	Greece
14	Afghanistan	44	Netherlands
15	Uzbekistan	45	Germany
16	Iran	46	Belgium
17	Iraq	47	France
18	Saudi Arabia	48	Switzerland
19	Israel	49	Italy
20	Syria	50	Ireland
21	Lebanon	51	United Kingdom
22	Cyprus	52	Portugal
23	Turkey	53	Spain
24	Egypt	54	USA
25	Ethiopia	55	Puerto Rico
26	Cameroon	56	Mexico
27	South Africa	57	Brazil
28	Western Africa	58	Ecuador
29	Australia	59	Peru
30	Samoa	60	Argentina
		61	Chile

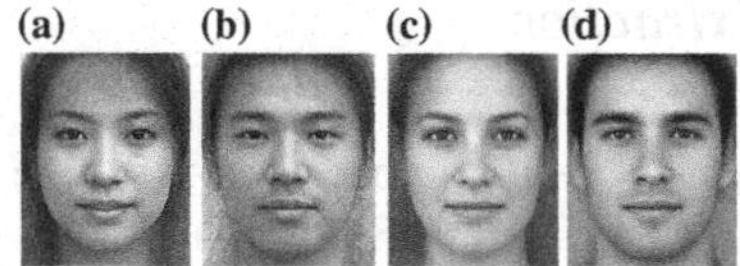

Fig. 5.2 Examples of average faces in the dataset. **a** Japanese female, **b** Japanese male, **c** Australian female, and **d** Australian male

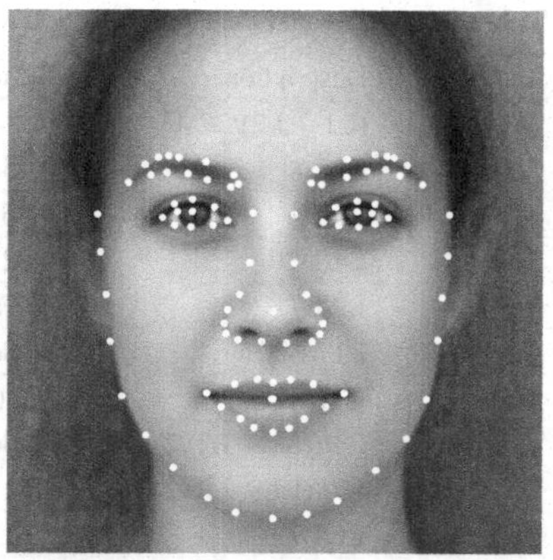

Fig. 5.3 98 landmarks to represent the facial geometry

Given the landmarks, it is thus convenient to calculate the ratios defined in the putative rules, because all key positions with clear biological meanings are included. Besides that, the x- and y-coordinates of the landmarks are concatenated to form a vector that represents the global geometric structure of the face, i.e.

$$G = (x_1, x_2, \ldots x_{98}, y_1, y_2, \ldots y_{98})^T, \tag{5.1}$$

which can be used to measure the global differences between face shapes (Zhang et al. 2011).

Facial beauty analysis requires accurate positions of landmarks, because a subtle variation may cause large differences in attractiveness. Therefore, automatically extracted landmarks are further manually adjusted to guarantee precision. In this chapter, the active shape model (ASM) method is also used to automatically locate the landmarks (Cootes et al. 1995).

5.2.3 Collection of Putative Ratio Rules

To the best of our knowledge, no work thoroughly summarizes the putative ratio rules. Therefore, it is necessary to review the relevant studies and provide a concise summary. Table 5.2 lists the 26 putative ratio rules which have appeared in the literature and can be calculated with the landmarks defined in Sect. 5.2.2, and Fig. 5.4 illustrates the distances used in defining these ratios. In Table 5.2, R1 corresponds to the horizontal fifths rule; R4 is the result of combining the golden ratio and vertical thirds, i.e., (3/2 × L21)/L4 = 1.618, where 3/2 × L21 is the face length according to the vertical thirds rule; Farkas et al. (1985) mentioned R2, R5, R8, R10, and R16 in their work; Schmid et al. (2008) made a more complete summary of

Table 5.2 Ratios and their reported ideal values in documented rules of beauty

Index	Description	Ideal value
R1	(L1 + L2)/2/L4	0.2[a]
R2	L7/L8	0.25 (Farkas et al. 1985)
R3	L5/L4	0.46 (Pallett et al. 2010)
R4	L4/L21	0.92[b]
R5	L3/L7	1 (Farkas et al. 1985)
R6	L17/L20	1 (Schmid et al. 2008)
R7	L11/L7	1.6 (Kiekens et al. 2008b)
R8	L3/((L1 + L2)/2)	1 (Schmid et al. 2008), 1.618 (Schmid et al. 2008)
R9	L7/((L1 + L2)/2)	1.618 (Schmid et al. 2008)
R10	L6/L7	1.618 (Schmid et al. 2008), 1.5 (Farkas et al. 1985)
R11	L6/L3	1.618 (Schmid et al. 2008)
R12	L5/L7	1.618 (Schmid et al. 2008)
R13	L5/L3	1.618 (Schmid et al. 2008)
R14	L22/L6	1.618 (Kiekens et al. 2008a)
R15	L4/L22	1.618 (Kiekens et al. 2008a)
R16	L20/L11	1.618 (Gunes et al. 2006), 1 (Farkas et al. 1985)
R17	L20/L19	1.618 (Schmid et al. 2008)
R18	L18/L19	1.618 (Gunes et al. 2006)
R19	L19/L12	1.618 (Gunes et al. 2006)
R20	L11/L12	1.618 (Gunes et al. 2006)
R21	(L14 + L16)/L7	1.618 (Schmid et al. 2008)
R22	(L14 + L16)/L3	1.618 (Schmid et al. 2008)
R23	L3/L16	1.618 (Schmid et al. 2008)
R24	L7/L16	1.618 (Schmid et al. 2008)
R25	(L1 + L2)/2/L12	1.618 (Schmid et al. 2008)
R26	L7/L12	1.618 (Schmid et al. 2008)

[a]Horizontal fifths

[b]Vertical thirds and golden ratio: 0.618 × 3/2

neoclassical and golden ratios, including R6, R8–R13, R17, and R21–R26; another 4 golden ratios, R16, R18–R20, were covered by Gunes and Piccardi (2006), who used the ratios to assess facial beauty; R7, R14, and R15 were provided by Kiekens et al. (2008a, b), who studied the norms of these ratios on Caucasoid faces for aesthetic plastic surgery; and R3 is the “new” golden ratio which was obtained according to human preference in a study by Pallett et al. (2010). As we can see, with the exception of R3, most of the ideal values in the rules are defined to be the golden ratio 1.618 or some simple proportion, such as 1/5, 1/4, 1, etc. For the same ratio, different documents supply different ideal values, e.g., R8, R10 and R16.

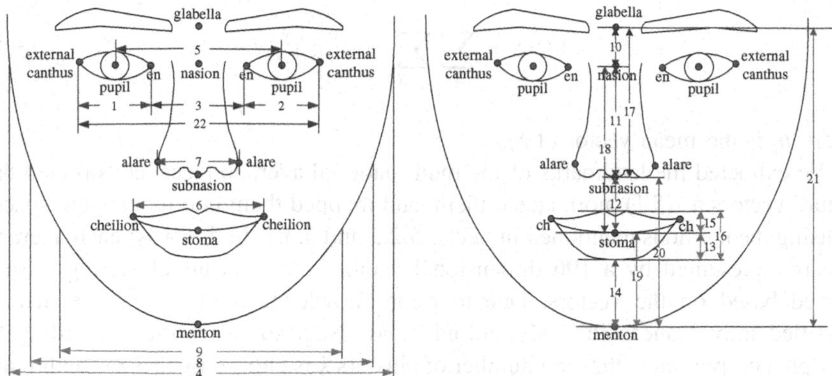

Fig. 5.4 Illustration of the distances

5.3 Multi-national Average Faces Clustering

5.3.1 Measurement of Shape Differences

The shape of an object is the geometrical information that remains when location, scale and rotation effects are filtered out (Dryden and Mardia 1998). Given the feature vectors as (5.1), a normalization step that follows the method proposed in Chen and Zhang (2010) is implemented to remove non-shape variations. The normalized feature vector is denoted by g. When the objects in a dataset are quite close in shape, the use of the Euclidean distance in the tangent space will be a good approximation to shape distances. It has been proven that human face shapes distribute in a very condensed subspace of the whole shape space (Zhang et al. 2011). Hence, we mapped the normalized feature vector into the tangent space and used the Euclidean distance as the measurement of shape differences. The constraint of the tangent space is $(\tilde{g} - \bar{g}) \cdot \bar{g} = 0$, where $\bar{g} = 1/n \sum_{i=1}^{n} g_i$. When $\|\bar{g}\| = 1$, which is the result of the normalization step, the corresponding feature vector in the tangent space will be $\tilde{g} = \frac{g}{g \cdot \bar{g}}$.

5.3.2 k-Means Clustering

Given a set of observations $(g_1, g_2, \ldots, g_n)$, where each observation is a d-dimensional real vector, k-means clustering aims to partition n observations into k $(k \leq n)$ sets $S = \{S_1, S_2, \ldots, S_k\}$ so as to minimize the within-cluster sum of squares (WCSS).

$$WCSS = \sum_{i=1}^{k} \sum_{g_j \in S_i} (g_j - \mu_i)^2, \tag{5.2}$$

where μ_i is the mean vector of S_i.

We extracted the landmarks of the multi-national average faces, constructed the feature vectors as (5.1), normalized them, and mapped them into the tangent space, by using the methods mentioned in Sects. 5.2.2 and 5.3.1. In this way, each average face is represented by a 196 dimensional vector, and k-means clustering is performed based on the vectors. Due to prior knowledge, humans can be mainly classified into 'Caucasoid', 'Mongoloid', and 'Negroid' categories according to their phenotypic traits, thus the number of clusters k is chosen to be 3 for both male and female.

If we use the demographic categories of faces from different countries (refer to Table 5.6 in Appendix 1) as a reference, the clustering result is summarized as follows: 91.7 % Mongoloid female and 92.3 % Mongoloid male average faces are in the same cluster; 80 % Negroid female and 100 % Negroid male average faces are in the same cluster; and 79.7 % Caucasoid female and 91.3 % Caucasoid male faces are in the same cluster. In other words, the three clusters mainly represent Mongoloid, Caucasoid and Negroid people. The images in each cluster are shown in Appendix 2.

5.3.3 Centers of Clusters

A cluster center represents the typical face of each cluster. Figure 5.5a shows the super-average faces of the three clusters, which are generated by warping the faces

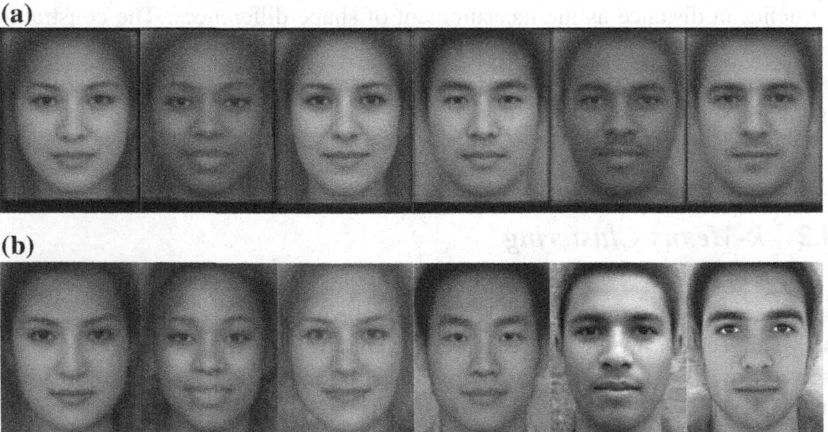

Fig. 5.5 Centers of clusters. **a** Super-average faces of the three clusters. **b** Average face closest to the center of each cluster

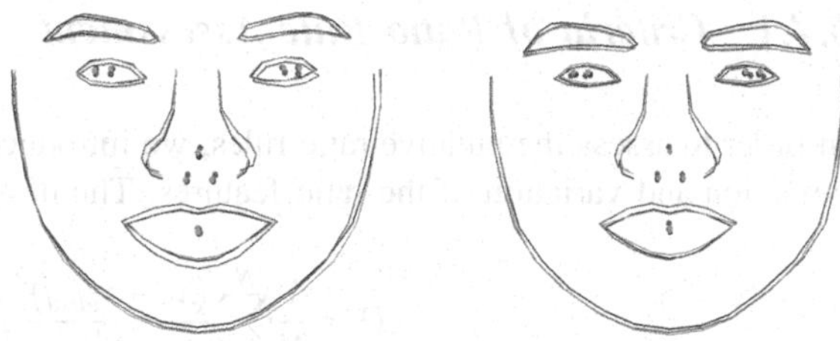

Fig. 5.6 Overlapped shapes of the three cluster centers, '*red*'—Negroid, '*blue*'—Mongoloid, and '*green*'—Caucasoid. *Left* female. *Right* male

Table 5.3 Significant differences between clusters with a significant level of 0.001

Cluster pairs	Female	Male
Mongoloid versus Negroid	R2, R7, R16, R20, R25	R6, R7, R16, R18
Mongoloid versus Caucasoid	R4, R6, R16, R18, R21, R22	R6, R18
Negroid versus Caucasoid	R2, R7	R2, R7, R9, R10, R12, R23, R26

in the same cluster to the mean shape of the cluster and averaging by pixels. The moving least square (MLS) method was used for warping, with the 98 landmarks as the control points (Schaefer and McPhail 2006). Figure 5.5b shows the average face in the dataset that is closest to the center of each cluster. The overlapped shapes of the three cluster centers are presented in Fig. 5.6. The centers of the three clusters are different in nose width, lip thickness, etc. In order to identify the differences with statistical significance, we performed two sample t-test on the 26 ratio features defined in Table 5.2. For significant level $\alpha = 0.001$, the significant differences between the clusters are listed in Table 5.3. Taking the female data as an example, we can see that the Negroid faces are significantly different from the other two clusters in nose shape (R2 and R7), and the vertical divisions of the Mongoloid faces are different from the other faces (R16, R6, R18, and R20), which implies that some of the putative ratio rules are race dependent.

5.4 Assessment and Correction of Putative Ratio Rules

One limitation of the previous work is that the rating scores of a small group of people were used to establish the ground truth on attractiveness (Schmid et al. 2008). Although strong agreement exists between raters, the insufficient number of raters may cause a bias. Another limitation is that the face images used were a specific group of people (e.g. Caucasoid) or generated with one virtual face image, so the conclusions may not be robust to race variations.

In this section, we will assess the ratio-based rules on both the whole dataset and individual clusters, select those with high universality, and finally, make appropriate corrections to the ideal values of the selected ratios to increase the accuracy.

5.4.1 Criteria of Ratio Rule Assessment

In order to assess the putative ratio rules, we introduce two indexes to measure the deviation and variation of the ratio features. The deviation is calculated using

$$D = \frac{1}{N}\sum_{i=1}^{N}\frac{(x_i - x_{ideal})^2}{\bar{x}^2}, \tag{5.3}$$

where x_i is the ratio value of image i, N is the number of average faces in the dataset, and $\bar{x} = \frac{1}{N}\sum_{i=1}^{N} x_i$. The variation is calculated by replacing x_{ideal} in (5.3) with $\bar{x}$, i.e.

$$V = \frac{1}{N}\sum_{i=1}^{N}\frac{(x_i - \bar{x})^2}{\bar{x}^2}. \tag{5.4}$$

Large deviation means that the ideal value is not accurate, while a larger variation implies that the rule is less universal. The deviation can be decomposed into a variation part and a bias part, i.e.

$$\begin{aligned} D &= \frac{1}{N\bar{x}^2}\sum_{i=1}^{N}(x_i - x_{ideal})^2 = \frac{1}{N\bar{x}^2}\sum_{i=1}^{N}(x_i - \bar{x} + \bar{x} - x_{ideal})^2 \\ &= \frac{1}{N\bar{x}^2}\sum_{i=1}^{N}\left[(x_i - \bar{x})^2 + 2(x_i - \bar{x})(\bar{x} - x_{ideal}) + (\bar{x} - x_{ideal})^2\right] \\ &= \frac{1}{N}\sum_{i=1}^{N}\frac{(x_i - \bar{x})^2}{\bar{x}^2} + \frac{1}{N}\sum_{i=1}^{N}\frac{(\bar{x} - x_{ideal})^2}{\bar{x}^2} \\ &= V + Bias. \end{aligned} \tag{5.5}$$

The variation part cannot be avoided regardless how well we estimate the ideal values, while bias can be reduced by correcting the ideal values of the rules. Therefore, the ratio features that have low variation are selected first, and then the ideal value of the selected ratios is adjusted to the corresponding sample means of the dataset.

5.4.2 Experimental Results on the Whole Dataset and Individual Clusters

We first perform k-means clustering on the average face dataset, and then examine the 26 rules with respect to the accuracy and universality on both the entire average face dataset and individual clusters.

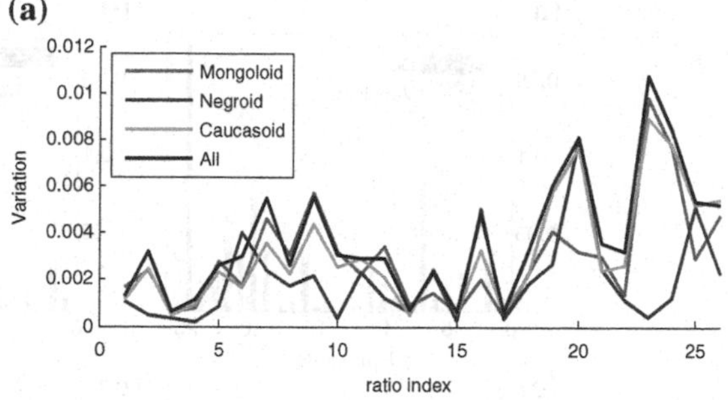

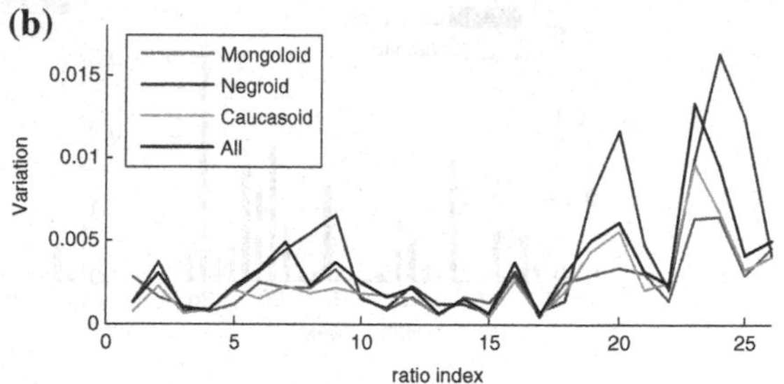

Fig. 5.7 Variation of the 26 ratio features on the three ethnic clusters. **a** Female. **b** Male

Table 5.4 Universal ratio features

Data	Top 5 universal ratio features	
	Female	Male
The whole dataset	R15, R3, R17, R13, R4	R17, R13, R15, R4, R3
Mongoloid cluster	R17, R15, R3, R4, R13	R17, R13, R4, R11, R3
Negroid cluster	R4, R15, R3, R10, R17	R15, R3, R17, R4, R11
Caucasoid cluster	R3, R13, R15, R17, R4	R15, R17, R13, R3, R1

Figure 5.7 shows the variations on the whole dataset and individual clusters. We can see that the variations in the Mongoloid, Negroid, and Caucasoid clusters are very similar. Moreover, the three clusters are consistent for the most universal ratio features, e.g., variations in R3, R4, R13, R15 and R17 are among the lowest for all of the curves shown in Fig. 5.7. Table 5.4 lists the top 5 universal ratios of the different clusters. Although the orders are a little bit different, the subsets are nearly the same, including 3 horizontal ratios for the eye level (R3, R13 and R15), 1 vertical ratio for lower part of face (R17), and 1 hybrid ratio between the face width and face height (R4). Interestingly, the female and male data obtain the same subset.

A comparison of the deviation and variation is shown in Fig. 5.8. For a large proportion of the features, the deviation is much larger than the variation. According to (5.5), this means that the ideal values of the corresponding rules of those features are biased. To minimize the deviation, we adjusted the ideal values of the universal features to the sample mean. Since the most universal features are consistent across the different clusters, we used all of the data to calculate the

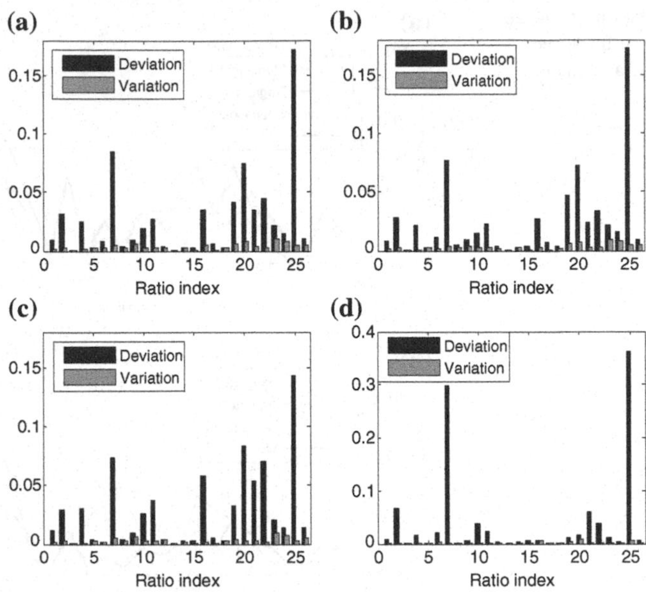

Fig. 5.8 Deviation and variation of the 26 rules on (female). **a** The whole dataset. **b** Caucasoid cluster. **c** Mongoloid cluster. **d** Negroid cluster

Table 5.5 Correction of the putative ratio rules of beauty

Index	Ideal value	Corrected value		p value (one sample t-test)	
		Female	Male	Female	Male
R3	0.46	0.466	0.4614	1.5409×10^{-5}	0.3707
R4	0.92	1.086	1.0571	7.4311×10^{-50}	1.9447×10^{-51}
R13	1.618	1.638	1.6393	2.1356×10^{-4}	2.1074×10^{-5}
R15	1.618	1.540	1.5865	1.1682×10^{-27}	2.8050×10^{-9}
R17	1.618	1.505	1.4959	1.2017×10^{-37}	1.2711×10^{-43}

sample mean. Table 5.5 shows the putative ideal values and the corrected values. In order to show the significance of the differences between them, one-sample t-test was implemented under the hypothesis that H_0: $X_{ideal} = X_{corrected}$ and H_1: $X_{ideal} \neq X_{corrected}$, which is equivalent to test if the sample mean is equal to a specified value X_{ideal}, because $X_{corrected} = \bar{X}$. The results show that except for R3 for male data, the hypothesis tests on the top 5 universal ratio features obtain small *p*-values, which means that the correction of the ideal value is necessary. Note that the putative ideal value of R3 is also obtained through statistical analysis on the preference of humans (Rhee and Lee 2010), instead of some divine number. Therefore, many putative rules have overestimated the effect of divine numbers, while the rules based on the measurements of real faces are more objective, accurate, and robust.

5.5 Testing of the Corrected Ratio Rules

In this section, we test the validity of the corrected rules on the synthesized face images and real face images, respectively.

The average faces of different ethnic groups are good representatives of beautiful faces of the corresponding races. So these average faces are then clustered into 3 groups by the *k*-means method. The result is consistent with the anthropology divisions, i.e., the clusters are dominated by Caucasoids, Negroids, and Mongoloids. Although the putative ratio rules are not very precise, they are popular and deserve further investigation. Therefore, we will collect putative ratio rules that have appeared in the literature and quantitatively evaluate their universality and precision on both a whole dataset and individual clusters. The results show that most of the ideal values defined in the putative rules are biased, and the subsets of the top 5 universal ratio features of the three clusters are nearly the same, which means the most universal ratio rules are robust to race variations. The precision of these rules can be further improved by adjusting the ideal values according to the data. In this way, we obtain a series of corrected ratio rules.

5.5.1 Testing on Synthesized Faces

In order to test the validity of the corrected ratio rules, we first prepared original faces, from which the ratios were altered to generate other face images.

As shown in Fig. 5.9, all synthesized faces have the same texture, but different geometric structures. Specifically, the face images in Fig. 5.9 differ in: (a) the distance between the eyes; (b) the face contour; (c) the ratio between face length and width; (d) the size of the eyes; and (e) the position of the mouth, among which Fig. 5.9a–e keep other facial parts unchanged, while Fig. 5.9c keeps other facial proportions unchanged. Figure 5.9a, b are used to test R3 (pupil distance/face width at eye level). The 7 images in each row correspond to the ideal value of R3 plus $[-9\sigma, -6\sigma, -3\sigma, 0, 3\sigma, 6\sigma, 9\sigma]$, where σ is the standard variation of R3 on the average face database. Similarly, Fig. 5.9c–e are used to test R4 (face width at eye level/face length), R13 (pupil distance/en-en distance), and R17 (lower face length/mouth-menton distance), respectively. Figure 5.9a, c also embed the variations in R15 (face width at eye level/ex-ex distance).

The 35 synthesized face images presented in Fig. 5.9 are shown in a random order as stimuli, and a total of 36 volunteers participated to judge the generated face images by their attractiveness with a 7-point scale, where '7' represents the most attractive and '1' represents the least attractive. Figure 5.10 shows a plot of the mean opinion score (MOS) of the face images in each row. The synthesized face images are generated by manipulating one ratio to fit and deviate from the rules while keeping the other facial features unchanged. Obviously, the faces that exactly fit the corrected ideal ratio obtain the highest MOS. As the ratio deviates from the ideal value, the MOS of the face

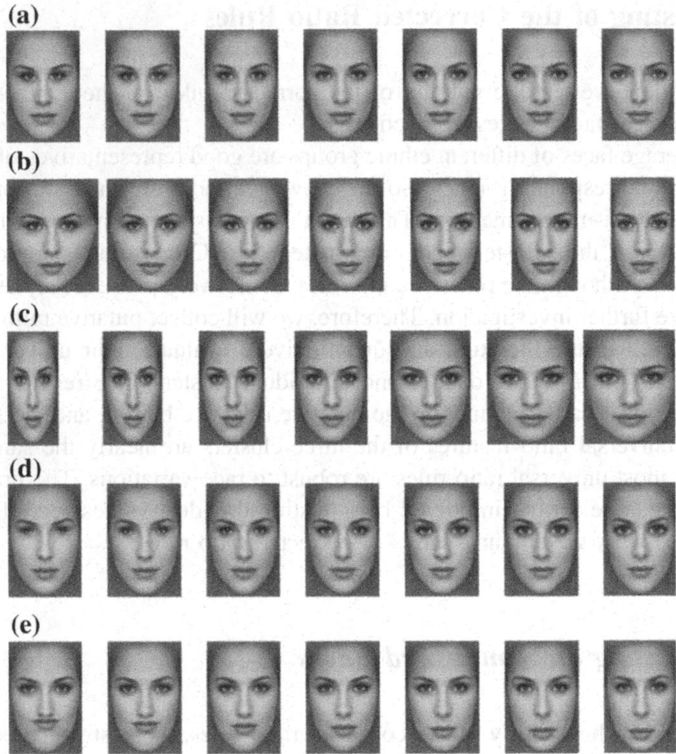

Fig. 5.9 Synthesized face images that differ in (**a**) the distance between the eyes; **b** the face contour; **c** the ratio between face length and width; **d** the size of the eyes; and **e** the position of the mouth. The 7 images in each row correspond to faces with an ideal ratio plus $[-9, -6, -3, 0, 3, 6, 9]\sigma$ respectively, where σ is the standard variation of the corresponding ratio on the average face database

image will decrease, although the rate of decrease is comparatively less when enlarging the eyes (row 4), enlarging the distance between the pupils (row 1), and changing only R4 while keeping other facial proportions constant (row 3). In other words, the synthesized face with most of the corrected rules obtains the highest score, and those with a ratio value larger or less than the ideal value by more than 3σ (σ is the standard variation on beautiful faces) obtain very low scores. The experiment result verifies the validity of the corrected ratio rules.

5.5.2 *Testing on Real Faces*

In this subsection, the corrected ratio rules are tested on real face images. In total, 390 face images of well-known beautiful women were collected, including the winners in Miss World and Miss Universe competitions, movie stars, and super models.

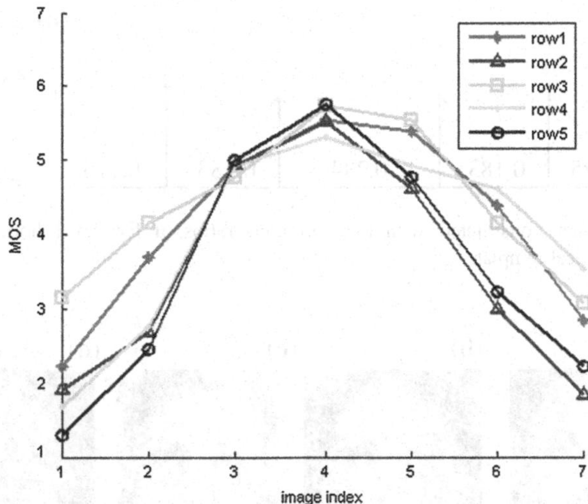

Fig. 5.10 The MOS of the synthesized face images

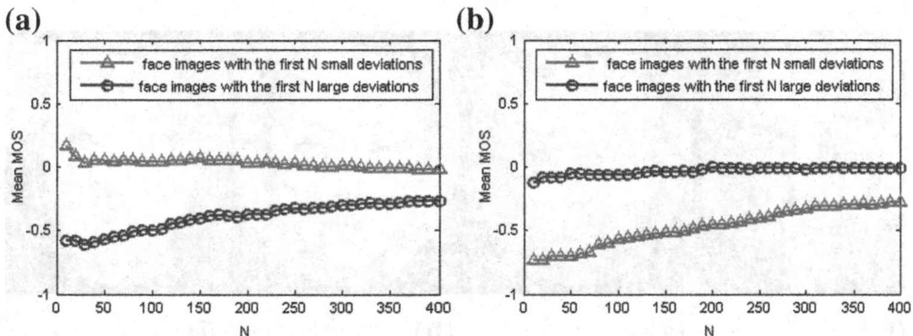

Fig. 5.11 The mean MOS of two groups of face images: images with the first *N* small deviations and those with the first *N* large deviations from (**a**) corrected ratio rules and (**b**) the putative ratio rules

Moreover, 409 frontal face images were selected from the M2VTS database and a Chinese database. The face images were shown in random order as stimuli and 36 volunteers gave their judgments of {−1, 0, 1} which represent not beautiful, common, and beautiful, respectively.

For each face image, we calculated the total deviation from the corrected ratios rules, selected the faces with the first *N* small deviations and those with the first *N* large deviations, and calculated their average MOSs. The result is shown in Fig. 5.11a. Faces with a small deviation have stable MOSs, while as the deviation grows larger, the MOSs will monotonically decrease. This reveals that when the deviation is small, the attractiveness of the face is determined by other features, such as the smoothness of the skin and the details of facial organ shapes. However, when

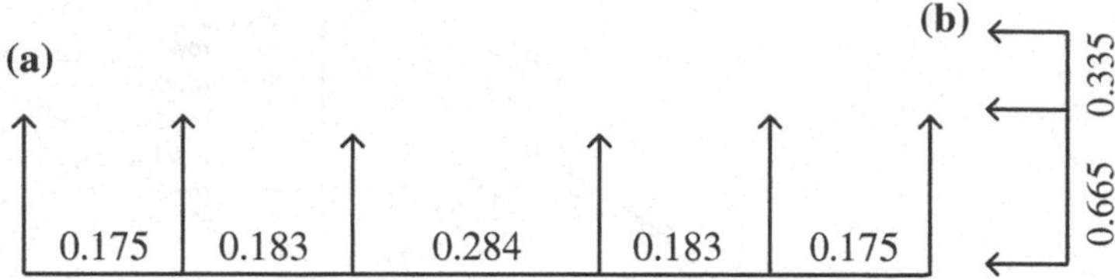

Fig. 5.12 Templates constructed with the corrected ratios. **a** Eye-level horizontal template. **b** Lower face vertical template

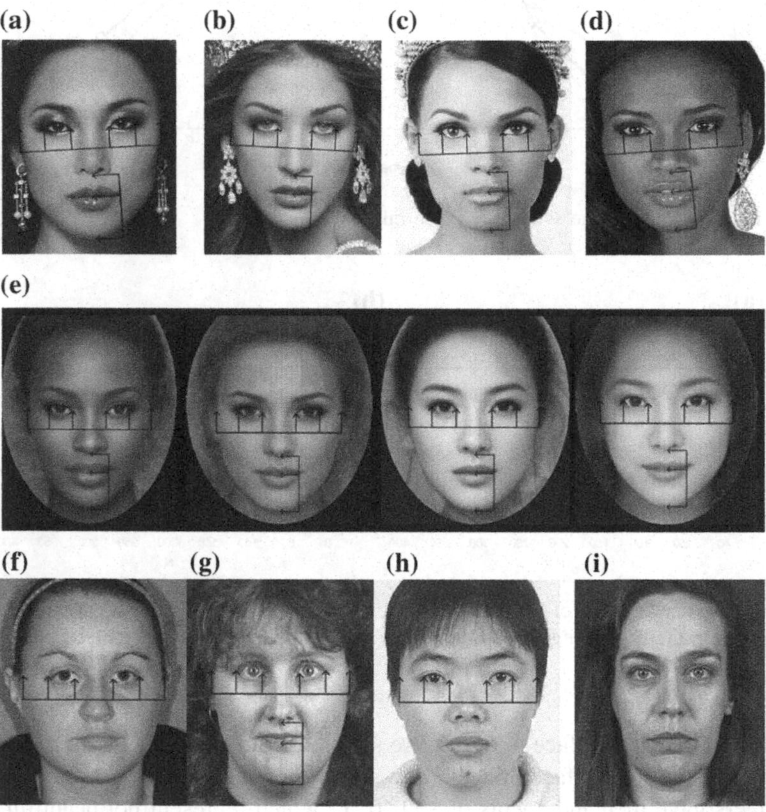

Fig. 5.13 Well-known beautiful faces coincide with the corrected rules. **a** Riyo Mori, Miss Universe 2007, Japan. D = 3.11. **b** Dayana Mendoza, Miss Universe 2008, Venezuela. D = 7.22. **c** Ada de la Cruz, Miss World 2007, Miss Universe 2009, Dominican. D = 9.72. **d** Leila Lopes, Miss Universe 2011, Angola. D = 6.16. **e** Average faces of attractive women of different races, generated by Rhee and Lee (2010). D = [2.93, 4.32, 4.70, 2.24]. **f–h** Examples deviated from the two templates. D = [41.7176, 49.4994, 23.1492]. **i** Example deviated from ideal ratio between face width and length of lower part of face. D = 73.4017

the deviation is large, the attractiveness is significantly affected by the ratio rules. For comparison purposes, the above procedure by using the putative ratio rules is implemented, and obtained a result which can be found in Fig. 5.11b, where there is a smaller deviation and hence lower MOS, which imply that the putative ratio rules are not accurate.

In order to intuitively show the validity of the corrected ratio rules, two templates, as shown in Fig. 5.12, were made, which indicate the ideal eye-level horizontal ratios and lower face vertical ratio, respectively. Figure 5.13 illustrates that the well-known beautiful faces of different ethnic groups coincide with the templates very well (e.g., Fig. 5.13a–e), but when the geometric structure of the face significantly deviates from the corrected ideal ratios, their attractiveness decreases (e.g., Fig. 5.13f–i).

5.6 Summary

In this chapter, we analyze and test the putative ratio rules in terms of the accuracy and universality. The results show that most of putative rules are somewhat subjective and arbitrary, overestimating the power of the magic numbers, e.g. 1, 1.618, etc., and the rules based on measurements of real faces are more objective, accurate, and robust. The top universal ratio features are consistent across different clusters, and the accuracy of the putative ratio rules can be improved by adjusting the ideal values. The validity of the corrected ideal facial proportions has been verified on both synthesized faces and well-known beautiful faces in the real world.

Appendix 1

Table 5.6 Division of average faces according to physical anthropology

Labels	Nationalities
Caucasoid	Afghani, Argentine, Austrian, Belgian, Czech, Dutch, Egyptian, English, Finn, French, German, Greek, Hungarian, Iranian, Iraqi, Irish, Israeli, Italian, Latvian, Lebanese, Polish, Romanian, Russian, Saudi Arabia, Serbian, South Indian, Spaniard, Swedish, Swiss, Turkish, Uzbek, White American, Syrian, Portuguese, Australia, Croatia
Negroid	African American, Cameroon, South African, West African
Mongoloid	Burmese, Cambodian, Chinese, Filipino, Japanese, Korean, Mongolian, Taiwanese, Thai, Tibetan, Vietnamese, Hong Kong
Mix	Brazilian, Ethiopian, Mexican, Peruvian, Puerto Rican, Ecuador, Chile, Indian

Note The population in some of the countries has several different origins. For example, Brazil is made up of the Aboriginals, and Portuguese, Black African, European, Arab and Japanese immigrants. For these countries, we label them as ‘Mix’

Appendix 2

The results of the *k*-means clustering are shown as follows. Each face has been marked with a country code which indicates his/her origin, e.g., the average face of the Hong Kong female is marked with an 'HK'.

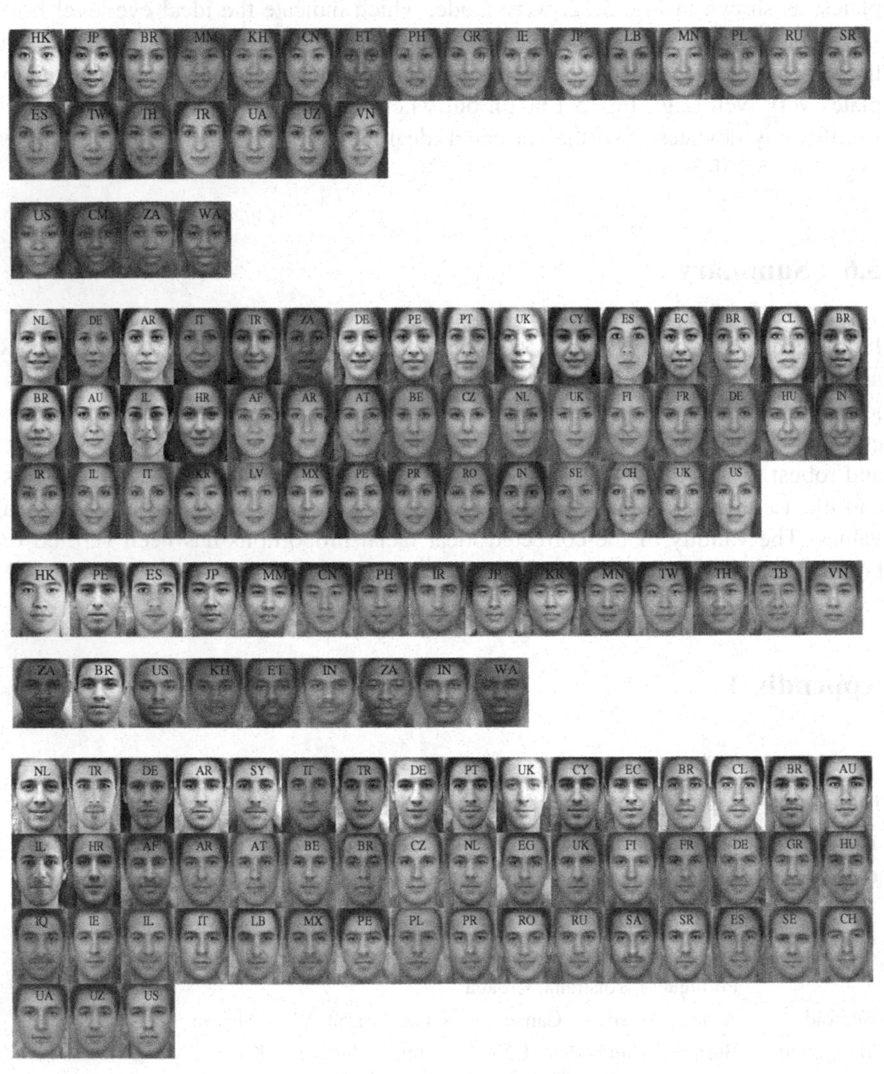

References

Chen F, Zhang D (2010) A benchmark for geometric facial beauty study. In: Proceedings of international conference on medical biometrics, pp 21–32

Cootes TF, Taylor CJ, Cooper DH, Graham J (1995) Active shape models—their training and application. Comput Vis Image Underst 61(1):38–59

Dryden IL, Mardia KV (1998) Statistical shape analysis. Wiley, New York

Etcoff NL (1994) Psychology, beauty and the beholder. Nature 368(6468):186–187

Fan J, Chau KP, Wan X, Zhai L, Lau E (2012) Prediction of facial attractiveness from facial proportions. Pattern Recogn 45:2326–2334

Farkas LG, Hreczko TA, Kolar JC, Munro IR (1985) Vertical and horizontal proportions of the face in young adult North American Caucasians: revision of neoclassical canons. Plast Reconstr Surg 75(3):328–337

Gaut B, Lopes DM (2001) The Routledge companion to aesthetics. Routledge, London

Gunes H, Piccardi M (2006) Assessing facial beauty through proportion analysis by image processing and supervised learning. Int J Hum Comput Stud 64(12):1184–1199

Jefferson Y (2004) Facial beauty-establishing a universal standard. Int J Orthod 15(1):9–22

Kiekens RM, Jagtman AMK, van 't Hof MA, van 't Hof BE, Manltha JC (2008a) Putative golden proportions as predictors of facial esthetics in adolescents. Am J Orthod Dentofac Orthop 134 (4):480–483

Kiekens RM, Jagtman AMK, van 't Hof MA, van 't Hof BE, Straatman H, Manltha JC (2008b) Facial esthetics in adolescents and its relationship to 'ideal' ratios and angles. Am J Orthod Dentofac Orthop 133(2):188.e1–8

Komori M, Kawamura S, Ishihara S (2009) Effect of averageness and sexual dimorphism on the judgment of facial attractiveness. Vis Res 49:862–869

Langlois JH, Roggman LA (1990) Attractive faces are only average. Psychol Sci 1:115–121

Pallett PM, Link S, Lee K (2010) New 'golden' ratios for facial beauty. Vis Res 50(2):149–154

Perrett DI, Lee KJ, Penton-Voak I, Rowland D, Yoshikawa S, Burt DM, Eenzi SP, Castles DL, Akamatsu S (1998) Effects of sexual dimorphism on facial attractiveness. Nature 394 (6696):884–887

Rhee SC, Lee SH (2010) Attractive composite faces of different races. Aesthet Plast Surg 34: 800–801

Schaefer S, McPhail T, Warren J (2006) Image deformation using moving least squares. In: Proceedings of ACM SIGGRAPH, pp 533–540

Schmid K, Marx D, Samal A (2008) Computation of a face attractiveness index based on neoclassical canons, symmetry, and golden ratios. Pattern Recogn 41(8):2710–2717

Wolf N (1990) The beauty myth. Morrow, New York

Zhang D, Zhao Q, Chen F (2011) Quantitative analysis of human facial beauty using geometric features. Pattern Recogn 44(4):940–950

Chapter 6
Beauty Analysis Fusion Model of Texture and Geometric Features

Most of previous studies use only one kind of features for facial beauty analysis. So do Chaps. 2, 3, 4 and 5 of this book, the knowledge of pattern recognition tells us fusion of features is usually beneficial to obtain better results. This chapter explores the issue to perform feature fusion for facial beauty analysis. As texture and geometric features usually contain different information, we integrate them for facial beauty analysis. This chapter is organized as follows: Sect. 6.1 gives a brief introduction to quantitative evaluation of facial beauty. Section 6.2 discusses feature extraction of face landmarks and describes the preprocessing procedure of face geometric feature extraction. In Sect. 6.3, the face texture feature extraction method based on the Block-LBP algorithm is introduced. Experimental results are shown in Sect. 6.4 and the conclusion is offered in Sect. 6.5.

6.1 Introduction

In the beauty pageant, participants evaluate face beauty based on their own tastes, which is often not convincing to the public. Aarabi et al. (2001) established an automatic scoring system for face beauty. They defined the face beauty in three levels, and chose 40 face images for training and other 40 face images for testing. They got the final classification accuracy of 91 % by using k nearest-neighbor (KNN) rule for classification. Iremet et al. (2007) proposed a two-level (beauty or not) model based on a training dataset with 150 female faces, in which the principal component analysis (PCA) and support vector machine (SVM) methods were used for feature extraction and classification, respectively. Finally, the highest accuracy of 89 % was achieved by using 170 female face images as the testing data. Gunes and Piccardi (2006) proposed a method based on supervised learning, in which 11 features were involved to describe the face beauty degree. Gray et al. (2010) proposed a model for predicting face beauty without landmarks, but it used only texture features to represent face beauty. In the research of Asian face beauty, to our

D. Zhang et al., *Computer Models for Facial Beauty Analysis*,
DOI 10.1007/978-3-319-32598-9_6

knowledge, current works mainly use geometric features to analyze face beauty (Zhang et al. 2011). Though the Gabor features are used in (Mao et al. 2011), it is complex and only uses texture features without considering geometric features. In summary, previous works have used image processing and machine learning techniques to analyze and recognize face beauty, and they have achieved initial success on some different data sets. However, there are few experiments on fusion of geometric and texture features to represent face beauty. In this chapter, we mainly discuss the feature fusion for facial beauty analysis.

6.2 Geometric and Texture Feature Extraction

In this section, we introduce the geometric and texture feature extraction method for the facial beauty study.

6.2.1 Geometric Feature Extraction

Chapter 4 presents an automatic geometric feature extraction method based on the active shape models (ASMs). In this chapter, we use this model to extract only 77 landmarks to represent the face shape. Figure 6.1a is an input image, and Fig. 6.1b shows the landmarks extracted by ASMs.

First, 40 geometric features (see Appendix 1) are defined, including the eye's width, mouth's length, face's length etc. In order to get robust features to describe face beauty, we normalize the geometric features by using the face width and face

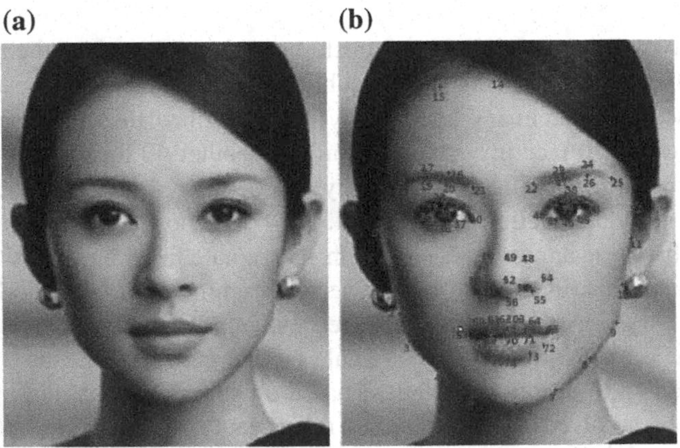

Fig. 6.1 Landmark extraction by using ASM. **a** An original image. **b** The extracted landmarks

height in horizontal and vertical direction, respectively. Then, the method of cross-crossover based on KNN (Liu et al. 2010) is used to choose the best combination of geometric features (Chen and Zhang 2010).

The processing details are as follows. Suppose that all the images are rated in terms of their attractiveness. In the initial stage, 40 geometric features are extracted from each image. However, there are some redundant features among them, the cross-crossover method is designed to select the best feature set. The whole sample is divided into 10 equal portions. A portion is randomly chosen as the testing sample and the others are treated as training samples. In testing, the KNN is used to learn a machine rater for each image and the Pearson correlation is used to evaluate the result. The testing procedure is as follows.

(1) Let A be a set including 40 starting geometric features, denoted by $A = \{a_1, a_2, a_3, \ldots, a_{40}\}$. B is used to store features and initialized as $B = \emptyset$.
(2) For each feature set A, the KNN is designed to learn a machine rater for each testing image and the Pearson correlation is used to evaluate the result. If a_1 gets the best result, then $A = \{a_2, a_3, \ldots, a_{40}\}$, $B = \{a_1\}$.
(3) Combining each feature of A with all the features of B to perform testing, Suppose that α_3 obtains the best result, then $A = \{a_2, a_4, \ldots, a_{40}\}$, $B = \{a_1, a_3\}$.
(4) Repeating (2) and (3) till $A = \emptyset$ and B includes the 40 starting geometric features. Then, the best combination of features can be gotten to describe the beauty face.

Figure 6.2 is the result of the best combination of features in each iteration, where the horizontal direction shows the feature number, and the vertical direction shows the Pearson correlation. It shows that when the number of features equals to 21, KNN achieves the highest correlation coefficient. The 21 selected features are shown in Fig. 6.3.

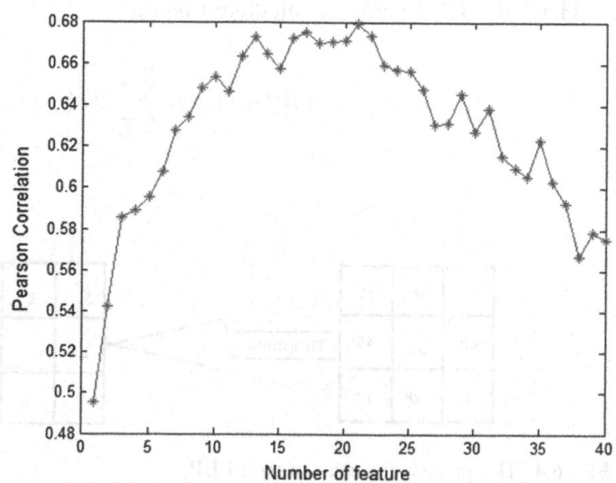

Fig. 6.2 The result of choosing the best combination of features

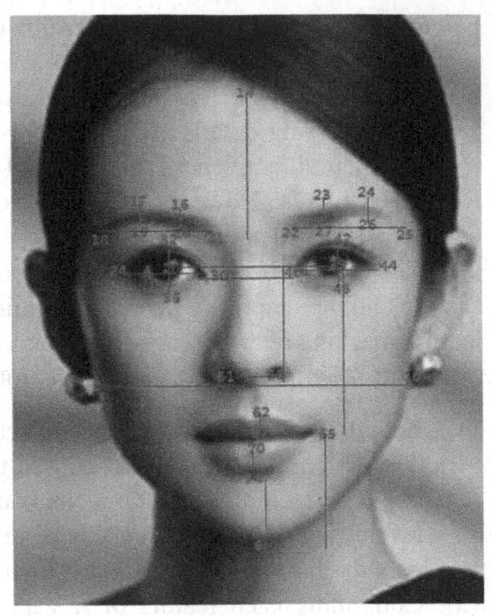

Fig. 6.3 The 21 selected geometric features

6.2.2 *Texture Feature Extraction*

6.2.2.1 LBP Features

The basic idea of Local Binary Patterns (LBP) (Huang et al. 2004) is to extract the local structure in an image by comparing each pixel with its neighborhoods. A pixel is taken as center and its neighbors are converted into 1 or 0. If the intensity of the center pixel is greater than or equal to its neighbor, then it is converted into 1; otherwise it is converted into 0. Then, we can end up with a binary number for each pixel, just like 11001111. Figure 6.4 shows a process to calculate the original LBP value of a pixel in 3 × 3 neighborhoods.

Here, the LBP value is calculated using

$$LBP(x_i, y_i) = \sum_{p=0}^{p-i} 2^p s(i_p - i_c) \tag{6.1}$$

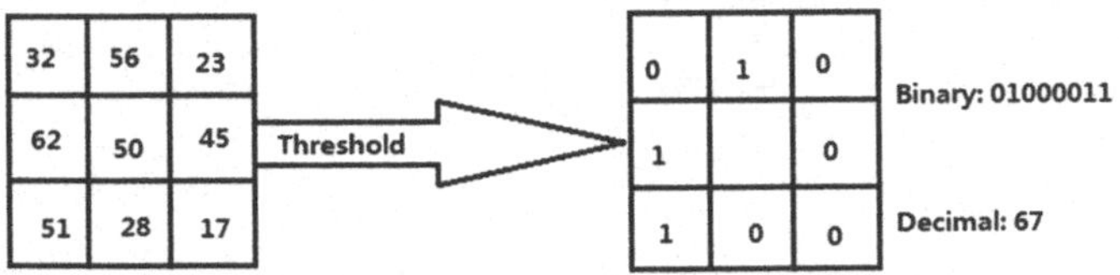

Fig. 6.4 The process for calculating a LBP

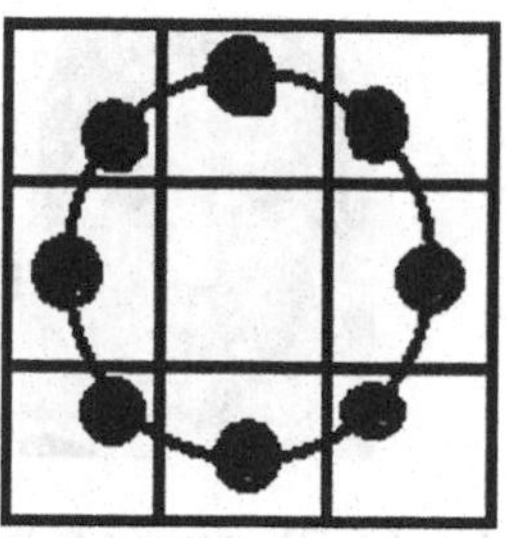

Fig. 6.5 A model for circular LBP operator

where (x_i, y_i) is the location in an image whose gray is i_c. i_p is the gray value of the pth neighbor of (x_i, y_i), and the original LBP algorithm sets $P = 8$. The function of $s(x)$ is a symbolic function and defined as

$$s(x) = \begin{cases} 1 & x \geq 0 \\ 0 & else \end{cases}. \tag{6.2}$$

Many researchers have proposed some extensions about the original LBP, such as the rotation invariance LBP which is based on a circular domain. Figure 6.5 is a circular LBP operator.

For a point (x_i, y_i), its neighboring point (x_n, y_n) can be calculated by

$$\begin{cases} x_n = x_i + R\cos\left(\frac{2\pi n}{p}\right) \\ y_n = y_i - R\sin\left(\frac{2\pi n}{p}\right) \end{cases}, \tag{6.3}$$

where R is the radius of the circular. If (x_n, y_n) is not on the image coordinates, its interpolation point can be calculated using

$$f(X,Y) \approx [1 - X \quad X]\begin{bmatrix} f(0,0) & f(0,1) \\ f(1,0) & f(1,1) \end{bmatrix}\begin{bmatrix} 1 - Y \\ Y \end{bmatrix}. \tag{6.4}$$

There is usually some background information which would impact the texture feature in a face image. We introduce a method to eliminate this impact via segmenting the face region out. The main steps are as follows:

(1) Use the ASMs method to get the landmarks, as shown in Fig. 6.1b.
(2) Find the location of face contour points, including the points from No. 0 to No. 15 in Fig. 6.1b.
(3) Use the face contour points to get a mask image, whose size should be the same with the face image.
(4) Segment the face image based on the mask image, so the hair and background can be removed. Figure 6.6 shows the process about the algorithm to locate the face region and LBPROT mapping.

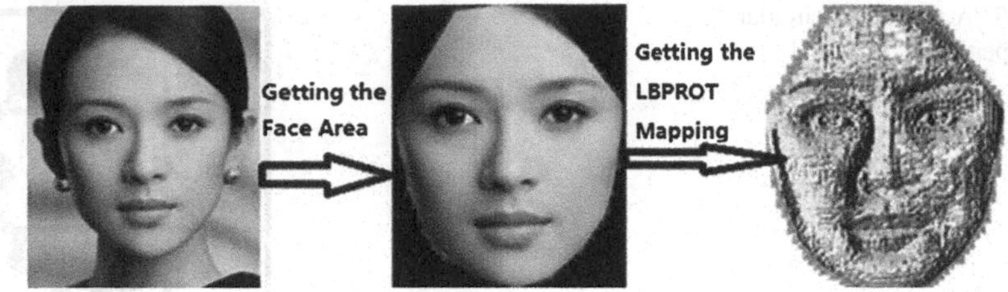

Fig. 6.6 The process to locate the face region and to perform LBPROT mapping

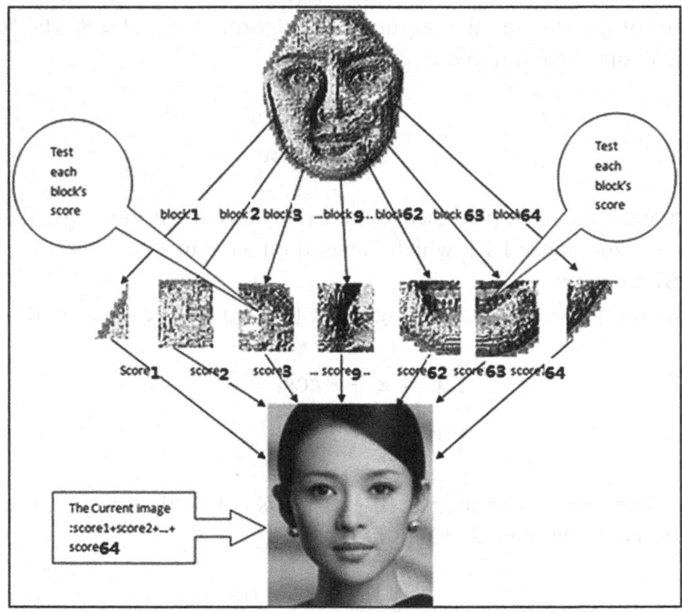

Fig. 6.7 The flowchart of BLBP extraction

6.2.2.2 Block-LBP

A face image will get low beauty score if there are some bad features on the face, such as scars. In this subsection, we present another Block Local Binary Patterns (BLBP) descriptor by using local features instead of global features to extract texture features (Guo et al. 2010). The details of the BLBP method are as follows. The flowchart is shown in Fig. 6.7.

(1) Divide each LBP image from the training set into smaller blocks. (Here the face image is divided into 64 blocks.)
(2) The first step of testing obtains the face region of the test images by the method introduced in Sect. 6.2.1. Then, the rotation invariance LBP of the

image is calculated. Finally, the images are divided into blocks. For each block, the most similar block is determined by Histogram Matching. The beauty score of the training sub-block is set to the human rated score of the corresponding face image. When testing the *i*th sub-block's score, we determine the most similar block according to each training sample's *i*th sub-block and set its score to the testing sub-block.

(3) The sum of each sub-block's score is treated as the testing image's final score.

Suppose I_i denotes the *i*th training image where $i = 1, 2, 3, \ldots, M$ and M is the number of training images. $P_{i,j} \in R^{256}$ denotes a vector which is a LBP image histogram for the *j*th block of I_i, where $i = 1, 2, 3, \ldots, N$, and N is the number of block. Let $A_j \in R^{M \times 256}$ be a histogram matrix and

$$A_j = \left[P_{1,j}, P_{2,j}, P_{3,j}, \ldots, P_{M,j}\right]'. \tag{6.5}$$

Let T_k be the *k*th testing image. $B_{k,j} \in R^{256}$ denotes a histogram vector of the *k*th block of T_k, and $S(i)$ denotes the *i*th mean human rater of the training image, the testing score of $B_{k,j}$ can be calculated by the following steps:

(1) Calculating the distances between $B_{k,j}$ and each row of A_j using

$$distance(i) = \sqrt{1 - \sum\nolimits_{f=0}^{255} \frac{\sqrt{B_{k,j}(f) * A_j(i,f)}}{\sum\nolimits_{r=0}^{255} B_{k,j}(r) * \sum\nolimits_{r=0}^{255} A_j(i,r)}}. \tag{6.6}$$

(2) Finding the min distance of $distance(i)$ by

$$flag = i \ where \ Min(distance(i)). \tag{6.7}$$

(3) The testing score for the *k*th block of T_k is

$$TS(j) = S(flag). \tag{6.8}$$

(4) The total score of T_k is

$$Score(T_k) = \sum\nolimits_{j=0}^{N} TS(j). \tag{6.9}$$

Finally, $Score(T_k)$ is used for evaluation.

6.3 Fusion Model Design

In this section, geometric and texture features are fused for facial beauty prediction. First, the 21 geometric features with Linear Regression or KNN are used to get machine ratings of the testing images, respectively. Then, the Histogram-Matching is applied to predict the score of face beauty for each sub-block in BLBP or BGabor models. Finally, a final score can be obtained by fusing these two scores. Let A be the machine rater using the 21 geometric features and B be the machine rater using the BLBP models. $A(i)$ and $B(i)$ are the beauty scores of the ith testing image, and the fusion score is

$$C(i) = a * A(i) + b * B(i), \tag{6.10}$$

where $a + b = 1$.

6.4 Experiments and Analysis

A beauty sorting database has been established for experiments. It contains 400 high-quality Asian female face images, including some well-known beautiful faces collected from some webs (e.g. Miss World, movie stars, and super models), several existing databases (the Shanghai database (Zhang et al. 2011)) and some profile pictures. The size of the face images is 480 × 600. The face images are confined to be frontal and they have neutral or gentle smile expressions. To obtain the human-rated beauty scores, an annotation interface was proposed, which displayed the face images in random order and asked the raters to give a score for each face image. The scores are integers from 1 to 10, where "10" means the most beautiful face, and "1" means the ugliest face. Nine volunteers attended the annotation task for all the images. Therefore, we obtained 9 annotations for each image. The average beauty ratings are considered as the human-rated beauty scores. In this chapter, 200 face images are chosen as the training set, and the remaining images are for the testing. Some face images are shown in Fig. 6.8.

Three experiments were performed to analyze face beauty. The first experiment used only the geometric feature to analyze face beauty. The second experiment used

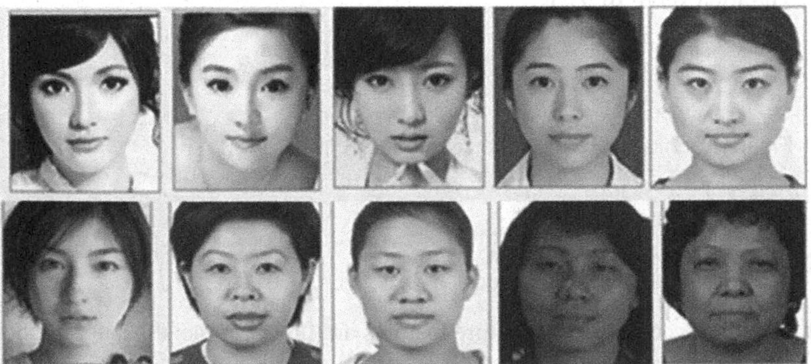

Fig. 6.8 Some examples of the image gallery

Table 6.1 The results obtained using the geometric features for face beauty analysis

	KNN	LR	SVM
Pearson Correlation	**0.806**	0.792	0.637

only the texture feature to analyze face beauty. The third experiment fused both geometric features and texture features to analyze face beauty. In this chapter, Pearson correlation is used for model evaluation (Pearson 1920; Rodgers and Nicewander 1988). Let $x_1, x_2, \ldots, x_n$ denote the beauty score of training samples (given by human rater). $\bar{x} = \frac{1}{n}\sum_{i=1}^{n} x_i$ is the mean value of $x_1, x_2, \ldots, x_n$. $y_1, y_2, \ldots, y_n$ denote the beauty scores of testing samples (given by machine learning rater). $\bar{y} = \frac{1}{n}\sum_{i=1}^{n} y_i$ is the mean value of $y_1, y_2, \ldots, y_n$. Then the Pearson Correlation of $x_1, x_2, \ldots, x_n$ and $y_1, y_2, \ldots, y_n$ is defined as

$$r = \frac{\sum_{i=1}^{n} (x_i - \bar{x})(y_i - \bar{y})}{\left[\sum_{i=1}^{n} (x_i - \bar{x})^2 \sum_{i=1}^{n} (y_i - \bar{y})^2\right]^{\frac{1}{2}}}. \tag{6.11}$$

6.4.1 Experiments Using Geometric Features

In this experiment, 21 geometric features are selected by the cross-crossover method, and different models, including KNN, SVM (Chen et al. 2001; Chang and Lin 2011) and Linear-Regression (LR) (Xie et al. 2002) are used to analyze face beauty. The results are evaluated by Pearson correlation, as shown in Table 6.1. We can see that KNN performs better than LR and SVM based on the geometric features, and a correlation coefficient of 0.806 can be gotten.

6.4.2 Experiments Using Texture Features

In this subsection, the BLBP method is compared with the Gabor texture feature extraction method. Firstly, the optimal block number of BLBP should be determined. We change this parameter from 1 * 1, 2 * 2... to 10 * 10, and the corresponding results are shown in Fig. 6.9. It shows that the best block number is 64, and the highest Pearson correlation is 0.866 under this parameter. The face regions do not need to be normalized to the same size. For example, let $m * n$ be the size of the face region, where m, n may be different for different images. When the block number is $N * N$, then each block size should be $\lfloor m/N \rfloor * \lfloor n/N \rfloor$.

Compared with LBP, Gabor, and Block-Gabor (BGabor) methods, the BLBP method has better performance in face beauty analysis. The results are listed in Table 6.2. BLBP can get a correlation coefficient of 0.866 in the Asian female face

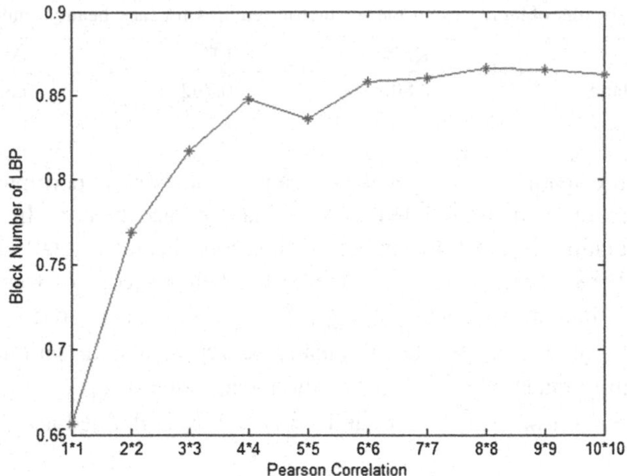

Fig. 6.9 Comparing with different block numbers in BLBP

Table 6.2 The results obtained using the texture feature for face beauty analysis

	LBP	BLBP(64)	Gabor	BGabor
Our database	0.656	**0.866**	0.571	0.655
Database in Zhang et al. (2011)	0.616	**0.789**	0.502	0.613

database which is first introduced in Sect. 6.4. Compared these methods on the database used in Zhang et al. (2011), the proposed BLBP also gets higher correlation coefficient.

6.4.3 Experiments on Fusion of Geometric and Texture Features

50 percent of the face images are randomly selected for training, and the remaining images are used for testing. Figure 6.10 shows the results, where "21(KNN): BLBP (HM)" means the fusion of the machine rater based on the 21 geometry features (learning rater by KNN) and BLBP texture features (learning rater by Histogram-Matching(HM)), similar to "21(KNN): BGabor(HM)", "21(LR): BBLBP(HM)" and "21(LR): BGabor(HM)". Figure 6.10 shows that for the combination of BLBP and KNN, the best Pearson correlation is 0.897. For the combination of BLBP with Linear Regression, the best Pearson correlation is 0.896. For the combination of BGabor with Linear Regression, the best Pearson correlation is 0.836. And for the combination of BGabor with KNN, the best Pearson correlation is 0.840. Figure 6.11 is the result of image sorting, which is based on the fusion

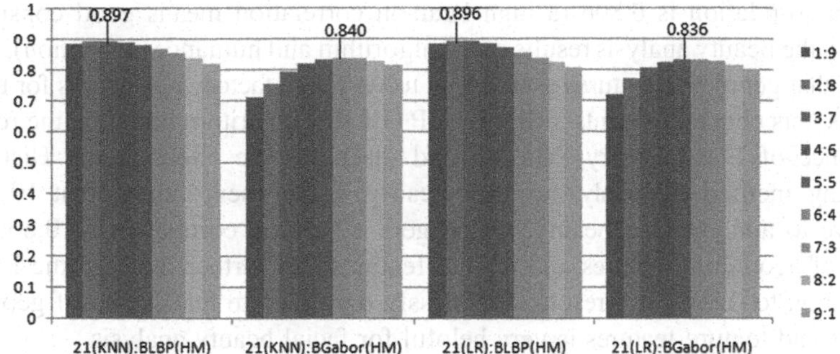

Fig. 6.10 The results obtained using different fusion schemes

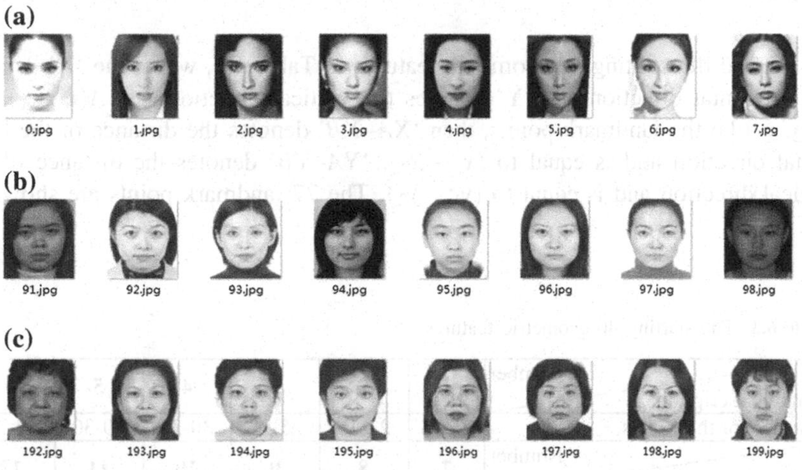

Fig. 6.11 The sorted results obtained using the proposed method. **a** The first 8 sorted face images. **b** The middle 8 sorted face images. **c** The last 8 sorted face images

scheme of 21(LR): BLBP(HM). Compared with the previous experimental results (only using the geometric or texture features), the fusion scheme can get a better result. It also shows the geometric and texture features are complementary for face beauty analysis.

6.5 Summary

This chapter aims to study facial beauty analysis by fusing the geometric and texture features of faces. For face beauty analysis, KNN, Linear Regression (LR) and SVM, are used for testing. Experiment shows that for geometric features the highest

Pearson correlation is 0.806 (a high Pearson correlation means good consistence between the beauty analysis results of the algorithm and humance perception), which tells us that geometric features do not lead to very satisfactory results. As for texture features, this chapter presents a Block-LBP (BLBP) algorithm based on the rotation invariance of Local Binary Patterns, and discusses the effect of the Histogram Matching method on analyzing face beauty. Experiments show that BLBP is effective to analyze face beauty, which gets a Pearson correlation of 0.866. The fusion of geometric features and texture features can further increase the Pearson Correlation to 0.897. The results doubtlessly demonstrate that fusion of geometric features and texture features is very helpful for facial beauty analysis.

Appendix 1

We defined the starting 40 geometric features in Table 6.3, where the 'X' denotes the horizontal direction and 'Y' denotes the vertical direction. Let $A(x_1, y_1)$ and $B(x_2, y_2)$ be the landmark points, then 'XA–XB' denotes the distance of the horizontal direction and is equal to $(x_1 - x_2)$, 'YA–YB' denotes the distance of the vertical direction and is equal to $(y_1 - y_2)$. The 77 landmark points are shown in Fig. 6.1b.

Table 6.3 The starting 40 geometric features

Feature description \ Number	**1**	**2**	**3**	**4**	**5**	**6**
Distance for the **X** axis	21-18	22-18	25-22	30-34	40-30	44-30
Feature description \ Number	**7**	**8**	**9**	**10**	**11**	**12**
Distance for the **X** axis	39-28	44-34	12-0	11-1	10-2	9-3
Feature description \ Number	**13**	**14**	**15**	**16**	**17**	**18**
Distance	**X8-X4**	**X7-X5**	**X54-X58**	**X53-X51**	**X65-X59**	**Y21-Y14**
Feature description \ Number	**19**	**20**	**21**	**22**	**23**	**24**
Distance for the **Y** axis	19-17	20-16	27-23	26-24	36-32	46-32
Feature description \ Number	**25**	**26**	**27**	**28**	**29**	**30**
Distance for the **Y** axis	56-21	62-56	74-70	67-62	6-74	6-14
Feature description \ Number	**31**	**32**	**33**	**34**	**35**	**36**
Distance for the **Y** axis	6-0	51-34	59-28	6-65	6-51	6-53
Feature description \ Number	**37**	**38**	**39**	**40**		
Distance for the **Y** axis	**Y6-Y65**	**Y65-Y39**	**Y53-Y39**	Y6-Y12		

References

Aarabi P, Hughes D, Mohajer K, Emami M (2001) The automatic measurement of face beauty. In: Proceeding of IEEE international conference on system man and cybernetics, pp 2644–2647

Chang CC, Lin CJ (2011) LIBSVM: a library for support vector machines. ACM Trans Intell Syst Technol 2(3):27. http://www.csie.ntu.edu.tw/_cjlin/libsvm

Chen F, Zhang D (2010) A benchmark for geometric face beauty study. Med Biometr 6165:21–32

Chen Y, Zhou X, Huang TS (2001) One-Class SVM for learning in image retrieval. In: Proceeding of international conference on image processing, vol 1, pp 34–37

Gray D, Yu K, Xu W, Gong Y (2010) Predicting face beauty without landmarks. In: Proceedings of European conference on computer vision, pp 434–447

Gunes H, Piccardi M (2006) Assessing face beauty through proportion analysis by image processing and. Int J Hum Comput Stud 64(12):1184–1199

Guo Z, Zhang L, Zhang D (2010) Rotation invariant texture classification using LBP variance (LBPV) with global matching. Pattern Recogn 43(3):706–719

Huang X, Li SZ, Wang Y (2004) Shape localization based on statistical method using extended local binary pattern. In: Proceeding of IEEE first symposium on multi-agent security and survivability, pp 18–20

Irem H, Turkmen Z, Kurt M, Karsligil M E (2007) Global feature based face beauty decision system. In: Proceedings of the 15th European signal processing conference, pp 1945–1949

Liu CL, Lee CH, Lin PM (2010) A fall detection system using. Expert Syst Appl 37(10): 7174–7181

Mao H, Chen Y, Jin L, Du M (2011) Evaluating face attractiveness: an gabor feature approach. J Commun Comput 8674–679

Pearson K (1920) Notes on the history of correlation. Biometrika 13(1):25–45

Rodgers JL, Nicewander WA (1988) Thirteen ways to look at the correlation. Am Stat 42(1):59–66

Xie K, Song Q, Zhou J (2002) A linear regress model based on least absolute criteria. J Syst Simul 14(2):189–192

Zhang D, Zhao Q, Chen F (2011) Quantitative analysis of human face beauty using. Pattern Recogn 44(4):940–950

Chapter 7
Optimal Feature Set for Facial Beauty Analysis

Because a number of features have been proposed for facial beauty analysis, it is significant to compare them under the same conditions. This is very useful for people to grasp advantages and shortcomings of different features and can provide guidance to the selection of features. In this chapter, we make a comprehensive comparison of putative ratios, shape parameters, eigenface, active appearance models (AAM), Gabor, local binary patterns (LBP) and PCANet features in terms of facial attractiveness prediction. This chapter is organized as follows. Section 7.1 gives a brief introduction to facial attractiveness prediction. Section 7.2 describes different facial features and the corresponding feature extraction methods. Section 7.3 introduces the feature selection algorithms to optimize each type of features. Section 7.4 presents an optimal combination method of multiple types of features. The experiments are described and reported in Sect. 7.5 and we conclude the chapter in Sect. 7.6.

7.1 Introduction

As many psychological studies show that a substantial beauty rating congruence exists over ethnicity, social class, age, and sex (Langlois and Kalakanis et al. 2000; Cunningham and Roberts et al. 1995). Image based facial attractiveness prediction becomes an emerging area in pattern recognition (Bottino and Laurentini 2010), which can promote many real-life applications such as aesthetic surgery planning, cosmetic recommendation and advertisement, photo retouching, and entertainment. The core of facial attractiveness prediction is to discover the relationship between low-level visual features and high-level perceived attractiveness. Hence, it is important to design effective low-level features.

Two categories of features, features suggested by putative rules and features borrowed from other face analysis tasks such as face recognition, have been adopted in existing works. It is known that although ratio based models are capable

D. Zhang et al., *Computer Models for Facial Beauty Analysis*,
DOI 10.1007/978-3-319-32598-9_7

of reproducing the average human judgment at some extent, only a small subset of ratio features is important for prediction of facial attractiveness (Schmid et al. 2008) and the putative ideal ratio values are not accurate (Fan and Chau 2012). Another category of features is inspired from face recognition studies, e.g., shape parameters, eigenface, Gabor filter responses (Liu and Wechsler 2002), local binary patterns (LBP) (Ahonen et al. 2006), etc. Researchers often combine multiple types of facial features to build regression models of facial attractiveness. For example, Eisenthal et al. (2006) and Kagian et al. (2008) combined geometric features, hair color, and skin smoothness into the regression model. Nguyen et al. (2013) concatenated LBP, Gabor filter responses, color moment, shape context, and shape parameters as a feature vector and apply principle component analysis (PCA) (Duda et al. 2000) to reduce the dimensionality. Inspired by the Hubel-Wiesel model (Hubel and Wiesel 1962), Gray et al. (2010) designed a multi-scale feature model by local filters and down-sampling, which can be seen as a form of convolutional neural network. Although so many handcrafted features have been used for facial attractiveness prediction, few works compare the discriminative power of different types of features and optimize the feature set. To our knowledge, only Whitehill and Movellan (2008) have compared eigenface, Gabor features, edge orientation histogram (EOH), and geometric features. They report that Gabor features delivered the best performance and adding a second feature type did not increase the performance. However, many potential features, such as LBP and active appearance models (AAM) (Cootes et al. 2001) parameters, are not considered in their research.

In this chapter, we conduct a comprehensive study on comparison and optimization of features for facial attractiveness prediction. Besides the commonly used features such as putative ratios, shape parameters, eigenface, Gabor, and LBP features, AAM parameters and PCANet features (Chan et al. 2014) are also employed. PCANet is a newly proposed feature extraction method based on a very simple deep learning network, which is reported to achieve state-of-the-art performance for many image classification tasks, such as face verification, hand-written digits recognition, and texture classification.

7.2 Feature Extraction

The features used in this chapter are shown in Table 7.1. These features can be classified into rule based features, global features, and local descriptor features. These features can also be classified into geometric features and appearance features. Different types of features emphasize different patterns. Therefore, combination of them is able to improve the prediction accuracy. In the following subsections, we will describe the extraction of each type of feature in detail.

Table 7.1 Overview of feature types

	Geometric	Appearance
Rule based	Putative ratios	–
Model based	Shape parameters	Eigenface, AAM parameters
Descriptor based	–	LBP, Gabor, PCANet

7.2.1 Ratio Features

Most putative rules on facial attractiveness are defined as ratios, e.g., neoclassical cannons, golden ratios, and traditional saying such as horizontal fifths and vertical thirds. In Sects. 5.2.2 and 5.2.3 of Chap. 5, we have introduced the putative 26 ratio rules in detail. In this chapter, we also extract these 26 ratio rules. Although the ideal values of the putative ratios may not be accurate, a set of ratio features that have potential relevance to facial attractiveness are defined.

In this chapter, we also use 98 landmarks model (see Chap. 3) for facial attractiveness prediction. All 98 landmark points are distributed on the major facial organs, including the face outline, eyebrows, eyes, nose, and mouth. Because all key positions are included in the landmark set, it is convenient to calculate the ratios.

7.2.2 Shape

The x- and y-coordinates of the 98 landmarks are concatenated to form a vector that represents the geometry of the face, i.e.,

$$G = [x_1, x_2, \ldots, x_{98}, y_1, y_2, \ldots, y_{98}]^T, \tag{7.1}$$

Given landmark vectors, shape features can be obtained by Procrustes superimposition (Dryden and Mardia 1998), which contains three steps, center alignment, scale normalization, and iterative rotation alignment (see Chen and Zhang 2010 for detail). The obtained shape vectors are also 196-dimensional. Then PCA is performed on the shape vectors to reduce the dimensionality to 50, which keeps 97 % of the total energy. The 50-dimensional component scores are called shape parameters.

7.2.3 Eigenface

Eigenface is a compact face representation method. A face is represented by a vector of pixel values. Suppose the input vectors are $I_1, I_2, \ldots, I_n$, the mean vector μ is subtracted from I_i and a data matrix $X = [I_1 - \mu, \ldots, I_n - \mu]$ is constructed.

Singular value decomposition (SVD) is applied on X, i.e., $X = U\sum V^T$. The column vectors in U are called eigenfaces. In our case, the eigenfaces corresponding to the largest 100 diagonal values in $\sum$ can explain 90 % of the variations. The input faces can be represented by $I = \mu + U^*b$, where U^* is composed of the first 100 eigenfaces, b is the low dimensional representation of I, and $b = U^{*T}(I - \mu)$.

7.2.4 AAM

AAM is a model based coding approach that parameterizes and combines the shape and texture of a face (Edwards et al. 1998). Shape parameters are obtained by performing PCA on the shape vectors s, so that

$$s = \bar{s} + P_s b_s, \tag{7.2}$$

where P_s is the projection matrix composed of eigenvectors, and b_s is the shape parameters. The first 100 eigenvectors are selected to construct P_s, which explains 99.2 % of the shape variations. To build a texture model, face images are warped to the mean shape (properly scaled and centered) and shape-free gray level images are obtained. Similar to the shape model, the gray level images are represented in vector form and PCA is performed. We construct the following formula

$$t = \bar{t} + P_t b_t, \tag{7.3}$$

where t denotes texture vectors; $\bar{t}$ is the mean texture; P_t is the projection matrix obtained using PCA; and b_t is the texture parameters. The first 200 eigenvectors of PCA are selected to construct P_t, which explains 97.6 % of the texture variations. The shape parameters b_s and the texture parameters b_t are combined by

$$b_c = [\beta b_s; b_t], \tag{7.4}$$

where $\beta = \sqrt{\sum_i \lambda_i^{(t)}} \Big/ \sqrt{\sum_i \lambda_i^{(s)}}$ is a scaling factor to balance the variances of b_s and b_t. After that, a final PCA is applied to obtain

$$b_c = \bar{b}_c + Pb, \tag{7.5}$$

where P is the projection matrix, and b represents the AAM parameters. Here we select the first 100 eigenvectors to construct P, which explains 97 % of the appearance variations. Hence, the AAM feature is of dimension 100. The corresponding eigenvalues are denoted by $\lambda_1^{(s)}, \lambda_2^{(s)}, \ldots, \lambda_{100}^{(s)}$.

7.2.5 Gabor

Gabor filters encode facial shape and texture information over a range of spatial scales. The Gabor filters can be defined as follows (Liu and Wechsler 2002)

$$\Psi_{\mu,\nu}(z) = \frac{\|k_{\mu,\nu}\|}{\sigma^2} e^{\|k_{\mu,\nu}\|^2/2\sigma^2} \left[e^{ik_{\mu,\nu}z} - e^{-\sigma^2/2} \right], \tag{7.6}$$

where μ and ν define the orientation and the scale of the Gabor kernels, $z = (x, y)$, $\|.\|$ denotes the norm operator, and the wave vector $k_{\mu,\nu}$ is defined as follows:

$$k_{\mu,\nu} = k_\nu e^{i\phi_\mu}, \tag{7.7}$$

where $k_\nu = k_{max}/f^\nu$ and $\phi_\mu = \pi\mu/8$. k_{max} is the maximum frequency, and f is the spacing factor between kernels in the frequency domain. Usually, five scales $\nu = \{0, \ldots, 4\}$ and eight orientations $\mu = \{0, \ldots, 7\}$ are used for face images (Liu and Wechsler 2002; Zou et al. 2007). Other parameters are set as $k_{max} = \pi, f = \sqrt{2}$, and $\sigma = 2\pi$. The Gabor representation of an image is the convolution of the image with a family of Gabor kernels, which is of very high dimensionality. For example, for a 128×128 image, the dimensionality of the feature vector is $40 \times 128 \times 128 = 655360$. After a down-sampling step with a factor of 16, the final Gabor feature vector is of dimension 40960.

7.2.6 LBP

In previous Sect. 6.2.1, we have presented the LBP features in detail. LBP operator encodes every pixel of an image with an 8-bit binary number by thresholding the neighborhood of the pixel with the center pixel value. The histogram of the labels is used as a texture descriptor. In our implementation, the face images are cropped and resized into 128×128 and divided into 7×7 local regions. Then the $\mathrm{LBP}_{8,2}^{u2}$ operator is applied to each region. We follow the same notation $\mathrm{LBP}_{P,R}^{u2}$ as in (Ahonen et al. 2006), where (P, R) means P sampling points on a radius of R, and $u2$ means uniform patterns. The histograms of the local regions are concatenated to obtain a 49×59 feature vector.

7.2.7 PCANet

PCANet is a simple deep learning network proposed by Chan et al. (2014). As shown in Fig. 7.1, it has three components, cascaded PCA filtering, binary hashing, and block-wise histogram. The PCA filter banks are learned in the training stage.

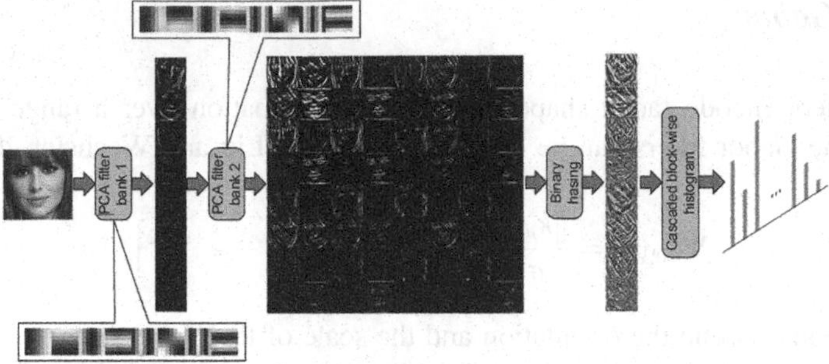

Fig. 7.1 Illustration of PCANet feature extraction

Each pixel of an input image is described by a local patch of size $k_1 \times k_2$ centered at the pixel. We subtract the patch mean from each patch and reshape it to vector form. If there are N training images of size 128×128, we will have $N \times 128 \times 128$ vectors of dimension $k_1 k_2$. Performing PCA on those vectors and reshaping the first L_1 eigenvectors into matrices of size $k_1 \times k_2$, we obtain the first layer PCA filter banks. The L_2 filters in the second layer are learned in a similar way. For each input image, the output of the first layer filtering is L_1 images, which are inputs for the second layer. Each of the L_1 input images has L_2 outputs, which are binarized and converted to a single integer-valued image by

$$I^{(3)} = \sum_{l=1}^{L_2} 2^{l-1} I_l^{(2)}. \tag{7.8}$$

The pixel value of $I^{(3)}$ is in the range $[0, 2^{L_2} - 1]$. The L_1 images in layer three are divided into 64 blocks of size 16×16. The histograms of the blocks are cascaded to obtain the final feature vector. In our implementation, $k_1 = k_2 = 7$, $L_1 = L_2 = 8$, and the PCANet feature is of dimension $8 \times 64 \times 256 = 131072$.

7.3 Feature Selection

It is natural to ask whether all the dimensions in each type of features are relevant and it is necessary to assess facial attractiveness and whether a subset of the dimensions can achieve similar or even better prediction performance. Because the number of training data is often limited, removing the irrelevant and redundant variables will alleviate computational burden. Therefore, feature selection within each type of feature is performed.

Feature selection methods are mainly divided into filters, wrappers, and embedded methods (Guyon and Elisseeff 2003). Filters rank variables with some criteria, wrappers assess subsets of variables in terms of the performance of a given predictor, and embedded methods optimize an objective function which has a goodness of fit term and a penalty term for the number of variables. Filters and embedded methods are efficient, whereas wrappers have high computational cost because they require extensive training and prediction implementations. In this chapter, we compare three feature selection methods, filter, sequential backward elimination, and the lasso (Hastie et al. 2009), representing the three categories of methods respectively. The criterion for the filter is the correlation coefficient between each variable and human rated attractiveness. In sequential backward elimination, initially all variables are used for attractiveness prediction. At each step, the variable with the least contribution to prediction accuracy is removed. The process is iterated till all the variables are ordered. The objective function of the lasso is

$$\widehat{\beta}^{Lasso} = \arg\min_{\beta} \left\{ \frac{1}{2} \|\boldsymbol{y} - \boldsymbol{X}\beta\|_2^2 + \lambda \|\beta\|_1 \right\} \quad (7.9)$$

where $\boldsymbol{X}$ is the input data matrix, $\boldsymbol{y}$ is the attractiveness score vector, and λ is the regularization parameter. The l_1 penalty will promote sparse solutions. To solve the entire lasso path, we use SpaSM (Sjostrand et al. 2012), a toolbox for sparse statistical modeling. The variables are then sorted in terms of the path. Given the sorted variables, a nested sequence of models can be obtained. To determine the optimal number of variables to keep, we train models with an increasing number of sorted variables. The first k variables are selected if none of larger feature subsets can significantly increase the prediction accuracy, which is determined by two-sample t-tests.

7.4 Score Level Fusion and Optimal Feature Set

As mentioned in Sect. 7.2, some types of features are complementary to each other. For example, the AAM features provide holistic information, whereas the LBP and PCANet features provide local information. In this section, we study combinations of multiple types of features for the goal to further increase the attractiveness prediction accuracy.

We focus on the seven types of features introduced in Sect. 7.2. Hence, there are totally 127 combinations ($C_7^1 + C_7^2 + \cdots + C_7^7 = 127$), which are represented by $Comb = [C_1, C_2, \ldots, C_{127}]$, where $C_1 = \{1\}$, $C_2 = \{1, 2\}$, ..., $C_{127} = \{1, 2, 3, 4, 5, 6, 7\}$. Different feature combinations are evaluated in terms of score level fusion performance. The outputs of the seven models are denoted by $y_1, y_2, \ldots, y_7$. For combination C_k, the score level fusion result is

$$\widehat{y} = \sum_{i \in C_k} \omega_i^{(k)} y_i. \quad (7.10)$$

Weight vector $\omega^{(k)}$ can be obtained by solving the least squares problem

$$\omega^{(k)} = \arg\min_{\omega} \left\| y - Y^{(k)}\omega \right\|, \tag{7.11}$$

where $Y^{(k)}$ is a $n \times |C_k|$ matrix including n entries of model outputs selected by C_k, and y is human rated attractiveness scores. The correlation between the predicted scores $\widehat{y}$ and human rated scores y is used to evaluate the prediction performance, i.e.,

$$r_{y,\widehat{y}} = \frac{cov(y,\widehat{y})}{\sigma_y \sigma_{\widehat{y}}} = \frac{E\left[(y-\mu_y)(\widehat{y}-\mu_{\widehat{y}})\right]}{\sigma_y \sigma_{\widehat{y}}}. \tag{7.12}$$

The optimal feature set is the least complex model with the most competitive performance.

7.5 Experiments Results

In this section, we make a comprehensive comparison of putative ratios, shape parameters, eigenface, active appearance models (AAM), Gabor, local binary patterns (LBP) and PCANet features in terms of facial attractiveness prediction. Firstly, different types of features are compared in terms of attractiveness prediction performance, which is measured by Pearson correlation between predicted attractiveness scores and human rated attractiveness scores. Secondly, dimensionality reduction and feature selection techniques are performed to optimize each type of feature. Thirdly, we discuss the optimal combination of multiple types of features which can further improve the performance.

7.5.1 Data Set and Preprocessing

In this chapter, all experiments are based on a newly built database, which includes 390 celebrity face images of Miss Universe, Miss World, movie stars, and super models collected from the web and 409 common face images collected from a face research website (http://faceresearch.org), Flicker, the XM2VTS database (Messer et al. 1999), and the Shanghai database (Zhang et al. 2011). All face images are confined to be female, frontal with neutral or gentle smile expressions. In order to collect human ratings, an interactive tool was developed, which displayed face images in random order. Totally 25 volunteers attended the rating procedure, most in their twenties. They were asked to rate the images with three scales:

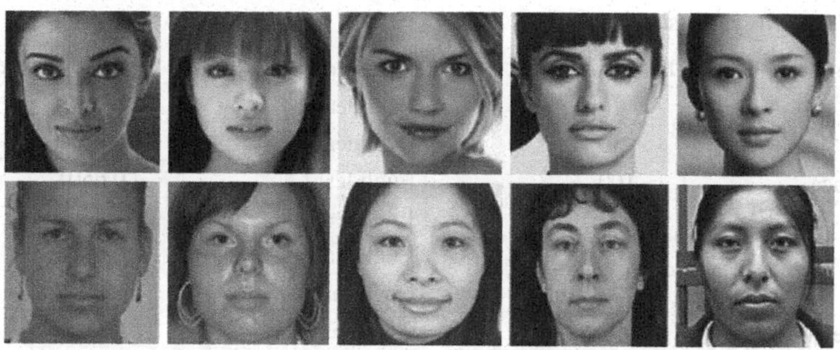

Fig. 7.2 Example face images after cropping. The *top row* shows celebrity faces and the *bottom row* shows common faces

−1 (unattractive), 0 (common), and 1 (attractive). One average, each person spent 40 min to rate all the 799 images. The attractiveness score of a face image is the mean of its ratings across all raters.

The collected face images were resized to 600 × 480 for landmark extraction. Active shape model (ASM) (Cootes et al. 1995) was used to detect landmarks. To further improve the precision of landmark positions, we also developed a tool for manual adjustment. The ratio, shape, and AAM features can be obtained with the landmarks. To extract eigenface, Gabor, LBP, and PCANet features, we cropped the images with a squared bounding box, which was determined by the landmarks, and resized the cropped image into 128 × 128. Figure 7.2 presents some examples after cropping, from which we can see the diversity of our database in attractiveness and race.

7.5.2 KNN Regression Results

Different types of features are compared in terms of attractiveness prediction performance. We take KNN regression as a baseline method. For an input face image, the predicted attractiveness score is the weighted average of the attractiveness scores of its k nearest neighbors in the training set. The weights are inversely proportional to the distances between the input face and its neighbors in the feature space. Euclidean distance is adopted for ratio, shape, eigenface, AAM, and Gabor features. Chi-squared distance, which is a common similarity measurement for histograms, is adopted for LBP and PCANet features. As original Gabor, LBP, and PCANet features are high-dimensional, we perform PCA for dimensionality reduction and denote them as Gabor-DR, LBP-DR, and PCANet-DR respectively. Euclidean distance is adopted for the ‘DR’ features.

Table 7.2 KNN regression result

Feature	Dimensionality	Distance measure	Performance
Ratio	26	Euclidean	0.7071
Shape	50	Euclidean	0.7429
Eigenface	100	Euclidean	0.6501
AAM	100	Euclidean	0.7540
Gabor	40960	Euclidean	0.6974
LBP	3776	Chi-squared	0.8052
PCANet	131072	Chi-squared	0.7828
Gabor_DR	100	Euclidean	0.7452
LBP_DR	100	Euclidean	0.7875
PCANet_DR	100	Euclidean	0.8419

In this experiment, 90 % of data are randomly selected for training and the remaining 10 % are used for testing. The correlation between predicted attractiveness scores and human rated scores are used to evaluate the prediction performance. The training and testing procedures are run 100 times, and the average prediction performances are shown in Table 7.2. We can see that dimensionality reduction significantly improves the performances of Gabor and PCANet features, and PCANet-DR achieves the best performance. Though the performance of LBP-DR is slightly lower than that of LBP, LBP-DR can reduce the dimensionality of when building more complex models. We apply dimensionality reduction to Gabor, LBP, and PCANet features in the following experiments and the '-DR' identifier is removed for simplicity.

In the above experiments, parameter k was obtained by search. Figure 7.3 shows the performances of KNN regression on different types of features with increasing value of k. The optimal k for Gabor feature is 6; the optimal k for eigenface, AAM, LBP, and PCANet features is about 10; and the optimal k for ratio and shape features is about 40.

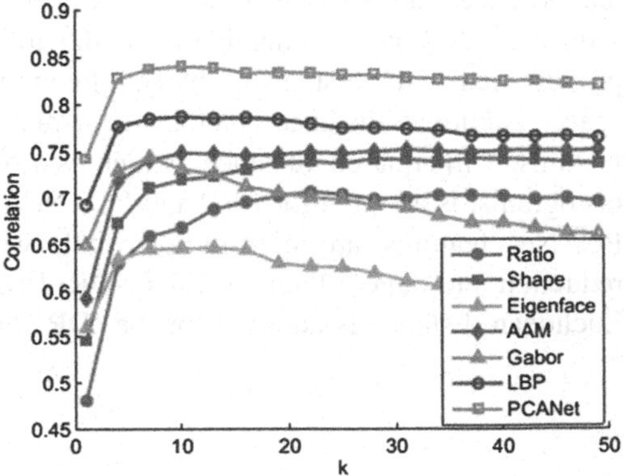

Fig. 7.3 KNN regression performance with different k

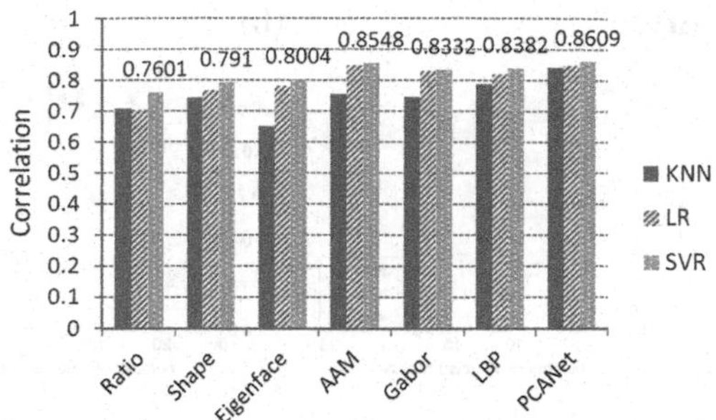

Fig. 7.4 Comparison of regression methods in terms of attractiveness prediction accuracy

7.5.3 Comparison of Regression Methods

Because KNN regression is simple and has fewest requirements to the features, it is used as a baseline method. However, the most commonly used regression methods in facial attractiveness prediction are linear regression (LR) (Duda et al. 2000) and support vector regression (SVR) with radial basis function (RBF) kernels (Vapnik 1995). It is necessary to investigate which regression method is better for a specific type of features. Similar to Sect. 7.5.2, the training and testing data were randomly divided and the training and testing procedures were run 100 times. The parameters of SVR were obtained by grid search. Figure 7.4 shows the average prediction accuracies of the three methods with different types of features. We can see that SVR achieves the best performance consistently.

7.5.4 Feature Selection Results

The three feature selection methods described in Sect. 7.3 are compared. They are filter, backward elimination and the lasso, respectively. A series of models were trained with an increasing number of features ordered by the three methods. The models were built with the SVR method, as shown in Sect. 7.5.3. The prediction performances of the models are shown in Fig. 7.5. We can see that the lasso outperforms the other two feature selection methods.

Hence, we used the lasso for feature selection. SVR models were trained with an increasing number of features sorted by the lasso. The training and testing procedures were the same as those in Sect. 7.5.2 and the average performances are plotted in Fig. 7.6. We can see that at first the performances of all types of features increase rapidly, and after about 20 % of the total features are chosen, the performance curves become flat. Hence, there are irrelative or redundant variables. The numbers of selected features are determined by multiple two-sample *t*-tests with significance level $\alpha = 0.05$. Table 7.3 gives the feature selection results. For most of the cases, about a half of features are discarded. However, the performances of the selected features are usually slightly better than those of original features (see Fig. 7.4; Table 7.3).

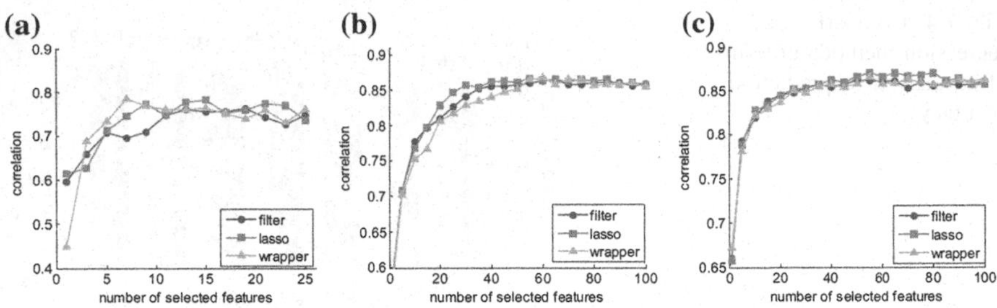

Fig. 7.5 Comparison of feature selection methods. The filter method is based on correlation criterion and the wrapper method is sequential backward elimination. **a** Ratio feature. **b** AAM feature. **c** PCANet feature. They represent rule based, model based, and descriptor based features respectively

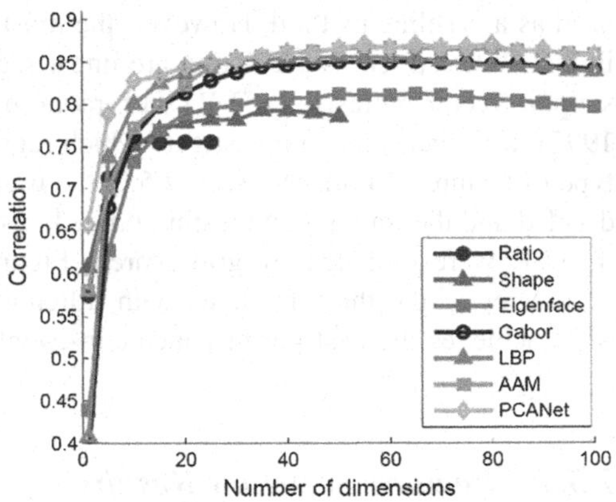

Fig. 7.6 Prediction performance with an increasing number of selected feature dimensions

Table 7.3 Feature selection results

Feature	#Dimension	Performance
Ratio	7	0.7554
Shape	33	0.7827
Eigenface	46	0.7979
AAM	55	0.8669
Gabor	50	0.8506
LBP	41	0.8561
PCANet	55	0.8708

7.5.5 Results of Score Level Fusion and Optimal Feature Set

Feature selection optimizes each type of feature, and in this section, we discuss the optimal combination of multiple types of features for facial attractiveness prediction. For seven types of features, there are 127 different combinations (see Sect. 7.4).

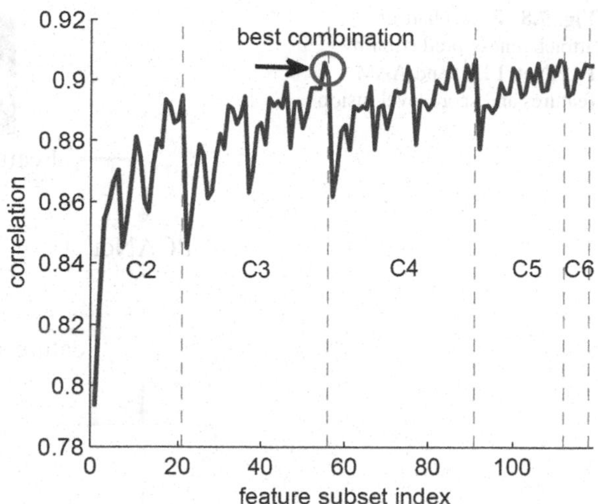

Fig. 7.7 Prediction performance of different feature combinations. For example, C2 means all combinations of two feature types, which has $C_7^2 = 21$ subsets

In order to obtain the combination weights defined in (7.11), we need to construct the single-type-feature output matrix *Y*. We randomly selected 700 faces to train seven models corresponding to the seven types of features (after feature selection). The models predicted attractiveness scores of the remaining 99 faces, so that there were 99×7 scores. Repeating this procedure for 10 times, we obtained a matrix of size 990×7, which served as matrix *Y*. Then by solving (7.11), we got the combination weights.

For each feature combination, score level fusion was performed. For example, if the combination has *n* types of features, then *n* SVR models are built on the training data, which predict *n* attractiveness scores for each of the testing data. The final score is weighted sum of the outputs of the *n* models (the weights are determined beforehand). We run 10-fold cross validation on our database and the average performances of different combinations are plotted in Fig. 7.7. The best feature combination is the most parsimonious one with competitive prediction accuracy, as marked in Fig. 7.7. Table 7.4 shows the optimal combinations constrained by the number of feature types. We can see that the best single-type feature is PCANet. The fusion of PCANet, LBP, and AAM can significantly improve the prediction performance, and the performance cannot be significantly increased by adding more types of features. Hence, the optimal feature set includes PCANet, LBP, and AAM features.

Table 7.4 Optimal combinations and score level fusion results

No. of types	Optimal combination	Performance
1	PCANet	0.8708
2	PCANet + LBP	0.8947
3	PCANet + LBP + AAM	0.9056
4	PCANet + LBP + AAM + Gabor	0.9067

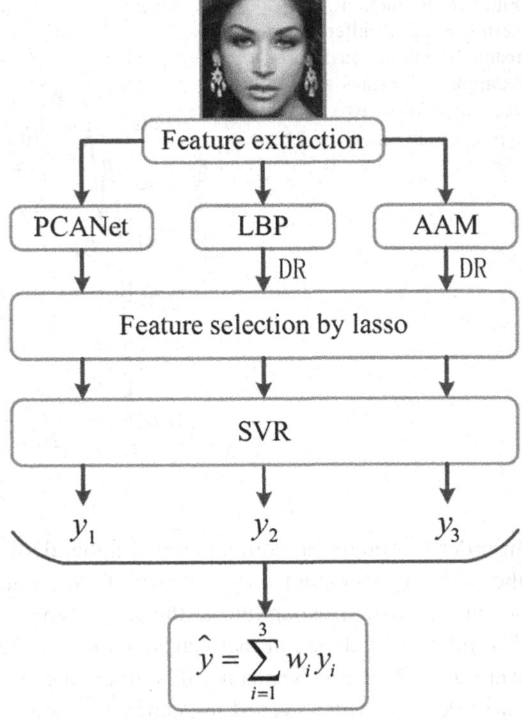

Fig. 7.8 Flow chart of attractiveness prediction by PCANet, LBP, and AAM features and score level fusion

Figure 7.8 illustrates a flow chart of our attractiveness prediction method, which includes the following steps: extraction of PCANet, LBP, and AAM features, dimension reduction, feature selection, SVR, and score level fusion.

7.5.6 Comparison with Other Works

In this section, we compare the score level fusion method with those proposed by other works. As facial attractiveness prediction is still an emerging topic, there is no public database for comparison. Therefore, we implemented the methods of other works on our database and make the comparison. As shown in Table 7.5, three methods are compared. Schmid et al. (2008) built a linear model with ratio features. Gray et al. (2010) trained a convolutional neural network for attractiveness prediction. Nguyen et al. (2013) cascaded shape, Gabor, LBP, and color moment features into a high-dimensional vector and performs PCA to reduce the feature dimension to 350. We did not include the color moment feature, because the images were collected from many sources and the various illumination conditions cover the true face colors. Besides, some of the data are gray-level images. For each method, 10-fold cross-validation was performed and the average prediction accuracy is

Table 7.5 Comparison with other works

Method	Feature	#Dimension	Performance
LR (Schmid et al. 2008)	Ratios	23	0.6958
Neural network (Gray et al. 2010)	convNet	–	0.7512
SVR (Nguyen et al. 2013)	Shape + Gabor + LBP	350	0.8185
SVR + fusion	AAM + LBP + PCANet	151	0.9056

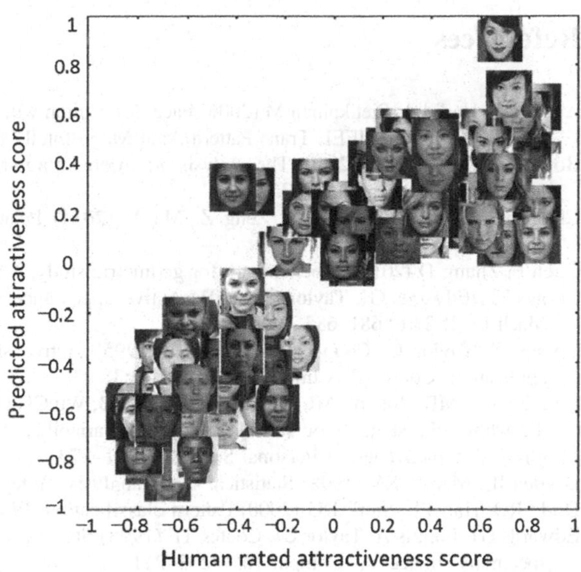

Fig. 7.9 Scatter plot of human rated scores and predicted scores obtained by our method

shown in Table 7.5. The results show that our method is much better than other methods. Figure 7.9 shows a scatter plot of human rated scores and predicted scores obtained by our method. We can see that most of the faces cluster around the diagonal line.

7.6 Summary

In this chapter, we give a comprehensive study on feature design for image based facial attractiveness prediction. Ratio, shape, eigenface, AAM, Gabor, LBP, and PCANet features are extracted and compared in terms of attractiveness prediction accuracy. It is found that dimensionality reduction and feature selection can promote the prediction performance. For feature selection, the lasso method performs better than filter and sequential wrapper methods. Then the optimal combination of multiple types of features is discussed. Experimental results show that PCANet is the best single-type feature, followed by AAM, LBP, and Gabor. Combining multiple types of features by score level fusion can significantly improve the performance, and the optimal feature set is constituted by PCANet, LBP, and AAM features. The model built on these features outperforms state-of-the-art methods and can serve as a competitive benchmark for further studies.

References

Ahonen T, Hadid A, Pietikainen M (2006) Face description with local binary patterns: application to face recognition. IEEE Trans Pattern Anal Mach Intell 28(12):2037–2041

Bottino A, Laurentini A (2010) The analysis of: an emerging area of research in pattern analysis. Image Anal Recognit 425–435

Chan TH, Jia K, Gao S, Lu J, Zeng Z, Ma Y (2014) Pcanet: a simple baseline for image classification? arXiv 1404.3606

Chen F, Zhang D (2010) A benchmark for geometric study. Med Biom 21–32

Cootes TF, Edwards GJ, Taylor CJ (2001) Active appearance models. IEEE Trans Pattern Anal Mach Intell 23(6):681–685

Cootes T, Taylor C, Cooper D, Graham J (1995) Active shape models: their training and application. Comput Vis Image Underst 61(1):38–59

Cunningham MR, Roberts AR, Barbee AP, Druen PB, Wu CH (1995) their ideas of beauty are, on the whole, the same as ours: consistency and variability in the cross-cultural perception of physical attractiveness. J Personal Soc 68(2):261–279

Dryden IL, Mardia KV (1998) Statistical shape analysis. Wiley

Duda RO, Hart PE, Stork DG (2000) Pattern classification. Wiley Interscience

Edwards GJ, Lanitis A, Taylor CJ, Cootes TF (1998) Statistical models of face images improving specificity. Image Vis Comput 16(3):203–211

Eisenthal Y, Dror G, Ruppin E (2006) Facial attractiveness: beauty and the machine. Neural Comput 18(1):119–142

Fan J, Chau KP, Wan X, Zhai L, Lau E (2012) Prediction of from facial proportions. Pattern Recogn 45(6):2326–2334

Gray D, Yu K, Xu W, Gong Y (2010) Predicting without landmarks. In: Proceedings of European conference on computer vision, pp 434–447

Guyon I, Elisseeff A (2003) An introduction to variable and feature selection. J Mach Learn Res 3:1157–1182

Hastie T, Tibshirani R, Friedman J (2009) The elements of statistical learning. Springer

Hubel DH, Wiesel TN (1962) Receptive fields, binocular interaction and functional architecture in the cat's visual cortex. J Physiol 160(1):106–154

Kagian A, Dror G, Leyvand T, Meilijson I, Cohen-Or D, Ruppin E (2008) A predictor of revealing humanlike psychophysical biases. Vis Res 48(2):235–243

Langlois JH, Kalakanis L, Rubenstein AJ, Larson A, Hallam M, Smoot M (2000) Maxims or myths of beauty? A meta-analytic and theoretical review. Psychol Bull 126(3):390

Liu C, Wechsler H (2002) Gabor feature based classification using the enhanced fisher linear discriminant model for face recognition. IEEE Trans Image Process 11(4):467–476

Messer K, Matas J, Kittler J, Luettin J, Maitre G (1999) Xm2vtsdb: The extended m2vts . In: Proceedings of international conference on audio and video-based biometric person authentication, vol 964, pp 965–966

Nguyen TV, Liu S, Ni B, Tan J, Rui Y, Yan S (2013) Towards decrypting attractiveness via multi-modality cues. ACM Trans Multimedia Comput Commun Appl 9(4):28

Schmid K, Marx D, Samal A (2008) Computation of a face attractiveness index based on, symmetry, and golden ratios. Pattern Recogn 41(8):2710–2717

Sjöstrand K, Clemmensen LH, Larsen R, Ersbøll B (2012) Spasm: a matlab toolbox for sparse statistical modeling. J Stat Softw (accepted for publication)

Vapnik V (1995) The nature of statistical learning theory. Springer

Whitehill J, Movellan J (2008) Personalized prediction. In: Proceedings of IEEE international conference on automatic face gesture recognition, pp 1–7

Zhang D, Zhao Q, Chen F (2011) Quantitative analysis of human using. Pattern Recogn 44 (4):940–950

Zou J, Ji Q, Nagy G (2007) A comparative study of local matching approach for face recognition. IEEE Trans Image Process 16(10):2617–2628

Part III
Hypotheses on Facial Beauty Perception

Chapter 8
Examination of Averageness Hypothesis on Large Database

The averageness hypothesis is one of the most known hypotheses. However, previous evaluation on this hypothesis is not very comprehensive. With this chapter, we mainly use a large scale database to test this hypothesis for obtaining convincing evaluation on it. The testing scheme and means are also applicable for other hypotheses. We first briefly introduce related works and the goal of the human facial beauty in Sect. 8.1. We present the human face shape modeling in detail in Sect. 8.2. In Sect. 8.3, we introduce the image processing techniques and face stimuli that we employ in the experiments, as well as the design of the perception experiments. In Sect. 8.4, we analyze the experimental results and main findings. The chapter is finally concluded in Sect. 8.5.

8.1 Introduction

Several facial beauty hypotheses, such as symmetrical faces and average faces, have been raised in the past studies. Among these hypotheses, the most influential and most investigated one is the averageness hypothesis. Some related works about the averageness hypothesis have discussed in Chap. 2. Despite the increasing public and professional interest and the extensive research in the field, the published studies have not yet reached consensus on those facial beauty hypotheses or on the characteristics that make human faces attractive. Moreover, there are some limitations in previous studies on facial beauty. First, the difference between face shapes was not quantified and it was consequently hard to quantitatively assess the impact of deviation from average face shapes on facial beauty. Second, they ignored the transformation, e.g. scaling and rotation, occurring to the faces during generation of face images. Such transformation can greatly affect the calculated distances between face shapes, and thus impair the reliability of the conclusions. They did not normalize the physical sizes of faces when evaluating their attractiveness, yet as common observations in our daily life tell us, the distance between a small-sized

D. Zhang et al., *Computer Models for Facial Beauty Analysis*,
DOI 10.1007/978-3-319-32598-9_8

face to a large-sized face could be very large, but the facial beauty perception of them could be similar. Third, most of them require intensive manual work, e.g. marking landmarks. Forth, most existing studies are based on human ratings of the attractiveness of faces. The quality of the collected human ratings severely affects the results. According to our experiments, if an absolute attractiveness score in a certain scale (e.g. 10-point scale (Schmid et al. 2008) or 7-point scale (Perrett et al. 1994; Eisenthal et al. 2006; Kagian et al. 2008) is required to assign to a face, large variation would be observed among different people. Unfortunately, only the averaging human ratings were used as ground truth in Eisenthal et al. (2006), Kagian et al. (2008), Leyvand et al. (2008), Schmid et al. (2008), but the variance of human ratings was not reported or analyzed. Moreover, when collecting the attractiveness scores of faces, they did not isolate the facial geometric features from other features. As a consequence, the collected attractiveness scores depend not only on geometric features, but also on other features such as textures. It is thus problematic to study the relationship between geometric features and facial beauty based on only such kind of attractiveness scores.

The goal of this preliminary study is to quantitatively analyze the effect of facial geometric features on the attractiveness of faces. In order to conquer the above-mentioned limitations of existing studies, we consider human faces in a feature space, namely human face shape space, which is defined by the facial geometric features and is a subspace of the unit hypersphere. Every human face after normalization is represented by a point in the space. The distance between two face shapes in the human face shape space is measured in terms of the angle between them, and an effective algorithm is applied to calculate it such that the measured distance is invariant to similarity transformation (i.e. translation, rotation, and scaling). Based on the established human face shape space and the distance measurement and by using advanced automatic image processing techniques, we present a method that enabled the human face shapes to be quantitatively evaluated and their contribution to the human facial beauty perception without interference of non-geometric features. Moreover, we employ a deductive approach in this chapter. In other words, human ratings are only used for evaluation experiments (instead of scoring each individual faces, participants are requested to choose out the most beautiful face from a set of faces which differ only in their geometric features).

8.2 Face Shape Space Modeling

8.2.1 Perception Function of Facial Beauty

In this section, two dimensional face images are used as stimuli. Given a face image I, we model the perception of its beauty by a function as follows

$$b = f(G, t, x), \tag{8.1}$$

where b is its beauty score, G and t are respectively the geometric and texture features extracted from face image I, and x denotes all other factors affecting the facial beauty perception (e.g. secondary sexual characteristics). These various factors make the facial beauty perception process quite complicated and so far, it is still not clear how these factors correlate with each other in determining the facial beauty. Hence, in this chapter we focus on the geometric feature driven perception of facial beauty. We keep all the determinants except the geometric feature constant between face images when comparing their attractiveness. As a result, the perception function of facial beauty considered in this section can be simplified to

$$b = f_G(G). \tag{8.2}$$

8.2.2 Geometric Feature Definition

In previous chapters, we have introduced the geometric feature in detail. In this chapter, we use the landmark model with 68 landmarks as an example. The landmark model with 68 points is shown in Fig. 4.2. Then the geometric feature of a face can be represented as

$$G = (x_1, y_1, x_2, y_2, \ldots, x_{68}, y_{68})^T, \tag{8.3}$$

where 'T' denotes the transpose operator.

8.2.3 Human Face Shape Space S_{FS}

The geometric feature simply uses the coordinates of landmarks defined in the coordinate system on the original image. It is thus not invariant to translation (i.e. the relative position of the face on the image) and scale. As a result, the geometric features of different faces would become incomparable due to their different positions or scales in the image coordinate system. Hence, they need to be normalized before comparison. We denote the normalized geometric feature as g. In order to make it invariant to translation, we subtract the average values of x- and y- coordinates of all landmarks on the face from the x- and y- coordinates of each landmark on a face respectively, i.e.

$$\begin{cases} \tilde{x}_i = x_i - \frac{1}{68}\sum_{i=1}^{68} x_i \\ \tilde{y}_i = y_i - \frac{1}{68}\sum_{i=1}^{68} y_i \end{cases} \quad i = 1, 2, \ldots, 68. \tag{8.4}$$

In other words, the center of the landmarks is moved to the origin of the coordinate system.

As discussed in the introduction, scale invariance is also desired for the facial geometric feature. For this purpose, we normalize the geometric feature vector to unit length by dividing its components by its norm such that $\|g\| = \sqrt{\sum_{i=1}^{136} g_i^2} = 1$. Finally, after the above normalization, every face is mapped to a point in the following space,

$$S_G = \{g|g \in R^{136}, \sum_{i=1}^{68} g_{2i-1} = 0, \sum_{i=1}^{68} g_{2i} = 0, \|g\| = 1\}, \quad (8.5)$$

which is the 136-dimensional unit hypersphere. The odd and even components (corresponding to the x- and y- coordinates of the landmarks defining the face shape) of the geometric feature vector both sum up to zero, because the landmarks have been centered (see Eqs. (8.3) and (8.4)) and the feature is translation invariant. However, due to the implicit constraints on human face shapes (e.g. there is one eye on either side of the nose), not all points in S_G correspond to a valid human face shape. Thus, the human face shape space, denoted by S_{FS}, composes a subspace of S_G (i.e. $S_{FS} \subset S_G$), which will be further demonstrated in the experiments later. Since all the normalized facial geometric features are in face shape space S_{FS}, they are also called "face shape". The perception function of facial beauty defined on S_{FS} becomes $b = f_G(G) = f_g(g)$.

8.2.4 Distance Measurement in S_{FS}

In the above-defined human face shape space S_{FS}, the representation of faces is invariant to translation and scaling. However, in-plane rotation of faces has so far not been considered, which can also make the calculated distances between face shapes inaccurate. Therefore, we have to eliminate the possible rotation between two face shapes when we calculate the distance between them. To this end, we first apply a rotation transformation R to each of the landmarks of one face shape such that it, after transformation, has the minimum Euclidean distance to the other face shape. The rotation transformation on a face shape g is fulfilled by rotating each of its landmarks, i.e.

$$\begin{pmatrix} \tilde{g}_{2i-1} \\ \tilde{g}_{2i} \end{pmatrix} = R \cdot \begin{pmatrix} g_{2i-1} \\ g_{2i} \end{pmatrix} = \begin{pmatrix} \cos\theta & \sin\theta \\ -\sin\theta & \cos\theta \end{pmatrix} \cdot \begin{pmatrix} g_{2i-1} \\ g_{2i} \end{pmatrix} \quad (8.6)$$

for $i = 1, 2, \ldots, 68$. Here, $\tilde{g}$ is the rotated result of g. For notation simplicity, we denote it by $\tilde{g} = R \circ g$. Given two face shapes g_1 and g_2 in S_{FS}, the optimal rotation R_{12}^* between them is estimated by solving the following optimization problem (its solution is given in the appendix),

$$R_{12}^{*} = \arg\min_{R} \|\tilde{g}_1 - g_2\|^2 = \arg\min_{R} \|R \circ g_1 - g_2\|^2. \tag{8.7}$$

The distance between these two shapes is then defined as[1]

$$d_{g_1 g_2} = \cos^{-1}(<\tilde{g}_1^{*}, g_2>) = \cos^{-1}(<R_{12}^{*} \circ g_1, g_2>), \tag{8.8}$$

where $<g_1, g_2> = g_1^T \cdot g_2$ represents the inner product. Note that the feature vectors in S_{FS} have unit length. The above distance measurement essentially measures the angles between feature vectors, or the arc length between corresponding points of the two face shapes on the unit hypersphere S_G. Moreover, according to the definition of S_G in (8.5) and the definition of the distance measurement in (8.8), it can be easily seen that this distance measurement is invariant to similarity transformation and thus makes the calculated distances between face shapes more reliable. Obviously, the range of the distance is between 0 and π in radian, or between 0 and 180 in degree (in the subsequent analysis, we will measure the distance in terms of radian).

8.2.5 Calculation of Average Face Shapes in S_{FS}

Given a set of face images, in order to calculate the average face shape of them, we first represent their face shapes in human face shape space S_{FS}. But we cannot get the average face shape simply by averaging each dimension because the rotation among the face shapes, if not handled, will result in a biased average face shape. As discussed in the last subsection, the face shape distance defined in (8.8) is invariant to similarity transformation. We define the average face shape of $\{g_1, g_2, \cdots, g_N\}$, a given set of face shapes in S_{FS}, as

$$\bar{g} = \arg\min_{g \in S_{FS}} \sum_{i=1}^{N} d_{g_i g}^2. \tag{8.9}$$

The average shape of a set of face shapes is the one which gives the minimum summation of squared distances between it and each of the given face shapes. According to the derivation in Dryden and Mardia (1998), when the given shapes lie on a small local patch, the above-defined average shape of them can be approximated by the eigenvector corresponding to the largest eigenvalue of the following matrix

[1] A concern here is whether this distance measurement is symmetric or not. Please see the Appendix I for the proof that it is.

$$\Lambda = \sum_{i=1}^{N} g_i g_i^T. \tag{8.10}$$

In the experimental results reported in the later section, we will show that the face shapes do cluster in a very compact region on the unit hypersphere. Hence, we can calculate the average face shapes by using the above method.

8.3 Methodology: Quantitative Analysis

8.3.1 Automatic Geometric Feature Extraction

In this chapter, we perfumed the automatic geometric feature extraction method presented in Sect. 4.2.2.2 to extract the geometric feature. The method can be briefly introduced as follows: we first detect the face in the image by using the VJ face detector, and then we use the method in Rowley et al. (1998) to detect the position of the eyes on the face, finally we use the active shape model (ASM) to locate the landmarks on the face. The geometric feature of the face is finally generated from these extracted landmarks based on the definitions given in Sect. 8.2.2 and the shape of the face is generated by mapping the geometric feature onto human face shape space S_{FS}. The mapping procedure is presented in Sect. 8.2.3.

8.3.2 Automatic Face Deformation

Given a face and its extracted geometric feature, for the purpose of quantitatively analyzing the effect of geometric feature on facial attractiveness, we have to change its geometric feature while keeping other features unchanged. This is basically a problem of image deformation on faces. To specify the deformation, we usually have to set up a set of control points on both the original and deformed face images, and the landmarks on the faces can naturally serve as the control points. Next, we first introduce how to specify the deformation by using the control points, and then how to implement the deformation.

With the landmarks as the control points, we need only to determine new positions of these landmarks to specify the deformation. Since this study aims to investigate the effect of average face shape in human facial beauty perception, we will deform a face to make its shape get close to or far away from average face shape $\bar{g}$. In other words, two new faces I_{near} and I_{far} with geometric features G_{near} and G_{far} will be generated from given original face $I_{original}$ whose geometric feature is $G_{original}$. The correspondent shapes of G_{near}, G_{far}, and $G_{original}$ in S_{FS} are g_{near}, g_{far}, and $g_{original}$, respectively. For fair comparison between I_{near} and I_{far}, it will be required that the distances between their shapes and the original shape should be nearly equal. To this end, we map the average face shape (which is calculated in the face shape space as defined in Sect. 8.2.5) back to the image coordinate system via scaling and translation with respect to the original face, getting the geometric feature, G_{near}. It has the same scale with the original face and their centers overlap in the image coordinate system. Note that G_{near} is thus defined in the image coordinate system and holds the shape of $\bar{g}$, i.e., $g_{near} = \bar{g}$. Hence its components directly correspond to the coordinates of the landmarks in image I_{near} to be generated. In other words, they give new positions of the landmarks in I_{near}.

In order to specify the positions of the landmarks in image I_{far} to be generated, we first fit the geometric feature of the original face to G_{near} via a rotation R, which can be estimated using Eq. (8.7), resulting in geometric feature $R \circ G_{original}$ and shape $R \circ g_{original}$. According to the distance metric in face space S_{FS}, the distance between g_{near} and $g_{original}$ equals to the angle between g_{near} and $R \circ g_{original}$, i.e., $d_{original,near} = \alpha_1 = \cos^{-1}(<R \circ g_{original}, g_{near}>)$, which is shown in Fig. 8.1. Then we define G_{far} as $G_{far} = 2 * R \circ G_{original} - G_{near}$, such that it is on the same line passing through G_{near} and $R \circ G_{original}$ and $R \circ G_{original}$ is the middle point of the segment connecting G_{near} and G_{far}. In S_{FS}, g_{far} can be obtained by normalizing vector $2 * R \circ g_{original} - g_{near}$ to unit scale, as shown in Fig. 8.1, where L_1 and L_2 can be seen as the Euclidean distance and $L_1 = L_2 = \left\| R \circ g_{original} - g_{near} \right\|$. Note that L_1 and L_2 are much smaller than the radii of S_G, i.e., $L_1 = L_2 \ll 1$ (we will show this in the experiments), so the difference between α_1 and α_2 is substantially small, although α_1 is always larger than α_2 by geometric constraint (the proof is given in Appendix II). The distance between g_{far} and $g_{original}$ is $d_{original,far} = \cos^{-1}(<R' \circ g_{original}, g_{far}>)$, where R' is the optimal rotation matrix between $g_{original}$ and g_{far}, i.e., $R' = \arg\min_R \left\| R \circ g_{original} - g_{far} \right\|$, so $d_{original,far} \leq \alpha_2 = \cos^{-1}(<R \circ g_{original}, g_{far}>) < \alpha_1 = d_{original,near}$. In this way, we ensure that the distance between $g_{original}$ and g_{far} is not larger than that between $g_{original}$ and g_{near}. In fact, the difference between these two distances is substantially small.

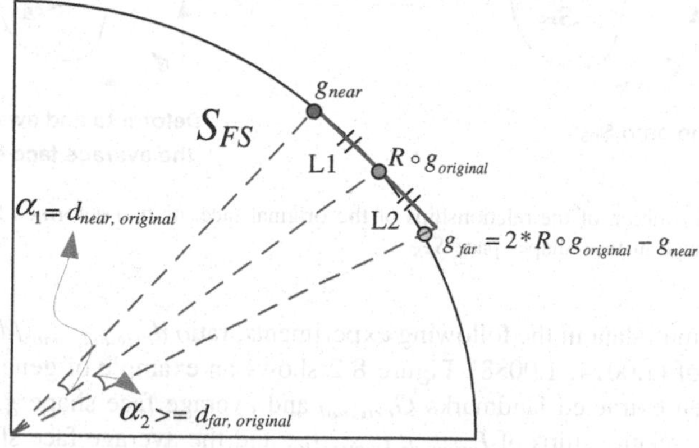

Fig. 8.1 Sketch for determining the new landmark positions of I_{far}

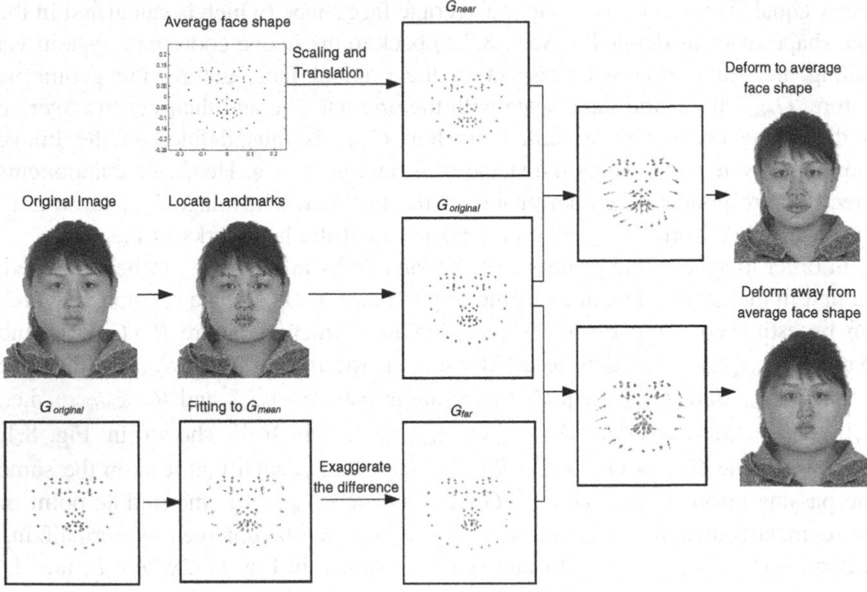

Fig. 8.2 An example of deforming an input image to and away from the average face shape

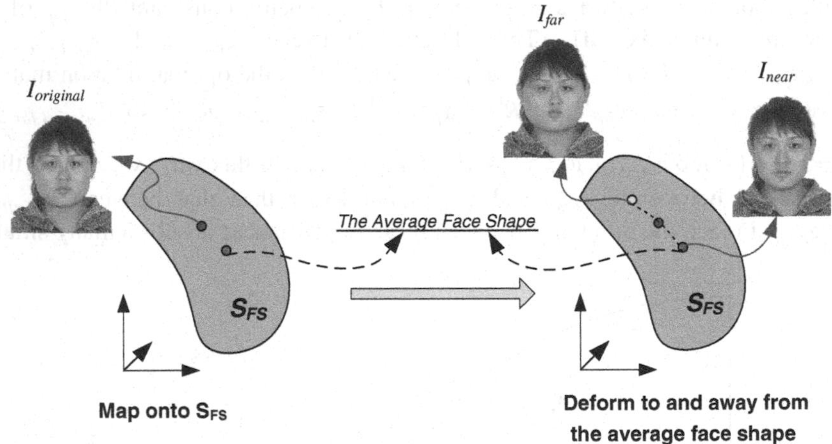

Fig. 8.3 An illustration of the relationships of the original face, its two deformed faces, and the average face shape in face shape space S_{FS}

As for the stimuli data in the following experiments, ratio $d_{original,\ near}/d_{original,\ far}$ is in the range of [1.0014, 1.0088]. Figure 8.2 shows an example of generating G_{near} and G_{far} given extracted landmarks $G_{original}$ and average face shape $\bar{g}$. Figure 8.3 illustrates the relationships of $I_{original}$, I_{near}, I_{far} and the average face shape in face shape space S_{FS}.

According to Igarashi et al. (2005), deformations for realistic shapes should be as rigid as possible. As for the control points based rigid transformation, please refer to the method in Schaefer et al. (2006) which is based on moving least squares (MLS). Taking the input image in Fig. 8.2 as an example, control points $G_{original}$ and G_{near} are used to specify and guide the deformation to the average face shape. If the deformation is viewed as a function f, it satisfies the following three properties (Schaefer et al. 2006): interpolation ($f(G_{original}) = G_{near}$), identity ($G_{original} = G_{near} \Rightarrow f(g) = g$), and smoothness. In this way, we generate two new faces as shown on the right of Fig. 8.2. One has a shape very close to $\bar{g}$, and the other has the shape far away from $\bar{g}$.

8.3.3 Stimuli Generation

We select images of 649 females and 658 males from the Shanghai database to test the presented algorithm. The geometric features of these faces were extracted and represented in S_{FS}. The average face shapes of female and male were then derived from all these female and male face samples, respectively. Figure 8.4a plots histograms of pair-wise distances between all these faces and their distances to the average face shapes. 50 female faces and 50 male faces were randomly chosen from the training data. From each of the faces, $I_{original}$, we generated two new faces, I_{near} and I_{far}, using the above-mentioned method. One of the two new faces became closer to the average face shape of its gender while the other one was moved far away. Moreover, the distances between these two new faces and the original one are ensured to be similar, i.e., $d_{original,near} \approx d_{original,far}$. As a result, 100 groups of face stimuli were obtained. In each group, there were three faces, one of which was the original face and the other two are newly generated faces with one obviously closer to the average face shape of its gender than the other one. Figure 8.4b and c show the histograms of the distances from g_{near} and g_{far}, respectively, to the original faces and the average face shapes.

8.3.4 Perception Experiment Design

The perception experiment aims to examine the role of average face shapes in human facial beauty perception by using the generated stimuli. For this purpose, 100 students in our university (63 males and 37 females, aged between 20 and 30) were requested to make forced-choice comparisons of beauty among the three faces in each group in the stimuli, i.e. they had to choose the one they thought more attractive than the other two. None of these participants was familiar to the faces in the training data. To facilitate the experiment, we implemented a web-based user interface. The participants viewed through the interface the face stimuli which were presented group by group and side by side (in random order and counterbalanced for side of presentation). They then submitted their choices directly on the interface. In the next section, we report the experimental results that we have obtained and carry out detailed analysis on the results.

8.4 Results and Analysis

8.4.1 Distribution of Human Face Shapes in S_G

We first investigated the distribution of human face shapes in S_G. According to the histogram of the pair-wise distances between the training data in the Shanghai database shown in Fig. 8.4, the face shapes distribute in a very compact region. Table 8.1 shows some statistics on these pair-wise distances between female faces (F-F), between male faces (M-M), and between all the faces (ALL). These results demonstrate that it is reasonable for us to assume that the human face shapes lie in a condensed subspace of S_G, or a small local patch of the unit hypersphere, as illustrated in Fig. 8.5. This observation justifies the method of calculating the average face shape sketched in Sect. 8.2.5 and shows that the Euclidean distance between any two face shapes is much smaller than the radii of S_G.

The observation of a very condensed space of human face shapes is not surprising. A shape, as a valid face shape of a real human face (here we refer to upright faces), has to conform to a number of constraints. For example, there should be two eyes residing nearly-symmetrically on the left and right parts of the face, and there should be one mouth below the only one nose on the face, etc. As a result, a random point in S_G (i.e. on the unit hypersphere) but outside the subspace of valid human face shapes will correspond to a shape that will not be perceived as a real human face.

8.4.2 Effect of Database Sizes on Average Face Shapes

To investigate the effect of database sizes on the accuracy of average face shapes, the following experiment on a larger dataset of Northeast China which contains 10,000 face images of each gender (this database is called the Northeast China database) was conducted. We first randomly chose two face images for each gender and calculated average face shapes based on them. We then gradually enlarged the dataset of each gender by doubling the number of samples of each gender and re-calculated the average face shapes. Specifically, we considered datasets with 2^i samples, where $i = 1, 2, \ldots, 13$. We repeated the above experiment by 100 times. The average differences between every two succeeding average face shapes and the

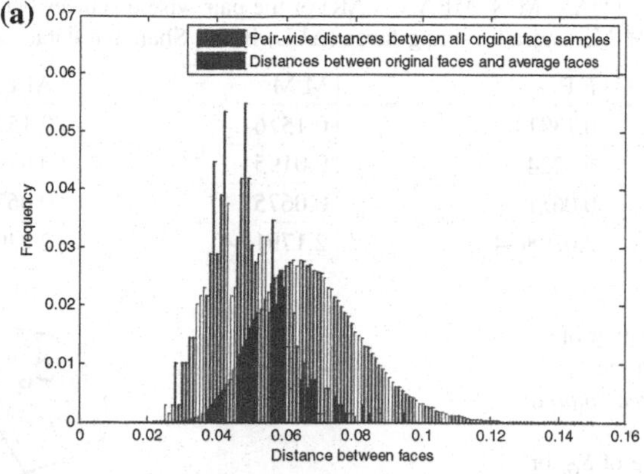

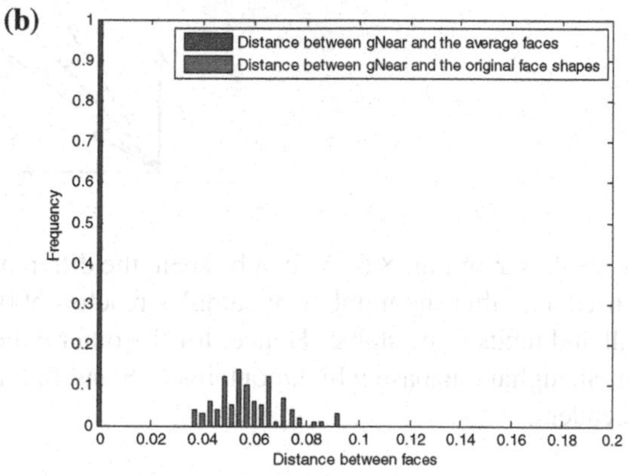

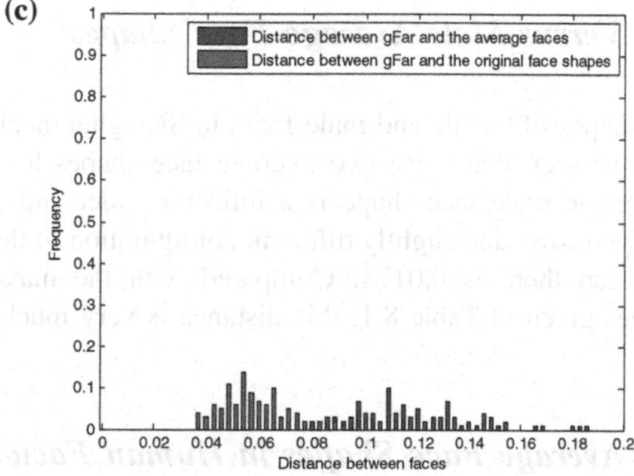

Fig. 8.4 Histograms of distances between face samples in the Shanghai database. **a** Histograms of pair-wise distances between all the original face samples and their distances to the average face shapes, **b** Histograms of distances from g_{near} to the original faces and the average face shapes, **c** Histograms of distances from g_{far} to the original faces and the average face shapes

Table 8.1 Statistics (MAX, MIN, MEAN, VAR) of the pair-wise distances between female faces (F-F), male faces (M-M), and all training faces (ALL) in the Shanghai database

	F-F	M-M	ALL
MAX	0.1391	0.1576	0.1576
MIN	0.0224	0.0195	0.0195
MEAN	0.0631	0.0675	0.0677
VAR	2.0298e-4	2.1791e-4	2.2402e-4

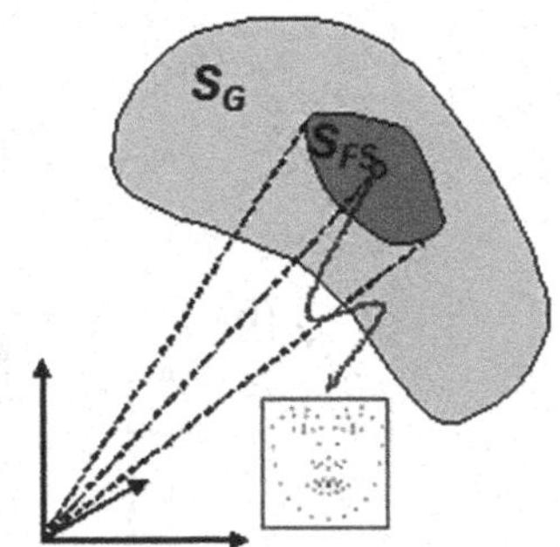

Fig. 8.5 An illustration of the space of human face shapes S_{FS} (the *green colored* region), which is a very condensed subspace of S_G, or a small local patch on the unit hypersphere

standard deviation are shown in Fig. 8.6. As can be seen, the difference decreases as more samples are used and after the number of samples reaches 500, the difference becomes very small and tends to be stable. Hence, for the other experiments in this chapter, we use the Shanghai database which contains 648 and 656 face samples of female and male genders.

8.4.3 Female Versus Male Average Face Shapes

The average face shapes of female and male faces in Shanghai database are shown in Fig. 8.7. It can be seen that these two average face shapes look quite similar except that the average male face shape is a little bit wider and longer and has relatively thicker eye-brows and slightly different configuration of the facial organs. The distance between them is 0.0174. Compared with the maximum distance between face shapes given in Table 8.1, this distance is very much smaller.

8.4.4 Role of Average Face Shapes in Human Facial Beauty

The beauty assessment results on the 100 groups of stimulus faces were collected from the 100 human observers who are required to test the role of average face

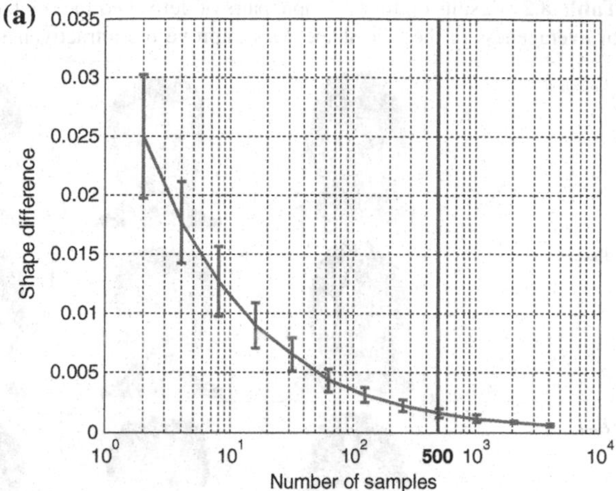

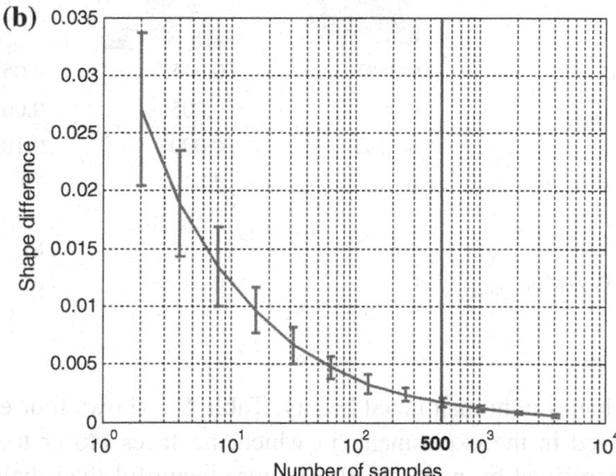

Fig. 8.6 Average differences and standard deviation between every two succeeding average face shapes calculated from datasets with 2, 4, 8, …, and 8192 face samples of **a** female and **b** male genders which are randomly chosen from the Northeast China database

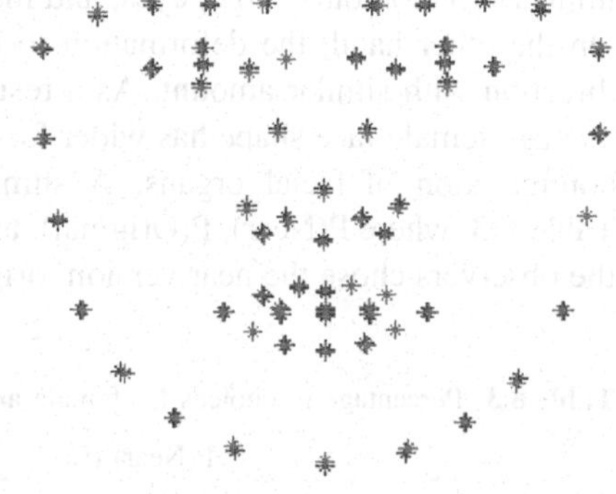

Fig. 8.7 Overlaid average female face shape (*red asterisk*) and average male face shape (*blue asterisk*)

Table 8.2 Results on four example pairs of deformed faces which demonstrate that the increasing of averageness in the face shape does improve the attractiveness of these faces

$g_{original}$				
g_{near}				
g_{far}	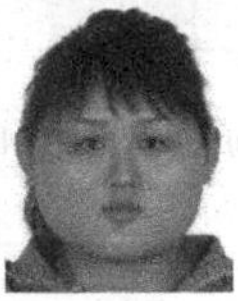			
$d_{g_{original}\bar{g}}$	0.0581	0.0453	0.0513	0.0560
$d_{g_{near}\bar{g}}$	0.0054	0.005	0.0055	0.0056
$d_{g_{far}\bar{g}}$	0.1162	0.0907	0.1016	0.1117
Votes for $g_{original}$	0	22	19	21
Votes for g_{near}	100	78	81	79
Votes for g_{far}	0	0	0	0

shapes in human facial beauty. Table 8.2 shows four example groups of such faces used in the experiment, in which the faces closer to the average face shapes are perceived by most people as more beautiful than their counterparts in the groups. We take the leftmost female face sample in Table 8.2 as an example. After deformation toward the average female face shape, the new face is characterized by thinner face contour, bigger eyes, and more scattered configuration of facial organs. On the other hand, the deformation to the other new face is toward the opposite direction with similar amount. As a result, the new face which is farther from the average female face shape has wider face contour, smaller eyes, and more crowded configuration of facial organs. A summary of observers' choices are listed in Table 8.3, where P(Near), P(Original), and P(Far) correspond to the percentage that the observers chose the near version, original version, and far version, respectively.

Table 8.3 Percentage of choices for female and male face images

	P(Near) (%)	P(Original) (%)	P(Far) (%)
Male face images	61.18	37.30	1.52
Female face images	70.59	28.55	0.86

We then considered the null hypothesis as $H_0 : f_g(g_A) = f_g(g_B)$ which claims that there is no significant difference in the attractiveness between the two faces g_A and g_B, and the alternative hypothesis $H_1 : f_g(g_A) > f_g(g_B)$ which supports that g_A is more attractive than g_B. In our experiments, we considered three different cases, i.e. $\{g_A = g_{near}, \; g_B = g_{far}\}$, $\{g_A = g_{original}, \; g_B = g_{far}\}$, and $\{g_A = g_{near}, \; g_B = g_{original}\}$. The alternative hypotheses in all these three cases support the averageness hypothesis (i.e. increasing the averageness of the geometric feature of a face will improve its attractiveness). For each of the 100 groups of faces, ratings were obtained from the 100 human observers, based on which, the percentages of observers who took g_{near}, $g_{original}$, or g_{far} as the more beautiful one were calculated, respectively. We denote them as P(Near|Faces), P(Original|Faces), and P(Far|Faces). Their histograms over the 100 groups of faces are given in Fig. 8.8a. Similarly, for each observer, the percentages of g_{near}, $g_{original}$, and g_{far} among all the 100 groups of faces that were chosen by him/her as the more beautiful one were also calculated. We denote them as P(Near|Observers), P(Original|Observers), and P(Far|Observers). Figure 8.8b shows the histograms of them over the 100 observers. From these histograms, we can clearly see that the percentage of choices has the relationship $g_{near} > g_{original} > g_{far}$ in general for both stimulus faces and observers. In other words, the faces that are closer to average face shapes are more likely to be perceived as more beautiful faces, and most people are more likely to prefer the faces that are more similar to average face shapes.

We finally computed the p-value based on the obtained beauty rating results under the three different hypotheses, i.e. (a) $\{H_0\colon f_g(g_{near}) = f_g(g_{far});\; H_1\colon f_g(g_{near}) > f_g(g_{far})\}$, (b) $\{H_0\colon f_g(g_{original}) = f_g(g_{far});\; H_1\colon f_g(g_{original}) > f_g(g_{far})\}$, and (c) $\{H_0\colon f_g(g_{near}) = f_g(g_{original});\; H_1\colon f_g(g_{near}) > f_g(g_{original})\}$. The histograms of p-value over the 100 stimulus faces and the 100 observers under these different cases are plotted in Fig. 8.9. At a significant level of 0.01, in case (a) when considering g_{near} and g_{far}, 99 % of the faces and 100 % of the observers accept H_1. In case (b) when considering $g_{original}$ and g_{far}, these percentages are 90 % and 98 %,

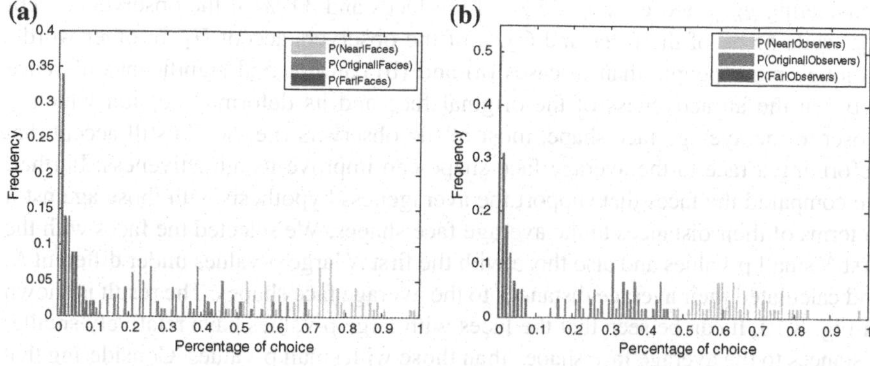

Fig. 8.8 Histograms of **a** P(Near|Faces), P(Original|Faces), and P(Far|Faces), and **b** P(Near|Observers), P(Original|Observers), and P(Far|Observers)

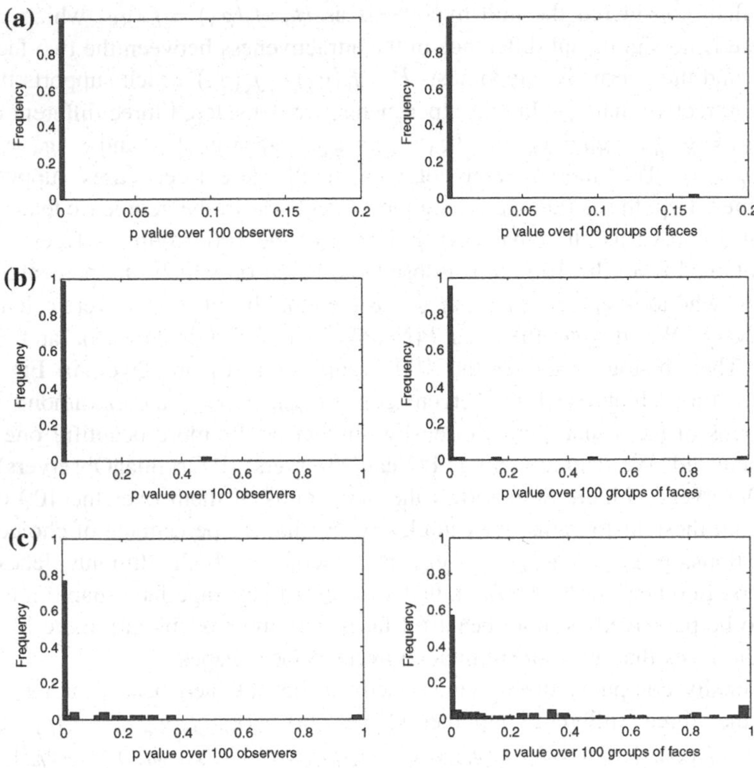

Fig. 8.9 Histograms of p-value over the 100 observers and the 100 groups of faces under the three different hypotheses, **a** $\{H_0{:}f_g(g_{near}) = f_g(g_{far});\ H_1{:}f_g(g_{near}) > f_g(g_{far})\}$, **b** $\{H_0{:}f_g(g_{original}) = f_g(g_{far});\ H_1{:}\ f_g(g_{original}) > f_g(g_{far})\}$, and **c** $\{H_0{:}\ f_g(g_{near}) = f_g(g_{original});\ H_1{:}\ f_g(g_{near}) > f_g(g_{original})\}$

respectively. The results in these two cases demonstrate that the average face shapes do have some positive contribution to the facial beauty. However, in case (c) when considering g_{near} and $g_{original}$, 45 % of the faces and 34 % of the observers accept H_0, while 55 % of the faces and 66 % of the observers accept H_1. In other words, although more people than in cases (a) and (b) can not find significant difference between the attractiveness of the original face and its deformed version which is closer to the average face shape, most of the observers (i.e. 66 %) still accept that deforming a face to the average face shape can improve its attractiveness. Further, we compared the faces that support the averageness hypothesis with those against it in terms of their distances to the average face shapes. We selected the faces with the first *N* small p-values and also those with the first *N* large p-values under different *N*, and calculated their average distances to the average face shapes. The result is shown in Fig. 8.10. It can be seen that the faces with large p-values have relatively smaller distances to the average face shapes than those with small p-values. Considering that the lower the p-value, the less likely the null hypothesis happens, this result provides us a deeper insight into the role of average face shapes in facial beauty perception:

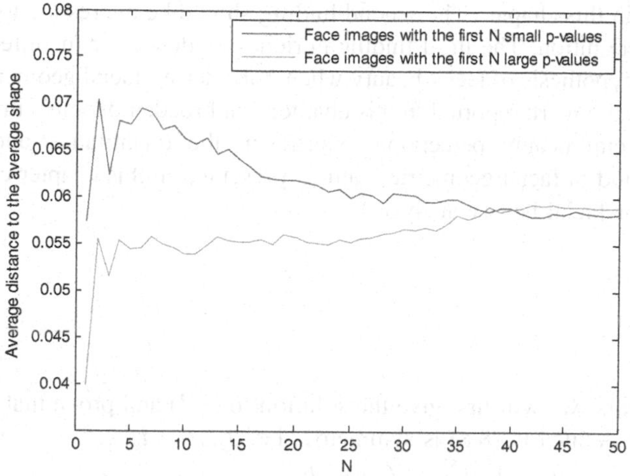

Fig. 8.10 The average distance to the average face shape of two groups of face images, i.e. images with the first N small p-values and images with the first N large p-values

given a face whose distance to the average face shape is already relatively small, making it closer to the average face shape may not be an effective approach to significantly improving its attractiveness. In general, an obvious/significant increase of averageness in a face shape will improve the attractiveness of the face.

8.5 Summary

In this chapter, the effect of the averageness hypothesis on human facial beauty has been quantitatively studied. We have defined a human face shape space in which every face is represented as a point on the unit hypersphere, and a distance measurement between two face shapes in the space which is invariant to similarity transformation. These enable us to quantitatively and more reliably (referring to the invariance to underlying transformation to face images) study the effect of average face shapes on the perception of human facial beauty. Extensive experiments have been conducted in which hundreds of Chinese female and male faces were used and one hundred human observers participated. The following several findings have been obtained from the experiments. (1) human face shapes distribute in a very compact region of the full geometric feature space, (2) female and male average face shapes are very similar, (3) the averageness hypothesis is in general effective with respect to the facial geometric feature driven perception of human facial beauty, given obvious/significant increases of averageness in face shapes. However, the attractiveness of a face whose distance to the average face shape is relatively small cannot be effectively improved by further deforming it toward the average face shape. The first finding justifies the method of calculating average face shapes that we used in this chapter. The second finding should be interesting to researchers of gender recognition. The third finding enriches evidence for the effectiveness of averageness hypothesis of facial beauty when considering facial geometric features. We hope that the work reported in this chapter can broaden people's understanding of human facial beauty perception. Moreover, the quantitative and automatic analysis method of facial geometric features presented in this chapter can be also a useful tool for facial beauty analysis.

Appendix I

In this appendix, we will first give the solution to (8.7) and prove that the distance measurement defined in (8.8) is symmetric, i.e. $d_{g_1g_2} = d_{g_2g_1}$.

Let $R = \begin{pmatrix} \cos\theta & \sin\theta \\ -\sin\theta & \cos\theta \end{pmatrix} = \begin{pmatrix} a & b \\ -b & a \end{pmatrix}$, then $\theta = \tan^{-1}\left(\frac{b}{a}\right)$, and according to (8.6), the optimization objective function in (8.7) becomes

$$\begin{aligned} E(a,b) &= \|R \circ g_1 - g_2\|^2 \\ &= \sum_i \left[(ag_{1,2i-1} + bg_{1,2i} - g_{2,2i-1})^2 + (-bg_{1,2i-1} + ag_{1,2i} - g_{2,2i})^2\right] \end{aligned}$$

Let $\partial E/\partial a = 0$ and $\partial E/\partial b = 0$, we get

$$a = \frac{\sum_i (g_{1,2i-1}g_{2,2i-1} + g_{1,2i}g_{2,2i})}{\sum_i (g_{1,2i-1}^2 + g_{1,2i}^2)} \text{ and } b = \frac{\sum_i (g_{1,2i}g_{2,2i-1} - g_{1,2i-1}g_{2,2i})}{\sum_i (g_{1,2i-1}^2 + g_{1,2i}^2)}.$$

Noting that $\|g_1\| = \|g_2\| = 1$, we have the solution to (8.7) as

$$a = \sum\nolimits_i (g_{1,2i-1}g_{2,2i-1} + g_{1,2i}g_{2,2i}) \text{ and } b = \sum\nolimits_i (g_{1,2i}g_{2,2i-1} - g_{1,2i-1}g_{2,2i}).$$

From the above derivation, it is easy to show that the solution $\{a_{12}, b_{12}\}$ to $\arg\min_R \|R \circ g_1 - g_2\|^2$ and the solution $\{a_{21}, b_{21}\}$ to $\arg\min_R \|g_1 - R \circ g_2\|^2$ satisfy $\begin{cases} a_{12} = a_{21} \\ b_{12} = -b_{21} \end{cases}$. Therefore,

$$\begin{aligned} <\tilde{g}_1^*, g_2> &= \sum_i \left[a_{12}(g_{1,2i-1}g_{2,2i-1} + g_{1,2i}g_{2,2i}) + b_{12}(g_{1,2i}g_{2,2i-1} - g_{1,2i-1}g_{2,2i})\right] \\ &= \sum_i \left[a_{21}(g_{1,2i-1}g_{2,2i-1} + g_{1,2i}g_{2,2i}) + b_{21}(g_{1,2i-1}g_{2,2i} - g_{1,2i}g_{2,2i-1})\right] = <\tilde{g}_2^*, g_1> \end{aligned}$$

This proves that $d_{g_1g_2} = d_{g_2g_1}$, i.e. the distance measurement defined in (8.8) is symmetric.

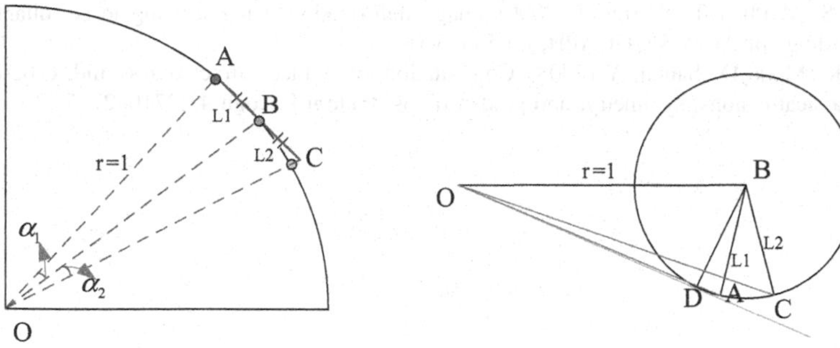

Fig. 8.11 Plots for the proof of $\alpha_1 > \alpha_2$

Appendix II

Here, we give proof to the statement in Sect. 8.3.2 that in Fig. 8.1. α_1 is always larger than α_2. As shown in Fig. 8.11a, ΔAOB and ΔBOC have two pairs of equal edges, $AB = BC$, $AO = BO$, and share the same vertex O and the same edge OB, and $\angle OAB < \pi/2 < \angle OBC$. If we reconstruct these relationships, as shown in Fig. 8.11b, first, we construct edge OB, and then draw a circle with the center B and radii *AB (BC)*. Second, from point O we draw a tangent line of the circle which intersects the circle at point D, i.e. $\angle ODB = \pi/2$. Since $\angle OAB = \angle OBA < \pi/2$, point A should be on the right of D. Moreover, because $\angle OBC > \pi/2$, point C should be on the right of A. Finally, we get the result shown in Fig. 8.11b. It's obvious that $\angle AOB$ is always larger than $\angle BOC$, i.e., α_1 is always larger than α_2.

References

Dryden IL, Mardia KV (1998) Statistical shape analysis. Wiley

Eisenthal Y, Dror G, Ruppin E (2006) Facial attractiveness: beauty and the machine. Neural Comput 18:119–142

Igarashi T, Moscovich T, Hughes JF (2005) As-rigid-as-possible shape manipulation. ACM Trans Graph 24(3):1134–1141

Kagian A, Dror G, Leyvand T, Meilijson I, Cohen-Or D, Ruppin E (2008) A machine learning predictor of facial attractiveness revealing human-like psychophysical biases. Vis Res 48: 235–243

Leyvand T, Cohen-Or D, Dror G, Lischinski D (2008) Data-driven enhancement of facial attractiveness. ACM Trans Graph 27(3): 38:1–9

Perrett DI, May KA, Yoshikawa S (1994) Facial shape and judgements of female attractiveness. Nature 368:239–242

Rowley HA, Baluja S, Kanade T (1998) Neural network-based face detection. IEEE Trans Pattern Anal Mach Intell 20(1):23–38

Schaefer S, McPhail T, Warren J (2006) Image deformation using moving least squares. In: Proceedings of ACM SIGGRAPH, pp 533–540

Schmid K, Marx D, Samal A (2008) Computation of a face attractiveness index based on neoclassical canons, symmetry, and golden ratios. Pattern Recogn 41:2710–2717

Chapter 9
A New Hypothesis on Facial Beauty Perception

The studies in Chap. 8 show that the averageness hypothesis is in general effective with respect to facial geometric feature driven perception of facial beauty. However, this hypothesis has its drawbacks. For example, the attractiveness of a face whose distance to the average face shape is relatively small cannot be effectively improved by further deforming it toward the average face shape. In this chapter, we mainly present a new hypothesis on facial beauty perception, which says that the weighted average of two facial geometric features is more attractive than the inferior one of them. This new hypothesis leads to a conclusion that attractive facial geometric features construct a convex set and derives a convex hull-based face beautification method, which is very useful for facial beautification. This chapter is organized as follows: in Sect. 9.1, we briefly introduce the background and related works of facial beauty perception. In Sect. 9.2, we define some notations and introduce the new hypothesis on facial beauty perception. In Sect. 9.3, we perform an empirical proof of the hypothesis. In Sect. 9.4, we present a corollary of the hypothesis and discuss the convex hull-based beautification method. Moreover, we compare it with state-of-the-art methods and analyze their intrinsic relationships. In Sect. 9.5, we discuss the compatibility between the new hypothesis and other hypotheses. Finally, we conclude the chapter in Sect. 9.6.

9.1 Introduction

Most researches aim at exploiting the general pattern of facial beauty perception. However, one important concern is whether beauty is in the eye of the beholder or beauty has a universal standard. Langlois et al. (2000) and Cunningham et al. (1995) demonstrated high beauty rating congruence over ethnicity, social class, age and gender. Mu (2013) reported that the inter-rater correlation mainly distributed at an interval of 0.4–0.7. These studies suggest that although some individual and

D. Zhang et al., *Computer Models for Facial Beauty Analysis*,
DOI 10.1007/978-3-319-32598-9_9

cross-cultural differences exist, people use similar criteria in their judgments of facial beauty. This is the rationale of facial beauty perception research.

For decades, the focus has been on what traits make a face attractive. A number of hypotheses have been proposed, among which the averageness hypothesis is the most influential and most investigated one. Langlois and Roggman (1990) demonstrated that composite faces were shown to be more attractive than most of the faces used to create them, and higher order composites were even more attractive. However, the averageness hypothesis has been widely debated. Perrett et al. (1994) found that composites of beautiful people were rated more appealing than composites from the larger, random population. Alley and Cunningham (1991) also supported the idea that there is not a unique beauty prototype. Hence, although average faces are attractive, attractive faces are mostly not average. Symmetry is another sufficiently investigated trait due to its potential biological benefit (Rhodes 2006). Studies measuring symmetry from unmanipulated faces have reported positive correlations with rated attractiveness (Perrett et al. 1999; Penton-Voak et al. 2001). However, Swaddle and Cuthill (1995) and Kowner (1996) demonstrated that low degree of facial asymmetry found in normal people did not affect attractiveness ratings. Schmid et al. (2008) and Chen and Zhang (2010) evaluated the contribution of symmetry in explaining the facial beauty concept by using datasets with hundreds of rated face images. They found that symmetry slightly increased the R^2 statistics, but the effect was weak. In addition to averageness and symmetry, golden ratios have been believed by some investigators to underlie the aesthetics of an ideal face (Atiyeh and Hayek 2008; Jefferson 2004). Marquardt (2002) constructed the Phi mask, as shown in Fig. 9.1, from a series of golden components and claimed that it was the perfect face shape. Nevertheless, the validity of these putative rules is still in question. Recent studies have shown that the most attractive ratios are not exactly golden ratio (Holland 2008; Peron et al. 2012). Fan et al. (2012) generated a synthesized face image that has neoclassical canons and most possible golden ratios, but it only received a below normal rating.

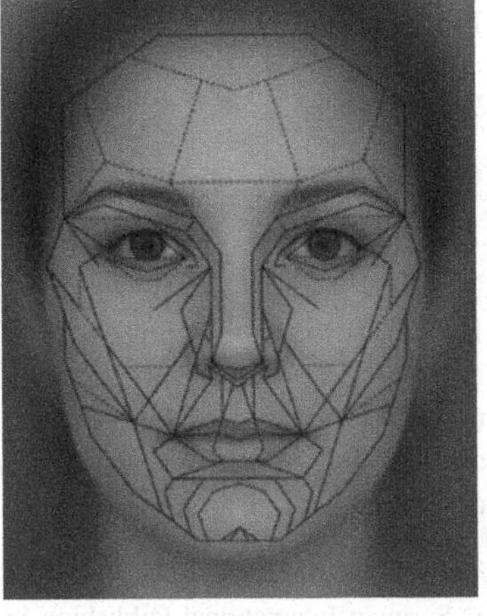

Fig. 9.1 An average face generated with 200 Caucasoid female faces overlapped with the Phi mask

Figure 9.1 also shows that the Phi mask does not fit the average face well, which implies that the averageness hypothesis and golden ratio hypothesis are not compatible. More recently, researchers began to build computational models of facial beauty by using multiple traits (e.g., averageness, symmetry, golden ratios, neoclassical canons, and skin smoothness) (Mu 2013; Schmid et al. 2008; Fan et al. 2012; Kagian et al. 2008; Eisenthal et al. 2006; Whitehill and Movellan 2008; Sutic et al. 2010; Gray et al. 2010). They first collected human ratings of the attractiveness of the face images in their databases and extracted the facial features, which quantitatively measured the traits. Then computational models were built using machine-learning methods such as linear regression and support vector regression (SVR) (Vapnik 1995). The models were usually evaluated by Pearson correlation between machine-predicted attractiveness scores and human ratings. Table 9.1 is a brief review of existing works on regression models of facial beauty. The performances are different due to various datasets as well as different features and learning methods. These models can be used to predict the attractiveness of a face, but they are not suitable for discovering or verifying a theory or understanding the inner structure of psychological phenomena (Thompson 1995; Cohen 2008).

Suppose attractiveness is a function of facial features, which is called the facial beauty perception function, and all previous works endeavor to discover the independent variables of the perception functions. In this chapter, we present the following new hypothesis on facial beauty perception: the weighted average of two facial geometric features is more attractive than the inferior (less attractive) one between them. Different from the previous works, the new hypothesis is about the characteristics of the perception functions. The underlying assumption is that though individual differences exist, the perception functions may share some identical properties. The hypothesis is defined on geometric features, assuming other factors are randomized, for the following reasons. First, geometric features

Table 9.1 Review of existing works on regression models of facial beauty

Author	Datasets			Features	Methods	Performance (Pearson's ρ)
	No.	Race	Annotation			
Eisenthal et al. (2006)	92	Caucasian	7-scale	Geometric	Linear regression	0.6
Schmid et al. (2008)	452	Caucasian	10-scale	Geometric	Linear regression	0.49
Kagian et al. (2008)	91	Caucasian	7-scale	Geometric	Linear regression	0.82
Whitehill and Movellan (2008)	1000	Diverse	4-scale	Texture	SVR	0.45
Gray et al. (2010)	2056	Caucasian	10-scale	Texture	Neural network	0.46
Fan et al. (2012)	432	Synthesized	9-scale	Geometric	Non-linear regression	0.8

play an important role in facial beauty perception, as shown in Table 9.1. Second, they are robust to illumination changes, resolution variations, and compression loss. Third, the mathematical operations of geometric features are easier to understand than texture and color features. In order to test the validity of the hypothesis, we built a database including 390 well-known beautiful face images and 409 common face images. The images are confined to be female, frontal, and with neutral or gentle smile expressions. They were rated by 25 volunteers based on their judgment on attractiveness. Statistical regression models are trained on this database. We test the hypothesis on 318,801 pairs of female images and obtain consistently supportive results. To our knowledge, this is the first time facial beauty perception has been investigated from the perspective of function characteristics. The new hypothesis gives us a deeper understanding of facial beauty perception.

One application of the hypotheses of facial beauty perception is face beautification. Each hypothesis corresponds to one approach. For example, the averageness hypothesis evokes a beautification method that warps the face to the average face shape (Zhang et al. 2011). It leads to similar results for every input face and loses personal details. The symmetry hypothesis corresponds to the method that makes a face ideally symmetry. It cannot guarantee that the results are beautiful. The golden ratio hypothesis corresponds to the method that makes a face to satisfy the most possible golden ratios. Similar to the method based on the averageness hypothesis, this method also enforces too many constraints on the beautified results. The regression models correspond to the method that warps a face image to the shape with a higher attractive score (Leyvand et al. 2008). The performance of this method depends on the accuracy of the regression models and has the local optimum problem.

9.2 The Weighted Averageness (WA) Hypothesis

In this section, we define some notations and give a new hypothesis on facial beauty perception. Note that we focus on geometric features, assuming other factors are randomized. In this chapter, we also use the landmark model with 98 points. The x- and y-coordinates of the landmarks are concatenated to form a vector, i.e.,

$$L = (x_1, x_2, \ldots, x_{98}, y_1, y_2, \ldots, y_{98})^T, \tag{9.1}$$

L is defined in the coordinate system on the original image. In order to filter out translation, rotation, and scale variations, we perform Procrustes superimposition on the landmark features (Dryden and Mardia 1998). It contains three steps, center alignment, scale normalization, and iterative rotation alignment (see (Chen et al. 2014) for detail). The results are defined as geometric features, which are denoted by g. If we use G to denote the set of geometric features of all valid faces, then G locates at a concentrated region in the 196-dimensional vector space (Zhang et al. 2011). For any g_1 and $g_2 \in G$, we assume the convex combination of them is also a geometric feature of a valid face, that is, $\theta g_1 + (1-\theta) g_2 \in G$, $0 \leq \theta \leq 1$.

Attractiveness s is a function of the geometric feature, that is,

$$s = f(g), \tag{9.2}$$

where f is called the facial beauty perception function. We now give the weighted average hypothesis, which is abbreviated to WA hypothesis.

Hypothesis 9.2.1 (Weighted Average). Given two distinct facial geometric features g_1 and $g_2 \in G$, the attractiveness of any weighted average of them is not less than that of the less attractive one, i.e., $f(\theta g_1 + (1-\theta)g_2) \geq \min\{f(g_1), f(g_2)\}, 0 \leq \theta \leq 1$.

9.3 Empirical Proof of the WA Hypothesis

To prove the WA hypothesis, we need to know G and $f(\cdot)$. However, we can get neither G nor $f(\cdot)$ exactly. What we have is a collection of facial geometric features and their corresponding attractiveness scores. Given those data as a training set, $f(\cdot)$ can be learned using statistical regression techniques, such as linear regression and SVR. The data can be considered as a sample from $(G, f(\cdot))$. Analogous to the empirical risk minimization (ERM) principle (Vapnik 1995), a loss function is defined as

$$R_{emp} = \frac{\sum_{g_1, g_2 \in G, g_1 \neq g_2} I(\gamma < \min\{f(g_1), f(g_2)\})}{\sum_{g_1, g_2 \in G, g_1 \neq g_2} 1}, \tag{9.3}$$

where $I(\cdot)$ is the indicator function and $\gamma = \min_{\theta} f(\theta g_1 + (1-\theta)g_2)$, R_{emp} measures the probability that the WA hypothesis fails.

In the following subsections, detailed implementation of the empirical proof is presented, including building a face image dataset, collecting attractiveness ratings, performing attractiveness score regression, and testing the WA hypothesis using (9.3).

9.3.1 Face Image Dataset

The data set for facial beauty study is required to have sufficient variability in attractiveness. As far as we know, none of the existing open face databases satisfies this requirement. There are few extremely beautiful faces in existing databases, and the faces often come from limited ethnic groups. In this experiment we use the dataset collected by our group. The dataset contains 390 celebrity face images of Miss Universe, Miss World, movie stars, and super models via Google, and 409 common face images from a face research website (http://faceresearch.org), Flicker, and other face databases (e.g., XM2VTS (Messer et al. 1999) and Shanghai (Zhang et al. 2011) databases). Please see Sect. 1.4 for the detailed introduction of the dataset.

9.3.2 Attractiveness Score Regression

Regression aims to find a smooth function f which maps a d-dimensional feature vector to a scalar value, that is, $f : R^d \rightarrow R$. Multivariate linear regression and SVR are two popular regression techniques in facial beauty study. Linear regression uses linear functions to model data, whereas by using various kernels, SVR can fit highly nonlinear functions. It is demonstrated by Leyvand et al. (2008) and Whitehill and Movellan (2008) that SVR with radial basis function (RBF) kernels outperforms other regression methods when modeling facial beauty perception.

Given a set of input feature vectors and their corresponding attractiveness scores, linear regression and SVR models can be constructed with well-established algorithms. Considering the high correlation between landmarks, we perform principal component analysis (PCA) on the geometric feature space for dimension reduction. Linear regression and SVR models are then trained on the PCA coefficient space. The linear regression is conducted by the least squares approach. The preset parameters for the SVR models are determined by grid search. In order to determine the number of the dimensions to use, we train the models with an increasing number of PCA coefficients, which are sorted by their corresponding eigenvalues, with the large eigenvalues ranked in the front. The experiment is performed with the setting of tenfold cross validation. The R^2 statistics, which is called coefficient of determination, is a statistical measure of how well a regression model fits the data. It measures the proportion of total variation of outcomes explained by the model. It is calculated as the square of the correlation coefficient between the outputs of the model and ground truth values. Figure 9.2 presents the experimental results. We can

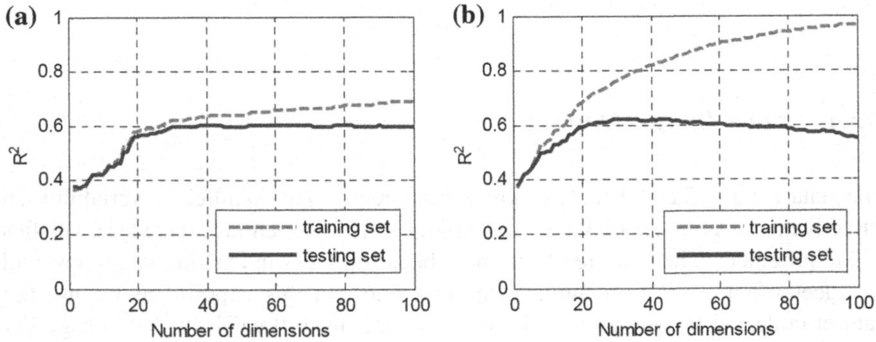

Fig. 9.2 R^2 statistic of **(a)** linear regression models and **(b)** SVR models trained with an increasing number of PCA coefficient features

see that the R^2 of the testing set stops growing when the number of dimensions reaches 30. However, the R^2 of the training set grows monotonously as the number of dimensions increases, which implies the occurrence of over fitting. Compared to linear regression, SVR has more serious over fitting problem. In order to alleviate over fitting, we reduce the dimensionality from 196 to 30 and conduct regression on the low dimensional space. The SVR model achieves an R^2 of 0.63 on the testing set; that is, the correlation between the predicted score and the ground truth is 0.79, which is slightly better than the linear regression model, whose R^2 is 0.6 and the correlation coefficient is 0.77.

9.3.3 Test the Hypothesis

Given an attractiveness function f and a face image dataset, it is straightforward to test the WA hypothesis using (9.3). There are totally C_N^2 possible pairs in a dataset with N face images. For each pair of face images, we should test whether $\min_\theta f(\theta g_1 + (1-\theta)g_2) \geq \min\{f(g_1), f(g_2)\}$ is true or not with $0 \leq \theta \leq 1$. For simplicity, θ is discretized into $0, 0.1, 0.2, \ldots, 1$.

A linear model is an affine function. For a line segment in the input space, the outcome of the model is still a line segment. Hence, the model outcomes of the points on the line segment are between those of the two endpoints. In this case, the WA hypothesis is inherently true.

A SVR model can capture nonlinearity, which is more complex than linear models. We substitute $f(\cdot)$ in (9.3) into the learned SVR model and obtain $R_{emp} = 0.0114$; that is, the WA hypothesis holds at a probability of 98.86 % under the SVR model. In order to measure the extent of the violation when the WA hypothesis fails, we define

$$\delta = \min_\theta f(\theta g_1 + (1-\theta)g_2) - \min\{f(g_1), f(g_2)\}. \tag{9.4}$$

Figure 9.3 shows the histogram of δ when the WA hypothesis fails ($\delta < 0$). The minimum of δ is -0.1411, and the median of the violation is -0.0095. Compared to

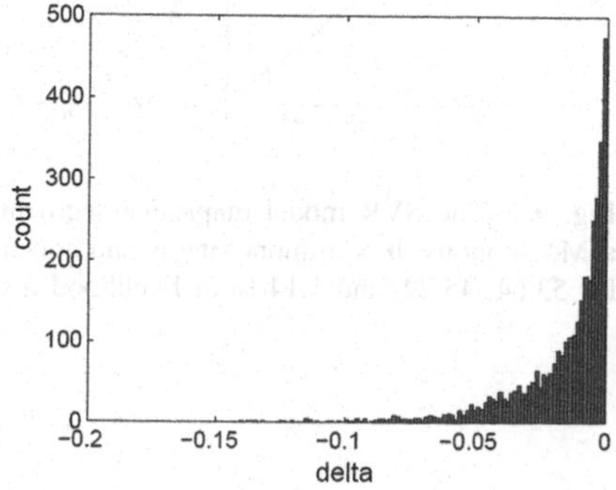

Fig. 9.3 Histogram of δ (the amount of violation) when the WA hypothesis fails ($\delta < 0$)

the whole attractiveness score scale of [−1, 1], the violation is small. Hence, both the probability and amount of violation are very small.

Furthermore, we explore the response curves of the SVR model in detail. Our dataset contains $C_{799}^2 = 318801$ pairs of images. Each pair of face images can construct a line segment in the feature space. The SVR model maps the line segments in the feature space into three categories of curves: (a) monotonous, (b) non-monotonous and concave, and (c) non-monotonous and convex, as illustrated in Fig. 9.4. The (a) and (b) categories of curves satisfy the hypothesis. They contribute 53.64 and 45.22 % of likelihood, respectively. The (c) category of curves violates the hypothesis. It accounts for 1.14 % of likelihood. In order to test whether these curves are consistent with human judgments, we generated image sequences corresponding to the three categories of curves, as shown in Fig. 9.5. The leftmost and rightmost images own geometric features g_1 and g_2, and the other images have geometric features $\theta g_1 + (1 - \theta)g_2$, with $\theta = 0.2, 0.4, \ldots, 0.8$. They are generated by warping the two original face images to a desired geometric feature and averaging their pixel values. For each category of curves, we randomly selected 20 sequences. The images corresponding to $\theta = 0$, $\theta = 0.5$, and $\theta = 1$ in each sequence make up a group of stimuli, as shown in Fig. 9.6. In total, 60 groups of stimuli were shown to 26 subjects (16 male, 10 female, ages 21–29), who were requested to choose the least attractive face among the three faces in each group. Within a group, the three images were presented in random order. Figure 9.7 shows the voting results. We can see that (a) and (b) categories of curves agree with the human judgments. However, for the stimuli corresponding to (c) categories of curves, almost all the subjects dislike images with $\theta = 0$, or $\theta = 1$ in comparison $\theta = 0.5$. This result disagrees with (c) categories of curves but supports the WA hypothesis. Therefore, it is more likely that the violation, that is, the (c) categories of curves, is caused by the artifacts of the SVR model. As we see in Fig. 9.4b, over fitting may exist in SVR models.

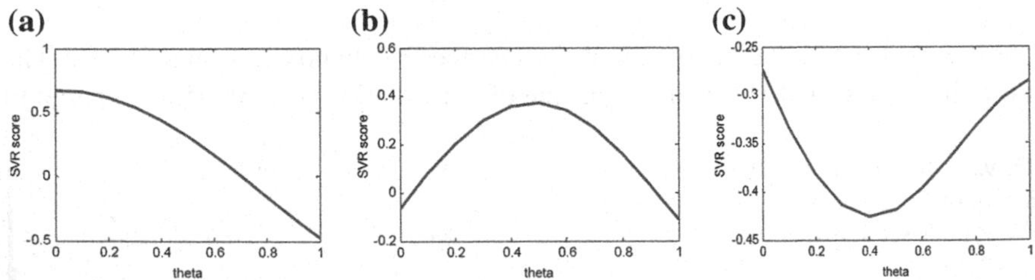

Fig. 9.4 The SVR model maps line segments in the feature space into three types of curves. **a** Monotonous. **b** Non-monotonous and concave. **c** Non-monotonous and convex. They account for 53.64, 45.22, and 1.14 % of likelihood respectively

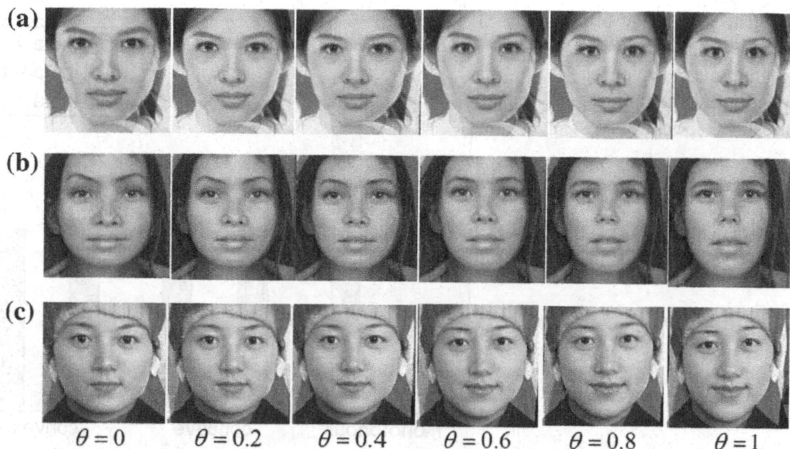

Fig. 9.5 Image sequences corresponding to the three categories of response curves. **a** Monotonous curves (Fig. 9.4a). **b** Non-monotonous and concave curves (Fig. 9.4b). **c** Non-monotonous and convex curves (Fig. 9.4c). The leftmost and rightmost images own geometric features g_1 and g_2, and the other images have geometric features $\theta_{g_1} + (1 - \theta)g_2$ $(\theta = 0.2, 0.4, \ldots, 0.8)$

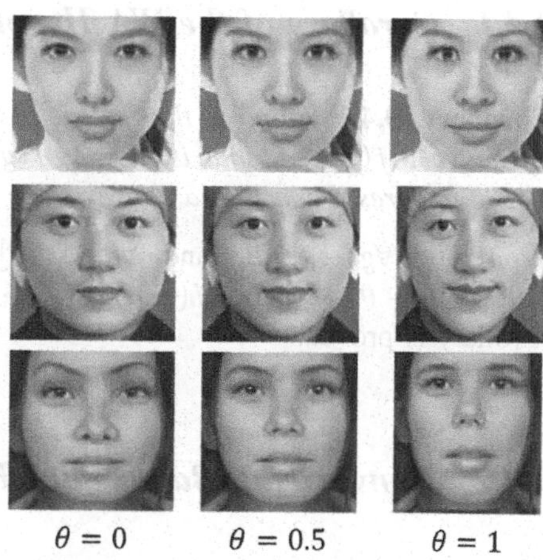

Fig. 9.6 Example stimuli for the perceptual experiment on response curves. Each row presents a group of stimuli with θ = 0, 0.5, and 1

In summary, statistical regression models trained on our dataset strongly agree with the hypothesis. Linear models are inherently consistent with the hypothesis. The SVR model agrees with the hypothesis at a probability of 98.86 %, and the small likelihood of violation is very likely to be caused by the artifacts of the SVR model.

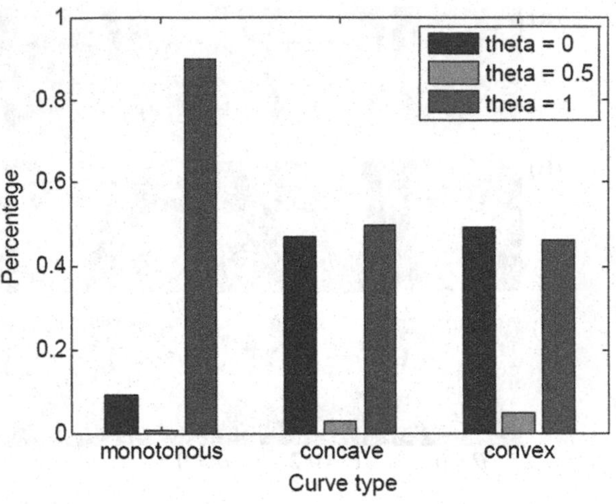

Fig. 9.7 The percentage of votes for the least attractive faces in the image sequences corresponding to the three categories of response curves

9.4 Corollary of the Hypothesis and Convex Hull Based Face Beautification

9.4.1 Corollary of the WA Hypothesis

Corollary 9.4.1 *Suppose that a facial geometric feature g is defined to be attractive if $f(g) > t$; that is, $B = \{g|f(g) > t\}$ is a set of attractive facial geometric features. Then B is a convex set.*

Proof For $\forall g_1, g_2 \in B$, and $\forall \theta \in [0, 1]$, according to the WA hypothesis, $f(\theta g_1 + (1-\theta)g_2) \geq \min\{f(g_1), f(g_2)\} > t$. Hence, $\theta g_1 + (1-\theta)g_2 \in B$. The corollary is proved.

9.4.2 Convex Hull-Based Face Beautification

Given a set of attractive examples $C = \{g_1, g_2, \ldots, g_M\}$, where $g_i \in B$, $i = 1, \ldots, M$, the convex hull of C, denoted by **conv***C*, is the set of all convex combinations of points in C, that is,

$$\mathbf{conv}C = \left\{\sum\nolimits_{i=1}^{M} \theta_i g_i | g_i \in C, \theta_i \geq 0, \sum\nolimits_{i=1}^{M} \theta_i = 1\right\}. \quad (9.5)$$

Definition of the smallest convex set to contain C: if B is a convex set that contains C, then $\mathbf{conv}C \subseteq B$ (Boyd and Vandenberghe 2004). Hence, the elements in **conv***C* are guaranteed to be attractive.

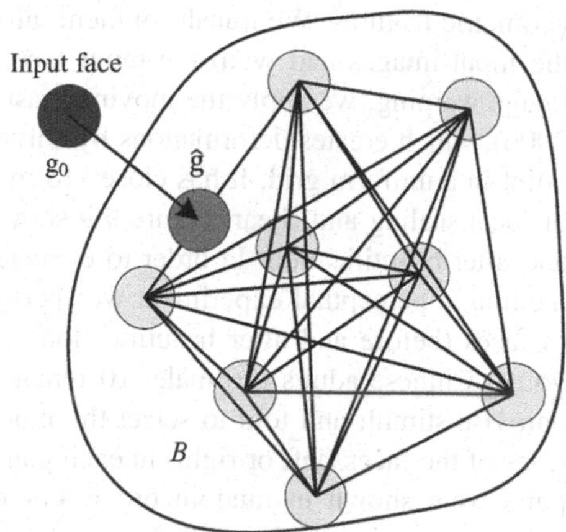

Fig. 9.8 Illustration of the convex hull-based face beautification method

In our dataset, the faces with attractiveness scores larger than 0.2 are considered as beautiful faces, which are assumed to have attractive geometric features. They are used to construct C. For any input face, which has a geometric feature g_0, its nearest point in **conv**C, denoted by $\widehat{g}$, is treated as the beautification result of g_0, i.e.,

$$\widehat{g} = \arg\min_{g \in \mathbf{conv}C} \|g - g_0\|, \tag{9.6}$$

where $\|\cdot\|$ is Euclidean distance. Figure 9.8 illustrates this convex hull-based face beautification method.

The problem in (9.6) can be recast and solved as the following norm approximation problem:

$$\text{minimize}\|A\theta - g_0\| \quad \text{s.t} \quad 0 \leq \theta_i \leq 1, i = 1, \ldots, M, 1^T\theta = 1, \tag{9.7}$$

where $A = [g_1, g_2, \ldots, g_M]$. Each column of A is a geometric feature in set C; thus, $A \in R^{196 \times M}$ and $A\theta = \theta_1 g_1 + \cdots + \theta_M g_M$. To solve (9.7), we use CVX, a package for specifying and solving convex programs (Grant and Boyd 2012, 2008). Then we obtain the optimal weighting vector $\widehat{\theta}$, and $\widehat{g} = A\widehat{\theta}$ is the beautification result of g_0.

9.4.3 Results

In our experiments, 232 face images whose attractiveness scores are larger than 0.2 are used to construct an attractive convex hull. The other 567 face images are to be beautified. We first detect facial landmarks and conduct Procrustes superimposition to obtain the geometric features. Then by solving (9.7), we obtain the beautified geometric features. We transform them into landmarks in the coordinate system on the input images and warp the input face images based on those landmarks. For image warping, we apply the moving least squares (MLS) method (Schaefer et al. 2006), which creates deformations by solving a small linear system (2×2) at each point in a uniform grid. It has closed-form solutions and can minimize the amount of local scaling and shear. Figure 9.9 shows some examples of face images before and after beautification. In order to evaluate the effectiveness of our beautification method, a perceptual experiment was performed. We randomly selected 200 pairs of faces (before and after beautification) as the stimuli. The participants were 26 young Chinese adults (16 male, 10 female, ages 21–29 years). They were shown pairwise stimuli and told to select the more attractive face in each pair. The positions of the faces (left or right) in each pair were determined randomly and the 200 pairs were shown in random order. For each pair of stimuli, the percentage of subjects selecting the beautified version was calculated (Fig. 9.10a). This produces 200 preference scores. The null hypothesis predicts the mean of these scores is 50 %. The preference scores were shown to be in favor of the beautified version (mean = 87.25 %, $t_{199} = 45.57$, $p < 0.005$). A complementary analysis was performed across subjects ($N = 26$) rather than across faces ($N = 200$). For each subject, the percentage of beautified version selections was calculated (Fig. 9.10b). One sample t-test showed that subjects preferred more of the beautified version than expected by chance (mean = 87.18 %, $t_{25} = 24.82$, $p < 0.005$). Analysis of variance (ANOVA) showed that the responses of male and female subjects had no significant difference ($F_{1,\ 24} = 0.027$, $p = 0.87$). The beautification results are convex combinations of beautiful faces. We see that the weighting vectors are sparse.

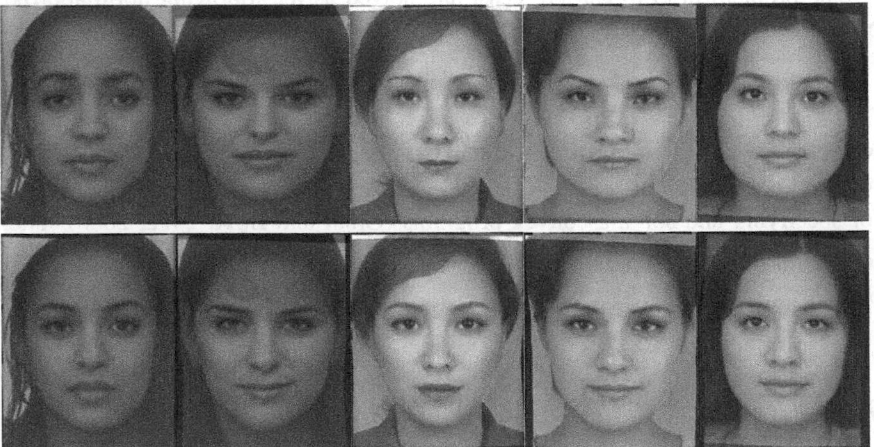

Fig. 9.9 Results of the convex hull based face beautification method. The *top* row contains face images before beautification, and the *bottom* row contains those after beautification. The first and second images are from the FERET database (Phillips et al. 1998), the third and fourth images are from the Shanghai database (Zhang et al. 2011), and the last image is from one of our authors. For privacy issue, the textures of the faces are mixed with that of the average face

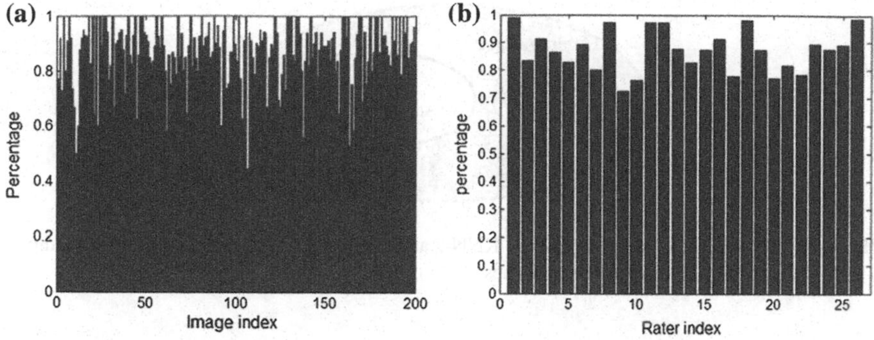

Fig. 9.10 The percentage of votes for the beautified version **a** across the 200 pairs of faces and **b** across the 26 raters

Specifically, there are only 2–20 nonzero elements in the weighting vectors, which is much less than the number of faces constructing the convex hull.

9.4.4 Comparison and Discussion

In this part, we compare the convex hull-based face beautification method with other geometric-based face beautification methods, including averageness-, KNN- and SVR-based methods, and discuss their intrinsic relationships.

The averageness-based beautification method (Zhang et al. 2011) makes all beautification results close to an average face. Since the average face is known to be attractive, it is in the convex hull. Hence, the solution set of the averageness-based method is a subset of that of the convex hull-based method. The KNN-based beautification method (Melacci et al. 2010) determines k nearest neighbors of an input face from a set of beautiful faces and warps the input face image to the weighted average of the k beautiful face shapes, that is:

$$\widehat{g} = \frac{\sum_{i=1}^{k} \frac{1}{d_i} g_i}{\sum_{i=1}^{k} \frac{1}{d_i}}, \tag{9.8}$$

where d_i is the distance between the input face shape and beautiful face shape g_i. The results of the KNN-based method are convex combinations of beautiful face shapes. Hence, the solution set of the KNN-based method is also a subset of that of the convex hull-based method. Figure 9.11 illustrates the relationships of the three methods. The solution sets of them are all guaranteed to be attractive, and the convex hull-based method has a larger solution set than the other two methods.

When the attractiveness is fixed, another desired property is keeping as many details of the original face as possible. A larger solution set gives more freedom to the beautification results and keeps more details. From this point of view, the

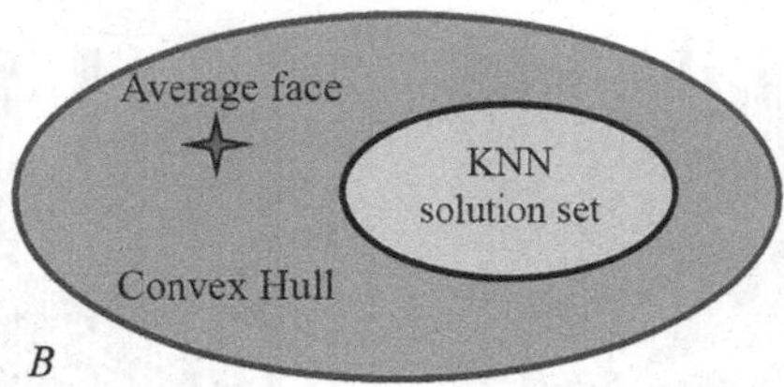

Fig. 9.11 Relationships of averageness-, KNN-, and convex hull-based beautification methods. *B* represents the set of beautiful face shapes

convex hull-based method is better than the averageness- and KNN-based methods. Figure 9.12 shows some beautification results. We can observe that (1) the averageness-based method leads to a similar result for every input face; and (2) the results of our method and the KNN-based methods are similar, but our method keeps more personalized details. For example, in Fig. 9.12a, the face shape of our beautification result is thinner and more similar to the original face, and in Fig. 9.12b, c, the mouth is a salient feature of the original faces and our method keeps more details on the mouth part in comparison with the other two methods. A perceptual experiment was carried out to compare the results of the three methods. The participants were 40 young Chinese adults (20 male, 20 female, ages 22–29 years). The original face image and beautification results of the three methods constituted a group of stimuli. We first compared the attractiveness of the results. Twenty participants (randomly selected 10 male and 10 female) were shown group-wise stimuli and told to select the most beautiful face in each group. The positions of the faces in each group were determined randomly. For each

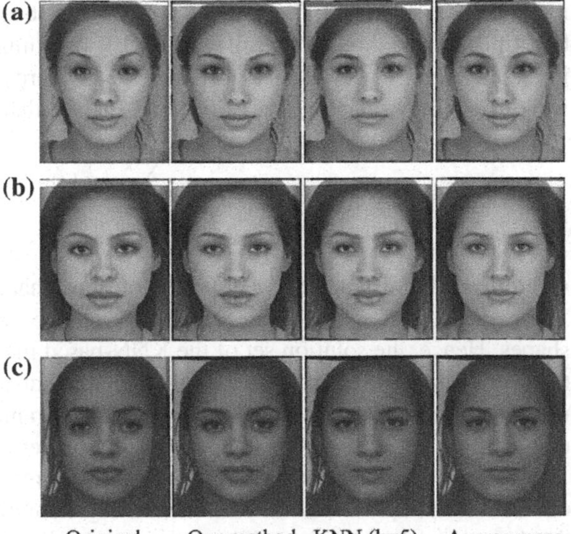

Fig. 9.12 Beautification results using avergeness-, KNN- and convex hull(our method)-based methods. The averageness-based method warped the original faces exactly to the shape of the average face. The original images of **a** and **b** are from the Shanghai database (Zhang et al. 2011), and the original image of **c** is from the FERET database (Phillips et al. 1998, 2000). For privacy issue, the textures of the faces are mixed with that of the average face

participant, the percentages of choices for the original faces and results of different beautification methods were calculated. The beautification results of all the three methods were preferred to the original images (t_{19} = 3.58, $p < 0.005$ for the averageness based method; t_{19} = 7.96, $p < 0.005$ for the KNN-based method; t_{19} = 13.29, $p < 0.005$ for the convex hull-based method). The beautification results of the convex hull-based and KNN-based methods were preferred to the averageness-based methods (t_{19} = 5.74, $p < 0.005$; t_{19} = 10.80, $p < 0.005$, respectively). The preferences of the beautification results of the convex hull-based and KNN-based methods have no significant differences (t_{19} = 1.778, $p = 0.091$). The male and female participants showed no significant difference between their responses ($F_{1,\ 18} = 0.31$, $p = 0.588$). Then, we compared the similarity between the beautification results and original faces. The original faces were shown on the left and the beautification results were shown on the right with random orders. The other 20 participants (10 male and 10 female) were shown the group-wise stimuli and told to select the face most similar to the original face in each group. Matched t-tests showed that the convex hull-based method obtained results more similar to the original faces than the averageness-based method (t_{19} = 8.59, $p < 0.005$) and the KNN-based method (t_{19} = 3.91, $p < 0.005$). The male and female participants had no significant difference between their responses ($F_{1,18} = 5.29$, $p = 0.034$). The results of the perceptual experiment agree with our analysis above.

Leyvand et al. (2008) proposed a SVR-based beautification method. They did not perform Procrustes superimposition but constructed 234-dimensional distance feature vectors by Delaunay triangulation on 84 facial landmarks for the reason that the distance features are easy to be normalized. The disadvantage of distance features is once a beautified distance vector is obtained, a distance embedding process is required, which is nontrivial and sometimes could not obtain a valid face (Leyvand et al. 2008). After Procrustes superimposition, our geometric features are congenitally invariant of translation, rotation and scale, so we can use them directly. Similar to Leyvand et al. (2008), we perform PCA on the geometric features to reduce the number of dimensions from 196 to 30, which can preserve 93.78 % of the total variations. Then a regression model is built using SVR with RBF kernels. The beautification is implemented by changing an input feature vector towards the direction that can increase the attractiveness score predicted by the SVR model. It is reported in Leyvand et al. (2008) that for some samples, the SVR-based method yields results which do not correspond to valid human faces. Hence, they added a regularization term to prevent the absolute feature values (PCA coefficients) from getting too large. However, according to our observation, for some instances, the directions are not appropriate from the beginning and in this case the regularization cannot help. For example, Fig. 9.13 shows some beautification results using the SVR-based method. The numbers below the image series are their attractiveness scores predicted by the SVR model. We can see that as the SVR-predicted attractive score increases, the faces become more and more strange and even unlike valid faces. This is because the SVR model has an over-fitting problem, especially for where the data are sparsely distributed. A perceptual experiment was performed to

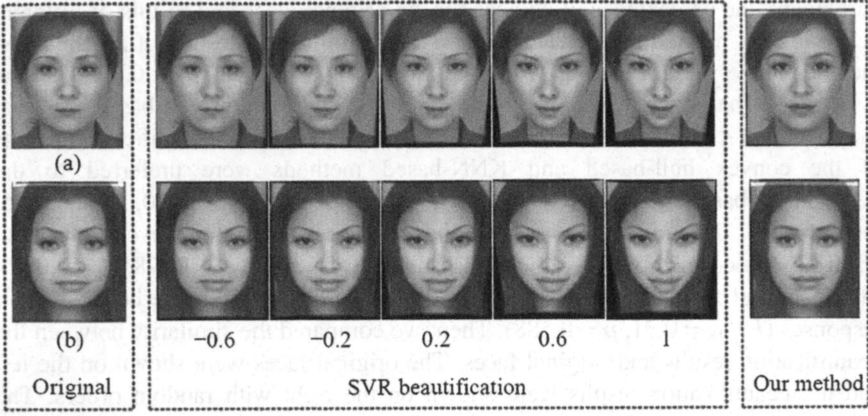

Fig. 9.13 Comparison between the SVR- and the convex hull-based (our method) methods. The numbers below the SVR beautification results are their corresponding predicted attractiveness scores. The SVR-based method leads to strange looking faces, while our method is more robust and always obtains valid results with higher attractiveness

validate this observation. For a fair comparison, we controlled the amount of deformations by the two methods to be the same, that is, $\|\widehat{g}_{svr} - g\| = \|\widehat{g}_{ch} - g\|$, where g is the geometric feature of the original face; $\widehat{g}_{svr}$ and $\widehat{g}_{ch}$ are beautified geometric features by the SVR- and convex hull-based methods, respectively. The stimuli were 20 pairs of beautification results obtained by the two methods. The participants were 30 Chinese adults (20 male, 10 female, ages 22–29 years). They were shown the pairwise stimuli and told to select the more attractive face in each pair. The positions of the faces in each pair were determined randomly. Matched t-test was carried out and showed that the convex hull-based beautification results were preferred to the SVR-based beautification results ($t_{29} = 19.35$, $p < 0.005$). The male and female participants had no significant difference between their responses ($F_{1,\ 28} = 0.30$, $p = 0.588$). Compared with the SVR-based method, the convex hull-based method does not need to train a regression model, has no free parameters to preset, and guarantees to obtain valid results with higher attractiveness.

9.5 Compatibility with Other Hypotheses

The WA hypothesis discovers a characteristic of facial beauty perception functions. We wonder if other existing hypotheses satisfy this characteristic. Suppose a function set F, which includes all perception functions that satisfy the WA hypothesis, that is:

$$F = \{f | f(\theta g_1 + (1-\theta) g_2) \geq \min\{f(g_1), f(g_2)\}\}, \tag{9.9}$$

where $0 \leq \theta \leq 1$. The averageness, symmetry, and golden ratio hypotheses can be modeled as functions of geometric features. In this section, we will discuss whether these functions belong to F.

9.5.1 Compatibility with the Averageness Hypothesis

The averageness hypothesis demonstrates that average faces are more attractive than the faces used to create them. A one-prototype model is suitable for this hypothesis, that is:

$$f_a(g) = -\|g - \bar{g}\|. \tag{9.10}$$

The faces near the average face will get a high attractiveness score, and those far away from the average face will get a low attractiveness score. For $\forall g_1, g_2 \in G$, and $\forall \theta \in [0, 1]$, we have $f_a(g_1) = -\|g_1 - \bar{g}\|$, $f_a(g_2) = -\|g_2 - \bar{g}\|$, and

$$\begin{aligned} f_a(\theta g_1 + (1-\theta) g_2) &= -\|\theta g_1 + (1-\theta) g_2 - \bar{g}\| \\ &= -\|\theta(g_1 - \bar{g}) + (1-\theta)(g_2 - \bar{g})\| \\ &\geq -\|\theta(g_1 - \bar{g})\| - \|(1-\theta)(g_2 - \bar{g})\| \\ &= -\theta\|g_1 - \bar{g}\| - (1-\theta)\|g_2 - \bar{g}\| \\ &\geq \min\{-\|g_1 - \bar{g}\|, -\|g_2 - \bar{g}\|\} \\ &= \min\{f_a(g_1), f_a(g_2)\} \end{aligned} . \tag{9.11}$$

Hence, $f_a(g) \in F$. The averageness hypothesis is compatible with the WA hypothesis.

We can also discuss the relationship between the two hypotheses from another perspective. It is easy to see that the WA hypothesis can be generalized to

$$f(A\theta) \geq \min\{f(g_1), f(g_2), \ldots, f(g_M)\}, \tag{9.12}$$

where $A = [g_1, g_2, \ldots, g_M]$, $\theta_i \geq 0$, $i = 1, \ldots, M$, and $1^T\theta = 1$. $A\theta$ is the weighted average of the geometric features of M subjects. The geometric feature of the average face, denoted by $\bar{g}$ is $A\theta$ with equal weights. According to the averageness hypothesis, $f(\bar{g})$ is larger than the attractiveness of most original faces; thus, it must be larger than the minimal among them. Therefore, the averageness hypothesis is compatible with the WA hypothesis.

9.5.2 Compatibility with the Symmetry Hypothesis

Human faces are axial symmetric. According to the symmetry hypothesis, asymmetry will decrease the attractiveness. The symmetry can be measured by

$$f_s(g) = -\|Sg\|, \tag{9.13}$$

where S is a 196 × 196 matrix, g is a 196 × 1 geometric feature. For example, if the symmetric axis is along the y-direction, the elements of S are −1, 1, and 0. Each row of S has at most one −1 and one 1, indicating the symmetric pairs. This is the simplest design of S. Certainly, S could be more complex, e.g., allowing the weighting scheme. Anyway, S is a linear transformation.

For $\forall g_1, g_2 \in G$, and $\forall \theta \in [0, 1]$, we have $f_s(g_1) = -\|Sg_1\|$, $f_s(g_2) = -\|Sg_2\|$, and

$$\begin{aligned} f_s({}_1 + (1-\theta)g_2) &= -\|S(\theta g_1) + (1-\theta)g_2\| \\ &= -\|S\theta g_1 + S(1-\theta)g_2\| \\ &\geq -\theta\|Sg_1\| - (1-\theta)\|Sg_2\| \cdot \\ &\geq \min\{-\|Sg_1\|, -\|Sg_2\|\} \\ &= \min\{f_s(g_1), f_s(g_2)\} \end{aligned} \tag{9.14}$$

Hence, $f_s(\cdot) \in F$. The symmetry hypothesis is compatible with the WA hypothesis.

9.5.3 Compatibility with the Golden Ratio Hypothesis

The golden ratio hypothesis demonstrates that when dozens of facial ratios equal to the golden ratio (1.618), the faces are attractive. Recent researches show that the ideal values of the ratios are not exactly 1.618, and they adjust the ideal values by measuring the collected face images. One approach to model the golden ratio hypothesis is based on the Phi mask, that is, $f_r(g) = -\|g - g_\phi\|$, where g_ϕ is the geometric feature of the Phi mask. Similar to the averageness hypothesis, it is also a one-prototype model and $f_r(\cdot) \in F$.

We can also examine each ratio separately. The ratio-based hypothesis can be modeled as

$$f_r(g) = -\|r(g) - r_0\|, \tag{9.15}$$

where $r(g)$ is the calculated ratio value given g, and r_0 is the ideal ratio value. For $\forall g_1, g_2 \in G$, and $\forall \theta \in [0, 1]$, we have $f_r(g_1) = -\|r(g_1) - r_0\|$, $f_r(g_2) =$

$-\|r(g_2) - r_O\|$. The ratio is calculated by horizontal or vertical measurements. Suppose $r(g_1) = l_1/l_2$, $r(g_2) = l_3/l_4$, then

$$r(\theta g_1 + (1-\theta)g_2) = \frac{\theta l_1 + (1-\theta)l_3}{\theta l_2 + (1-\theta)l_4}. \tag{9.16}$$

We can see that when $\theta = 0$, $r(\theta g_1 + (1-\theta)g_2) = r(g_2)$; when $\theta = 1$, $r(\theta g_1 + (1-\theta)g_2) = r(g_1)$. Besides, $r(\theta g_1 + (1-\theta)g_2)$ is a monotonic function of θ. Hence, $r(\theta g_1 + (1-\theta)g_2)$ is between $r(g_1)$ and $r(g_2)$, and $-\|r(\theta g_1 + (1-\theta)g_2) - r_O\| \geq \min\{-\|r(g_1) - r_O\|, -\|r(g_2) - r_O\|\}$, i.e., $f_r(\theta g_1 + (1-\theta)g_2) \geq \min\{f_r(g_1), f_r(g_2)\}$. Therefore, $f_r(\cdot) \in F$. The golden ratio hypothesis is compatible with the WA hypothesis.

9.6 Summary

In this chapter, a new hypothesis on facial beauty perception is presented. Instead of exploiting what traits make a face attractive, the new hypothesis focuses on discovering the general characteristic of the perception functions: the weighted average of two facial geometric features is more attractive than the inferior one between them. We first test the WA hypothesis by examining computational models learned from data and receive consistently supportive results. Then perceptual experiments are carried out to further validate the hypothesis. A corollary of the WA hypothesis is that attractive facial geometric features construct a convex set. This corollary derives a convex hull-based face beautification method. It is more flexible than the averageness- and KNN-based beautification method, and more robust than the SVR-based beautification method. Furthermore, we prove that the mainstream hypotheses on facial beauty perception are compatible with the weighted average hypothesis. Therefore, the WA hypothesis is more general than other existing ones. This chapter also shows mutual promotion between computer science and psychology. On one hand, image processing and statistical learning techniques are used to test psychological hypothesis. On the other hand, the validated hypothesis enlightens a new face beautification method, which can facilitate many real-life applications (e.g., aesthetic plastic surgery planning, photo retouching, entertainment, etc.).

Several issues need to be investigated. First, the WA hypothesis has been validated with female faces in this work. Whether the hypothesis is also valid with male faces requires further research. Second, aside from geometric features, texture and color features are also important to facial beauty perception. How to quantify and normalize these features, from the perspective of facial beauty, is still unsolved. Third, in addition to finding the discriminative traits, discovering the function characteristics may attract more attention. This chapter is a beginning, not an end.

References

Alley TR, Cunningham MR (1991) Averaged faces are attractive, but very attractive faces are not average. Psychol Sci 123–125

Atiyeh BS, Hayek SN (2008) Numeric expression of aesthetics and beauty. Aesthet Plast Surg 32 (2):209–216

Boyd S, Vandenberghe L (2004) Convex optimization. Cambridge University Press, Cambridge

Chen F, Zhang D (2010) A benchmark for geometric facial beauty study. Med Biometr 21–32

Chen F, Xu Y, Zhang D (2014) A new hypothesis on facial beauty perception. ACM Trans Appl Percept 11(2):8

Cohen BH (2008) Explaining psychological statistics. Wiley, New York

Cootes TF, Taylor CJ, Cooper DH, Graham J (1995) Active shape models-their training and application. Comput Vis Image Underst 61(1):38–59

Cunningham MR, Roberts AR, Barbee AP, Druen PB, Wu CH (1995) "Their ideas of beauty are, on the whole, the same as ours": consistency and variability in the cross-cultural perception of female physical attractiveness. J Pers Soc Psychol 68(2):261–269

Dryden IL, Mardia KV (1998) Statistical shape analysis. Wiley, Chichester

Eisenthal Y, Dror G, Ruppin E (2006) Facial attractiveness: beauty and the machine. Neural Comput 18(1):119–142

Fan J, Chau KP, Wan X, Zhai L, Lau E (2012) Prediction of facial attractiveness from facial proportions. Pattern Recogn 45(6):2326–2334

Grant MC, Boyd SP (2008) Graph implementations for nonsmooth convex programs. Recent advances in learning and control. Springer, London, pp 95–110. http://stanford.edu/~boyd/graph_dcp.html

Grant M, Boyd S (2012) CVX: Matlab software for disciplined convex programming, version 2.0 beta. http://cvxr.com/cvx

Gray D, Yu K, Xu W, Gong Y (2010) Predicting facial beauty without landmarks. In: Proceedings of European conference on computer vision, pp 434–447

Holland E (2008) Marquardt's Phi mask: pitfalls of relying on fashion models and the golden ratio to describe a beautiful face. Aesthet Plast Surg 32(2):200–208

Jefferson Y (2004) Facial beauty-establishing a universal standard. Int J Orthod-Milwaukee 15 (1):9–26

Kagian A, Dror G, Leyvand T, Meilijson I, Cohen-Or D, Ruppin E (2008) A machine learning predictor of facial attractiveness revealing human-like psychophysical biases. Vis Res 48 (2):235–243

Kowner R (1996) Facial asymmetry and attractiveness judgment in developmental perspective. J Exp Psychol-Hum Percept Perform 22(3):662–674

Langlois JH, Roggman LA (1990) Attractive faces are only average. Psychol Sci 1(2):115–121

Langlois JH, Kalakanis L, Rubenstein AJ, Larson A, Hallam M, Smoot M (2000) Maxims or myths of beauty? A meta-analytic and theoretical review. Psychol Bull 126(3):390

Leyvand T, Cohen-Or D, Dror G, Lischinski D (2008) Data-driven enhancement of facial attractiveness. ACM Trans Graph 27(3):38

Marquardt SR (2002) Dr. Stephen R. Marquardt on the Golden Decagon and human facial beauty. Interview by Dr. Gottlieb. J Clin Orthod: JCO 36(6):339–347

Melacci S, Sarti L, Maggini M, Gori M (2010) A template-based approach to automatic face enhancement. Pattern Anal Appl 13(3):289–300

Messer K, Matas J, Kittler J, Luettin J, Maitre G (1999) XM2VTSDB: the extended M2VTS database. In: Proceedings of international conference on audio and video-based biometric person authentication, vol 964, pp 965–966

Mu Y (2013) Computational facial attractiveness prediction by aesthetics-aware features. Neurocomputing 99:59–64

Penton-Voak I (2011) In retreat from nature? Successes and concerns in Darwinian approaches to facial attractiveness. J Evol Psychol 9(2):173–193

Penton-Voak IS, Jones BC, Little AC, Baker S, Tiddeman B, Burt DM, Perrett DI (2001) Symmetry, sexual dimorphism in facial proportions and male facial attractiveness. Proc R Soc Lond B: Biol Sci 268(1476):1617–1623

Peron APLM, Morosini IC, Correia KR, Moresca R, Petrelli E (2012) Photometric study of divine proportion and its correlation with facial attractiveness. Dental Press J Orthod 17(2):124–131

Perrett DI, Burt DM, Penton-Voak IS, Lee KJ, Rowland DA, Edwards R (1999) Symmetry and human facial attractiveness. Evol Hum Behav 20(5):295–307

Perrett DI, May KA, Yoshikawa S (1994) Facial shape and judgements of female attractiveness. Nature 368(6468):239–242

Phillips PJ, Moon H, Rizvi SA, Rauss PJ (2000) The FERET evaluation methodology for face-recognition algorithms. IEEE Trans Pattern Anal Mach Intell 22(10):1090–1104

Phillips PJ, Wechsler H, Huang J, Rauss PJ (1998) The FERET database and evaluation procedure for face-recognition algorithms. Image Vis Comput 16(5):295–306

Rhodes G (2006) The evolutionary psychology of facial beauty. Annu Rev Psychol 57:199–226

Schaefer S, McPhail T, Warren J (2006) Image deformation using moving least squares. ACM Trans Graph 25(3):533–540

Schmid K, Marx D, Samal A (2008) Computation of a face attractiveness index based on neoclassical canons, symmetry, and golden ratios. Pattern Recogn 41(8):2710–2717

Sutic D, Breskovic I, Huic R, Jukic I (2010) Automatic evaluation of facial attractiveness. In: Proceedings of international convention, pp 1339–1342

Swaddle JP, Cuthill IC (1995) Asymmetry and human facial attractiveness: symmetry may not always be beautiful. Proc R Soc Lond B Biol Sci 261(1360):111–116

Thompson B (1995) Stepwise regression and stepwise discriminant analysis need not apply here: a guidelines editorial. Educ Psychol Meas 55(4):525–534

Vapink V (1995) The nature of statistical learning theory. Springer

Whitehill J, Movellan JR (2008) Personalized facial attractiveness prediction. In: Proceedings of international conference on automatic face gesture recognition, pp 1–7

Zhang D, Zhao Q, Chen F (2011) Quantitative analysis of human facial beauty using geometric features. Pattern Recogn 44(4):940–950

Part IV
Computational Models of Facial Beauty

Chapter 10
Beauty Analysis by Learning Machine and Subspace Extension

Compared with features based methods, dedicated data-driven facial beauty modeling methods have a major advantage that it may be able to directly perform facial beauty analysis from raw data. As a result, data-driven facial beauty modeling methods allow facial beauty analysis to be more easily carried out. Moreover, they may enable the corresponding system to be more convenient for use. One main characteristic of data-driven facial beauty modeling is that we may pay less attention on rules or principles on beauty analysis and we can achieve satisfactory facial beauty analysis by just collecting enough raw data, performing proper training and selecting a suitable learning algorithm. The success of deep learning techniques sufficiently demonstrates the potential of data-driven learning. In this sense, it is worth to study data-driven methods for facial beauty analysis. Data-driven facial beauty modeling methods can also work for facial beauty analysis by virtue of conventional features. A data-driven method is referred to as generalized data-driven method if it is workable for both raw data and conventional features.

This chapter mainly presents an evolutionary cost-sensitive extreme learning machine (ECSELM) which simultaneously learns a classifier and cost matrix by leveraging a backtracking search algorithm for both robust recognition and regression. Section 10.1 introduces three extreme learning machine (ELM) algorithms including conventional ELM, kernel ELM and weighted ELM. The ECSELM and its optimization algorithms are formulated in Sect. 10.3. The extension of evolutionary cost-sensitive (ECS) framework to discriminative subspace analysis (i.e. ECSLDA) and its algorithmic framework are presented in Sect. 10.3. The experiments for multi-modal beauty analysis involving facial, dressing, and vocal attractiveness are presented in Sect. 10.4. The performance analysis including face analysis, parameter sensitivity analysis and computational complexity analysis are discussed in Sect. 10.5. Finally, Sect. 10.6 concludes the chapter.

D. Zhang et al., *Computer Models for Facial Beauty Analysis*,
DOI 10.1007/978-3-319-32598-9_10

10.1 Introduction

Extreme learning machine (ELM) was proposed by Huang et al. (2006a) for generalized single-hidden-layer feed-forward neural networks (SLFN) in order to overcome the drawbacks of gradient-based methods, such as the local minima, learning rate, stopping criteria and learning epochs. As Huang et al. has further provided the rigorous proof of universal approximation of ELM with much milder condition that almost any nonlinear piecewise continuous function can be used as the activation functions in hidden nodes of ELM (Huang et al. 2006a, b; Huang and Chen 2007, 2008). Different from traditional learning algorithms, ELM not only tends to reach the smallest training error but also its smallest norm of the output weights leads to better generalization performance of SLFN, according to the Bartlett's theory (Bartlett 1998).

Different versions of improved ELM have been proposed. Inspired by Mercer condition, a kernel ELM was proposed for robust classification (Huang et al. 2008). Since ELM randomly selects the input weights and biases that associate with the output weights, in Zhu et al. (2005), a differential evolutionary based ELM was proposed to select the input weights and achieved a good generalization performance with more compact networks. Because imbalanced data sets are quite common in various applications, a weighted ELM, in which each training sample was assigned with larger weight to strengthen the impact of minority class and smaller weight to weak the impact of majority class, was proposed with two weighting schemes (W^1ELM vs. W^2ELM) (Zong et al. 2013). Further, a boosting weighted ELM was proposed with an AdaBoost framework for sample imbalance (Li et al. 2014). ELM has recently drawn a significant amount of interest from researchers in various fields such as face recognition (Bartlett 1998; Zong and Huang 2011), activity recognition (Deng et al. 2014), action recognition (Iosifidis et al. 2013), and handwritten character recognition (Chacko et al. 2012).

10.1.1 SLFN and ELM

ELM, in which the input weights and hidden biases were randomly selected and the output weights were analytically determined using Moore-Penrose generalized inverse, has also been proved to be efficient and effective for regression and classification tasks (Huang et al. 2008, 2010; Mohammed et al. 2011). However, ELM requires more hidden neurons than gradient descent algorithms and leads to ill-conditioned problem due to randomly selected input weights and hidden biases (Zhu et al. 2005).

Given N samples $[\mathbf{x}_1, \mathbf{x}_2, \ldots, \mathbf{x}_N]$ and their corresponding targets $[\mathbf{t}_1, \mathbf{t}_2, \ldots, \mathbf{t}_N]$, where $\mathbf{x}_i = [x_{i1}, x_{i1}, \ldots, x_{in}]^{\mathrm{T}} \in \mathbf{R}^n$ and $\mathbf{t}_i = [t_{i1}, t_{i1}, \ldots, t_{im}]^{\mathrm{T}} \in \mathbf{R}^m$, standard SLFN with L hidden nodes and activation function $\mathcal{H}(\mathbf{x})$ is modeled as

$$\sum_{j=1}^{L} \boldsymbol{\beta}_j \mathcal{H}(\mathbf{w}_j \cdot \mathbf{x}_i + b_j) = \mathbf{t}_i, i = 1, \ldots, N, \tag{10.1}$$

where $\mathbf{w}_j = [w_{j1}, w_{j2}, \ldots, w_{jn}]^{\mathrm{T}}$ is the input weight vector connecting the j-th hidden node and the n input nodes, $\boldsymbol{\beta}_j = [\beta_{j1}, \beta_{j2}, \ldots, \beta_{jm}]^{\mathrm{T}}$ is the output weight vector connecting the j-th hidden node and the m output nodes, b_j is the bias of the j-th node in the hidden layer. It is worth noting that, in ELM, input weights $\mathbf{w}$ and hidden neuron biases $\mathbf{b}$ are randomly generated and are independent of the training data.

The representation (10.1) can be written compactly as

$$\mathbf{H} \cdot \boldsymbol{\beta} = \mathbf{T}. \tag{10.2}$$

where $\boldsymbol{\beta} = [\boldsymbol{\beta}_1, \boldsymbol{\beta}_2, \ldots, \boldsymbol{\beta}_L]^{\mathrm{T}}$, $\mathbf{T} = [\mathbf{t}_1, \mathbf{t}_2, \ldots, \mathbf{t}_N]^{\mathrm{T}}$, $\mathbf{H}_{N \times L}$ is the hidden layer output matrix, and the i-th column of $\mathbf{H}$ is the output of the i-th hidden neuron w.r.s inputs $\mathbf{x}_1$, $\mathbf{x}_2$, …, $\mathbf{x}_N$. To obtain the *minimum norm least square* solution of the linear system (10.2) is equivalent to train a SLFN. When the number of hidden neurons $L = N$, $\mathbf{H}$ is a square matrix and invertible. Then the SLFN may have zero error. However, in most cases $L \ll N$ and $\mathbf{H}$ is non-square, therefore, the *minimum norm least square* solution can be obtained as

$$\widehat{\boldsymbol{\beta}} = \mathbf{H}^{\dagger}\mathbf{T}, \tag{10.3}$$

where $\mathbf{H}^{\dagger}$ is the Moore-Penrose generalized inverse of $\mathbf{H}$.

ELM (Huang et al. 2006b) aims to minimize the training error and the ℓ_2-norm of the output weights. The optimization of ELM with constraint can also be rewritten as

$$\begin{cases} \text{minimize } \mathcal{L}_{\mathrm{ELM}} = \frac{1}{2}\|\boldsymbol{\beta}\|^2 + C \cdot \frac{1}{2} \cdot \sum_{i=1}^{N} \|\boldsymbol{\xi}_i\|^2 \\ \text{subject to} : \mathcal{H}(\mathbf{x}_i)\boldsymbol{\beta} = \mathbf{t}_i - \boldsymbol{\xi}_i, i = 1, \ldots, N \end{cases}, \tag{10.4}$$

where C is the regularization parameter. By solving problem (10.4), the output weights can be analytically determined as

$$\boldsymbol{\beta}_B = \mathbf{H}^{\dagger}\mathbf{T} = \begin{cases} \mathbf{H}^{\mathrm{T}}\left(\frac{1}{c} + \mathbf{H}\mathbf{H}^{\mathrm{T}}\right)^{-1}\mathbf{T}, N < L \\ \left(\frac{1}{c} + \mathbf{H}\mathbf{H}^{\mathrm{T}}\right)^{-1}\mathbf{H}^{\mathrm{T}}\mathbf{T}, N \geq L \end{cases}, \tag{10.5}$$

where $\mathbf{I}$ is the identity matrix.

10.1.2 Kernel ELM

One can apply Mercer's condition to ELM, and formulate it as a kernel ELM (Huang et al. 2012). A kernel matrix in ELM is defined as

$$\Omega_{\mathrm{ELM}} = \mathbf{H}\mathbf{H}^{\mathrm{T}}, \tag{10.6}$$

where $\Omega_{\mathrm{ELM}i,j} = \mathcal{H}(\mathbf{x}_i) \cdot \mathcal{H}(\mathbf{x}_j) = K(\mathbf{x}_i, \mathbf{x}_j)$

Then, for the case where the number of training samples is not huge (i.e. $N < L$), the output of the ELM classifier (10.6) with respect to **x**, can be represented as

$$\begin{aligned} y &= \mathcal{H}(\mathbf{x})\mathbf{H}^{\mathrm{T}}\left(\frac{1}{c} + \mathbf{H}\mathbf{H}^{\mathrm{T}}\right)^{-1}\mathbf{T} \\ &= \begin{bmatrix} K(\mathbf{x}, \mathbf{x}_1) \\ \vdots \\ K(\mathbf{x}, \mathbf{x}_N) \end{bmatrix}^{\mathrm{T}} \left(\frac{1}{c} + \Omega_{\mathrm{ELM}}\right)^{-1}\mathbf{T} \end{aligned}. \tag{10.7}$$

10.1.3 Weighted ELM

The weighted ELM was proposed to address the problem of imbalanced samples (Zong et al. 2013). In contrast to the ELM, a weight matrix **W** associated with the number of each class is embedded in the objective function. Therefore, the optimization problem can be rewritten as

$$\begin{cases} \text{minimize } \mathcal{L}_{\mathrm{WELM}} = \frac{1}{2}\|\boldsymbol{\beta}\|^2 + C \cdot \mathbf{W} \cdot \frac{1}{2} \cdot \sum_{i=1}^{N} \|\xi_i\|^2 \\ \text{subject to} : \mathcal{H}(\mathbf{x}_i)\boldsymbol{\beta} = \mathbf{t}_i - \xi_i, i = 1, \ldots, N \end{cases}. \tag{10.8}$$

Generally, each training sample was assigned with larger weight to strength the impact of minority class and smaller weight to weak the impact of majority class. Specially, two weighted schemes based ELM called as W¹ELM and W²ELM were defined as follows.

$$\mathrm{W^1ELM} : W_{ii} = \frac{1}{\#\mathrm{Class}\ i}, \tag{10.9}$$

$$\mathrm{W^2ELM} : W_{ii} = \begin{cases} \frac{0.618}{\#\mathrm{Class}\ i}, & \text{if } \#\mathrm{Class}\ i > AVG(\#\mathrm{Class}\ i) \\ \frac{1}{\#\mathrm{Class}\ i}, & \text{else} \end{cases}, \tag{10.10}$$

where #Class i is the number of samples belonging to class i, AVG(#Class i) is the average number of samples for each class.

10.2 Evolutionary Cost-Sensitive Extreme Learning Machine

Up to now, ELM has been widely used for classification and regression with different versions of improvements for higher classification accuracy and lower error rate. However, all the existing ELM based recognition methods tend to achieve lower error rate with assumption of the same loss for any misclassification, which, however, may not hold in many applications. For instance, in the face recognition based access control system, different misclassification may lead to different loss or cost. Specifically, misclassifying an impostor as a genuine user and allowing the subject to enter the room may result in more serious loss than misclassifying a genuine user as an imposter and not allowing the subject to enter the room. The different losses in a face recognition system have been first given by formulating a cost-sensitive classification task in Zhang and Zhou (2010).

It is known that subspace learning such as principal component analysis (PCA) (Turk and Pentland 1991) and linear discriminant analysis (LDA) (Belhumeur et al. 1997), manifold learning such as locality preserving projections (LPP) (He et al. 2005) and margin fisher analysis (MFA) (Yan et al. 2007c), and their weighted, kernelized, and tensorized variants (Yan et al. 2007a, b) have been proposed for face recognition. Recently, their cost-sensitive versions, such as CSPCA, CSLDA, CSLPP, and CSMFA have also been surveyed for face recognition in Lu and Tan (2010, 2013). Though cost sensitive learning can reduce the misclassification loss with a predefined cost matrix which quantifies how severe one type of mistake against another type of mistake, in many realistic cases the cost matrix is unknown or difficult to define by users (Zhang and Zhou 2010), so that the learned subspace (e.g. discriminative subspace) is not optimal and result in poor classification performance. Liu and Zhou (2010) first attempt to address the problem of cost matrix definition using a cost interval instead of a precise cost value, however, it brings a large computational cost, and a pre-interval should be manually defined such that the proposed problem has always been an open topic in cost-sensitive learning. Therefore, refining the cost matrix or learning a cost matrix is extremely desired and to be resolved for a cost-sensitive system.

Motivated by the above open problems of ELM and cost-sensitive learning, an evolutionary cost-sensitive extreme learning machine (ECSELM) is presented in this chapter. The evolutionary cost-sensitive (ECS) framework can effectively learn a cost information matrix seeking for the optimal classifier or predictor which not only addresses the sample imbalance, but also takes into consideration the false recognition loss during ELM learning. Furthermore, inspired by subspace learning, an evolutionary cost-sensitive linear discriminant analysis (ECSLDA) is also presented as extension for robust discriminative subspace learning. Finally, the ECSELM and ECSLDA approaches are tested in a variety of cost-sensitive tasks including biometrics (e.g. human beauty analysis), computer vision (e.g. face analysis).

10.2.1 Cost-Sensitive Extreme Learning Machine

Cost-sensitive learning is also an important topic in machine learning. However, cost-sensitive ELM (CSELM) is first proposed in ELM based methods.

The cost matrix $\boldsymbol{M}$ of N samples can be shown as

$$\boldsymbol{M} = \begin{bmatrix} 0 & M_{12} & \cdots & M_{1q} & \cdots & M_{1N} \\ M_{21} & 0 & \cdots & M_{2q} & \cdots & M_{2N} \\ \vdots & \vdots & \ddots & \vdots & \cdots & \vdots \\ M_{q1} & M_{q2} & \cdots & 0 & \cdots & M_{qN} \\ \vdots & \vdots & \cdots & \vdots & \ddots & \vdots \\ M_{N1} & M_{N2} & \cdots & M_{Nq} & \cdots & 0 \end{bmatrix}_{N\times N}, \tag{10.11}$$

where $M_{i,j}$ denotes the misclassification loss caused by erroneously classifying the i-th sample as the j-th sample, and the diagonal elements of zero denote the zero loss of the correct classification.

Then, the CSELM for recognition and regression is shown as

$$\begin{cases} \text{minimize}\, \mathcal{L}_{\text{CSELM}} = \frac{1}{2}\|\boldsymbol{\beta}\|^2 + C\cdot \text{diag}(\boldsymbol{B})\cdot\frac{1}{2}\cdot\sum_{i=1}^{N}\|\boldsymbol{\xi}_i\|^2 \\ \text{subject to}: \mathcal{H}(\mathbf{x}_i)\boldsymbol{\beta} = \mathbf{t}_i - \boldsymbol{\xi}_i, i = 1,\ldots,N \end{cases}, \tag{10.12}$$

where $\boldsymbol{B}$ is a cost information vector with entries $\boldsymbol{B}_i = \sum_j (\boldsymbol{W}\cdot\boldsymbol{M})_{ij}$, $\boldsymbol{W}_{N\times N}$ is a diagonal weighted matrix assigned for each training sample whose coefficient can be calculated as (10.9), such that the cost information vector $\boldsymbol{B}$ on the error term is also an effective tradeoff between the samples' imbalance and the loss of misclassification. $\mathbf{t}_i$ and $\boldsymbol{\xi}_i$ denote the label vector and error vector with respect to the sample $\mathbf{x}_i$, for multi-class recognition. If $\mathbf{x}_i$ belongs to the k-th class, the k-th position of $\mathbf{t}_i$ is set as 1, i.e. $t_i^k = 1$, and other bits are set as -1 (e.g. $\mathbf{t}_i = [1, -1, -1, \ldots, -1]^T$ when $\mathbf{x}_i$ belongs to class 1).

With a fixed $\boldsymbol{B}$, the representation (10.12) is a convex optimization problem, which can be solved by minimizing the following objective function

$$\begin{aligned} \mathcal{L}_{\text{CSELM}}(\boldsymbol{\beta}, \boldsymbol{\xi}_i, \alpha_i) = \frac{1}{2}\|\boldsymbol{\beta}\|^2 + C\cdot\text{diag}(\boldsymbol{B})\cdot\frac{1}{2}\cdot\sum_{i=1}^{N}\|\boldsymbol{\xi}_i\|^2 \\ - \alpha_i\cdot(\mathcal{H}(\mathbf{x}_i)\boldsymbol{\beta} - \mathbf{t}_i + \boldsymbol{\xi}_i) \end{aligned}. \tag{10.13}$$

where α_i is the Lagrange multiplier.

To derive the output weights, we calculate the derivatives of $\mathcal{L}_{\text{CSELM}}$ with respect to $\boldsymbol{\beta}$, $\boldsymbol{\xi}_i$, α_i as follows

$$\begin{cases} \frac{\partial\mathcal{L}(\boldsymbol{\beta},\xi_i,\alpha_i)}{\partial\beta} = 0 \rightarrow \boldsymbol{\beta} = \mathbf{H}^{\mathrm{T}}\boldsymbol{\alpha} \\ \frac{\partial\mathcal{L}(\boldsymbol{\beta},\xi_i,\alpha_i)}{\partial\xi_i} = 0 \rightarrow \alpha_i = C\cdot \mathrm{diag}(\boldsymbol{B})\cdot\xi_i, i=1,\ldots,N. \\ \frac{\partial\mathcal{L}(\boldsymbol{\beta},\xi_i,\alpha_i)}{\partial\alpha_i} = 0 \rightarrow \mathcal{H}(\mathbf{x}_i)\boldsymbol{\beta} - \mathbf{t}_i + \xi_i, i=1,\ldots,N \end{cases} \tag{10.14}$$

Then the output weights associated with $\boldsymbol{B}$ can be solved as follows.

$$\boldsymbol{\beta}_{\boldsymbol{B}} = \mathbf{H}^{\dagger}\mathbf{T} = \begin{cases} \mathbf{H}^{\mathrm{T}}\cdot\left(\frac{1}{c} + \mathrm{diag}(\boldsymbol{B})\mathbf{H}\mathbf{H}^{\mathrm{T}}\right)^{-1}\cdot \mathrm{diag}(\boldsymbol{B})\cdot\mathbf{T}, N<L \\ \left(\frac{1}{c} + \mathbf{H}^{\mathrm{T}}\mathrm{diag}(\boldsymbol{B})\mathbf{H}\right)^{-1}\cdot\mathbf{H}^{\mathrm{T}}\cdot\mathrm{diag}(\boldsymbol{B})\cdot\mathbf{T}, N\geq L \end{cases}, \tag{10.15}$$

where $\mathbf{H}^{\dagger}$ is the Moore-Penrose generalized inverse of $\mathbf{H}$, which can be represented as

$$\mathbf{H} = \begin{bmatrix} \mathcal{H}(\mathbf{w}_1\mathbf{x}_1+b_1) & \mathcal{H}(\mathbf{w}_2\mathbf{x}_1+b_2) & \cdots & \mathcal{H}(\mathbf{w}_L\mathbf{x}_1+b_L) \\ \mathcal{H}(\mathbf{w}_1\mathbf{x}_2+b_1) & \mathcal{H}(\mathbf{w}_2\mathbf{x}_2+b_2) & \cdots & \mathcal{H}(\mathbf{w}_L\mathbf{x}_2+b_L) \\ \vdots & \vdots & \vdots & \vdots \\ \mathcal{H}(\mathbf{w}_1\mathbf{x}_N+b_1) & \mathcal{H}(\mathbf{w}_2\mathbf{x}_N+b_2) & \cdots & \mathcal{H}(\mathbf{w}_L\mathbf{x}_N+b_L) \end{bmatrix}. \tag{10.16}$$

In this chapter, the "radbas" function is empirically used as the feature mapping (activation) $\mathcal{H}(\cdot)$, which is shown as

$$\mathcal{H}(\mathbf{w},\mathbf{b},\mathbf{x}) = \exp(-\|\mathbf{w}\cdot\mathbf{x}+\mathbf{b}\|^2). \tag{10.17}$$

Sigmoid, Laplacian, polynomial function, etc. can also be used as hidden layer activation function.

Therefore, in cases of a few samples and huge samples output $\mathbf{z}$ of a test instance $\mathbf{y}$ can be solved by

$$\begin{aligned} \mathbf{z} &= \mathcal{H}(\mathbf{y})\cdot\boldsymbol{\beta}_{\boldsymbol{B}} \\ &= \begin{cases} \mathcal{H}(\mathbf{y})\cdot\mathbf{H}^{\mathrm{T}}\cdot\left(\frac{\mathrm{I}}{C} + \mathrm{diag}(\boldsymbol{B})\mathbf{H}\mathbf{H}^{\mathrm{T}}\right)^{-1}\cdot\mathrm{diag}(\boldsymbol{B})\cdot\mathbf{T}, N<L \\ \mathcal{H}(\mathbf{y})\cdot\left(\frac{\mathrm{I}}{\mathrm{C}} + \mathbf{H}^{\mathrm{T}}\mathrm{diag}(\boldsymbol{B})\mathbf{H}\right)^{-1}\cdot\mathbf{H}^{\mathrm{T}}\cdot\mathrm{diag}(\boldsymbol{B})\cdot\mathbf{T}, N\geq L \end{cases}. \end{aligned} \tag{10.18}$$

Similarly, the kernel version of ECSELM can also be introduced as (10.6). In the testing process of multi-class classification, one can then declare the predicted label of test instance $\mathbf{y}$ as

$$\widehat{k} = \arg\max_{k\in\{1,\ldots,c\}} \{\mathbf{z}\in\Re^c|\mathbf{z} = \mathcal{H}(\mathbf{y})\cdot\boldsymbol{\beta}_{\boldsymbol{B}}\}_c, \tag{10.19}$$

where c denotes the number of classes.

Notably, it can be figured out from (10.15) and (10.18) that the output weight and final decision have dependency on cost information vector $\boldsymbol{B}$ which can be calculated by weighting matrix $\boldsymbol{W}$ and cost matrix $\boldsymbol{M}$, and hence, the next step is to solve cost information vector $\boldsymbol{B}$ instead of the cost matrix and weighting matrix.

10.2.2 Evolutionary CSELM

The ECSELM introduces the evolutionary optimization in the framework of CSELM for decision level optimization. As mentioned before, the cost matrix was generally determined in an empirical way which will easily result in poor generalization performance. To address this problem, the cost matrix is determined by optimization through an evolutionary algorithm (EA).

On the basis of the CSELM, the ECSELM seeks the optimal cost matrix $\boldsymbol{M}$ which can make a better prediction through output weights $\boldsymbol{\beta}_M$ with respect to $\boldsymbol{M}$ such that the loss between the predicted value and ground truth reaches the minimum as follows

$$\begin{aligned} &\min_{\boldsymbol{M}} \sum_i \mathcal{L}\{\mathbf{t}_i, f_{\text{CSELM}}(\mathbf{x}_i, \boldsymbol{\beta}_M)\} \\ &\text{s.t. } l_1 \le \boldsymbol{M}_{i,j} \le l_2, \boldsymbol{M}_{i,i} = 0, i = 1, \ldots, N; j = 1, \ldots, N, \end{aligned} \tag{10.20}$$

where l_1 and l_2 are the low and upper bounds, N is the number of training samples, $\mathcal{L}$ is the classification or regression loss function, $\mathbf{t}_i$ is the label vector of sample $\mathbf{x}_i$, and f_{CSELM} denotes the CSELM classifier or predictor.

However, it can be found that output weight matrix $\boldsymbol{\beta}$ in (10.15) is associated with $\boldsymbol{B}$, which is indeed calculated by multiplying an unknown/known weighted matrix $\boldsymbol{W}$ with unknown cost matrix $\boldsymbol{M}$. For convenience, optimization problem (10.20) seeking for $\boldsymbol{M}$ can thus be intuitively transformed as the following problem

$$\begin{aligned} &\boldsymbol{B}^* = \arg \min_{\boldsymbol{B}} \sum_i \mathcal{L}\{\mathbf{t}_i, f_{\text{CSELM}}(\mathbf{x}_i, \boldsymbol{\beta}_B)\}, \\ &\text{s.t. } l'_1 \le \boldsymbol{B}_i \le l'_2 \end{aligned} \tag{10.21}$$

where l'_1 and l'_2 are the new bounds.

By solving (10.21), i.e. the optimization of the CSELM classifier/predictor model in the decision level, the optimal output weight matrix $\boldsymbol{\beta}_B$ can be obtained simultaneously with respect to the optimal cost information vector $\boldsymbol{B}^*$.

Then, the predicted output in the decision level of test instance $\mathbf{y}$ can be represented as

$$\widehat{k} = \arg \max_{k \in \{1,\ldots,c\}} \{\mathbf{z} \in \Re^c | \mathbf{z} = \mathcal{H}(\mathbf{y}) \cdot \boldsymbol{\beta}_{B^*}\}. \tag{10.22}$$

The ECSELM is summarized in Algorithm 10.1.

Algorithm 10.1. ECSELM

Input: Training set $\{\mathbf{x}_i\}_{i=1}^{N}$, and test instance $\mathbf{y}$, training target matrix $\mathbf{T}$.

Initialize: weighting matrix $\boldsymbol{W}$ and cost matrix $\boldsymbol{M}$.

Procedure:

1. Randomly select input weights $\mathbf{w}$ and hidden biases $\mathbf{b}$.
2. Compute cost information vector $\boldsymbol{B}$ with $\boldsymbol{B}_i = \sum_j (\boldsymbol{W} \cdot \boldsymbol{M})_{ij}$.
3. Compute the hidden layer output matrix $\mathbf{H}$ of training set and feature mapping $\mathrm{H}(\mathbf{y})$ using (10.16) and (10.17).
4. Compute output weights $\boldsymbol{\beta}_{\boldsymbol{B}}$ using (10.15).
5. Obtain the optimal $\boldsymbol{B}^*$ by solving the optimization problem (10.21) using Algorithm 10.2.
6. Compute the optimal output weights $\boldsymbol{\beta}_{\boldsymbol{B}^*}$ by substituting $\boldsymbol{B}^*$ to (10.15).

Output: $\boldsymbol{\beta}_{\boldsymbol{B}^*}$ and predicted label $\widehat{k}$ of test instance $\mathbf{y}$.

10.2.3 Optimization

Evolutionary algorithm (EA) is employed to seek the optimal $\boldsymbol{B}$ under the boundary constraint. EA is a population based stochastic search strategy that search for near-optimal solution. EA tries to evolve an individual into a new individual with better fitness by a trial individual, which can be generated using various genetic operators on the raw individuals such that ongoing effort is made on EA. In this chapter, we leverage a new evolutionary algorithm i.e. backtracking search optimization algorithm (BSA) (Civicioglu 2013) to address the cost matrix and classifier/predictor learning with few parameters. BSA, as a random search method with three basic genetic operators: selection, mutation and crossover used to generate trial individuals, has simple structure such that it is effective, fast and capable of solving multimodal problems. It can be briefly described as four stages in implementation: *initialization*, *selection-I*, *recombination* and *selection-II*. The basic steps of BSA are formulated as follows.

(1) *Initialization*: generation and evaluation of a population $\boldsymbol{P}$.

$$\boldsymbol{P}_{i,j} \sim \mathrm{U}(l_d^j, l_u^j), i = 1, \ldots, N; j = 1, \ldots D \tag{10.23}$$

$$F_i = \mathrm{ObjFun}(\boldsymbol{P}_i), i = 1, \ldots, N, \tag{10.24}$$

where $\boldsymbol{P}$ is encoded by the solution form of $\boldsymbol{B}$, N and D respectively denote the population size and problem dimension, l_d^j and l_u^j denote the low and upper bounds with respect to the j-th element, U denotes uniform distribution, and ObjFun(·) denotes the objective function (10.21).

(2) *Selection-I*: update step for historical population $\boldsymbol{Q}$

$$\boldsymbol{Q}_{i,j} \sim \mathrm{U}(l_d^j, l_u^j) \tag{10.25}$$

$$\text{if } a < b \text{ then } \boldsymbol{Q} = \boldsymbol{P}, \forall a, b \sim \mathrm{U}(0,1) \tag{10.26}$$

$$\boldsymbol{Q}' = permuting(\boldsymbol{Q}), \tag{10.27}$$

where *permuting* (·) is a random shuffling function. The historical population involves some memory characteristics.

(3) *Recombination*: update step for solution population $\boldsymbol{P}'_{new}$.

$$Binary\, mapping\, matrix\, \boldsymbol{C}_{\boldsymbol{N}\times\boldsymbol{D}}|0-1 \tag{10.28}$$

$$\boldsymbol{P}_{new} = \boldsymbol{P} + 3r \cdot C \odot (\boldsymbol{Q}' - \boldsymbol{P}) \tag{10.29}$$

$$P'_{new(i,j)} = \begin{cases} \begin{cases} l_d^j, & \text{if } rand^1 < rand^2 \text{ and } P_{new(i,j)} < l_d^j \\ rand \cdot (l_u^j - l_d^j) + l_d^j, & \text{otherwise} \end{cases} \\ \begin{cases} l_u^j, & \text{if } rand^1 < rand^2 \text{ and } P_{new(i,j)} > l_u^j \\ rand \cdot (l_u^j - l_d^j) + l_d^j, & \text{otherwise} \end{cases} \end{cases},$$

$$i = 1, \ldots, N; j = 1, \ldots, D \tag{10.30}$$

where $P'_{new(i,j)}$ represents the j-th element of the i-th individual, $\odot$ denotes dot product, $r \sim N(0,1)$, $rand^1$ and $rand^2 \sim \mathrm{U}(0,1)$, and $N(0,1)$ denotes the standard normal distribution.

Then, the new population is evaluated by calculating

$$F'_i = \mathrm{ObjFun}_i(\boldsymbol{P}'_{new}\{i\}), i = 1, \ldots, N, \tag{10.31}$$

where $\boldsymbol{P}'_{new}\{i\}$ denotes the i-th individual in the population.

(4) *Selection-II*: update step for new solution population $\boldsymbol{P}''_{new}$, global minimum F_{gmin}, and the optimal solution $\boldsymbol{g}_{opt}$.

$$\boldsymbol{P}''_{new} = \boldsymbol{P}'_{new}\{F'_i < F_i\} \cup \boldsymbol{P}\{F'_i \geq F_i\}, i = 1, \ldots, N \tag{10.32}$$

$$F_{gmin} = \min\{F\{F'_i \geq F_i\} \cup F'\{F'_i < F_i\}\}, i = 1, \ldots, N \tag{10.33}$$

$$\boldsymbol{g}_{opt} = \boldsymbol{P}''_{new}\{ind_{opt} | ind_{opt} = \arg_i \min\{F\{F'_i \geq F_i\} \cup F'\{F'_i < F_i\}\}\}. \tag{10.34}$$

The ECS framework of the solution is presented in Algorithm 10.2.

Algorithm 10.2. ECS framework

Input: The population size *N*, problem dimension *D*, lower and upper bounds l_d and l_u, the maximal iterations *epoch*;

Procedure:

1. *Initialization*:
   1.1. Population generation $\boldsymbol{P}_{i,j} \leftarrow \mathrm{U}\left(l_d^j, l_u^j\right)$ using (10.23);
   1.2. Objective function evaluation using (10.24);

while *iteration<epoch* **do**

2. *Selection-I*: *update step for historical population.*
   2.1. Historical population $\boldsymbol{Q}_{i,j} \leftarrow \mathrm{U}\left(l_d^j, l_u^j\right)$ using (10.25);
   2.2. Redefine $\boldsymbol{Q} \leftarrow \boldsymbol{P}$ using 'if-then' rule in (10.26);
   2.3. Permute $\boldsymbol{Q}' \leftarrow permuting(\boldsymbol{Q})$ by shuffling (10.27);
3. *Recombination*: *update step for solution population.*
   3.1. Generate crossover mapping matrix using (10.28);
   3.2. Mutate for new population using (10.29);
   3.3. Boundary control with (10.30);
   3.4. Objective function evaluation with the new population using (10.31);
4. *Selection-II: update step for new solution population, global minimum and optimal solution.*
   4.1. Update population using (10.32);
   4.2. Update the global minimum $\boldsymbol{F}_{best}$ using (10.33)
   4.3. Update the optimal solution using (10.34)

end while

Output: $\boldsymbol{B}^*$.

10.2.4 Parameters Setting

In experiments, number L of hidden neurons is selected from 100 to 500, and penalty parameter C is selected from 2^0 to 2^{30} without extra parameters setting. The parameter sensitivity of the algorithms has been explored in Sect. 10.5.2 by changing the C value and number L for presenting the best results. Both the maximum population size and the search epochs are set as 100, and the lower and upper boundary is set as −1 and 1, respectively. Notably, the population size and epochs can be accordingly adjusted in specific problems.

10.3 Discriminative Subspace Extension: ECSLDA

In this section, the evolutionary cost-sensitive framework is further extended to subspace analysis motivated by the existing cost-sensitive subspace methods, and consequently an ECSLDA method is proposed to learn an optimal discriminative subspace by alternative optimization of the cost matrix and to improve the recognition performance.

Cost matrix N of c classes is defined by

$$N = \begin{bmatrix} 0 & N_{12} & \cdots & N_{1q} & \cdots & N_{1c} \\ N_{21} & 0 & \cdots & N_{2q} & \cdots & N_{2c} \\ \vdots & \vdots & \ddots & \vdots & \cdots & \vdots \\ N_{q1} & N_{q2} & \cdots & 0 & \cdots & N_{qc} \\ \vdots & \vdots & \cdots & \vdots & \ddots & \vdots \\ N_{c1} & N_{c2} & \cdots & N_{cq} & \cdots & 0 \end{bmatrix}_{c\times c}, \tag{10.35}$$

where $N_{i,j}$ denotes the misclassification loss caused by erroneously classifying the i-th class as the j-th class, and the diagonal elements of zero denote the zero loss of the correct classification. To measure the cost of the k-th class, an importance function $\sigma(k)$ is defined as (Lu and Tan 2013)

$$\sigma(k) = \sum_{i=1}^{c} N_{k,l}, k = 1, \ldots, c. \tag{10.36}$$

Algorithm 10.3. ECSLDA

Input: Training set $\{\mathbf{x}_i\}_{i=1}^{N}$, test instance $\mathbf{y}$, training target matrix $\mathbf{T}$, and cost matrix N;

Procedure:

1. Compute $S_{b(N)}$ using (10.37).
2. Compute $S_{w(N)}$ using (10.38).
3. Obtain the subspace projection $\mathbf{w}_N^*$ by solving (10.39).
4. Obtain the optimal cost matrix N^* by solving (10.40) using Algorithm 10.2.
5. Obtain the optimal $\mathbf{w}_{N^*}^*$ by substituting N^* into (10.39).

Output: $\mathbf{w}_{N^*}^*$ and predicted label $\widehat{k}$ of $\mathbf{y}$ obtained using the NN classifier.

The cost-sensitive between-class scatter matrix and the cost-sensitive within-class scatter matrix of ECSLDA can be defined as

$$S_{b(N)} = \sum_{k=1}^{c}\sum_{l=1}^{c} N_{k,l}(\mathbf{m}_k - \mathbf{m}_l)(\mathbf{m}_k - \mathbf{m}_l)^{\mathrm{T}}, \tag{10.37}$$

$$S_{w(N)} = \sum_{k=1}^{c}\sum_{i=1}^{N_k} \sigma(k)(\mathbf{x}_i - \mathbf{m}_k)(\mathbf{x}_i - \mathbf{m}_k)^{\mathrm{T}}, \tag{10.38}$$

where $\mathbf{m}_k$ and $\mathbf{m}_l$ denote the center of class k and class l, N_k denotes the number of samples in class k, and $\mathbf{x}_i$ denotes the i-th sample vector from class k.

Then, the ECSLDA can be formulated as

$$\mathbf{w}_N^* = \arg\max_{\mathbf{w}_N} \frac{\mathbf{w}_N^T S_{b(N)} \mathbf{w}_N}{\mathbf{w}_N^T S_{w(N)} \mathbf{w}_N}, \tag{10.39}$$

where $\mathbf{w}_N$ denotes discriminative subspace of ECSLDA with respect to cost matrix N.

The ECSLDA seeks the optimal cost matrix N^* that yields an optimal subspace $\mathbf{w}_N^*$ by solving the following sub-problem

$$\begin{aligned} N^* &= \arg\min_{N} \sum_{n} \mathcal{L}\{t_n, g_{\mathrm{NN}}(\mathbf{x}_{\mathrm{n}}^{\mathrm{T}}\mathbf{w}_N^*)\} \\ s.t.\quad & l_1 \le N_{i,j} \le l_2, N_{i,i} = 0, i = 1,\ldots,c; j = 1,\ldots,c \end{aligned}, \tag{10.40}$$

where $g_{\mathrm{NN}}(\cdot)$ denotes the nearest neighbor (NN) classifier, $\mathcal{L}$ is the classification loss function, t_n is the label of sample x_n. Finally, the predicted label of test instance $\mathbf{y}$ can be obtained by the NN classifier. The formula is

$$\widehat{k} = g_{\mathrm{NN}}(\mathbf{y}^{\mathrm{T}}\mathbf{w}_{N^*}^*). \tag{10.41}$$

The ECSLDA algorithm is summarized in Algorithm 10.3.

10.4 Multi-modality Human Beauty Data Analysis

Facial attractiveness assessment using geometric and appearance based features coupled with pattern recognition techniques have been studied separately (Zhang et al. 2011; Fan et al. 2012; Gray et al. 2010; Eisenthal and Dror 2006). We explore human beauty analysis in this chapter because it is recognized as a cost-sensitive learning task (Yan 2014), and it is therefore used to evaluate the cost-sensitive methods.

Recently, a public multi-modality beauty (M^2B) database which includes three sub data sets (facial images, dressing images and vocal data, of female persons from eastern and western cultural races) have been released online for human beauty study (Nguyen et al. 2012; Nguyen et al. 2013). In this section, we will test the ECSELM and ECSLDA methods on the M^2B database for human beauty study consisting of three tasks: facial, dressing and vocal attractiveness assessment.

10.4.1 M^2B Database

In M^2B database, the facial, dressing and vocal features were from 620 eastern females (i.e. Chinese, Korean and Japanese) and 620 western females (i.e. Caucasian, consisting of Angles, Celtic, Latin and Germanic). For facial beauty analysis, geometric (landmark) and appearance based features were studied separately. The specific details of facial, dressing and vocal feature extraction methods and the attractiveness score acquisition in different modality can be found in (Nguyen et al. 2012). In this chapter, we just expand the study based on the well extracted features. The facial, dressing and vocal features with 300, 300 and 50 dimensions after PCA reduction were used. Some examples of facial images of eastern and western females with landmark points have been shown in Figs. 10.1 and 10.2, respectively. Some examples of dressing images of eastern and western females have been shown in Fig. 10.3. We observe that from Figs. 10.1 and 10.2 the facial images in M^2B database contain similar noise such as illumination, poses, occlusions, and expressions with face recognition. However, these features may have also some relationship with facial attractiveness which is different from the existing work that only fontal faces with restricted setting were used in facial beauty analysis, such that the M^2B data is exploited in this work. The attractiveness scores (ground truth) of facial, dressing and vocal features for each person were normalized within [1, 10] from *k*-wise ratings of raters (Nguyen et al. 2013). The dashed lines in Fig. 10.4 demonstrate that the histogram of facial, dressing, and vocal attractiveness scores statistic belongs to Gaussian distribution.

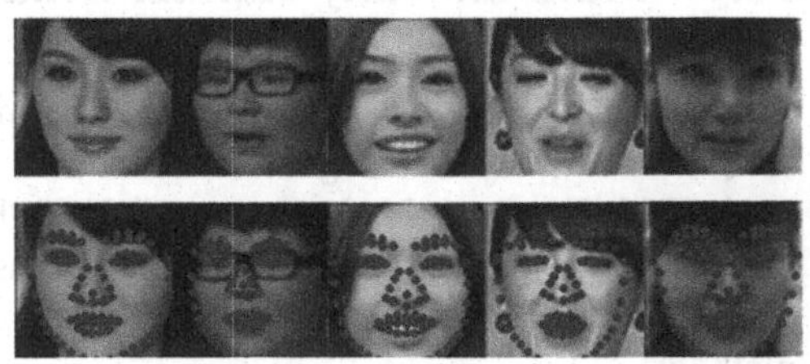

Fig. 10.1 Examples of facial images with landmarks of eastern females

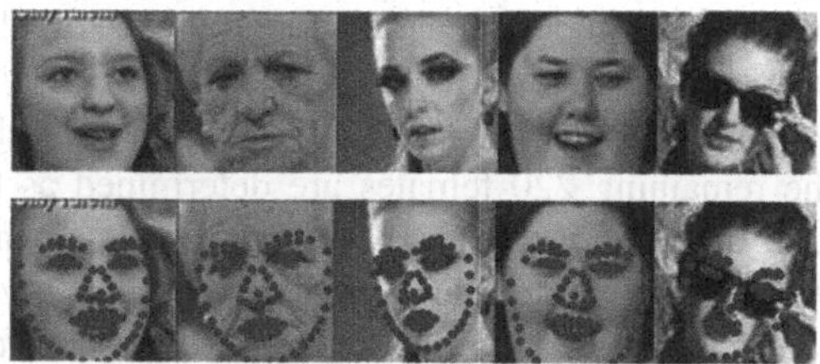

Fig. 10.2 Examples of facial images with landmarks of western females

Fig. 10.3 Examples of eastern (*first row*) and western (*second row*) dressing images in M^{2}B database. Database

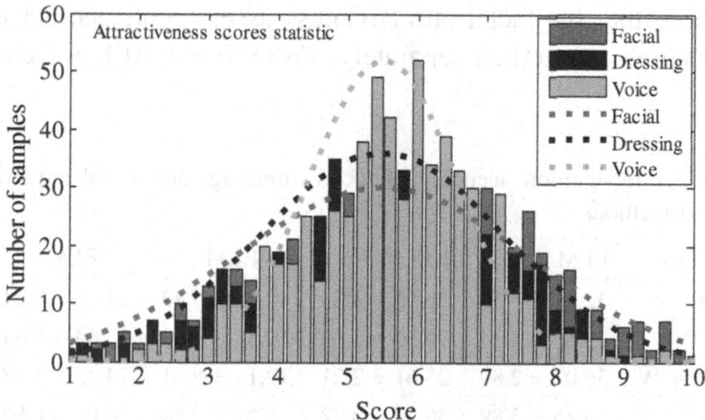

Fig. 10.4 Statistic histogram of facial, dressing and vocal attractiveness scores

10.4.2 Attractiveness Assessment: Beauty Recognition

To qualitatively evaluate the beauty, the raw attractiveness scores within [1, 10] for facial, dressing and vocal features have been divided into five levels, 1 (1–2), 2 (2–4), 3 (4–6), 4 (6–8), and 5 (8–10) which correspond to the beauty quality of "poor", "fair", "good", "very good", and "excellent", respectively. In experiments, the attractiveness assessment of eastern (denoted as "E") and western (denoted as "W") females is studied separately. 400 females are randomly selected as the training set, and the remaining 220 females are determined as the testing set. To share the information between eastern and western females in model training, we fuse the training set of the eastern and western females together (denoted as "E + W"). We do the same on the testing set, so 800 and 440 females are used in the training and testing sets, respectively. Then, for each experiment we run each procedure 10 times, and the average rank-1 recognition accuracy and the standard deviation of each method are provided. The compared methods are divided into the following three categories.

- ELM based methods including ELM, KELM, W^1ELM, and W^2ELM are exploited for each task, in which coefficient C is set to 2^{10}.
- Subspace methods and their cost-sensitive extensions including CSPCA, CSLDA, CSLPP, and CSMFA are studied.
- Generic classifiers including KNN, SVM and LSSVM. We also test CISVM (Liu and Zhou 2010) which was first proposed for addressing the cost-sensitive matrix problem using cost interval. Additionally, we have also compared a cost-sensitive ordinal regression (CSOR) (Yan 2014) that was specially proposed for facial beauty analysis.

Rank-1 recognition rate, which is defined as the ratio of the number of correctly recognized testing samples to the number of total testing samples is adopted to evaluate performance of methods. The rank-1 recognition results of facial, dressing, and vocal attractiveness obtained using ELM based methods are presented in Table 10.1. Note that for facial attractiveness assessment, geometric and appearance based features are studied separately. From Table 10.1, we can find that the

Table 10.1 Rank-1 recognition accuracy of facial, dressing, and vocal attractiveness obtained using ELM based methods

Feature	Race	ELM	KELM	W^1ELM	W^2ELM	ECSELM
Facial (geometric)	E	32.91 ± 5.50	26.05 ± 3.23	19.68 ± 5.42	24.91 ± 8.21	48.51 ± 1.30
	W	33.50 ± 4.34	26.36 ± 5.83	19.55 ± 7.39	23.64 ± 6.41	49.36 ± 1.61
	E + W	36.07 ± 2.89	23.61 ± 2.21	19.11 ± 8.31	24.45 ± 8.68	47.10 ± 1.45
Facial (appearance)	E	33.45 ± 3.89	36.36 ± 8.72	21.91 ± 9.54	24.00 ± 6.98	50.45 ± 0.81
	W	35.23 ± 10.5	34.14 ± 7.70	21.32 ± 9.32	23.77 ± 2.11	52.27 ± 0.92
	E + W	35.45 ± 2.99	38.77 ± 3.36	17.77 ± 3.36	22.43 ± 2.14	45.45 ± 0.84
Dressing	E	37.05 ± 5.80	39.68 ± 14.5	22.91 ± 5.09	28.09 ± 8.09	55.45 ± 1.21
	W	30.09 ± 3.01	35.09 ± 3.71	17.27 ± 6.90	23.55 ± 9.26	47.27 ± 0.98
	E + W	35.75 ± 1.87	38.41 ± 1.84	17.18 ± 3.04	21.43 ± 3.37	50.10 ± 0.82
Vocal	E	44.05 ± 7.08	41.41 ± 2.49	27.91 ± 6.41	30.91 ± 5.79	56.18 ± 0.93
	W	37.14 ± 2.94	35.73 ± 7.41	21.73 ± 9.70	25.45 ± 5.49	54.76 ± 1.13
	E + W	40.84 ± 3.12	34.09 ± 2.02	19.18 ± 3.51	23.57 ± 4.57	50.45 ± 0.91

recognition accuracy obtained by ECSELM for each task is about 20 % higher than other ELMs. Besides, the standard deviation of ECSELM is also much smaller such that the stability of ELM is well improved. It can also be observed that appearance based features are more useful than geometric feature in facial attractiveness assessment.

The results of the ECSLDA method and other subspace methods i.e. PCA, LDA, LPP, MFA, CSPCA, CSLDA, CSLPP, and CSMFA, are shown in Table 10.2. From this table we can see that the accuracy of ECSLDA is about 10 % higher than those of other subspace learning methods, which demonstrates that the evolutionary cost-sensitive framework is effective for determining the optimal projection and the cost matrix plays an important role in cost-sensitive learning mechanism.

Table 10.3 presents the comparisons with the generic classifiers (e.g. KNN, SVM and LSSVM) and two cost-sensitive methods (e.g. CISVM and CSOR) for beauty analysis. The number of nearest neighbors is empirically set as 30. From the results, we have the following conclusions.

- For different tasks, CISVM seems to be worse than other methods. The reason may be that though CISVM attempts to address the problem of cost matrix using available cost interval instead of a precise cost value, the cost interval is still needed to be predefined which may degrade the performance if the cost interval is not selected well. In addition, the training complexity of SVM is incremented, which depends on the specific size of the cost interval.
- Though CSOR is improved in comparison with SVM by introducing cost-sensitive concept, the cost matrix construction is prior defined and lack of flexible property for different tasks and new environments.

Both ECSELM and ECSLDA perform better than the other methods, while ECSELM obtains the best recognition accuracy and its accuracy is about 10 % higher than those of the other methods.

In human attractiveness assessment with 5 level scores from 1 to 5, the cumulative score, which has been tested in (Fu and Huang 2008; Guo et al. 2008; Geng et al. 2007), is also used to measure the aesthetic performance of the proposed methods. The cumulative score can be defined as

$$CumScore(\theta) = N_{es\theta}/N_{test} \times 100\,\%, \tag{10.42}$$

where θ denotes the error level, $N_{es\theta}$ denotes the number of testing instances on which absolute error e between the predicted label and true label less than θ ($\theta = 0, 1, 2, \ldots, c-1$), and N_{test} denotes the number of total testing instances. It is clear that $CumScore(0)$ is equivalent to the rank-1 recognition. The *CumScore* curves of facial, dressing and vocal attractiveness recognition by using ELM and subspace based methods have been illustrated in Figs. 10.5, 10.6, and 10.7, respectively, from which, we can see that the proposed ECSELM and ECSLDA have higher cumulated scores than other methods, and always perform better than others under different error levels.

Table 10.2 Recognition accuracy of facial, dressing, and vocal attractiveness obtained using subspace based methods

Fea	Ra-ce	PCA-NN	CSPCA-NN	LDA-NN	CSLDA-NN	LPP-NN	CSLPP-NN	CSMFA-NN	ECSLDA-NN
Geo	E	29.50 ±1.85	30.27 ±1.96	27.45 ±3.59	28.64 ±2.47	28.86 ±2.28	29.90 ±3.05	29.09 ±3.51	39.54 ±1.01
	W	29.23 ±2.64	29.23 ±2.41	30.22 ± 2.77	30.50 ±2.51	30.77 ±3.91	29.50 ±2.49	29.41 ±1.91	42.73 ±0.91
	E + W	29.16 ±1.27	28.77 ±1.13	29.61 ±1.84	30.18 ±1.90	30.11 ±1.75	30.66 ±1.07	28.82 ±1.56	39.10 ±0.52
App	E	31.41 ±2.38	32.68 ±2.22	28.45 ±0.84	29.41 ±2.19	30.36 ±2.56	30.41 ±2.75	31.82 ±2.48	44.55 ±1.26
	W	28.55 ±2.94	28.55 ±2.26	26.09 ±2.99	26.59 ±2.44	28.91 ±2.34	28.00 ±3.28	31.50 ±2.85	44.55 ±1.80
	E + W	30.11 ±2.47	29.09 ±2.02	34.02 ±1.16	34.48 ±1.87	32.93 ±1.38	33.80 ±1.49	30.84 ±2.18	40.91 ±0.67
Dre	E	35.45 ±3.60	30.41 ±2.78	32.14 ±2.17	33.14 ±2.83	38.68 ±2.96	39.95 ±1.47	37.86 ±4.48	43.18 ±0.75
	W	27.27 ±3.72	24.82 ±2.64	23.55 ±2.12	24.41 ±2.45	23.73 ±4.18	29.09 ±3.34	29.82 ±2.47	38.18 ±1.71
	E + W	29.93 ±1.19	29.57 ±2.31	34.18 ±1.96	33.43 ±2.63	31.41 ±9.67	33.00 ±3.29	31.84 ±1.85	41.51 ±0.77
Voc	E	37.77 ±2.25	38.36 ±3.86	39.77 ±3.46	39.05 ±2.81	43.09 ±3.32	41.59 ±3.12	40.63 ±2.67	53.64 ±0.90
	W	33.14 ±3.50	33.59 ±3.03	34.41 ±2.80	33.91 ±4.33	34.68 ±2.14	34.50 ±2.37	36.77 ±3.07	44.09 ±1.51
	E + W	35.89 ±2.81	35.36 ±1.88	36.61 ±2.12	36.55 ±3.29	38.39 ±2.13	36.32 ±1.30	35.70 ±1.59	43.41 ±0.92

Note Geo-geometric, App-appearance, Dre-dressing, Voc-vocal, Fea-feature

Table 10.3 Recognition accuracy of facial, dressing, and vocal attractiveness obtained using baseline classifiers

Attribute	Race	KNN	SVM	LSSVM	CISVM	CSOR	ECSLDA-NN	ECSELM
Appearance	E	36.45 ±3.03	36.59 ±1.59	36.23 ±2.17	34.91 ±2.79	39.61 ±1.19	44.55 ±1.26	50.45 ±0.81
	W	37.64 ±3.57	38.64 ±2.37	39.59 ±3.11	37.20 ±3.01	42.78 ±1.64	44.55 ±1.80	52.27 ±0.92
	E + W	38.25 ±1.53	37.27 ±1.94	38.52 ±1.58	35.53 ±2.82	40.54 ±1.22	40.91 ±0.67	45.45 ±0.84
Dressing	E	41.13 ±3.22	39.82 ±3.12	40.68 ±2.39	39.59 ±5.23	42.20 ±2.03	43.18 ±0.75	55.45 ±1.21
	W	35.68 ±2.35	36.18 ±2.05	33.50 ±2.75	35.45 ±3.17	35.71 ±2.15	38.18 ±1.71	47.27 ±0.98
	E + W	37.95 ±1.60	35.16 ±1.38	39.68 ±1.43	33.90 ±2.55	41.22 ±1.02	41.51 ±0.77	50.10 ±0.82
Vocal	E	43.30 ±2.97	46.59 ±1.89	47.27 ±3.08	45.50 ±3.15	49.95 ±2.02	53.64 ±0.90	56.18 ±0.93
	W	38.23 ±3.90	39.05 ±3.25	37.18 ±3.09	37.82 ±3.70	40.67 ±2.30	44.09 ±1.51	54.76 ±1.13
	E + W	42.25 ±2.16	40.98 ±1.78	40.05 ±1.07	40.20 ±2.43	42.92 ±1.09	43.41 ±0.92	50.45 ±0.91

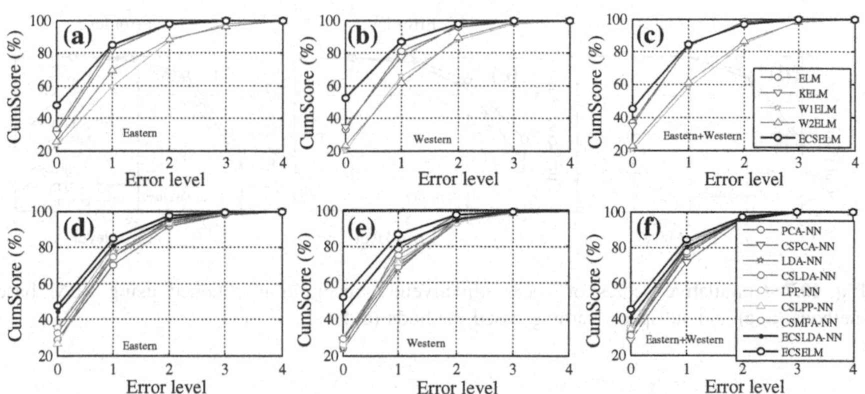

Fig. 10.5 Cumulative scores of facial attractiveness recognition obtained using ELM based methods **(a–c)** and subspace based methods **(d–f)**

Besides the classification, ECSELM is specifically tested in attractiveness score estimation, and further comparisons with the NN, ridge regression, neural network, DFAT (Nguyen et al. 2012), and LDFAT (Nguyen et al. 2013) methods are exploited by strictly following Nguyen et al. (2013) with a standard 2-fold cross validation test in experiments. The cross-validation process is repeated 10 times and the average value is presented to be the final results. In estimation of the attractiveness scores which is scaled within [1 10], the mean absolute error (*MAE*)

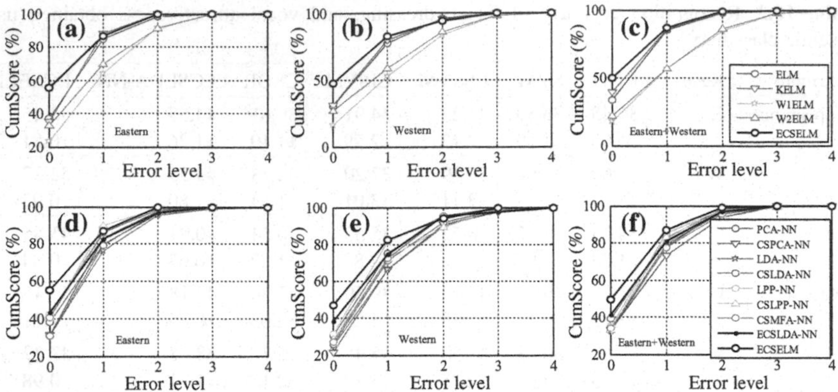

Fig. 10.6 Cumulative scores of dressing attractiveness recognition obtained using ELM based methods (**a**–**c**) and subspace based methods (**d**–**f**)

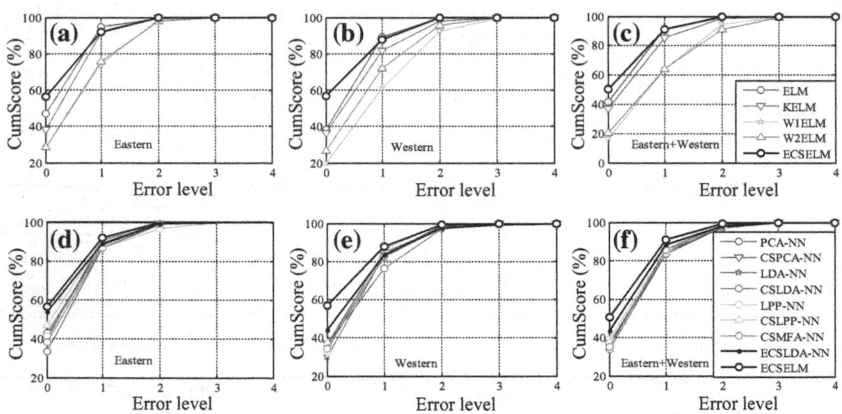

Fig. 10.7 Cumulative scores of vocal attractiveness recognition obtained using ELM based methods (**a**–**c**) and subspace learning based methods (**d**–**f**)

defined as $MAE = \sum_{i=1}^{N_{test}} |\widehat{y}_i - t_i| \Big/ N_{test}$ is used for performance measurement and comparison, where N_{test} is the number of test instances, $\widehat{y}_i$ and t_i are the estimated score and the ground truth of instance i, respectively.

The results of facial, dressing, and vocal attractiveness score estimation are shown in Table 10.4. Note that the appearance based features of facial images are used in facial attractiveness score estimation, and the results of all methods except for the ELM methods are from Nguyen et al. (2012) and Nguyen et al. (2013). It can be found that the ECSELM obtains better estimation performance than LDFAT, which has a more complex structure embedded with an attribute layer for multi-task learning. Vocal attractiveness score prediction is better than prediction of dressing

Table 10.4 MAE of attractiveness score estimation

Method	Facial		Dressing		Vocal	
	E	W	E	W	E	W
NN	2.10	1.91	1.50	2.02	1.39	1.78
Ridge regression	1.89	1.83	1.39	1.76	1.15	1.37
Neural network	1.82	1.75	1.37	1.62	1.12	1.38
DFAT	1.52	1.48	1.26	1.46	1.01	1.24
LDFAT	1.46	1.46	**1.14**	1.37	**0.96**	1.14
ELM	1.55	1.53	1.29	1.56	1.04	1.27
KELM	1.72	1.52	1.32	1.51	1.33	1.77
W^1ELM	1.82	1.79	1.56	1.69	1.54	1.61
W^2ELM	1.71	1.76	1.50	1.69	1.45	1.58
ECSELM	**1.40**	**1.43**	**1.14**	**1.36**	0.97	**1.13**

Table 10.5 MAE of cross-culture attractiveness estimation

Method	Facial		Dressing		Vocal	
	E → W	W → E	E → W	W → E	E → W	W → E
DFAT	1.91	2.22	2.55	2.71	1.55	1.62
LDFAT	1.57	**1.43**	1.61	1.40	1.44	1.32
ELM	1.52	1.56	1.50	1.29	1.27	1.03
KELM	1.57	1.53	1.62	1.52	1.76	1.78
W^1ELM	1.74	1.80	1.73	1.72	1.75	1.60
W^2ELM	1.66	1.71	1.70	1.66	1.72	1.56
ECSELM	**1.47**	1.51	**1.46**	**1.25**	**1.23**	**0.99**

attractiveness, and facial attractiveness score prediction performance is inferior. This may result from the complex features of faces.

To study the aesthetic difference between cultures or races, we have also conducted the cross culture validation experiment, that is, we learn a model from the one culture (eastern/western) and tests on the other culture (western/eastern), denoted as E → W and W → E, alternatively. The attractiveness score estimation results of between-culture are shown in Table 10.5, from which, we can see that ECSELM has the lowest MAE except for the case of W → E in facial attractiveness score prediction in which LDFAT gets the lowest MAE. After comparisons among the three modalities (tasks), the prediction of vocal attractiveness is still better than dressing, and the worst result is for facial attractiveness score estimation.

In summary, for attractiveness recognition, we have compared the ECSELM and ECSLDA methods with ELM methods, subspace analysis methods and popular classifiers. For attractiveness score regression, the results compared with conventional regressions and the newly presented DFAT and LDFAT are given. These results and comparisons fully prove that ECSLDA can make effective discrimination in facial, dressing, and vocal attractiveness by seeking for an optimal projection subspace.

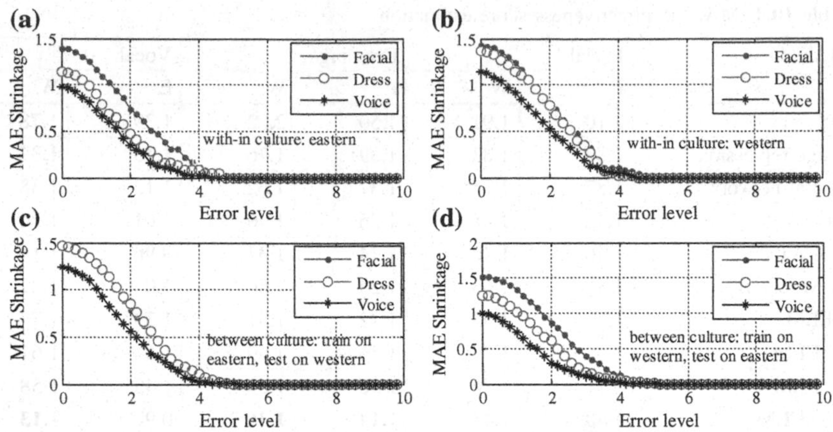

Fig. 10.8 MAE shrinkage: within culture (**a–b**) and between culture (**c–d**) tests

Moreover, ECSELM has the best performance in both recognition and estimation in human beauty assessment.

To study the estimation performance of ECSELM in different error level, a shrinkage error similar to *CumScore* in recognition is conducted. The shrinkage error is defined as

$$ShrinkageError(\rho) = \sum_{k} \left| \widehat{y}_k - t_k \right|_{e \geq \rho} \Big/ N_{test}, \tag{10.43}$$

where ρ denotes the error level, $\widehat{y}$ and t denote the estimated score and ground truth of an instance, and k denotes the index number of instances with the absolute error e higher than ρ ($\rho = 0, 0.2, 0.4, \ldots, 9.8$). It's clear that *ShrinkageError*(0) is equal to MAE.

The *ShrinkageError* curves including within-culture and between-culture cases using ECSELM are described in Fig. 10.8. It is interesting that error of attractiveness score estimation can be ranked as facial, dressing and vocal in descending order, which is in accordance with the Gaussian width shown in Fig. 10.4.

10.5 Performance Analysis

10.5.1 Face Analysis

In this section, we will employ face analysis including face recognition and face verification experiments using the presented methods, and evaluate their potentials in face analysis application. This section aims to test the usefulness of the presented method, whilst the comparisons with those face recognition methods are not concentrated because this work is not specifically presented for face recognition. Therefore, we select two benchmark face data sets, the AR face database (Martinez and Benavente 1998) that contains the faces of 100 persons (50 males and 50 females) and the challenging labeled faces in the wild (LFW) database (Huang et al. 2007) that consists of 13,233 images of 5749 people in unrestricted environments, to test the presented methods.

10.5.1.1 Experiment on AR Dataset

We use the same features as Yang et al. (2011) in which 7 facial images of each person with illumination and expression changes from session 1 were used for training and the other 7 images with the same condition from session 2 were used for testing. Note that the features used in our experiment are the 300-dimensional Eigenface (Turk and Pentland 1991). For fair comparisons, we implement all methods for the same train/test split.

We have compared the evolutionary cost-sensitive methods with generic classifiers (e.g. nearest neighbor, nearest subspace, and linear SVM), cost-sensitive subspace analysis based methods (e.g. CSPCA, CSLPP, CSMFA, and CSLDA), and ELM based methods (e.g. ELM, KELM, and WELM). In addition, three specialized cost sensitive face recognition methods (e.g. mckNN Zhang and Zhou 2010, mcSVM Lee et al. 2004, and mcKLR Zhang and Zhou 2010) are also compared in this chapter. The kernel case of ECSELM is considered in FR application. It's worth noting that the SVM is performed in a linear way and the reported results for baselines are from existing literature (Yang et al. 2011), because the baseline classifiers have been implemented for many times in AR dataset.

The results of the ELM with penalty coefficient $C = 2^5$ and subspace based methods presented in this work are shown in Table 10.6, from which we have the following conclusions.

- KELM shows an obvious advantage in accuracy, which demonstrates that the kernel method may have positive effect on the AR database. More significantly, the cost-sensitive ELM achieves an accuracy of 89.4 % with 2.3 % improvement in comparison with KELM. Hence, the effect of cost-sensitive learning in ELM is demonstrated.
- Among the subspace based methods, CSLPP performs the worst. The possible reason is that in the AR database the low-dimensional features obtained using

Table 10.6 Recognition rates of ELM and cost-sensitive subspace based methods

Methods	ELM	KE-LM	WE-LM	CS-ELM	CS-PCA	CS-LPP	CS-MFA	CS-LDA	ECS-LDA
Recognition rate	81.9	87.1	82.7	**89.4**	68.8	45.5	69.5	86.4	**88.9**

Table 10.7 Comparisons with baselines and state-of-the-art cost-sensitive face recognition methods

Methods	NN	NS	SVM	CISVM	mckNN	mcSVM	mcKLR	ECSELM
Recognition rate	71.4	76.0	87.1	–	83.2	86.6	92.2	**92.7**

LPP is not dominant. Compared with CSPCA and CSMFA, CSLDA achieves much better recognition performance (86.4 %), which shows the discriminative ability of LDA.

The ECSLDA has a 2.5 % improvement in accuracy in comparison with CS-LDA, which demonstrates the significance of the cost matrix.

To evaluate our ECSELM method, we present the results of several popular classifiers and three cost sensitive face recognition methods in Table 10.7, from which we have following conclusions.

- The cost-sensitive face recognition methods (e.g. mckNN, mcSVM and mcKLR) outperform the conventional classifiers. McKLR obtains an accuracy of 92.2 %. McSVM obtains an inferior accuracy of 86.6 %. The results also demonstrate that kernel trick is beneficial to recognition of faces in the AR database.
- The ECSELM method shows the best accuracy of 92.7 % on the AR database among all the existing methods presented in this chapter. Compared with CSELM in Table 10.6, a further improvement of 3.3 % recognition accuracy is obtained. The superior performance demonstrates that the evolutionary cost-sensitive extreme learning machine presented in this chapter is also effective for face recognition. Another merit of ECSELM is that, it can predict the label of a given instance without leveraging the multi-class voting mechanism coupling with multiple binary classifiers (e.g. SVM).

Note that the result of CISVM is not given because there is no report for its use in face recognition. Furthermore, the cumulated score in recognition is calculated using (10.42) with θ in the range of 0 to 99 (there are 100 classes in total). The *CumScore* curves are depicted in Fig. 10.9, which clearly demonstrates that the

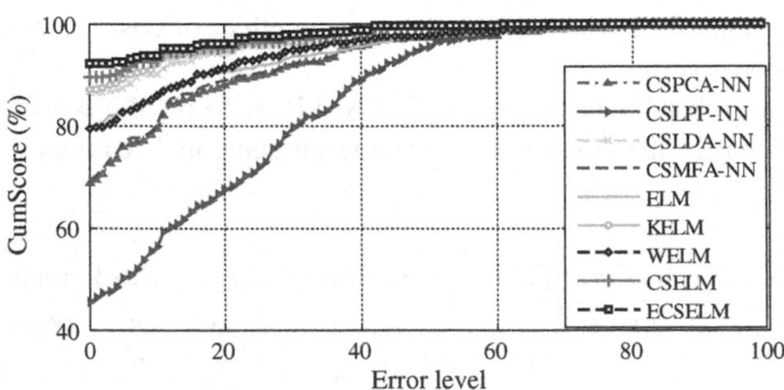

Fig. 10.9 CumScore curves of all the methods

CSELM and ECSELM outperform other methods, and CSLPP method shows the worst performance among all methods. These results prove that ECSELM has a good potential in FR application.

10.5.1.2 Experiment on the LFW Dataset

In this section, we evaluate the ECSELM method on the LFW dataset which is commonly regarded as a challenging dataset for unrestricted face verification and matching. The face images show large variations in poses, illuminations, expressions, and ages, etc. Several sample faces are shown in Fig. 10.10. The aligned version of all faces in LFW, referred to as "funneled" is available. The dataset is organized into two views, view 1 and view 2.

- In *view* 1, a set consisting of 2200 pairs for training and 1000 pairs for testing is developed for model and parameter selection.
- In *view* 2, 6000 pairs for 10-fold cross-validation are developed. In each fold, 600 pairs including 300 similar pairs and 300 dissimilar pairs are set.

Note that the experimental setup for this data set is different from conventional face recognition and most people has only one face image, so it is impossible to take some face images for training, and to use some face images for testing. Therefore, the decision on each pair is generally made as "same" (positive pair) or "not same" (negative pair) without knowing the identity information of each person. Hence, it indeed becomes a binary classification problem.

For this data set, state-of-the-arts methods including metric learning and side information based LDA (Cao et al. 2013; Kan et al. 2011; Nguyen and Bai 2010; Davis et al. 2007; Guillaumin et al. 2009; Ying and Li 2012) are generally explored over intra-personal subspace instead of the generic classifiers (e.g. SVM). To make the evolutionary cost-sensitive extension method suitable for LFW, the appropriate feature vector that can reflect the similarity information should be set for each pair. We conduct the experiments by following the standard protocol of LFW, and the experimental setup is presented as follows.

For each aligned face image, two facial descriptors, local binary patterns (LBP) and scale invariant feature transformation (SIFT), are used to extract features, respectively, and PCA is used for dimension reduction and a obtained 300-dimensional vector is used to represent each face image. The features are generated by authors in (Cao et al. 2013). Due to the lack of full class label

Fig. 10.10 Sample images of one "same" pair and one "not same" pair from LFW

information, for evaluating the above methods in this scenario, we represent a face pair using five similarity metrics, correlation coefficient, Euclidean distance, cosine distance, Mahalanobis distance and bilinear similarity function with positive semi-definite (p.s.d.) matrix learned in Cao et al. (2013). Hence, a 5-dimensional vector is formulated to represent each similar/dissimilar pair, and a binary classifier is trained using the ECSELM method.

Following the 10-fold cross-validation protocol of performance evaluation on *view* 2, 9 folds are used for training, and the remaining folds are used for testing. The average verification accuracy and the standard deviation of 10 times are reported for each method. For performance comparisons, we first compare ELMs with penalty coefficient $C = 2^{10}$ with cost-sensitive subspace analysis based methods presented in this chapter. The results of ELMs and cost-sensitive space methods are shown in Table 10.8, from which we have the following conclusions

- ELM based methods outperform the subspace methods. Nevertheless, the standard deviations of ELMs are higher than those of others methods. The possible reason is that the hidden layer output matrix is activated with randomly generated input weight matrix and bias, which can be improved by the ECS strategy.
- CSMFA shows the worst face verification performance among all the methods. The possible reason is that the constructed locality graph using k nearest neighbors of each input sample may perform badly for the LFW database consisting of many face pairs and the intra sample information is lost.
- Though the ECSLDA outperforms other cost-sensitive subspace methods and demonstrates the effectiveness of the ECS strategy, the ELMs have greater positive effect on face verification and show better potentials.

Further, we compare the ECSELM with recently proposed state-of-the-art metric learning methods including SILD (Kan et al. 2011), KISSME (Kostinger et al. 2012), CSML (Nguyen and Bai 2010), ITML (Davis et al. 2007), LDML (Guillaumin et al. 2009), DML-eig (Ying and Li 2012), and LMLML (Bohne et al. 2014) that have obtained good performance for LFW. The comparison results are shown in Table 10.9, from which we have the following conclusions.

Table 10.8 Recognition rates of ELM and cost-sensitive subspace based methods

Method	LBP descriptor	SIFT descriptor
ELM	85.40 ± 2.81	83.40 ± 1.43
KELM	85.72 ± 3.07	84.37 ± 2.55
WELM	**85.93 ± 2.24**	**84.85 ± 1.35**
CSPCA	82.87 ± 1.18	78.65 ± 1.14
CSLDA	82.45 ± 1.69	79.27 ± 1.23
CSLPP	84.30 ± 1.45	81.65 ± 1.74
CSMFA	53.18 ± 1.70	52.76 ± 1.35
ECSLDA	**85.77 ± 0.83**	**83.43 ± 1.50**

Table 10.9 Comparisons on LFW face verifications

Method	LBP descriptor	SIFT descriptor
SILD	80.07 ± 1.35	80.85 ± 0.61
ITML	83.98 ± 0.48	81.45 ± 0.46
LDML	82.27 ± 0.58	81.05 ± 0.48
CSML	85.57 ± 0.52	–
KISSME	83.37 ± 0.54	83.08 ± 0.56
DML-eig	82.28 ± 0.41	81.27 ± 2.30
SubSML	86.73 ± 0.53	85.55 ± 0.61
LMLML	86.13 ± 0.53	–
ECSELM	**87.97 ± 1.37**	**86.60 ± 1.25**

- SubSML shows better performance in the presented metric learning methods on both descriptors, which reflects the effect of the Mahalanobis distance and bilinear similarity metrics in SubSML. Notably the results on SIFT features were not reported in CSML and LMLML.
- The ECSELM algorithm performs the best among the state-of-the-art metric learning methods for both descriptors. It also presents a new metric re-learning prospective for face verification, with group metrics as input features.

10.5.2 Parameter Sensitivity Analysis

In the ECSELM method, there is only one parameter, i.e. trade-off coefficient C. For different datasets, the parameter variation may show different performance. So, we use different values from the set $\{2^0, 2^5, 2^{10}, 2^{20}, 2^{30}\}$. Figure 10.11 shows the performance variations with different penalty coefficient C, from which we see that the ECSELM and standard ELM are not sensitive to the trade-off parameter variation, and better performance for AR and LFW is obtained when C is set as 2^5, 2^{10}, and 2^{20}, respectively. Notably, WELM is denoted by W^2ELM.

Additionally, we also study the performance variation with different numbers of hidden neurons i.e. L. By fixing the best C for each data, we select L from the set $\{100, 200, 300, 400, 500\}$, and run the ELMs. The results are shown in Fig. 10.12, from which we observe that the there is no large performance variation of the

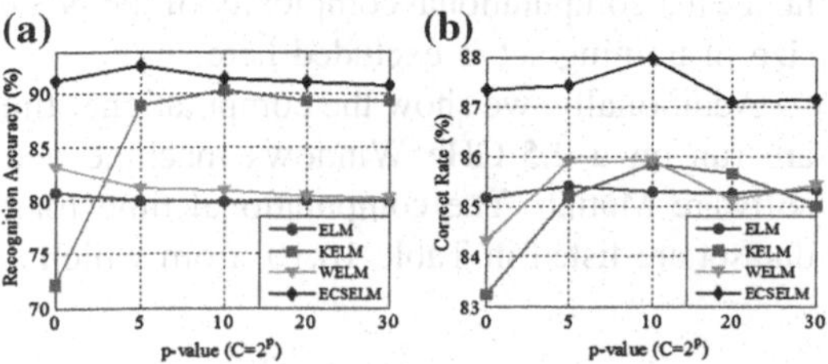

Fig. 10.11 Performance variation w.r.t. the trade-off parameter C = 2p in ELM based methods: **a** AR with L = 300; **b** LFW with L = 100

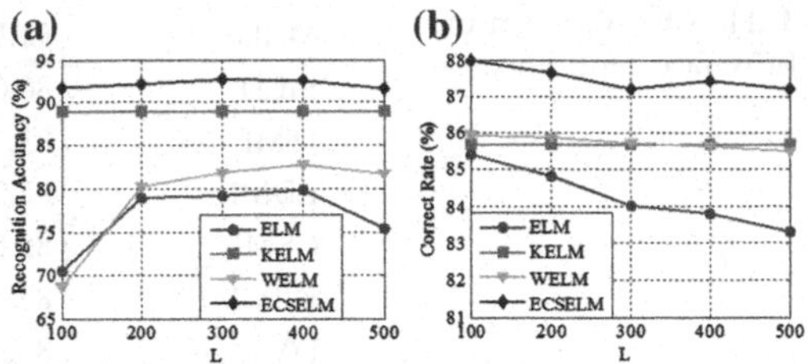

Fig. 10.12 Performance variation w.r.t. the number of hidden neurons L in ELMs: **a** AR with C = 25; **b** LFW with C = 210

ECSELM w.r.t. *L*, whereas the performance of standard ELM drops dramatically for LFW when *L* is larger than 200. So, the best *L* for AR, LFW can be set as 300, 100, and 200. Note that the hidden layer output matrix of KELM generated from the training samples through a kernel mapping is not associated with *L*, and the recognition performance of KELM is invariable. In summary, the ECSELM method is quite robust to the variation of model parameter *C* and the number *L* of hidden neurons. Therefore, the parameter selection is free for our method and can be empirically determined.

10.5.3 Computational Complexity Analysis

The CSELM, ECSELM and ECSLDA algorithms are computationally efficient. For ECSELM, the main steps of Algorithm 10.1 are involved in computing the matrix inverse $(\frac{1}{c} + diag(\boldsymbol{B})\mathbf{H}\mathbf{H}^{\mathrm{T}})^{-1}$ or $(\frac{1}{c} + \mathbf{H}^{\mathrm{T}} diag(\boldsymbol{B})\mathbf{H})^{-1}$, and the search of the optimal multiplier vector $\boldsymbol{B}$ representing cost information using Algorithm 10.2. The hidden layer output matrix **H** can be pre-computed. The matrix multiplication for two matrices of size $m \times n$ and $n \times p$ has a computational cost of $O(mnp)$. The complexity of Algorithm 10.2 depends on population size *N*, problem dimension *D* (i.e. the length of vector $\boldsymbol{B}$), and the number *epochs* of iterations in loop, i.e. $O(N \cdot epochs)$. In the ECSELM method, the above matrix computing is embedded into the loop of optimization, so the computational cost is $O(N \cdot epochs \cdot m \cdot n \cdot p)$.

For the evolutionary cost-sensitive extension to LDA, it only involves the computational complexity of Algorithm 10.2, related with population size *N* and the number epochs for loop. Therefore, compared with LDA, the evolutionary cost-sensitive extension to LDA has the extra complexity of $O(N \cdot epochs)$. Note that the nearest neighbor classifier for recognition is used for all subspace methods, and hence the computational complexity of the NN classifier that depends largely on the size of training set is excluded here.

Additionally, we show the computational time of the algorithms. The algorithms are run on a 2.5 GHz Windows machine and are implemented on the basis of software Matlab. The computational time for face verification on the large LFW dataset are listed in Table 10.10, from which we have the following conclusions.

Table 10.10 Computational time on the LFW data set for training and testing in one fold

Method	ELM	KELM	WELM	CSPCA	CSLDA	CSLPP	CSMFA	ECSLDA	ECSELM
Time(s)	2.61	58.48	4.47	412.08	26.39	331.77	6731.9	2318.1	237.81

- KELM needs more computations than ELM and WELM. This is caused by computing the output weights on a higher-dimensional kernel matrix.
- CSPCA and CSLPP cost too much time comparably. For the former, the time is mainly spent on computation of the covariance matrix with a large training set. For the latter, most time is spent by constructing a nearest neighbor graph on the training set. ELMs have much higher computational efficiency than subspace methods, especially for large scale datasets. The subspace methods taken most time in the NN classifier which shows low efficiency when the size of the training set is larger.
- The CSMFA spends the most time among all the methods. The reason is that the time is mostly spent on the computation of the locality graph where k nearest neighbors should be searched for each input vector.
- The ECSLDA method spends much computational time (2318.1 s) with a continuous search in a solution space. Nevertheless, ECSELM still inherits the very low computational complexity of conventional ELM.

10.6 Summary

In this chapter, we first introduce the conventional ELM, kernel ELM and weighted ELM algorithms. Then we focus on an evolutionary cost-sensitive extreme learning machine (ECSELM) to address the robust recognition and regression of ELM in attractiveness analysis and related tasks. Specifically, the evolutionary cost-sensitive framework is explored for guiding the users to free determine the cost information matrix. A subspace extension of linear discriminant analysis (i.e. ECSLDA) is also presented for improvement of those conventional cost-sensitive subspace learning methods (e.g. CSLDA). Experiments in a variety of fields on cost-sensitive learning tasks such as multi-modal human beauty analysis (e.g. facial, dressing and vocal attractiveness assessment) and face analysis fully demonstrate the efficiency, effectiveness and generality of the ECSELM and ECSLDA methods.

References

Bartlett PL (1998) The sample complexity of pattern classification with neural networks: the size of the weights is more important than the size of the network. IEEE Trans Inf Theory 44 (2):525–536

Belhumeur PN, Hespanha J, Kriegman DJ (1997) Eigenfaces vs. fisherfaces: recognition using class specific linear projection. IEEE Trans Pattern Anal Mach Intell 19(7):711–720

Bohné J, Ying Y, Gentric S, Pontil M (2014) Large margin local metric learning. In: Proceedings of European conference on computer vision, pp 679–694

Cao Q, Ying Y, Li P (2013) Similarity metric learning for face recognition. In: Proceedings of IEEE international conference on computer vision, pp 2408–2415

Chacko BP, Krishnan VV, Raju G, Anto PB (2012) Handwritten character recognition using wavelet energy and extreme learning machine. Int J Mach Learn Cybernet 3(2):149–161

Civicioglu P (2013) Backtracking search optimization llgorithm for numerical optimization problems. Appl Math Comput 219(15):8121–8144

Davis J, Kulis B, Jain P, Sra S, Dhillon I (2007) Information theoretic metric learning. In: Proceedings of international conference on Machine learning, pp 209–216

Deng WY, Zheng QH, Wang ZM (2014) Cross-person activity recognition using reduced kernel extreme learning machine. Neural Networks 53:1–7

Eisenthal Y, Dror G (2006) Facial attractiveness: beauty and the machine. Neural Comput 18 (1):119–142

Fan J, Chau KP, Wan X, Zhai L, Lau E (2012) Prediction of facial attractiveness from facial proportions. Pattern Recogn 45(6):2326–2334

Fu Y, Huang TS (2008) Human age estimation with regression on discriminative aging manifold. IEEE Trans Multimedia 10(4):578–584

Geng X, Zhou ZH, Smith-Miles K (2007) Automatic age estimation based on facial aging patterns. IEEE Trans Pattern Anal Mach Intell 29(12):2234–2240

Gray D, Yu K, Xu W (2010) Predicting facial beauty without landmarks. In: Proceedings of European conference on computer vision, pp 434–447

Guillaumin M, Verbeek J, Schmid C (2009) Is that you? Metric learning approaches for face identification. In: Proceedings of IEEE international conference on computer vision, pp 498–505

Guo G, Fu Y, Dyer C, Huang T (2008) Image-based human age estimation by manifold learning and locally adjusted robust regression. IEEE Trans Image Process 17(7):1178–1188

He X, Yan S, Hu Y, Niyogi P, Zhang HJ (2005) Face recognition using Laplacianfaces. IEEE Trans Pattern Anal Mach Intell 27(3):328–340

Huang G, Ramesh M, Berg T, Learned-Miller E (2007) Labeled Faces in the Wild: a database for studying face recognition in unconstrained environments. Technical Report, Amherst

Huang GB, Chen L (2007) Convex incremental extreme learning machine. Neurocomputing 70 (16):3056–3062

Huang GB, Chen L (2008) Enhanced random search based incremental extreme learning machine. Neurocomputing 71(16):3460–3468

Huang GB, Chen L, Siew CK (2006a) Universal approximation using incremental constructive feedforward networks with random hidden nodes. IEEE Trans Neural Networks 17(4):879–892

Huang GB, Zhu QY, Siew CK (2006b) Extreme learning machine: theory and applications. Neurocomputing 70:489–501

Huang GB, Ding XJ, Zhou HM (2010) Optimization method based extreme learning machine for classification. Neurocomputing 74(1–3):155–163

Huang GB, Zhou H, Ding X, Zhang R (2012) Extreme learning machine for regression and multiclass classification. IEEE Trans Syst Man Cybern Part B 42(2):513–529

Iosifidis A, Tefas A, Pitas L (2013) Dynamic action recognition based on dynemes and extreme Learning Machine. Pattern Recogn Lett 34(15):1890–1898

Kan M, Shan S, Xu D, Chen X (2011) Side-information based linear discriminant analysis for face recognition. In: Proceedings of British machine vision conference, pp 1–12

Kostinger M, Hirzer M, Wohlhart P, Roth P M, Bischof H (2012) Large scale metric learning from equivalence constraints. In: Proceedings of IEEE conference on computer vision and pattern recognition, pp 2288–2295

Lee Y, Lin Y, Wahba G (2004) Multicategory support vector machines, theory, and application to the classification of microarray data and satellite radiance data. J Am Stat Assoc 99(465):67–81

Li K, Kong X, Lu Z, Liu W, Yin J (2014) Boosting weighted ELM for imbalanced learning. Neurocomputing 128:15–21

Liu X Y, Zhou Z H (2010) Learning with cost intervals. In: Proceedings of ACM SIGKDD international conference on Knowledge discovery and data mining, pp 403–412
Lu J, Tan Y P (2010) Cost-sensitive subspace learning for face recognition. In: Proceedings of IEEE conference on computer vision and pattern recognition, pp 2661–2666
Lu J, Tan YP (2013) Cost-sensitive subspace analysis and extensions for face recognition. IEEE Trans Inf Forensics Secur 8(3):510–519
Martinez A, Benavente R (1998) The AR face database. CVC Technical Report 24
Mohammed AA, Minhas R, Wu QMJ, Sid-Ahmed MA (2011) Human face recognition based on multidimensional PCA and extreme learning machine. Pattern Recogn 44(10):2588–2597
Nguyen H V, Bai L (2010) Cosine similarity metric learning for face verification. In: Proceedings of Asian conference on computer vision, pp 709–720
Nguyen T V, Liu S, Ni B, Tan J, Rui Y, Yan S (2012) Sense beauty via face, dressing, and/or voice. In: Proceedings of ACM international conference on multimedia, pp 239–248
Nguyen T V, Liu S, Ni B, Tan J, Rui Y, Yan S (2013) Towards decrypting attractiveness via multi-modality cues. ACM Trans Multimedia Comput Commun Appl **9**(4):28:1–28:20
Turk M, Pentland A (1991) Eigenfaces for recognition. J Cogn Neurosci 3(1):71–86
Yan H (2014) Cost-sensitive ordinal regression for fully automatic facial beauty assessment. Neurocomputing 129:334–342
Yan S, Liu J, Tang X, Huang T (2007a) A parameter-free framework for general supervised subspace learning. IEEE Trans Inf Forensics Secur 2(1):69–76
Yan S, Xu D, Yang Q, Zhang L, Tang X, Zhang H (2007b) Multilinear discriminant analysis for face recognition. IEEE Trans Image Process 16(1):212–220
Yan S, Xu D, Zhang B, Zhang H, Yang Q, Lin S (2007c) Graph embedding and extensions: a general framework for dimensionality reduction. IEEE Trans Pattern Anal Mach Intell 29 (1):40–51
Yang M, Zhang L, Feng X, Zhang D (2011) Fisher discrimination dictionary learning for sparse representation. In: Proceeding of international conference on computer vision, pp 543–550
Ying Y, Li P (2012) Distance metric learning with eigenvalue optimization. J Mach Learn Res 13 (1):1–26
Zhang D, Zhao Q, Chen F (2011) Quantitative analysis of human facial beauty using geometric features. Pattern Recogn 44(4):940–950
Zhang Y, Zhou ZH (2010) Cost-sensitive face recognition. IEEE Trans Pattern Anal Mach Intell 32(10):1758–1769
Zhu QY, Qin AK, Suganthan PN, Huang GB (2005) Evolutionary extreme learning machine. Pattern Recogn 38(10):1759–1763
Zong W, Huang GB (2011) Face recognition based on extreme learning machine. Neurocomputting 74(16):2541–2551
Zong W, Huang GB, Chen Y (2013) Weighted extreme learning machine for imbalance learning. Neurocomputing 101:229–242

Chapter 11
Combining a Causal Effect Criterion for Evaluation of Facial Beauty Models

As a data-driven facial beauty modeling method, evolutionary cost-sensitive extreme learning machine presented in Chap. 10 shows the potential of the machine learning methodology in facial beauty analysis. As we know, machine learning methods usually depend on a large amount of data to obtain the conclusion or reasoning. For facial beauty analysis, it is always difficult to collect extensive facial images and to label them. As a result, the means to sufficiently exploit limited data to perform learning is crucial. With this chapter, we pay our main attention on generating more available training data and exploiting original and generated data to conduct model learning on facial beauty analysis. The proposed method can be viewed as a data-driven model learning method based on the causal effect criterion. This chapter is organized as follows. Section 11.1 introduces the related work of facial attractiveness study. In Sect. 11.2, we present a novel model assessment method with a causal effect criterion and we present two approaches to measure it. Section 11.3 describes the method of facial beauty modeling. Section 11.4 presents a model based facial beauty manipulation method. Experimental results are shown in Sect. 11.5, and we conclude the chapter in Sect. 11.6.

11.1 Introduction

Compared with other facial analysis tasks (e.g., face recognition, facial expression classification, age estimation, etc.), facial attractiveness study has the following challenges. First, data collection is difficult. It is partly because the face images are required to cover a wide range of attractiveness, especially sufficient beautiful faces. As far as we know, no public face database satisfies this requirement. And it is partly because collecting labels (e.g. human ratings) is extremely laborious and expensive. Second, due to the scarcity of beautiful faces in daily life, the images used in facial attractiveness study are often collected from the web. There are uncontrollable external variations such as illuminations, occlusions, and image

D. Zhang et al., *Computer Models for Facial Beauty Analysis*,
DOI 10.1007/978-3-319-32598-9_11

quality. Third, the aims of facial attractiveness study are beyond prediction. As shown in Fig. 11.1, the three modules are closely related. The understanding module can promote the researches on prediction (Eisenthal et al. 2006; Gunes and Piccardi 2006; Schmid et al. 2008; Fan et al. 2012) and manipulation (Liao et al. 2012) by supplying empirical knowledge, and the performances of prediction and manipulation modules can verify the validity of the understanding (Perrett et al. 1994; Pallett et al. 2010; Zhang et al. 2011). A valid computational model of facial attractiveness could promote all the three modules, e.g., deepening the understanding of facial attractiveness perception, estimating the attractiveness of an input face image, and guiding the manipulation on the face image to enhance its attractiveness.

As introduced in Chap. 9, different kinds of features were extracted and used to build computational models of facial attractiveness by supervised learning methods. Existing works depend only on associations of features to obtain high prediction accuracy. However, association is not causation. Hence, a model with high prediction accuracy may fail in interpretation and manipulation. It is easy to understand that a model with strong causal effect is more likely to approach the true attractiveness perception rules. Moreover, knowing the causal effect, we can expect the outcomes of different manipulations on face images. However, almost no work considers the causal effect when building facial attractiveness models. In this chapter, we present a model assessment method by using a causal effect criterion and we also present two approaches to measure it. The post-intervention images and the original ones constitute two groups of stimuli. Then we ask participants to give judgments to the stimuli and evaluate the effect of the intervention by analyzing the judgment results. Though this approach is reliable, the cost of perceptual experiments is very high. Hence, we present another approach to estimate the causal

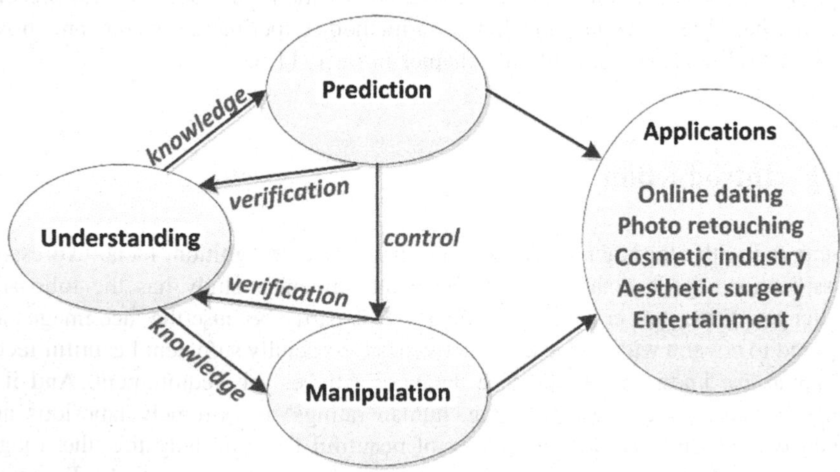

Fig. 11.1 Relationships between understanding, prediction, and manipulation modules in facial attractiveness study

effect. The original and post-intervention images are represented in the feature space. Given a training set, a joint distribution between features and attractiveness can be estimated. Based on this distribution, we estimate the post-intervention attractiveness. The difference between the post-intervention attractiveness and original attractiveness is used to measure the causal effect.

11.2 Causal Effect Criterion

A computational model of facial attractiveness can be represented by a function, i.e., $Y = f(X)$, where X is a feature vector and Y is the attractiveness score predicted by the model. Obviously, the model is determined by feature vector X and function form f. By using different features and function forms, we can obtain different models. A question is which model is better. A commonly used criterion to assess a model is the prediction accuracy of the model, which is measured by the correlation between the predicted scores and ground truth scores given by human ratings. This criterion is competent for the attractiveness prediction problem. However, it is problematic for attractiveness manipulation problems such as face beautification. For example, suppose the feature vector is two-dimensional, a set of training data is denoted by $[x_1, y_1, x_2, y_2, \ldots, x_n, y_n]$, as shown in Fig. 11.2a. The attractiveness scores are represented by the colors from blue to red, where red represents high scores. We can learn a model illustrated in Fig. 11.2b by linear regression. In Fig. 11.2c, we normalized the features into unit variance and obtained the model shown in Fig. 11.2d. Because X and f are different, the two models are different. They will achieve the same performance in terms of the prediction accuracy

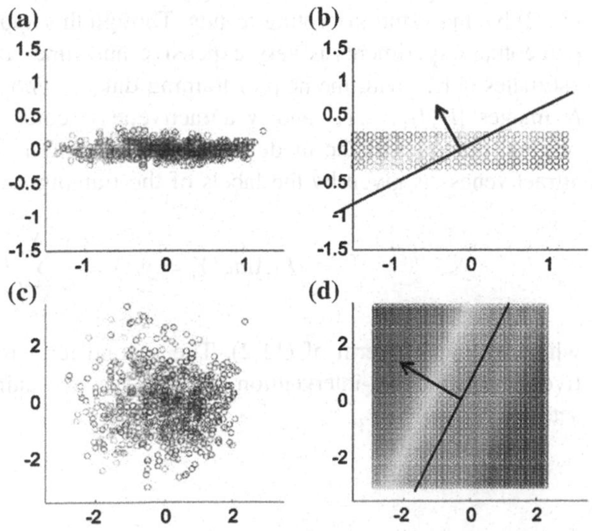

Fig. 11.2 Illustration of the difference between prediction accuracy and causal effect criteria. **a** Scatter plot of training data. **b** Attractiveness function learned from (**a**). **c** Normalization of (**a**). **d** Attractiveness function learned from (**c**). The two models have the same prediction performance but different causal effects

criterion. We wonder whether they also perform the same for attractiveness manipulation or not. Unluckily, the answer is no. Given a model $f(x)$, attractiveness manipulation is guided by the derivative of the model, i.e., moving x along the direction that increases the attractiveness fastest. As shown in Fig. 11.2b, d, the two directions are different. In Fig. 11.2b, due to the finite definition domain in the feature space, it cannot increase the attractiveness much, whereas in Fig. 11.2d, the attractiveness of most data points can be largely increased. Hence, the second model is better than the first one when used for attractiveness manipulation.

As we know, the prediction problem is determined by association, whereas the manipulation problem is determined by causation. Hence, causal effect is also an important index when we verify and evaluate computational models. The causal effect of X_i on Y is defined as

$$E(Y|do(X_i = x_i + 1)) - E(Y|do(X_i = x_i)), \tag{11.1}$$

where $E(Y|do(X_i = x_i))$ is the post-intervention average value of Y that would occur if we forced $X_i = x_i$ by external intervention, and $do(\cdot)$ is Pearl's *do*-operator. In this chapter, we want to measure the causal effect of model $Y = f(X)$ on attractiveness A. Note that Y is the outcome of the model, whereas A is the perceived attractiveness. The average causal effect can be measured by

$$E(A|do(Y_i = y_i + 1)) - E(A|do(Y_i = y_i)), \tag{11.2}$$

where $Y_i = f_i(X)$. We use subscript i to distinguish different models. $do(Y_i = y_i + 1)$ means to modify each face image to increase the model outcome by 1.

Here we show how to quantify (11.2). A straightforward approach imposes interventions according to the model and generates post-intervention face images. Taking the original images and post-intervention images as two groups of stimuli, we ask participants to give their judgments, e.g., make a vote. Then we can quantify (11.2) by analyzing the voting results. Though this approach is reliable, performing perceptual experiments is very expensive and time consuming. Another approach estimates (11.2) with the help of training data. Suppose that a training set contains N images $[I_1, I_2, \ldots, I_N]$ and N attractiveness scores $[l_1, l_2, \ldots, l_N]$. Let y_i be the original outcome of the model, i.e., no intervention is performed. The perceived attractiveness is given by the labels of the training set and is defined by

$$E(A|do(Y_i = y_i)) = \frac{1}{N}\sum_{n=1}^{N} l_n, \tag{11.3}$$

which is the first term of (11.2). The second term is the mean perceived attractiveness of the post-intervention images. We can estimate it utilizing the training set, i.e.,

$$E(A|do(Y_i = y_i + 1)) = \frac{1}{N} \sum_{n=1}^{N} \sum_{x_k \in N(x_n + \Delta x_n)} w_k l_k \quad (11.4)$$

where Δx_n satisfies

$$f_i(x_n + \Delta x_n) = f_i(x_n) + 1, \quad (11.5)$$

$x_n + \Delta x_n$ is the feature of the face image after intervention. x_k is the feature of the training data that locates at the neighborhood of $x_n + \Delta x_n$. w_k is the weight which is inversely proportional to the square of the distance between x_k and $x_n + \Delta x_n$, i.e.,

$$w_k \propto \frac{1}{\|x_n + \Delta x_n - x_k\|^2}, \quad \sum_k w_k = 1. \quad (11.6)$$

We can see that the attractiveness of the post-intervention face is estimated by the weighted average of the attractiveness of the faces in its neighborhood. Then the average causal effect (11.2) can be obtained by (11.3) and (11.4).

11.3 Facial Beauty Modeling

A computational model is determined by features and a function. In this section, we first analyze and compare different facial features for facial attractiveness modeling. Then we apply manifold embedding algorithms for dimensionality reduction and build models by regression methods.

11.3.1 Feature Extraction

In this chapter, the geometric features and texture features which have been introduced in Sect. 6.2 of Chap. 6 are extracted for facial attractiveness prediction. Geometric features include the ratios and shape. The ratio features often come from putative rules, such as golden ratio rules, vertical thirds, and horizontal fifths. We have introduced the ratio feature in detail in Sect. 5.2.3 of Chap. 5. The shape feature is represented by a set of landmarks. In this chapter, we also use the face landmark model with 98 landmarks which is introduced in Chap. 3. The x- and y- coordinates of the landmarks are concatenated to form a vector, i.e.,

$$G = (x_1, x_2, \ldots, x_{98}, y_1, y_2, \ldots, y_{98}). \quad (11.7)$$

Procrustes superimposition (Dryden and Mardia 1998) is performed to filter out the location, scale, and rotation variations. The results are called shape features, denoted by X_s. The implementation details can be found in Chen and Zhang (2010). Texture features include eigenface representation (Kirby and Sirovich 1990), Gabor filter response (Liu and Wechsler 2002), and local binary patterns (LBP) (Ahonen et al. 2006). Eigenface was adopted for facial attractiveness prediction in Eisenthal et al. (2006). Face images are represented in vector form and PCA is performed to obtain a set of bases. Projecting an input face vector to these bases, we can obtain a low-dimensional representation of the face image, which is called eigenface representation. Gabor and LBP features are very popular in the field of face recognition and were used for facial attractiveness prediction (Nguyen et al. 2013). Gabor filters encode facial shape and texture information over a range of spatial scales (Liu and Wechsler 2002). The LBP operator encodes every pixel of an image with an 8-bit binary number by thresholding the neighborhood of the pixel with the center pixel value (Ahonen et al. 2006), and the histogram of the labels is used as a texture descriptor.

As facial attractiveness depends on both the shape and the texture of a face, AAM features also have potential for facial attractiveness modeling, although it has not been used in existing works. AAM is a model-based coding approach, which parameterizes and combines the shape and the texture of a face (Cootes et al. 2001). The shape, eigenface, AAM, Gabor and LBP features have introduced in detail in Sect. 7.2 of Chap. 7.

The first step of building the model is to determine which feature is better. We examine the features from two aspects. One is discriminative power, which is quantified by classification and regression performances. Different classifiers and regression methods are tested and the best performance achieved by each type of feature is reported in Table 11.1. In our implementation, the face images are aligned and cropped when extracting eigenface, Gabor, and LBP features. The parameters of the Gabor filters are set following Liu and Wechsler (2002). When extracting the LBP features, the face images are divided into 7×7 local regions and the $\mathrm{LBP}_{8,2}^{u2}$ operator is applied to each region. The notation of the LBP operator follows Ahonen et al. (2006). The original Gabor and LBP features are of very high dimensions. To avoid the effects of the curse of the dimensionality, we perform PCA to reduce the dimensionality to 100. From Table 11.1, we can see that AAM

Table 11.1 Comparison of facial features

Feature	Classification (%)	Regression (r)	Manipulation
Ratio	87.14	0.7601	Available
Shape	90.47	0.7910	Available
Eigenface	91.23	0.8004	Available
AAM	**95.06**	**0.8593**	Available
$\mathrm{LBP}_{8,2}^{u2}$	94.57	0.8332	Not available
Gabor	95.04	0.8382	Not available

features outperform other features for both classification and regression cases. The second aspect is manipulation convenience, i.e., analyzing if we can generate post-intervention images by manipulating the features. This character is important for causal effect measurement and attractiveness manipulation problems. By using image warping methods, such as moving least squares (MLS) (Schaefer and McPhail 2006) and thin plate splines (TPS) (Bookstein 1989), we can modify the ratio and shape features of face images. Eigenface and AAM features are compact representations of face images. Given the modified features after intervention, it is convenient to reconstruct face images by linear transformations. However, the extraction of LBP and Gabor features has unrecoverable information loss and it is hard to reconstruct images from them. Hence, we cannot obtain the post-intervention face images after manipulating LBP and Gabor features.

Table 11.1 presents a summary of the comparison of different features. We can see that AAM features have both competitive discriminative ability and manipulation convenience. Therefore, in this chapter, we select AAM features to build the computational models.

11.3.2 Manifold Learning and Attractiveness Regression

AAM features form a compact representation of face images. However, not every element in the AAM features is related to attractiveness because there are many external variations such as illumination. In order to isolate the unrelated variations and reduce the feature dimensionality, we apply manifold learning algorithms on the AAM features.

Suppose the image space is sampled by a set of face images $X = \{x_i : x_i \in R^D\}_{i=1}^n$ with feature dimension D. The attractiveness scores given by human raters provide a ground truth set $L = \{l_i : l_i \in R\}_{i=1}^n$. The goal of attractiveness manifold learning is to find a low-dimensional representation in the embedded subspace, capturing the intrinsic structures within data and its representation $U = \{u_i : u_i \in R^d\}_{i=1}^n$ with $d < D$, which is a one to one mapping to X. In this chapter, we focus on linear manifold, i.e., the objective is to find an $D \times d$ matrix P satisfying

$$U = P^T X, \tag{11.8}$$

where $U = \{u_1, \ldots, u_n\}$, $X = \{x_1, \ldots, x_n\}$, $P = \{p_1, \ldots, p_d\}$, and $d < n$. PCA, LDA, and LPP are three typical linear manifold embedding methods based on different optimization criteria. PCA seeks a projection that best represents the data in a least-squares sense. LDA (Duda et al. 2000) seeks a projection that best separates the data in a least-squares sense. LPP (He and Niyogi 2003) seeks a projection that best preserves the neighborhood structure. PCA is an unsupervised method, whereas LDA and LPP are supervised methods. We perform the three methods on our database. Experimental results show that the LDA manifold outperforms the PCA and LPP manifolds in attractiveness prediction (see Sect. 11.5.1 for details). The LDA projection matrix is given by maximizing the criterion function

$$J(P) = \frac{|P^T S_B P|}{|P_T S_W P|}, \tag{11.9}$$

where S_B is the between-class scatter matrix, and S_W is the within-class scatter matrix. The attractiveness scores can be discretized into c levels, and

$$S_B = \sum_{k=1}^{c} n_k (m_k - m)(m_k - m)^T, \tag{11.10}$$

$$S_W = \sum_{k=1}^{c} \sum_{x \in D_k} (x - m_k)(x - m_k)^T, \tag{11.11}$$

where n_k is the number of samples in level k, m_k is the mean vector of level k, and m is the mean vector of all data. Projection matrix P can be solved by finding the generalized eigenvectors that correspond to the largest eigenvalues in

$$S_B p_i = \lambda_i S_W p_i. \tag{11.12}$$

Given a set of face images embedded in a linear manifold, an attractiveness function can be learned, which models the relationship between the images and the attractiveness scores, i.e.,

$$y = f(u), \tag{11.13}$$

where y is the attractiveness score, u is a point in the manifold. Linear regression (LR) (Chatterjee and Hadi 1986) and SVR (Vapnik 1995) are two popular techniques to estimate attractiveness function f (Schmid et al. 2008; Leyvand et al. 2008). Using LR, we can obtain the attractiveness function in an explicit form as

$$y = w^T u + w_0, \tag{11.14}$$

where w and w_0 are model parameters. With radial basis function (RBF) kernels, SVR can model nonlinearity structure, but the model cannot be explicitly expressed. We build models with both regression methods and find that the prediction performance, causal effect of the linear model and the SVR model are very similar (see Sect. 11.5 for details).

11.3.3 Feature Normalization and Model Causality

It is worth emphasizing that a normalization step before manifold learning and attractiveness regression is critical to the causality of the model and the performance of attractiveness manipulation. Without this step, the learned model will give large weights on insignificant feature components and result in small causal effect. The performance of attractiveness manipulation is closely related to the model causality. The normalized AAM features can be obtained by

$$X = \sum{}^{-1} b, \tag{11.15}$$

where $\sum = diag(\lambda_1, \lambda_2, \ldots, \lambda_{100})$, b is the AAM features (The AAM features is introduced in detail in Sect. 7.2.4 of Chap. 7). For manifold learning, feature normalization has no effect on the data distribution in the LDA manifold. However, the PCA and LPP manifolds learned on the normalized features will be much different from those learned on the original features, because feature normalization changes the distance metric.

11.4 Model Based Facial Beauty Manipulation

Guided by facial attractiveness models, we can manipulate the features to increase the attractiveness score y. For linear models defined in (11.14), the gradient of y with respect to feature x is

$$\nabla_x y = \nabla_x w^T u = \nabla_x w^T P^T x = Pw, \tag{11.16}$$

which indicates the manipulation orientation. The amount of movement can also be controlled. Suppose we want to increase the attractiveness score by t, then the modified features will be

$$\tilde{x} = x + t\frac{Pw}{\|pw\|_2^2}. \tag{11.17}$$

For the nonlinear model obtained by SVR, the manipulation orientation is calculated by numerical differentiation. In the gradient descent/ascent way, we move the features to approach the desired attractiveness. If there is a normalization step before learning the model, $\tilde{x}$ has to be weighted to obtain the final AAM features, i.e.,

$$b = \sum \tilde{x}, \tag{11.18}$$

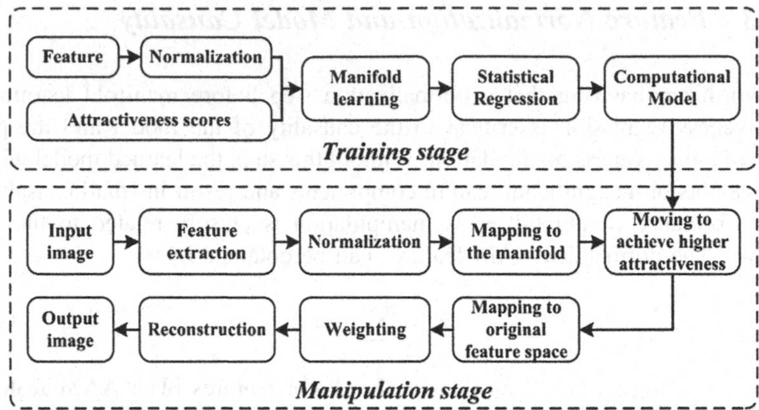

Fig. 11.3 The framework of model based facial attractiveness manipulation

where $\sum = diag(\lambda_1, \lambda_2, \ldots, \lambda_{100})$, which is the same as in (11.15). Then we can obtain the shape and texture parameters by using the AAM which has introduced in Sect. 7.2.4 to reconstruct the modified face image.

Figure 11.3 presents the whole framework of model based facial attractiveness manipulation. In the training stage, we learn the computational model based on a training data set, and in the manipulation stage, we modify the features with the guidance of the model to control the attractiveness of the input face. A straightforward application of attractiveness manipulation is automatic face beautification. Another important usage of attractiveness manipulation is to generate post-intervention face images, which can serve as stimuli when evaluating causal effect by perceptual experiments, as we mentioned in Sect. 11.2.

11.5 Experimental Results

The database which we used for the experiment in this chapter is the same with the database which has been used and introduced in Sect. 7.5.1 of Chap. 7. Firstly, we perform experiments to investigate the attractiveness manifold. Secondly, we build computational models and use them to manipulate facial attractiveness. Thirdly, we compare different models under prediction performance and causal effect criteria.

11.5.1 Results of Attractiveness Manifold Learning

We perform PCA, LDA, and LPP manifold learning algorithms on the AAM features. Because the extraction of AAM features contains a PCA step, thus the elements of AAM features just correspond to the principal components on the PCA manifold. To learn the LDA and LPP manifold, the attractiveness scores are discretized into 8 levels with equal intervals. The neighborhood size for LPP embedding is set as $k = 5$, and 'heat kernel' with $t = 1$ is used to calculate the edge weight. We use all the available labeled data for the manifold embedding algorithms. Figure 11.4a–c display the 2-D manifolds learned by the PCA, LDA, and LPP algorithms. The data points of attractiveness from −1 to 1 are colored from blue to red. We can observe that the LDA and LPP manifolds are more discriminative than the PCA manifold, which is easy to understand because LDA and LPP are supervised methods while PCA is unsupervised. The first component of LPP manifold is not discriminative. It is because the images in our database have large external variations, e.g., the illumination variation, so that the images in a neighborhood may only have similar illumination but not look like each other. As mentioned in Sect. 11.3.3, a feature normalization step is necessary before building the model. Hence, we also perform manifold learning on the normalized features and use N-PCA, N-LDA, and N-LPP for distinction. The results are shown in Fig. 11.4d–f. We can see that the normalization step does not change the manifold learned by LDA algorithm. However, the manifolds learned by PCA and LPP algorithms change significantly. It is because the optimization criteria of PCA and LPP depend on the distance metric between data points, whereas feature normalization changes this distance metric. Obviously, the N-LDA manifold is more discriminative than the N-PCA and N-LPP manifolds.

Besides the scatter plots shown in Fig. 11.4, we also compare the manifolds quantitatively. The manifold that can achieve higher attractiveness regression accuracy is preferred. We perform LR and SVR on the PCA, LDA, and LPP manifolds using different number of training data which are randomly selected. The remainder data are used for testing. The SVR is based on RBF kernels and the

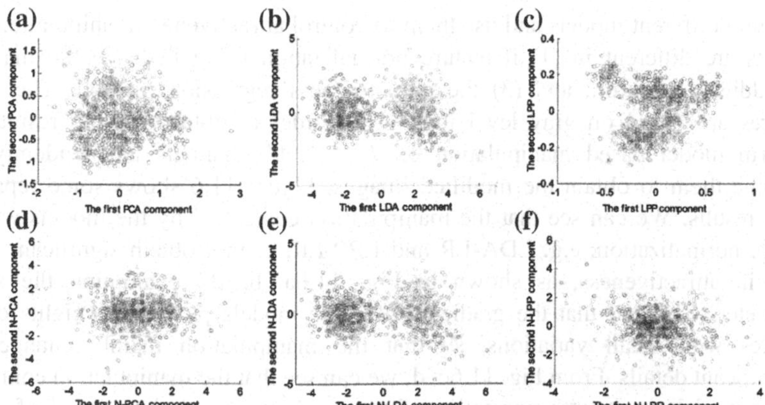

Fig. 11.4 Attractiveness manifold visualization (2-D). **a** PCA manifold. **b** LDA manifold. **c** LPP manifold. **d** N-PCA manifold. **e** N-LDA manifold. **f** N-LPP manifold. The data points of attractiveness from −1 to 1 are colored from *blue* to *red*

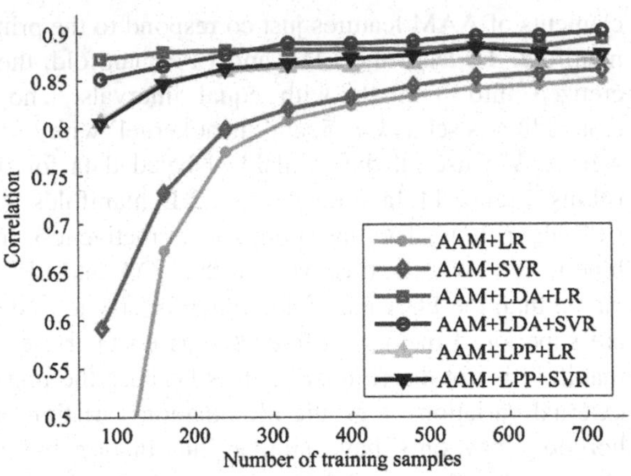

Fig. 11.5 Comparison of different manifolds in terms of attractiveness regression performance. The correlation between the predicted attractiveness scores and the ground truth scores is used to evaluate the regression performance

parameters are optimized by grid search. The correlation between the predicted attractiveness scores and the ground truth scores is used to evaluate the regression accuracy. We run each method 20 times. The average performances of different settings are shown in Fig. 11.5. We can see that the LDA manifold is better than the LPP and PCA manifolds; SVR is slightly better than LR when there are enough training data. As we know, feature normalization cannot increase the discriminative power of the manifolds or the performance of attractiveness regression. The N-LDA manifold is the same as the LDA manifold, and it can be inferred that N-LDA manifold is better than N-PCA and N-LPP manifolds.

11.5.2 Facial Attractiveness Manipulation

We build different models and use them to control attractiveness manipulation. The models are different in (1) if feature normalization is applied; (2) the manifold embedding algorithm; and (3) the attractiveness regression method. The AAM features are based on gray level images. In order to obtain colored results, we perform model based manipulation on L^*, a^*, b^* channels independently and combine them to obtain the modified images. Figure 11.6 shows some representative results. We can see that the manipulation controlled by the models without feature normalization, e.g. LDA-LR and LPP-LR, cannot obtain significant variations in attractiveness, as shown in Fig. 11.6a, b. By examining the model parameters, we find that the gradients of these models put large weights on the features with small variations, so that the manipulation mainly changes the insignificant details. From Fig. 11.6c, d, we can see that the manipulation controlled by the models built with normalized features shows an obvious trend of attractiveness. The learned models prefer bigger and brighter eyes, soft angled eyebrows, thinner chins, and fuller lips, which is consistent with our intuition. To better illustrate the difference caused by feature normalization, Fig. 11.7 shows two

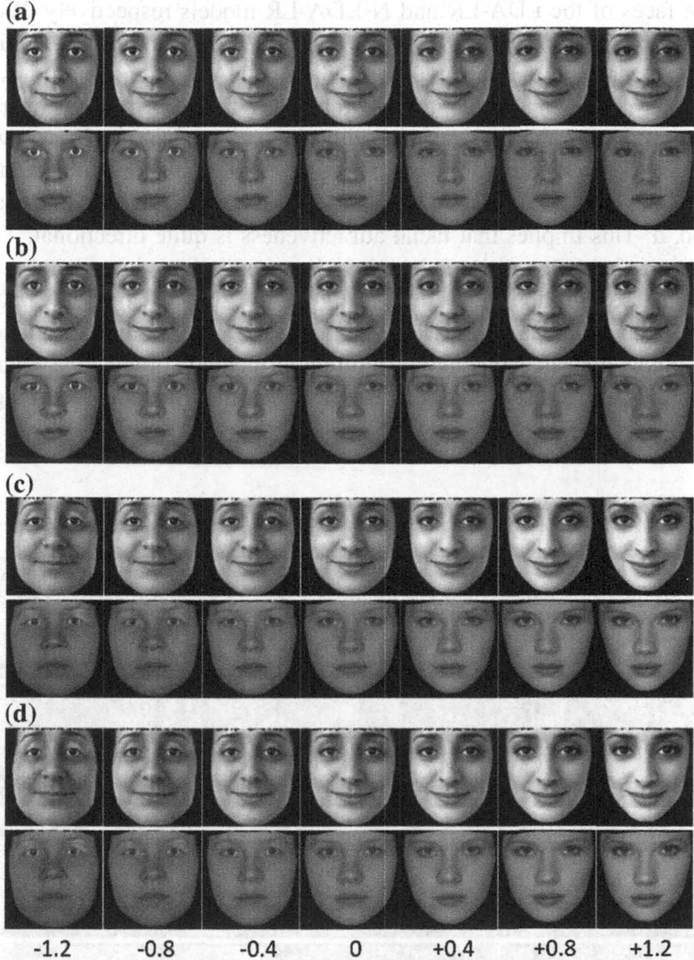

Fig. 11.6 Face image manipulation under the control of different models. **a** LDA-LR model. **b** LPP-LR model. **c** N-LDA-LR model. **d** N-SVR model. The face images in the *middle* are the original images. They are manipulated along the gradient orientations of the models. The *numbers* under the images indicate the amount of change in attractiveness

Fig. 11.7 Derivative faces of **a** LDA-LR model and **b** N-LDA-LR model. The example is based on the grayscale image of the second face in Fig. 11.6

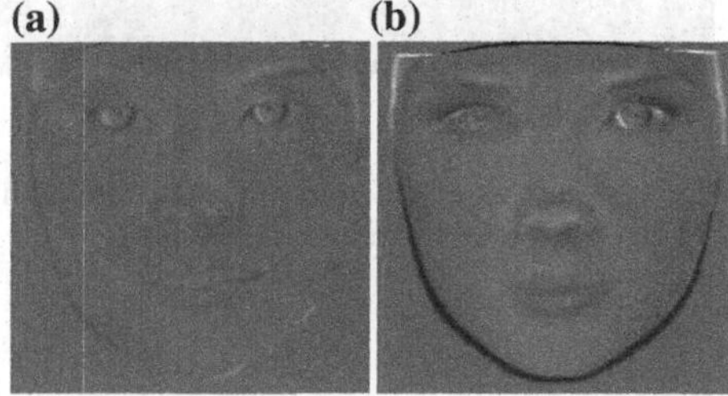

derivative faces of the LDA-LR and N-LDA-LR models respectively. We can see that the derivative face of the LDA-LR model is more uniform and difficult to interpret, whereas the derivative face of the N-LDA- LR model shows obvious patterns, e.g., modifying the contour of the lower face, wearing eyeliner and eye shadow, highlighting the lip, and deepening the color of the eyebrows, which are similar to a makeup process. It is interesting to find that manipulation results of the N-SVR model and the N-LDA-LR model are nearly the same, as shown in Fig. 11.6c, d. This implies that facial attractiveness is quite directional. To test the effectiveness of the learned model, we also manipulate face images from the FERET database (Phillips et al. 2000) using the N-LDA- LR model learned on our database. Some results are shown in Fig. 11.8. We can see that the model is also effective to new images. Note that the amount of manipulation can be controlled. In practical applications, users can decide how much modification according to their preference.

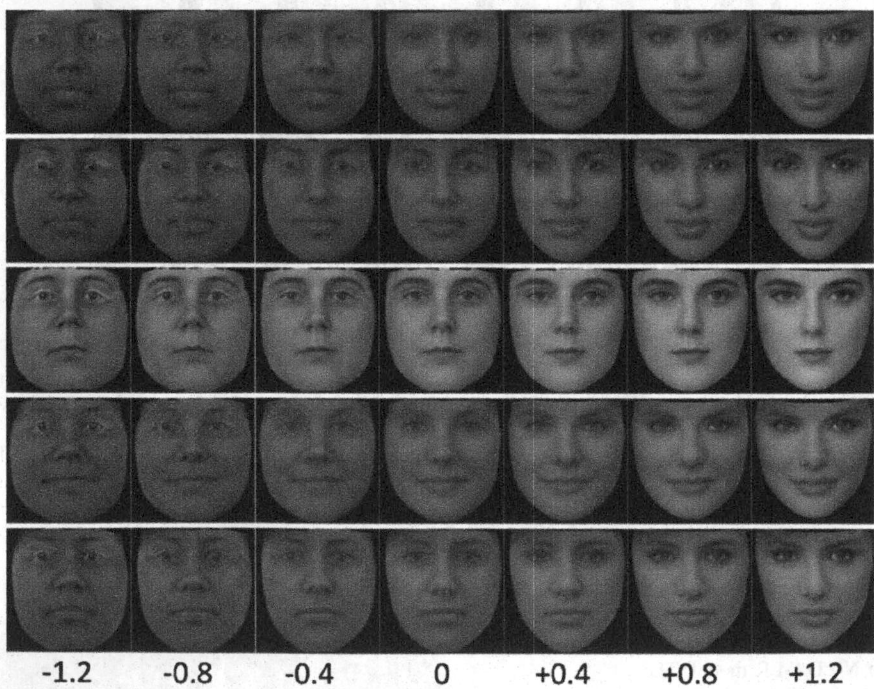

Fig. 11.8 Facial attractiveness manipulation on images from the FERET database guided by the N-LDA-LR model learned on our database

11.5.3 Quantitative Comparison Under Prediction Performance and Causal Effect Criteria

The previous section shows that not all the models are capable of controlling attractiveness manipulation, which implies that the causal effects of some models are insignificant. Here we give a quantitative comparison between different models in terms of attractiveness prediction performance and causal effect. For attractiveness prediction, we run 10-fold cross validation on our database and calculate the mean absolute error (MAE) of different models. The results are shown in Table 11.2. We can see that the LDA-LR and N-LDA-LR models achieve the best performance, followed by the LPP-LR and N-LPP-LR, which shows that manifold embedding can increase prediction accuracy and feature normalization does not affect prediction performance.

To quantify the causal effects of the models, we apply the two approaches introduced in Sect. 11.2. For each model, we calculate the causal effect by (11.2)–(11.6). The number of neighborhood in (11.4) is set to be 10. The results are shown in Table 11.2. We can see that the models with feature normalization have significant larger causal effects than those without feature normalization. The results are consistent with our observation of Fig. 11.6. The N-SVR model obtained the best causal effect, which is slightly better than the N-LDA-LR model. However, compared with the N-SVR model, the N-LDA-LR model has the following advantages: it has no parameters to train; it has explicit formulation; and the manipulation can be achieved by linear transformations, which is easier and faster.

The second approach to quantify the causal effect is performing perceptual experiment. The stimuli include the post-intervention face images as the experimental group, which are generated by the attractiveness manipulation method presented in Sect. 11.4, and the original face images as the control group. We randomly selected 50 pairs of face images to make up the stimuli. The participants were 30 university students (15 male, 15 female). They were told to choose the more attractive face in each pair. The positions of the faces in each pair (left or right) were determined randomly and the 50 pairs were shown in random order. If the original face images are denoted by $I_1, I_2, \ldots, I_N$ and the post-intervention face images are denoted by $\tilde{I}_1, \tilde{I}_2, \ldots, \tilde{I}_N$, the causal effect is measured by the percentage of votes for the two groups of stimuli, i.e.,

Table 11.2 Comparison of models by two criteria

Model	Prediction (MAE)	Causal effect
LR	0.2209	0.2694
LPP-LR	0.2048	0.2674
LDA-LR	0.1944	0.2682
N-LR	0.2272	0.5700
N-LPP-LR	0.2062	0.5276
N-LDA-LR	0.1938	0.5709
N-SVR	0.2101	0.5973

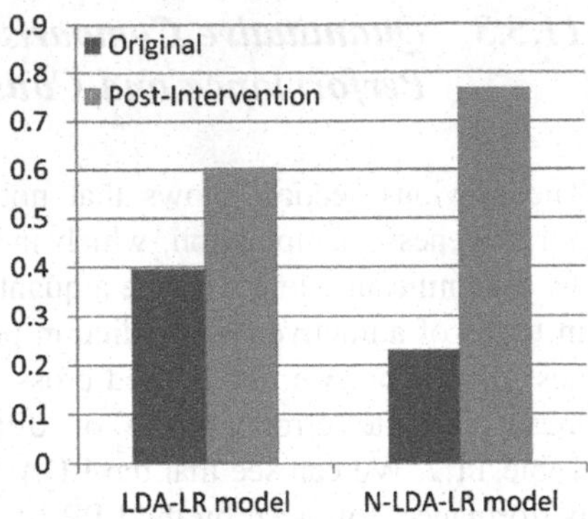

Fig. 11.9 The percentage of votes for the original images and the post-intervention images

$$E(A|\tilde{I}) - E(A|I) = \frac{1}{N}\sum_{i=1}^{N} P(\tilde{I}_i) - P(I_i), \tag{11.19}$$

where N is the number of stimuli and $P(I)$ means the percentage of participants that prefer image I. We select the LDA-LR mod- el and N-LDA-LR models to do the perceptual experiments, because they can represent the two categories of models, i.e. with or without feature normalization. The voting results are shown in Fig. 11.9. It is obvious that the N-LDA-LR model has a stronger causal effect than the LDA-LR model. By using (11.19), we obtain the quantified causal effect of 0.2080 for the LDA-LR model and 0.5380 for the N-LDA-LR model.

Considering prediction accuracy, causal effect, and ease of implementation, we conclude that the N-LDA-LR model is a good choice for facial attractiveness modeling.

11.6 Summary

Attractiveness is an important attribute of a face that can be understood, predicted, and manipulated. In this chapter, we point out that facial attractiveness study includes understanding, prediction, and manipulation problems. The commonly used prediction accuracy criterion is not sufficient to evaluate the computational models of facial attractiveness. Hence, we add a causal effect criterion and present two ways to measure it. Different models are built and compared under the two criteria. A model based facial attractiveness manipulation method is presented and tested. The experiments show that AAM features are effective for facial attractiveness modeling, although they have not been used in previous works; dimensionality reduction by manifold learning can increase the prediction performance; and feature normalization is essential for model causality. The model selected by the two criteria works well in both attractiveness prediction and manipulation problems. The derivative face generated by the model has obvious patterns that are consistent to our daily experience.

References

Ahonen T, Hadid A, Pietikainen M (2006) Face description with local binary patterns: application to face recognition. IEEE Trans Pattern Anal Mach Intell 28(12):2037–2041

Bookstein F (1989) Principal warps: thin-plate splines and the decomposition of deformations. IEEE Trans Pattern Anal Mach Intell 11(6):567–585

Chatterjee S, Hadi AS (1986) Influential observations, high leverage points, and outliers in linear regression. Stat Sci 1(3):379–393

Chen F, Zhang D (2010) A benchmark for geometric facial beauty study. Springer, pp 21–32

Cootes TF, Edwards GJ, Taylor CJ (2001) Active appearance models. IEEE Trans Pattern Anal Mach Intell 23(6):681–685

Dryden IL, Mardia KV (1998) Statistical shape analysis. Wiley

Duda RO, Hart PE, Stork DG (2000) Pattern classification. Wiley Interscience

Eisenthal Y, Dror G, Ruppin E (2006) Facial attractiveness: beauty and the machine. Neural Comput 18(1):119–142

Fan J, Chau KP, Wan X, Zhai L, Lau E (2012) Prediction of facial attractiveness from facial proportions. Pattern Recogn 45(6):2326–2334

Gunes H, Piccardi M (2006) Assessing facial beauty through proportion analysis by image processing and supervised learning. Int J Hum Comput Stud 64(12):1184–1199

He X, Niyogi P (2003) Locality preserving projections. In: Proceedings of neural information processing systems, vol 16, p 153

Kirby M, Sirovich L (1990) Application of the karhunen-loeve procedure for the characterization of human faces. IEEE Trans Pattern Anal Mach Intell 12(1):103–108

Leyvand T, Cohen-Or D, Dror G, Lischinski D (2008) Data-driven enhancement of facial attractiveness. ACM Trans Graph 27(3):38

Liao Q, Jin X, Zeng W (2012) Enhancing the symmetry and proportion of 3d face geometry. IEEE Trans Visual Comput Graphics 18(10):1704–1716

Liu C, Wechsler H (2002) Gabor feature based classification using the enhanced fisher linear discriminant model for face recognition. IEEE Trans Image Process 11(4):467–476

Nguyen TV, Liu S, Ni B, Tan J, Rui Y, Yan S (2013) Towards decrypting attractiveness via multi-modality cues. ACM Trans Multimedia Comput Commun Appl 9(4):28

Pallett PM, Link S, Lee K (2010) New "golden" ratios for facial beauty. Vis Res 50(2):149–154

Perrett D, May K, Yoshikawa S (1994) Facial shape and judgements of female attractiveness. Nature 368(6468):239–242

Phillips PJ, Moon H, Rizvi SA, Rauss PJ (2000) The feret evaluation methodology for face-recognition algorithms. IEEE Trans Pattern Anal Mach Intell 22(10):1090–1104

Schaefer S, McPhail T, Warren J (2006) Image deformation using moving least squares. ACM Trans Graph 25(3):533–540

Schmid K, Marx D, Samal A (2008) Computation of a face attractiveness index based on neoclassical canons, symmetry, and golden ratios. Pattern Recogn 41(8):2710–2717

Vapnik V (1995) The nature of statistical learning theory. Springer

Zhang D, Zhao Q, Chen F (2011) Quantitative analysis of human facial beauty using geometric features. Pattern Recogn 44(4):940–950

Chapter 12
Data-Driven Facial Beauty Analysis: Prediction, Retrieval and Manipulation

In this chapter, we present a generalized data-driven facial beauty analysis framework that contains three application modules, prediction, retrieval, and manipulation. Readers are able to grasp main aspects and practical functions of facial beauty analysis via this framework. The framework is also helpful for us to design and implement applicable facial beauty analysis systems. It clearly shows relationship of different modules on the basis of the data flow and hierarchical structure of a resultant system. The chapter is organized as follows. Section 12.1 first introduces the related work of facial beauty analysis, and then gives a briefly description of the framework of facial beauty analysis. Section 12.2 describes the preprocessing and feature extraction procedures of the framework. Section 12.3 gives the definition of the beauty model. In Sect. 12.4, the facial beauty prediction method is presented. In Sect. 12.5, we discuss the beauty-oriented face retrieval problem and propose the search criteria for two application scenarios. Section 12.6 presents the facial beauty manipulation algorithm. Experimental results are shown in Sect. 12.7. We finally conclude the chapter in Sect. 12.8.

12.1 Introduction

Data-driven facial beauty analysis aims to build computational models of facial beauty and give solutions to real-world applications with the help of learned models.

A basic point of facial beautification is to manipulate the target characteristic and to keep other characteristics intact. The images before and after manipulation form a group of stimuli, and participants are asked to make judgments according to their preferences. The findings of these studies are limited to verifying the relevance between predefined characteristics and facial beauty. Although the findings provide evidence for explaining human behavior and evolutionary theories (Little et al. 2011), they are far from adequate for developing application systems.

D. Zhang et al., *Computer Models for Facial Beauty Analysis*,
DOI 10.1007/978-3-319-32598-9_12

Recent psychological studies have found that there is a high degree of agreement on facial beauty perception across ethnic groups, social classes, ages, and genders (Langlois et al. 2000; Cunningham et al. 1995). Based on these findings, data-driven facial beauty analysis has been developed by computer scientists. A category of studies has focused on facial beauty prediction (Eisenthal et al. 2006; Gunes and Piccardi 2006; Schmid et al. 2008; Fan et al. 2012; Gray et al. 2010; Nguyen et al. 2013). First, hundreds of facial images are collected and facial beauty is quantified by the mean opinion scores of human raters. Then, different kinds of features are extracted, and supervised learning methods are employed to build computational models of facial beauty.

Although some progress has been made in data-driven facial beauty analysis, compared with other facial image analysis tasks, research on facial beauty is still in its infancy. For example, the beauty model can be embedded as an important component in many application systems. However, most existing works only use the model in the most straightforward way, that is, beauty prediction. In this chapter, we present a facial beauty analysis framework that contains three application modules: prediction, retrieval, and manipulation, which can support different real-life applications. The framework is shown in Fig. 12.1. We will analyze the framework in the following section in detail.

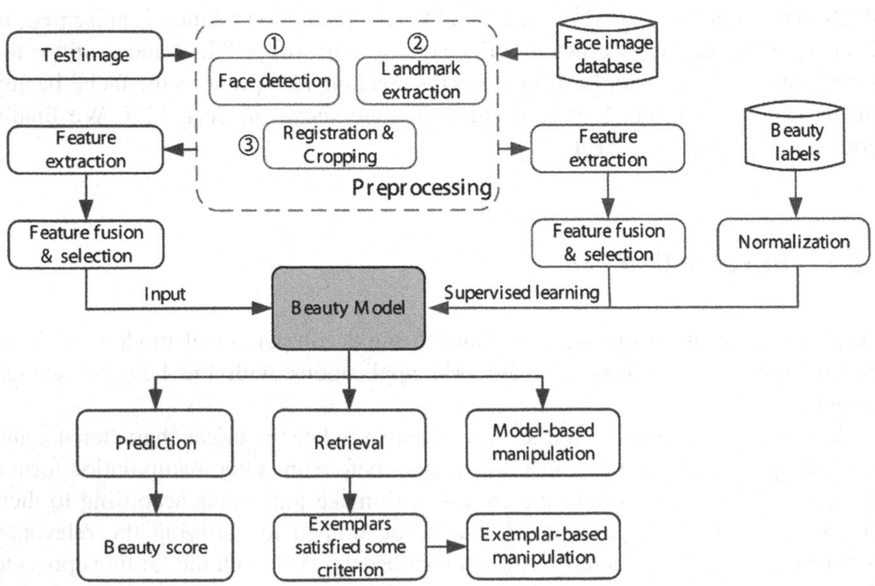

Fig. 12.1 An overview of our facial beauty analysis framework

12.2 Facial Image Preprocessing and Feature Extraction

As shown in Fig. 12.1, facial image preprocessing is the first step of the facial beauty analysis framework, which is important for robust feature extraction. The procedure is illustrated in Fig. 12.2 and contains two main steps, the first step is face detection and landmark extraction, and the second step is face registration and cropping.

Feature extraction is an important part of the facial beauty analysis framework. In this chapter, we introduce four representative low-level features, from global to local, from geometry to appearance, and from popular (LBP) to new (PCANet) (see Table 12.1). In addition, we consider soft biometric traits for beauty prediction and beauty-oriented facial image retrieval.

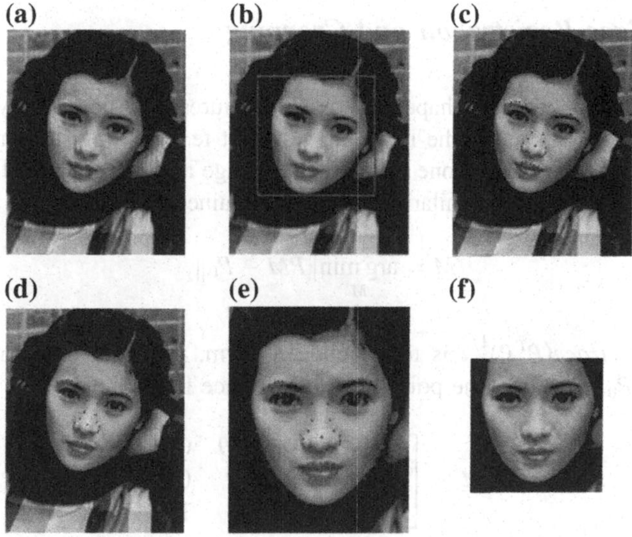

Fig. 12.2 Illustration of the facial image preprocessing procedure. **a** Original image. **b** Face detection by Viola-Jones detector. **c** Landmark extraction by ASM. **d** Manual adjustment. **e** Registration. **f** 128 × 128 crop and resize

Table 12.1 Representative low-level features

	Geometry	Appearance
Global	Shape	AAM
Local	–	LBP, PCANet

12.2.1 Face Detection and Landmark Extraction

Similar to the landmark extraction method presented in Sect. 4.2.2.2, we also first detect the face in the image using Viola-Jones face detector (Viola and Jones 2001), and then use the active shape models (ASMs) (Cootes and Taylor 1995) to locate the landmarks. We use 98 landmarks to represent the face shape (see Fig. 12.2). The landmarks are distributed on the main facial organs and are denser at the contours with high curvatures. The ASM algorithm is semi-automatic. First, a subset of facial images is manually labeled to train the shape model and the profile model. Then, the ASM algorithm can iteratively fit the model to new images. It works well on most of frontal faces. However, when the illumination is nonuniform, the accuracy of the automatic extracted landmarks will decrease. To deal with this problem, we design an interface for manual adjustment of the landmarks (see Fig. 12.2c, d).

12.2.2 Face Registration and Cropping

Given the landmarks, the shape and AAM features can be reliably extracted. However, before extracting the LBP and PCANet features, registration and cropping are required. We select one frontal facial image as a reference and align other facial images to it with a similarity transform obtained by

$$\hat{M} = \arg\min_{M} \|PM - P_0\|, \tag{12.1}$$

where $\|P\| = trace(P^T P)^{1/2}$ is the Euclidean norm. P and P_0 are corresponding points, and P_0 represents the points of the reference facial image.

$$M = \begin{bmatrix} s\cos\theta & -s\sin\theta & 0 \\ s\sin\theta & s\cos\theta & 0 \\ tx & ty & 1 \end{bmatrix} \tag{12.2}$$

M is the similarity transform matrix. P is also a $k \times 3$ matrices in the form of

$$P = \begin{bmatrix} x_1 & y_1 & 1 \\ \vdots & \vdots & \vdots \\ x_k & y_k & 1 \end{bmatrix}. \tag{12.3}$$

Here the landmarks can serve as the corresponding points. Equation (12.1) is a quadratic optimization problem and can be analytically solved (see details in Dryden and Mardia 1998). Figure 12.2e shows an example of face registration. We define a square region with the face in the center and crop the registered images accordingly. The cropped facial images are resized to 128 × 128 for LBP and PCANet feature extraction (see Fig. 12.2f).

12.2.3 Low-Level Face Representations

The low-level representations include shape parameters, active appearance model (AAM) (Cootes et al. 2001) representation, LBP, and PCANet (Chan et al. 2014), which are from global to local and from geometry to appearance. The shape parameters, AAM, LBP and PCANet were introduced in detail in Sects. 7.2.2, 7.2.4, 7.2.6 and 7.2.7 of Chap. 7, respectively.

12.2.4 Soft Biometric Traits

Recently, soft biometrics has been used in human-machine interaction, face retrieval, and person re-identification. We expect that the use of soft biometric traits can improve the performance of facial beauty prediction and beauty-oriented face retrieval. Four soft biometric traits are considered: race, age, expression, and makeup. We label race into four categories (Caucasian, Asian, Negroid, and unknown), label age into four categories (20–29, 30–39, 40–49, and over 50), label expression into two categories (neutral and smile), and label makeup into three categories (heavy, light, and none). Currently the traits are manually labeled. Forty volunteers attended the labeling task and the labels were determined by a majority vote. In practical applications, the labels of the soft biometric traits can either be given by users or be automatically annotated with pre-trained classifiers. We analyze the effect of manually and automatically annotated labels of soft biometric traits in Sect. 12.7.3.

12.3 Facial Beauty Modeling

As shown in Fig. 12.1, the core of the framework is the beauty model. With carefully designed features, the model can be built for different purposes, such as prediction, beauty-oriented face retrieval and manipulation. In the following sections, we will present in detail the corresponding beauty models for the above three purposes.

12.3.1 Problem Formulation

Suppose a facial image I_i is represented by a feature vector x_i, and its beauty score is denoted by y_i, $y_i \in [-1, 1]$, where '1' means the most beautiful. Given a set of training data $D = \{(x_1, y_1), (x_2, y_2), \ldots, (x_n, y_n)\}$, a beauty model can be learned by supervised learning, i.e.,

$$y = f(x). \tag{12.4}$$

The model can be used to predict the attractiveness of facial images, retrieve faces that satisfy a certain beauty level, and guide the manipulation of facial images. By using specifically designed features, we can build different models for different goals. In the following sections, we will present the details of how to build and use the beauty model in the three applications.

12.3.2 Regression Methods

Given a set of training data, multivariate linear regression (LR) (Chatterjee and Hadi 1986) and SVR (Vapnik 1995) can be used to learn the beauty model defined in (12.4). Using LR, we can obtain the beauty model in an explicit form as

$$y = \omega^T \mathrm{x} + \omega_0, \tag{12.5}$$

where ω and ω_0 are model parameters. With radial basis function (RBF) kernels, SVR can model a nonlinear structure, but the model cannot be explicitly expressed. We use LibSVM (Chang and Lin 2011) to train the SVR model, and the parameters are optimized by grid search.

12.4 Facial Beauty Prediction

In this section, we investigate the optimal feature set to build the beauty model for facial beauty prediction. The performance of the model is evaluated by the correlation between the predicted scores and the ground truth scores given by human ratings. First, we independently compare different types of features, and then we try to improve the prediction performance by feature fusion and selection.

Because the amount of training data is often limited, to increase the computational efficiency and alleviate the problem of dimensionality, PCA is performed on the shape, LBP, and PCANet features. After PCA, all types of features are of dimension 100. Experimental results show that the best single-type feature is

Table 12.2 Comparison of low-level features in terms of facial beauty prediction

Feature	#Dim	Regression performance		
		KNN	LR	SVR
Shape	100	0.7356	0.7415	0.7763
AAM	100	0.7751	0.8332	0.8459
LBP	100	0.7435	0.7977	0.8075
PCANet	100	0.7987	0.8508	**0.8615**

Table 12.3 Comparison of outputs of models built with different features

Correlation	Shape	AAM	LBP	PCANet
Shape	1	0.8595	0.6800	0.7362
AAM	0.8595	1	0.7253	0.7958
LBP	0.6774	0.7253	1	0.8025
PCANet	0.7362	0.7958	0.8025	1

PCANet, which is better than the features used in previous works (see Tables 12.2 and 12.5).

It can be seen that the outputs of the models built with AAM, LBP, and PCANet features have low correlations with each other, compared with their prediction performances (see Table 12.3), which implies that the three types of features are complementary. However, the shape feature is embedded in the AAM feature by definition. Therefore, we propose to combine AAM, LBP, and PCANet features as well as the soft biometric traits to further improve the performance. The combined feature vector is of dimension 304. It can be asked whether all the dimensions of the feature vector are relevant and necessary to assess facial beauty or whether a subset of the dimensions can achieve similar or even better prediction performance. Therefore, we apply the lasso (Hastie et al. 2009) which have introduced in Sect. 7.3 for feature selection. Before that, the features are normalized to zero mean and unit variance.

12.5 Beauty-Oriented Face Retrieval

Most existing face retrieval systems are designed for forensic applications (Jain et al. 2012), in which similarity is the searching criterion. However, there are some applications where the beauty of the face plays an important role. For example, an online dating site would like to recommend potential partners to users, who usually have personal requirements about facial beauty. Another example is that when people need to beautify their faces, either by aesthetic plastic surgery or by just modifying photos, it would be good to be given some exemplars. In Sect. 12.6.1, we show that the exemplars can be used to generate a manipulation plan. In this section, we discuss the face retrieval problem in these two scenarios. As facial beauty is an essential factor, we call it beauty-oriented face retrieval.

12.5.1 Retrieval for Face Recommendation

A user may want to find a potential partner that has (1) a high beauty score, (2) a similar beauty score to the user, (3) specific race, (4) specific age group, and (5) other requirements. The user can give some verbal descriptions to the system, and then the system searches the database and returns a series of faces that satisfy the user's criteria. Suppose the image set in the database is $U = \{I_1, I_2, \ldots, I_N\}$, and the features of the images are represented by $X = \{x_1, x_2, \ldots, x_N\}$. Here we adopt the model built with the optimized feature set, i.e., after feature fusion and selection. First, the beauty scores of the facial images in the database are estimated by the model, and the top-n images whose scores are nearest to the desired value are returned. Then, the returned images are filtered by other constraints, such as the race and age group.

12.5.2 Retrieval for Face Beautification

The retrieved examples can be used to guide face beautification. Chen et al. (2014) proved that convex combinations of beautiful face shapes are guaranteed to be beautiful, i.e., if $B = \{x | f(x) \geq y_0\}$, where x is the shape feature, then $f(\sum_{x_i \in B} \theta_i x_i) \geq y_0$, where $\theta_i \geq 0$ and $\sum_i \theta_i = 1$. Here y_0 can be treated as the lower bound of a user's desired beauty score. For a query face with shape x_q, our task is to find a set of faces whose beauty scores are larger than y_0 and a convex combination of their shapes that is the closest to x_q. The latter is to keep as much personal details of the query face as possible. Given a beauty model, we can estimate the beauty scores of the faces in the database and return a subset of faces whose beauty scores are larger than y_0, denoted by C. Then, we solve the following norm approximation problem:

$$\hat{\theta} = \arg\min_{\theta} \|A\theta - \mathrm{x}_q\| \quad s.t. \quad \theta_i \geq 0, \sum\nolimits_i \theta_i = 1, \tag{12.6}$$

where $A = \{\mathrm{x}_{c1}, \mathrm{x}_{c2}, \ldots, \mathrm{x}_{cn}\}$ is composed of the shape features of the faces in C. To solve (12.6) we use CVX, a package for specifying and solving convex programs (Grant and Boyd 2012; Grant et al. 2008). Experimental results show that the weighting vector $\hat{\theta}$ is often sparse, with 2–20 nonzero elements. The faces corresponding to the nonzero weights are treated as the retrieval results.

12.6 Facial Beauty Manipulation

Another application is data-driven facial beauty manipulation. One can automatically beautify the geometry and texture of a query face and preview the results. The amount of beauty manipulation can be controlled. If the feature of the query face is x_q, and the estimated beauty score is $f(x_q)$, then the desired beauty score is calculated by

$$y_0 = f(\mathrm{x}_q) + [1 - f(\mathrm{x}_q)] \times \alpha, \tag{12.7}$$

where $\alpha \in [0, 1]$ is a parameter to indicate the amount of manipulation (from 0 to 100 %), and $y_0 \in [f(\mathrm{x}_q), 1]$. The task is to modify the input facial image to make its beauty score equal or larger than y_0 while keeping as many personal details as possible. The following two approaches can achieve this goal.

12.6.1 Exemplar-Based Manipulation

In Sect. 12.5.2, we obtained a series of facial images whose beauty scores are larger than y_0 and a weighting vector $\hat{\theta}$. We modify the shape of the input face to $\hat{\mathbf{x}} = A\hat{\theta}$, where A follows the same definition as in (12.6). Because $\hat{\theta}$ is sparse, $\hat{\mathbf{x}}$ is a convex combination of the shapes of the retrieved exemplars. The shape $\hat{\mathbf{x}}$ is aligned to the landmarks on the query face image by a similarity transformation, that is, $\hat{\mathbf{x}}$ is transformed to the same coordinate system as the query facial image. After that, we perform image deformation by the moving least squares (MLS) (Schaefer and McPhail 2006) method using the landmarks as the control points.

The above is called exemplar-based manipulation. It is designed for facial geometry manipulation, with the weighted average hypothesis proved in Chen et al. (2014) as the groundwork. This approach is not suitable for appearance features, because convex combinations of appearance features will lose the identity information of the query face.

12.6.2 Model-Based Manipulation

We can also manipulate facial beauty with the guidance of a beauty model. Model-based manipulation can be applied to modify both facial geometry and appearance. Specifically, facial geometry is manipulated with the guidance of the model built with the shape parameters (shape feature after PCA), whereas facial appearance is manipulated with the guidance of the model built with the AAM feature.

If the model is in linear form as in (12.5), the gradient of the function indicates the manipulation direction. When the desired beauty score is y_0, the new feature can be calculated by

$$\hat{\mathbf{x}} = \mathbf{x}_q + (y_0 - y_q)\frac{\omega}{\|\omega\|_2^2}, \tag{12.8}$$

where $\mathbf{x}_q$ is the feature of the query face image and $y_q = f(\mathbf{x}_q) = \omega^T\mathbf{x}_q + \omega_0$ is the estimated beauty score. If the model does not have an explicit expression, such as the nonlinear SVR model, the manipulation direction can be obtained by numerical differentiation. In the gradient descent/ascent way, we move the feature to approach the desired beauty score.

It is worth noting that in the case of facial beauty manipulation, the features should be normalized before training the beauty models. Both the shape parameters and the AAM feature have zero mean and diagonal covariance matrices. If the covariance matrix is denoted by $\sum$, the normalized features are $\sum^{-1/2}\mathbf{x}$, and the modified feature $\hat{\mathbf{x}}$ should be transformed to $\tilde{\mathbf{x}} = \sum^{1/2}\hat{\mathbf{x}}$ before reconstructing the modified facial image.

Finally, we can obtain the desired shape, if $\tilde{\mathbf{x}}$ is a shape parameter vector or desired shape and texture by the AAM algorithm. If $\tilde{\mathbf{x}}$ is an AAM feature, then, by applying MLS warping, we reconstruct the modified facial image. Note that the image reconstructed by the AAM feature will lose personal details, because the PCA operation filters out the high frequency information of the original image. To solve this problem, we can record the texture residual between the original shape-free image and that reconstructed by the texture parameters, and superpose the texture residual to the desired texture before image warping.

12.7 Experiments

12.7.1 Data Set

We built a database that contains 1,609 high-quality female face images, which is an extension of that used in our previous work (Chen et al. 2014). The images include well-known beautiful faces collected from the web (e.g., Miss Universe, Miss World, movie stars, and super models) and facial images from several existing databases (e.g., the XM2VTS database Messer et al. 1999, FERET database Phillips et al. 2000, and the Shanghai database Zhang et al. 2011). The facial images are confined to be frontal and have neutral or gentle smile expressions. The ethnicities of the faces are diversified. To obtain the human-rated beauty scores and the labels of the soft biometric traits, we developed an annotation interface, which displayed the facial images in random order and instructed the raters to make multiple choices. We used a 10-point integer scale for beauty rating, where '10' means the most beautiful. Forty volunteers attended the annotation task. Each person was assigned 400 images. Hence, we obtain about 10 annotations for each image. The average beauty-ratings across the raters are considered as the human-rated beauty scores, which are normalized to [−1, 1].

12.7.2 Evaluation of Features for Facial Beauty Prediction

In this section, we compare the low-level features in terms of facial beauty prediction. Linear regression models and SVR models are trained with different types of features and used to estimate beauty scores of the test data. We randomly select 90 % of the face images for training, and the remaining images are used for testing. The KNN regression method serves as a baseline. The experiment was run 100 times, and the average correlations between the predicted scores and human-rated scores are shown in Table 12.2. It can be seen that the PCANet feature achieves the best performance, followed by the AAM and LBP features. For the regression method, SVR is better than LR, and both are much better than KNN regression. It can also be seen that the outputs of the models built by AAM, LBP, and PCANet features are not very correlated with each other, compared with the prediction performance (see Table 12.3). This finding verifies our argument in Sect. 12.2 that they are representative and complementary.

12.7.3 Benefit of Soft Biometric Traits

The effect of soft biometric traits for facial beauty prediction is investigated. As mentioned in Sect. 12.2.4, the labels of the soft biometric traits can be given by the users or be automatically annotated with pre-trained classifiers. Experiments were conducted under these two conditions. Similar to the previous experiment, 90 % of the data are randomly selected for training the classifiers of soft biometric traits and the beauty model. The remaining data are used for testing. In the first case, the manually labeled soft biometric traits are combined as additional features. In the second case, the labels of the soft biometric traits of the test data are estimated by linear discrimination analysis, which fits a multivariate normal density to each group and classifies the test data by the *maximum* a posteriori probability (MAP) criterion. We run the experiment 10 times and the average performances of the shape, AAM, LBP, and PCANet features combined with automatically extracted and manually labeled soft biometric traits are shown in Fig. 12.3. The performances of the original features are also shown for comparison. It can be seen that soft biometric traits can promote the prediction performance in all cases, especially when the original feature is less informative, such as the shape feature. The automatically extracted soft biometric traits are only slightly inferior to manually labeled ones. Hence, in practical applications, users can make free choices on giving the soft biometric information.

12.7.4 Results of Feature Fusion and Selection

We perform feature fusion and selection to further improve the prediction performance. Table 12.4 shows the results of different feature fusion schemes, which are evaluated by 10-fold cross validation. It can be seen that as expected, feature fusion can improve the prediction performance. However, as the number of feature dimensions increases, the problem of dimensionality occurs. As shown in the table, the performance of combining AAM, PCANet, and soft biometric traits is better

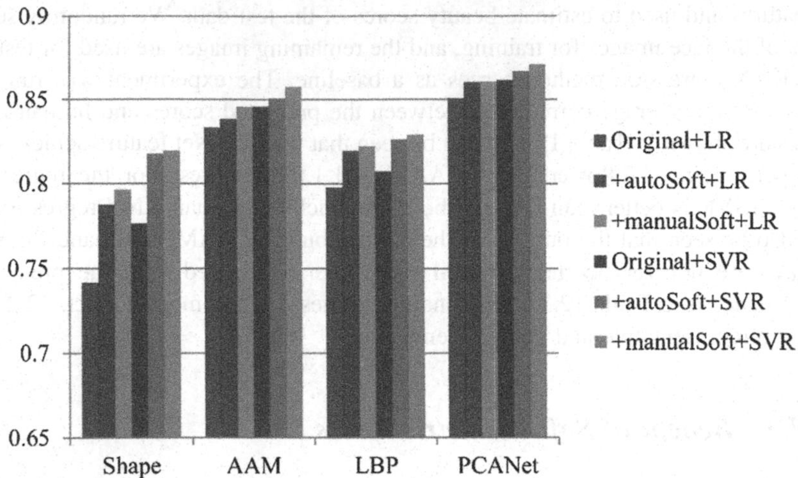

Fig. 12.3 Comparison of features combined with automatically extracted and manually labeled soft biometric traits in terms of facial beauty prediction performance

Table 12.4 Prediction performances of feature fusion and selection

Fusion scheme	LR	FS + LR	SVR	FS + SVR
LBP + AAM	0.8564	0.8694	0.8656	0.8772
LBP + PCANet	0.8469	0.8647	0.8586	0.8695
AAM + PCANet	0.8742	0.8838	0.879	0.8875
AAM + LBP + PCANet	0.8642	0.8875	0.8751	0.8912
AAM + PCANet + Soft	0.8756	0.8853	0.8881	0.8925
AAM + LBP + PCANet + Soft	0.8701	0.8902	0.8857	0.8954

than that of combining all four types of features. To alleviate the problem of dimensionality, feature selection is performed on each fusion scheme. In Table 12.4, FS stands for feature selection. It can be seen that after feature selection, the combination of the AAM, LBP, PCANet, and soft biometric traits achieves the best performance for facial beauty prediction.

Table 12.5 compares our optimized model with the methods used in other works in terms of facial beauty prediction. The results are based on 10-fold cross validation. In Schmid et al. (2008), 6 classical canons and 17 golden ratios were defined. Our landmarks can extract 5 out of the 6 canons and 14 out of the 17 golden ratios, among which two canons and golden ratios have the same definitions. Hence, 17 ratio features were used to build the model. In the implementation of the work presented by Gray et al. (2010), we used the Deep Learning Toolbox (Palm 2012) to train the convolutional neural network. For the work presented by Nguyen et al. (2013), we only compared their facial representation method with ours, although it also models dressing, accessories, hairstyle, and voice, which are out of

Table 12.5 Comparison of facial beauty prediction performance with other works

Work	Feature	Dimension	Method	Performance
Schmid et al. (2008)	Ratios	17	LR	0.6547
Gray et al. (2010)	convNet	–	Neural network	0.7677
Nguyen et al. (2013)	Shape + Gabor + LBP + Color	350	Fusion + SVR	0.8416
Our	AAM + LBP + PCANet + Soft	160	Fusion + FS + SVR	0.8954

the scope of this chapter. The results show that our method significantly outperforms previous works. That is mainly because the AAM and PCANet features are more discriminative, and the soft biometric traits provide auxiliary information.

12.7.5 Results of Beauty-Oriented Face Retrieval

First, we tested the beauty-oriented retrieval for face recommendation, i.e., given verbal descriptions on beauty score and additional requirements such as race, the algorithm returns a series of facial images. Half of the data are used for training the beauty model and the soft biometric classifiers, and the remaining images are used for retrieval. Figure 12.4 gives an example of the retrieval results. Because the size of the database is limited, we only use one filtering condition (race in this example). If the database is large and diverse enough, the retrieved results can be filtered by multiple external conditions.

Second, we tested the beauty-oriented retrieval for face beautification. Similar to the previous experiment, half of the data are used to train the beauty model, and the model is used to estimate the beauty scores of the remaining images. For the images whose beauty scores are less than −0.2, we search the beautification exemplars by solving (12.6). The desired beauty score y_0 is determined by (12.7), where α is set to

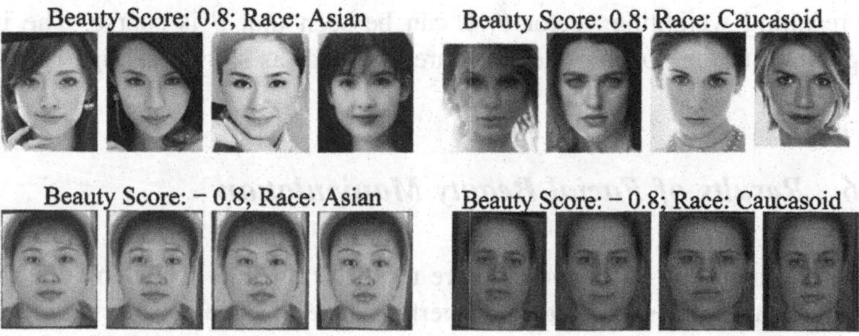

Fig. 12.4 An example of beauty-oriented face retrieval according to verbal descriptions. Because facial beauty is a sensitive topic, the images in the *bottom row* are with synthesized textures to conceal the identities

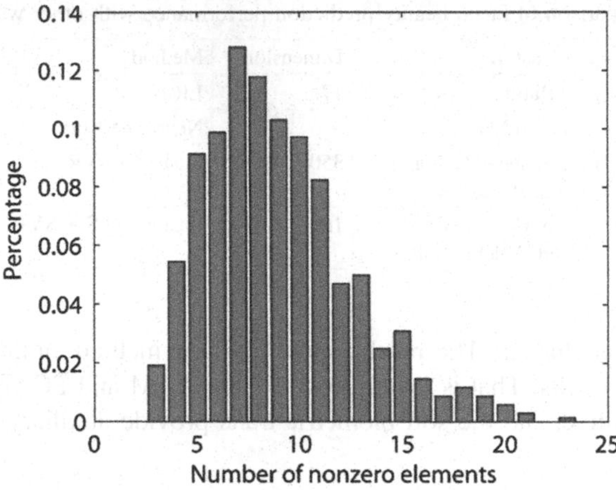

Fig. 12.5 Distribution of the number of nonzero elements in the weighting vector $\hat{\theta}$

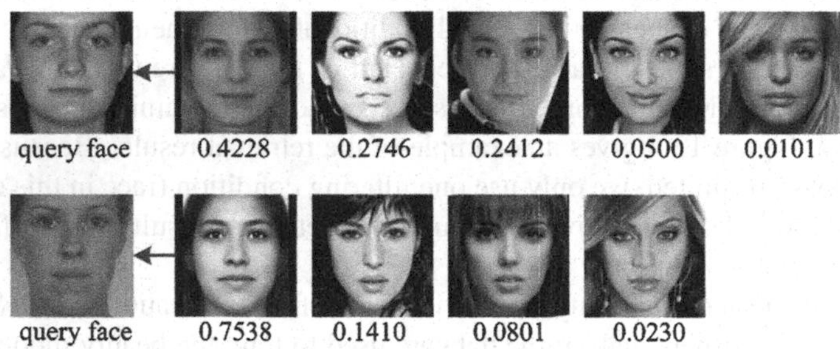

Fig. 12.6 The retrieved exemplars for face beautification. The *number* below the *face images* are their corresponding weights

0.5. Figure 12.5 shows the distribution of the number of nonzero elements (>0.001) in the resulting weighting vector $\hat{\theta}$. It can be seen that $\hat{\theta}$ is sparse. The images corresponding to the nonzero elements are returned, as shown in Fig. 12.6.

12.7.6 Results of Facial Beauty Manipulation

In this experiment, 50 % of the data are used to train the beauty model, and the remaining images are used to test the performance of facial beauty manipulation. The beauty scores of the test images are predicted by the model. For the images whose predicted beauty scores are less than −0.2, we perform different manipulation strategies: (1) exemplar-based geometry (EG) beautification, (2) model-based

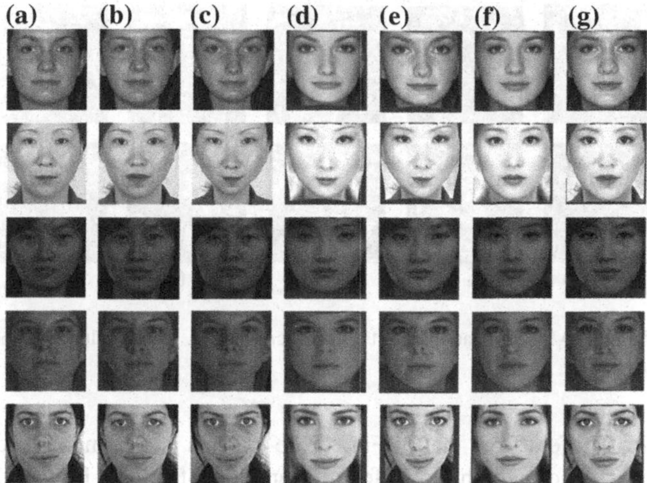

Fig. 12.7 Facial beauty manipulation results (α = 0.6). **a** Original faces. **b** Exemplar-based geometry (EG) beautification (Chen et al. 2014). **c** Model-based geometry (MG) beautification (Leyvand et al. 2008). **d** Model-based appearance (MA) beautification. **e** MA beautification superposed with texture residual. **f** Exemplar-based geometry beautification and model-based appearance (EGMA) beautification. **g** EGMA beautification superposed with texture residual

geometry (MG) beautification, (3) model-based appearance (MA) beautification, and (4) exemplar-based geometry and model-based appearance (EGMA) beautification. For the model-based approaches, the results of LR models and SVR models are very similar, so we can adopt the simpler LR model. For the MA and EGMA methods, two versions of results are generated: one is superposed with the texture residual, and the other is not. The AAM feature introduced in Sect. 7.2.4 is based on gray-scale images. To obtain colored manipulation results, we transform the images into CIELAB color space and independently perform the MA and EGMA manipulation in the three channels. Some results are shown in Fig. 12.7. It can be seen that model-based methods are not robust for facial geometry beautification, e.g., for the MG and MA results of the second image, the chins are too narrow, and the mouths are too small. This is because the learned beauty model is not perfect, especially when the data are sparsely distributed (e.g., strange faces). Compared with model-based methods, the exemplar-based method is more robust for facial geometry beautification. Different from facial geometry, the effects of model-based manipulation on facial texture are consistent and directional: brightening the skin tone, putting on eye liner, and improving the color saturation of the eyes and the lips, which is like a makeup process. The EGMA method uses the exemplar-based method to obtain the desired shape and uses the model-based method to obtain the desired texture. Hence, the results are more effective and robust. Comparing Fig. 12.7d–g, it can be seen that Fig. 12.7d, f lose the personal details, e.g., the hair and collar are blurred, and the facial skin is over smoothed, whereas Fig. 12.7e, g keep the above details and are easier to identify. It may be argued that the attractiveness

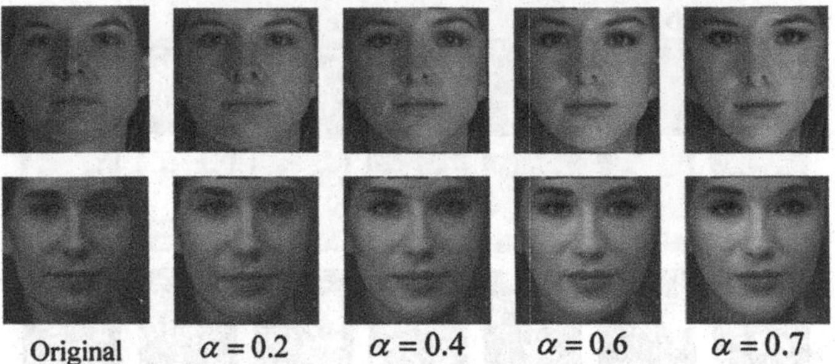

Fig. 12.8 The EGMA beautification results with increasing α. The results are superposed with texture residual

of Fig. 12.7d–f differs from that of Fig. 12.7e–g. This is reasonable because facial beauty is determined by both global features and local features. Figure 12.7d–f, e–g have the same global features (shape and AAM features) but different local features. Moreover, the amount of manipulation can be controlled by the parameter α defined in (12.7), as illustrated in Fig. 12.8. In practical applications, developers can choose the manipulation strategy according to their needs, and users can choose the amount of manipulation according to their preferences.

12.8 Summary

In this chapter, we present a data-driven facial beauty analysis framework. The beauty model is the core of the framework. With carefully designed features, the model can be built for different applications: facial beauty prediction, beauty-oriented face retrieval, and facial beauty manipulation. We combine low-level features AAM, LBP, and PCANet as well as soft biometric traits for facial beauty prediction. The features are further optimized by feature selection. The model built with the optimized features achieves a correlation of 0.8954 with the average human judgments. Then, we discuss two application scenarios of beauty-oriented face retrieval. One is for face recommendation with requirements on facial beauty, and the other is to find exemplars for guiding face beautification. Finally, we present an exemplar-based approach and a model-based approach for facial beauty manipulation. Experimental results show that the exemplar-based approach is more robust for facial geometry beautification, whereas the model-based approach can improve the attractiveness of facial texture. Hence, the combination of them can produce better results. Comparing the results of different manipulation strategies, it can be seen that facial beauty is determined by facial geometry, global texture variation, and local flaws (e.g., wrinkles and scars), corresponding to the shape feature, the AAM feature, and the texture residual.

References

Chang CC, Lin CJ (2011) LIBSVM: a library for support vector machines. ACM Trans Intell Syst Technol 2:27:1–27:27. http://www.csie.ntu.edu.tw/cjlin/libsvm

Chatterjee S, Hadi AS (1986) Influential observations, high leverage points, and outliers in linear regression. Stat Sci 1(3):379–393

Chen F, Xu Y, Zhang D (2014) A new hypothesis on facial beauty perception. ACM Trans Appl Percept 11(2): 8:1–8:20

Cootes T, Taylor C, Cooper D, Graham J (1995) Active shape models-their training and application. Comput Vis Image Underst 61(1):38–59

Cootes TF, Edwards GJ, Taylor CJ (2001) Active appearance models. IEEE Trans Pattern Anal Mach Intell 23(6):681–685

Cunningham MR, Roberts AR, Barbee AP, Druen PB, Wu CH (1995) Their ideas of beauty are, on the whole, the same as ours: consistency and variability in the cross-cultural perception of female physical attractiveness. J Pers Soc Psychol 68(2):261–279

Dryden IL, Mardia KV (1998) Statistical shape analysis. John

Eisenthal Y, Dror G, Ruppin E (2006) Facial attractiveness: beauty and the machine. Neural Comput 18(1):119–142

Fan J, Chau KP, Wan X, Zhai L, Lau E (2012) Prediction of facial attractiveness from facial proportions. Pattern Recogn 45(6):2326–2334

Grant MC, Boyd SP (2008) Graph implementations for nonsmooth convex programs. Recent advances in learning and control. Springer, London, pp 95–110. http://stanford.edu/boyd/graph_dcp.html

Grant M, Boyd S (2012) CVX: matlab software for disciplined convex programming, version 2.0 beta. http://cvxr.com/cvx, sep

Gray D, Yu K, Xu W, Gong Y (2010) Predicting facial beauty without landmarks. In: Proceedings of international conference on computer vision, pp 434–447

Gunes H, Piccardi M (2006) Assessing facial beauty through pro- portion analysis by image processing and supervised learning. Int J Hum Comput Stud 64(12):1184–1199

Hastie T, Tibshirani R, Friedman J (2009) The elements of statistical learning. Springer

Jain AK, Klare B, Park U (2012) Face matching and retrieval in forensics applications. IEEE Multimedia 19(1):20–28

Langlois JH, Kalakanis L, Rubenstein AJ, Larson A, Hal-lam M, Smoot M (2000) Maxims or myths of beauty? A meta-analytic and theoretical review. Psychol Bull 126(3):390–423

Leyvand T, Cohen-Or D, Dror G, Lischinski D (2008) Data- driven enhancement of facial attractiveness. ACM Trans Graph 27(3):38:1–38:9

Little AC, Jones BC, DeBruine LM (2011) Facial attractiveness: evolutionary based research. Philos Trans R Soc B: Biol Sci 366(1571):1638–1659

Messer K, Matas J, Kittler J, Luettin J, Maitre G (1999) Xm2vtsdb: the extended m2vts database. In: Proceedings of international conference on audio and video-based biometric Person authentication, vol 964, pp 72–77

Nguyen TV, Liu S, Ni B, Tan J, Rui Y, Yan S (2013) Towards decrypting attractiveness via multi-modality cues. ACM Trans Multimedia Comput Commun Appl 9(4):28

Palm RB (2012) Prediction as a candidate for learning deep hierarchical models of data. Technical University of Denmark, Palm 25

Phillips PJ, Moon H, Rizvi SA, Rauss PJ (2000) The ferret evaluation methodology for face-recognition algorithms. IEEE Trans Pattern Anal Mach Intell 22(10):1090–1104

Schaefer S, McPhail T, Warren J (2006) Image deformation using moving least squares. ACM Trans Graph 25(3):533–540

Schmid K, Marx D, Samal A (2008) Computation of a face attractiveness index based on neoclassical canons, symmetry, and golden ratios. Pattern Recogn 41(8):2710–2717

Vapnik V (1995) The nature of statistical learning theory. Springer

Viola P, Jones M (2001) Rapid object detection using a boosted cascade of simple features. In: Proceedings of IEEE conference on computer vision and pattern recognition, pp 511–518
App store, photo and video. https://itunes.apple.com/hk/genre/ios-photo-video/id6008?mt=8
Keepcap. http://www.keepcap.com/
Picbeauty in google play. https://play.google.com/store/apps/details?id=com.ywqc.picbeauty&hl=zh_HK
Zhang D, Zhao Q, Chen F (2011) Quantitative analysis of human facial beauty using geometric features. Pattern Recogn 44(4):940–950

Part V
Application System

Chapter 13
A Facial Beauty Analysis Simulation System

Precedent chapters provide solid bases for system design and implementation on facial beauty analysis. These bases include various facial features, models, rules and decision making algorithms for beauty analysis. This chapter introduces our face beautification system, which is very useful and many readers will be interested in. In order to assess the face beauty index, we establish this face beauty prediction model and system based on the *Geo + PCANet* method, which can quickly and effectively estimate beauty indexes for new images. In terms of face beautification, we mainly achieve three functions. First, the shape of the face contour, mouth, eyes, nose, and eyebrows are represented by facial landmark points. We propose a method that can effectively adjust the positions of the landmark points to beautify the facial geometry. Then, we improve the moving least squares (MLS) method to warp the original face image by virtue of the new landmark positions and obtain the beautification result. Second, this system enables us to perform face skin beautification, including face speckle removal, wrinkle removal, skin whitening, etc. The system uses the improved multi-level median filtering for face skin beautification. Third, the average face beautification is implemented. We propose a simple method to achieve average face beautification. Experimental results showed that the proposed system can significantly improve facial attractiveness of most of face images.

13.1 Introduction

With the development of the image processing technology, more and more scholars study face aesthetic and have obtained some achievements on facial beauty prediction, face shape beautification, and face skin beautification etc., but there are few systems that implement these functions, which may be viewed as the most useful side of facial beauty analysis.

D. Zhang et al., *Computer Models for Facial Beauty Analysis*,
DOI 10.1007/978-3-319-32598-9_13

In facial beauty prediction, Aarabi et al. (2001) established an automatic scoring system. They defined facial beauty in three levels and chose 40 face images for training and used other 40 face images for testing. Then, they got a classification accuracy of 91 % by using KNN. Turkmen et al. (2007) treated facial beauty prediction as a two-class (beauty or not) problem. They trained a classifier based on a training dataset with 150 female faces and respectively used principal component analysis (PCA) and support vector machine (SVM) for feature extraction and classification. The highest accuracy was obtained by using 170 female face images as the testing data. Also Eisenthal et al. (2006) and Kagian et al. (2006) did similar studies on facial beauty prediction. Gunes et al. (2006) put forward a method based on supervised learning, in which 11 features were used to measure facial beauty. Schmid et al. (2008) focused on the geometry of a face and used actual faces for analysis. They showed that there were some differences in the criteria suitable for analysis of facial attractiveness of males and females. Gray et al. (2010) proposed a method that predicted face beauty without landmarks, in which only texture features were used to describe facial beauty. Zhang et al. (2011) used geometric features to analyze face beauty, and they quantitatively discussed the effect of facial geometric features on human facial beauty by using a similarity transformation invariant shape distance measurement and advanced automatic image processing techniques. Mao et al. (2011) proposed a computational method for estimating facial activeness based on Gabor features and SVM. Experimental results showed that the Feature Point Gabor features performed best and obtained a correlation of 0.93 with average human ratings, but only 100 Chinese female faces were used in the experiment. Gan et al. (2014) utilized deep self-taught learning to learn the concept of facial beauty and produced human-like predictors, but its algorithm is relatively complex. To summarize, existing works on facial beauty prediction took advantage of the image processing and machine learning technique, and scholars have achieved promising results, but there were still some problems. For example, the number of face images in the experiments was inadequate. The facial beauty degrees were not widely distributed.

For face shape beautification, Leyvand et al. (2008) studied the data-driven facial beautification, where the authors beautified frontal face images with the guidance of the SVR model learned from the training data. Melacci et al. (2010) proposed a template-based face beautification system, V.EN.US, which depended on a celebrity beauty database. For face skin beautification, Han et al. (2010) used a binariszation algorithm to roughly separate feature zones on faces, and used an improved multi-level median filtering for face skin beautification. Liang et al. (2014) presented an adaptive edge-preserving energy minimization model with a spatially variant parameter and a high-dimensional guided feature space for mask generation, and then used the adaptive region-aware masks for face skin beautification.

This chapter focuses on our face beauty simulation system. It also includes studies on facial beauty prediction, face shape beautification, face skin beautification and average face beautification. We analyze facial beauty by using geometric features, texture features and some popular facial feature models such as gold ratios model and average face model. In terms of geometric features, we first collect

42 features based on the ASMs model. Then we use the cross-validation method to obtain the optimal 24 geometric features. For prediction of facial beauty index, we compare *K* nearest neighbors (KNN) (Song et al. 2007), linear regress (LR) (Zhou et al. 2012), and support vector regression (SVR) methods (Khalfe 2008). The best result is obtained by KNN. As for texture features, we test the BLBP and *PCANet* (Chan et al. 2014). Fusing the geometric features (*Geo*) and *PCANet* feature (*Geo + PCANet*), we obtain a good result and the Pearson correlation of the obtained facial beauty index and human ratings is so high as 0.869. For face shape beautification, an improved average face beautification algorithm based on the moving least square method is proposed. First, it can automatically retrieve training samples which own similar geometric features with the test sample. Then average landmark points of these training samples are used as the test sample objective control points. The details will be introduced later. Finally, the moving least squares (MLS) method is applied for image warping to obtain the beautification result. For face skin beautification, this chapter uses an improved multi-level median filtering, which can realize speckle removal, wrinkle removal and skin whitening.

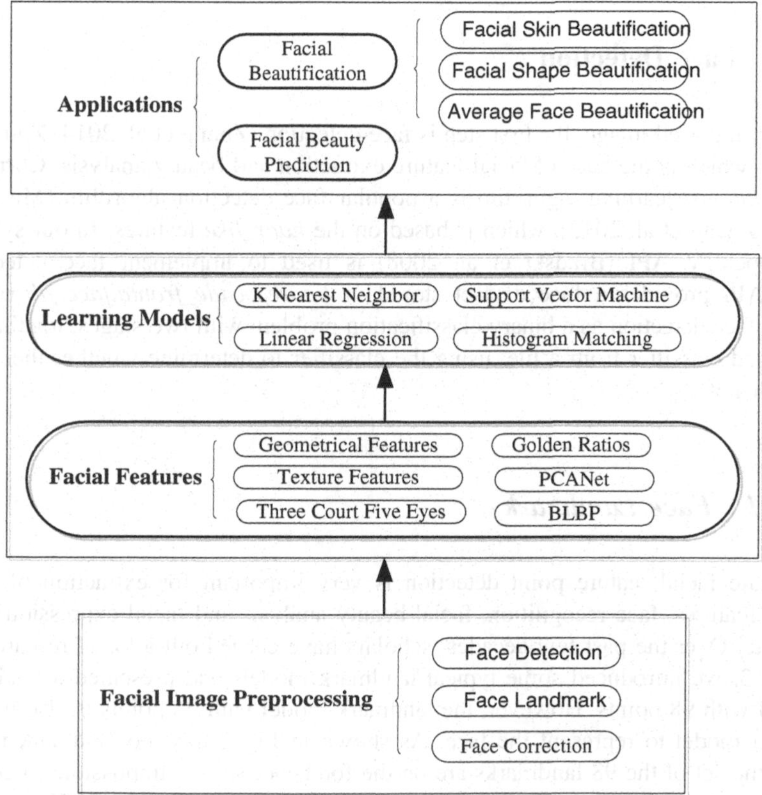

Fig. 13.1 The framework of the simulation system for face aesthetics

For average face beautification, the testing image and a standard model are first divided into the same number of triangles by virtue of ASMs landmark points and each triangle is numbered. Then we map the testing image to the standard model by requiring that the vertex of the corresponding two triangles with the same No. of the standard model and testing image have the same coordinates. Finally, the weighted sum of the new images and our average face template images is obtained to achieve the average face beautification. The framework of the simulation system is shown in Fig. 13.1.

The remainder of the chapter is organized as follows. Section 13.2 describes face image preprocessing including face detection, face landmark and face correction. In Sect. 13.3, we introduce the facial feature extraction methods, including extraction methods on geometric features, texture features, and some facial feature models, such as BLBP, *PCANet*, average face model, gold ratio model, and three court five eye model. These features are helpful for facial beauty prediction. Section 13.4 introduces the details of face shape beautification, face skin beautification and average face beautification. The experiments are shown in Sect. 13.5. Section 13.6 provides the conclusions.

13.2 Face Detection

For an imported image, the first step is face detection (Zhang et al. 2014; Zhu et al. 2012), which is the base of facial feature extraction and beauty analysis. Currently the *Adaboost* learning algorithm is a popular face detection algorithm (Ma et al. 2010; Zhang et al. 2013), which is based on the *haar_like* features. In our system, the OpenCV API (Bradski et al. 2008) is used to implement face detection. This API provides a face dataset stored in *haarcascade_frontalface_alt.xml.* It views face detection as a binary classification problem with two stages, loading the provided classifier from a file, using the classifier to determine whether there is a face or not.

13.2.1 Face Landmark

Accurate facial feature point detection is very important for extraction of good facial features, face recognition, facial beauty analysis and facial expression analysis etc. Over the past few decades, scholars have carried out a lot of research. In Chap. 3, we introduced some typical landmark models and presented a landmark model with 98 points. However, the landmark model with 98 points is also not the perfect model to represent the face. As shown in Fig. 13.2a, no landmark points from the set of the 98 landmarks are on the forehead, so it is impossible to get the skin pattern of the forehead directly by virtue of the landmark points. We improve this model to obtain 101 landmark points on the face, as shown in Fig. 13.2b.

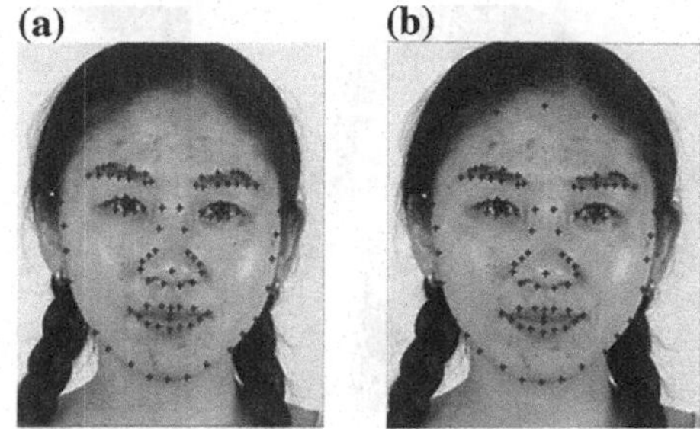

Fig. 13.2 Landmark model. **a** Landmark model with 98 landmark points. **b** Landmark model with 101 landmark points

Here we compare the two landmark models. With the model with 101 landmark points, we propose a simple face region segmentation model (FRSM) to obtain the face region, which would be helpful for facial skin beautification. The main steps of the FRSM are as follows.

1. Using the ASM method to get the 101 landmarks;
2. Catching the location of face contour points;
3. Using the face contour points to achieve a mask image;
4. Segment the face image based on the mask image, and then the hair and background are removed.

After we obtain the face region, we could achieve facial skin beautification with the multilevel median filter model (the detail is presented in Sect. 13.4.2.2). Based on these two landmark models, we obtain different results. As shown in Figs. 13.3 and 13.4, we know that the 101 landmark point model is better, because it is more convenient to beautify the forehead skin.

13.2.2 Face Image Correction

In our face image database, there are different degrees of inclination. An example is shown in Fig. 13.5. So we should identify them and align face images for obtaining

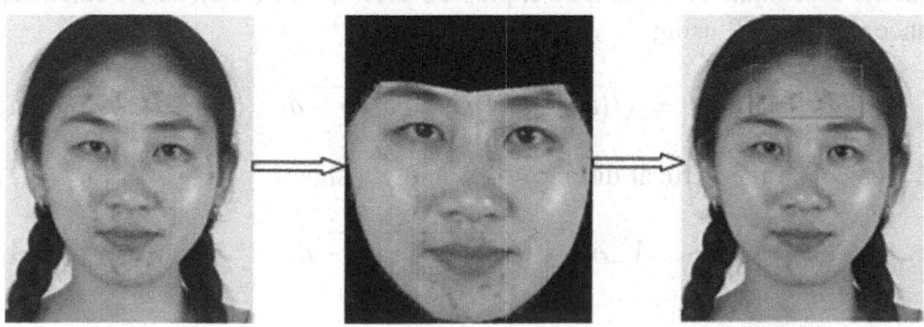

Fig. 13.3 Facial skin beautification result based on the 98 landmark point model

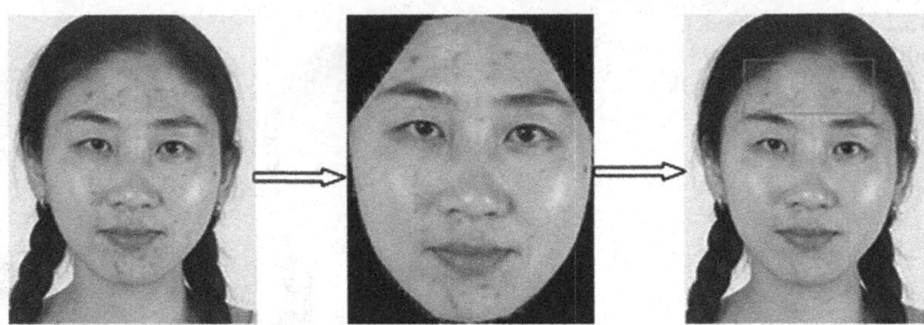

Fig. 13.4 Facial skin beautification result based on the 101 landmark point model

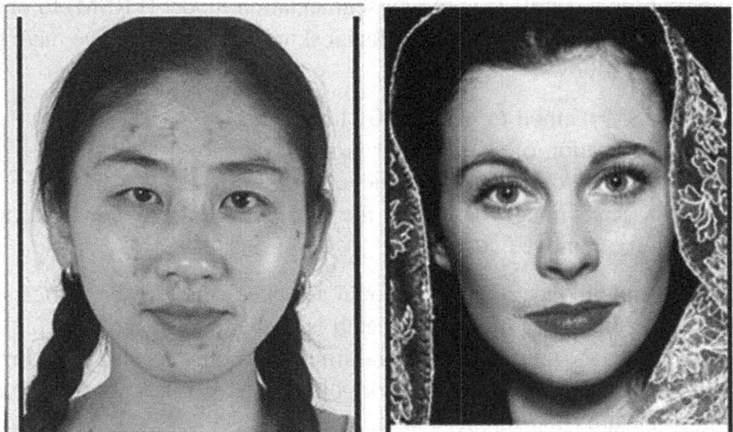

Fig. 13.5 Inclination image instances

better results. Here we use the ASM model with 101 landmark points to align the face including the position of eyes, mouth, nose etc. We choose the center position of the two eyes to determine inclination of face images. As shown in Fig. 13.6, we use A and B as the reference points and perform face inclination correction based on them.

Let the coordinate of A and B be expressed as $A(a, b)$, $B(c, d)$, so we calculate the distance of A and B using

$$Dis\_AB = \sqrt{(a-c)*(a-c)+(b-d)*(b-d)} \tag{13.1}$$

We calculate the vertical distance of A and B using

$$V\_AB = \sqrt{(b-d)*(b-d)} \tag{13.2}$$

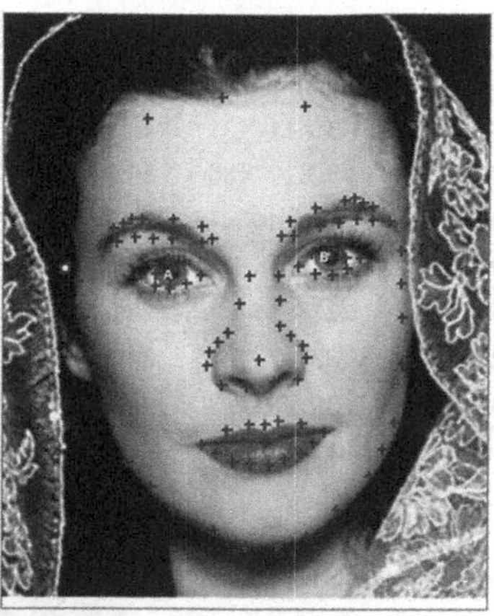

Fig. 13.6 Landmark points on the face

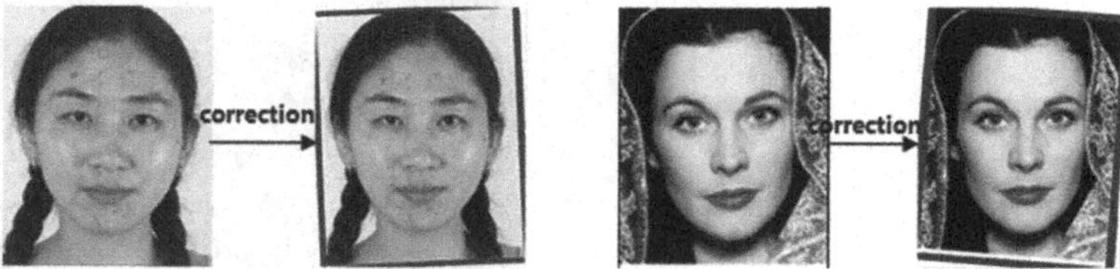

Fig. 13.7 The face alignment result

We see that the tilt angle of faces is usually smaller than 10°, so we obtain the inclination degree by directly calculating the sine value using

$$degree = (HDis_{AB}/(Dis_{AB} * 2 * \pi)) * 360° \tag{13.3}$$

After obtaining the tilt angle, we can easily perform face alignment. Figure 13.7 shows the alignment result.

13.3 Facial Beauty Analysis

13.3.1 Beauty Analysis by Geometry Features

In this section, we use facial geometric features to describe the facial beauty. Based on landmarks, we can exploit some geometric features to describe the face beauty. First, we choose 42 geometric features, which are shown in Table 13.1, including the eye's width, mouth's length, face's length etc. We take the following feature as an example. "**8**:X45-X35" means the 8th feature whose value is the distance in the

Table 13.1 The original 42 geometric features

	Characteristic expression: type number in bold					
Description	**1**:X8-X1	**2**:X21-X8	**3**:X14-X21	**4**:X31-X27	**5**:X41-X31	**6**:X35-X36
Description	**7**:X37-X41	**8**:X45-X35	**9**:X27-X80	**10**:X98-X37	**11**:X62-X47	**12**:X55-X54
Description	**13**:X61-X48	**14**:X60-X49	**15**:X46-X45	**16**:X58-X51	**17**:X97-X81	**18**:X70-X64
Description	**19**:X94-X84	**20**:X95-X83	**21**:X98-X80	**22**:X93-X85	**23**:Y12-Y14	**24**:Y10-Y6
Description	**25**:Y25-Y17	**26**:Y23-Y19	**27**:Y54-Y47	**28**:Y56-Y45	**29**:Y33-Y29	**30**:Y43-Y39
Description	**31**:Y8-Y100	**32**:Y54-Y8	**33**:Y70-Y45	**34**:Y67-Y55	**35**:Y78-Y67	**36**:Y89-Y70
Description	**37**:Y89-Y54	**38**:Y84-Y35	**39**:Y83-Y80	**40**:Y74-Y79	**41**:Y89-Y74	**42**:Y63-Y100

Note The number in bold stands for the type of the feature

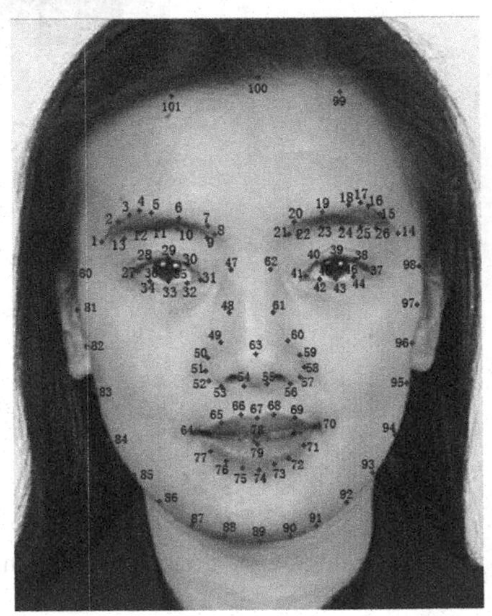

Fig. 13.8 The No. of each landmark point

horizontal direction between the 35th and 45th points. "35" and "45" are corresponding to the numbers in Fig. 13.8. In order to obtain the best geometric features to describe face beauty, we use a method based on *KNN* to choose the best combination of features. The obtained best combination of features Nos. are 18, 16, 1, 17, 4, 8, 23, 24, 25, 26, 31, 11, 7, 22, 5, 32, 33, 29, 30, 33, 34, 35, 40, 41 which are from Table 13.1.

The procedure to obtain the best combination of features is presented below. 42 initial geometric features are obtained for each image. Among the 42 initial geometric features there are redundant features, so we should seek the best combination of features. In the proposed systems, we adopt the feature selection algorithm presented in Sect. 6.2.1 of Chap. 6 to select the best combination of features for facial beauty analysis. The steps can be briefly summarized as follows: first, we randomly divide all images into 10 equal portions. Then we randomly view a portion as the test sample, and treat the others as training samples. The result of 10-fold cross validation is viewed as the final result. We use the KNN to get a machine rater for each image and exploit the Pearson correlation of the machine rater and human rater to evaluate the result. The rule to select a feature is that the higher of the correlation the better of the feature.

13.3.2 Beauty Analysis by Texture Features

As for the facial texture features, we use the LBP features. Specifically, we use the BLBP model and *PCANet* model to analyze facial beauty. The BLBP has some advantages. For example, it can generate more samples based on the current sample. Moreover, in aesthetic research of human faces, the main means is to exploit human faces with similar beauty to obtain their common properties, rather than to identify a human face. Experiments show that it is more reliable to exploit the local facial skin similarity than to exploit holistic facial skin similarity. BLBP defines a new scoring model which is very different from the usual scoring model. Specially, more detailed information about the BLBP has presented in Sect. 6.2.2.2, and the *PCANet* model is introduced in Sect. 7.2.7.

13.3.3 Beauty Analysis by Popular Feature Model

In the study of facial aesthetics, there are some popular facial feature models such as the average face model, the gold ratio model, and the three court five eyes model. These models first obtain some facial geometric features, and then describe the facial beauty by them. We present some applications of these models in facial beauty prediction below.

Model1–Average face model (AFM): the average face model first generates an average face as a template, and then extracts the corresponding geometric features. In this chapter, Fig. 13.11 in Sect. 13.4.2 shows a template. We first extract 24 geometric features which are presented in Sect. 13.3.1 for each facial image, then we calculate their similarity by distance matching.

Let $TE = [t_1, t_2, t_3 \ldots t_{24}]$ be the geometric feature vector of the template. N is the test sample number. $TT = [tt_1, tt_2, tt_3 \ldots tt_N]$ is the matrix composed of geometric feature vectors of the test samples, and $tt_i = [tt_{i1}, tt_{i2}, tt_{i3} \ldots tt_{i24}]$ denotes the ith test sample. Then we calculate the ith similarity with the template by

$$S_i = \sum_{j=1}^{24} (t_j - tt_j) * (t_j - tt_j) \tag{13.4}$$

Table 13.2 Some gold ratios from Schmid et al. (2008)

Ratio number	Numerator points	Denominator points	Description
1	X41-X31	X45-X35	Interocular distance to mideye distance
2	X57-X52	X45-X35	Nose width to mideye distance
3	X41-X31	X70-X64	Interocular distance to mouth width
4	X37-X1	X41-X31	Eye fissure width to interocular distance
5	X37-X41	X57-X52	Eye fissure width to nose width
6	X97-X81	Y89-Y100	Width of face to length of face
7	X57-X52	X70-X64	Nose width to mouth width

Table 13.3 The features of three court five eyes model

Ratio number	Numerator points	Denominator points	Value
1	D1 = Y8-Y100	H = Y89-Y100	D1/H
2	D2 = Y54-Y8	H = Y89-Y100	D2/H
3	D3 = Y89-Y54	H = Y89-Y100	D3/H
4	D4 = X27-X80	W = X98-X80	D4/W
5	D5 = X31-X27	W = X98-X80	D5/W
6	D6 = X41-X31	W = X98-X80	D6/W
7	D7 = X37-X41	W = X98-X80	D7/W
8	D8 = X98-X41	W = X98-X80	D8/W

S_i is normalized to [1, 10] and we obtain $S = [S_1, S_2, S_3 \ldots S_N]$. When an image is more beautiful, we usually assign a higher score to it. Thus, we take $SSS = 10 - SS = [SSS_1, SSS_2, SSS_3 \ldots SSS_N]$ as the result, i.e. score. Finally, we calculate the Pearson correlation of SSS and scores from the human rater.

Model2–Gold ratios model (TGRM): The gold ratio model selects some gold ratios to analyze facial beauty. In this chapter, we choose 7 gold ratios from Schmid et al. (2008) (the detail description is shown in Table 13.2), where the number after X or Y is corresponding to those of the landmark points in Fig. 13.8. Then we also calculate their similarity by distance matching. This is similar with the average face model. But in the gold ratio model, the initial feature vector of the template is fixed e.g. $TE = [0.618, 0.618, 0.618, 0.618, 0.618, 0.618, 0.618]$.

Model3–Three court five eyes model (TCFEM): The three court five eye model uses eight facial geometric features, which are shown in Table 13.3, where the number after X or Y is corresponding to those of the landmark points in Fig. 13.8. Then we also calculate their similarity by distance matching. In this model, the initial feature vector is fixed e.g. $TE = [0.333, 0.333, 0.333, 0.200, 0.200, 0.200, 0.200, 0.200]$.

13.4 Facial Aesthetics Applications

13.4.1 Facial Beauty Prediction Model

After we obtain the face geometric (*Geo*) features and texture features, we can build a face beauty prediction model. The used learning models include KNN, SVR, LR, histogram matching (HM) (Shen 2007) and distance matching (DM) (Cormode et al. 2007). In this chapter, the 10 fold cross-validation is used as the experiment scheme (Golub et al. 1979). In the field of face aesthetics, the Pearson correlation coefficient (Lee et al. 1988; Pearson 1920) is one of the most widely used evaluation indices, so we use the Pearson Correlation and the running time as evaluation indices. Table 13.4 shows the experiment results on our image set. Based on the results in Table 13.4, our Face Beauty Analysis System selects the *PCANet* fusion geometric features (*Geo + PCANet*) to predict the face beauty in terms of the accuracy. In the system, we chose the fusion method presented in Sect. 6.3 for facial prediction. For example, let *A* be the scores of the KNN model on the 24 geometric features. Let *B* be the scores of the SVR model on the *PCANet* features. *A* (*i*) and *B*(*i*) correspond to the same image machine rater and *i* denotes the *ith* test image. We obtain final scores by formula (13.5).

$$C(i) = a * A(i) + b * B(i) \tag{13.5}$$

where $a + b = 1$, Then we obtain the Pearson Correlation of *C* and human rater scores.

Table 13.4 The experiments results for prediction face beauty for different learning model

	Pearson correlation	Running time (s)	Learning model
Geo	0.762	<2	KNN
BLBP	0.852	<35	HM
PCANet	0.858	<2	SVR
Average face model	0.452	<1	DM
Gold ratios	0.323	<1	DM
Three court five eyes	0.441	<1	DM
Geo + BLBP	0.864	<36	KNN + HM
BLBP + PCANet	0.882	<37	HM + SVR
Geo + PCANet	**0.869**	**<3**	**KNN + SVR**
PCANet + Geo + BLBP	0.889	<38	SVR + KNN + HM

Bold is the results obtained by the method used in our Face Beauty Analysis System

13.4.2 Facial Beautification Model

13.4.2.1 Facial Shape Beautification Model

We use the moving least squares (MLS) method (Schaefer et al. 2006) based on the control points to achieve face shape beautification. The MLS method can well determine effective target control points. In the implementation of the system, we use the average face hypothesis and MLS to obtain the corresponding target control points for each image and achieve facial shape beautification. For a test face image, we first predict its beauty index by our learning model. Then we search similar faces that have higher prediction scores from our training data set. Finally, we get the target control points by virtue of the mean of the landmark points of the similar faces. The details are as follows.

Let I be a test image. $P = [p_1, p_2, p_3, \ldots, p_{101}]$ is its landmark points set and $X = [x_1, x_2, x_3, \ldots, x_{24}]$ is its geometric features. y is the prediction score of the *PCANet + KNN* model. Let N be the number of training samples. *PL* is a matrix to represent the set of landmark points of all training samples and each row of *PL* represents a sample. In other words, $PL = [pl_1, pl_2, pl_3, \ldots, pl_N]$ is landmarks of the ith sample and $i \leq N$, Let $Y = [y_1, y_2, y_3, \ldots, y_N]$ be the set of training sample rater scores. $PF = [pf_1, pf_2, pf_3, \ldots, pf_N]^T$ and $pf_i = [f_{i,1}, f_{i,2}, f_{i,3}, \ldots, f_{i,24}]$ is geometric features of the ith sample. Then we can find the most similar image of test image x_i by

$$\begin{aligned} &\min \sum_{j=1}^{N} \sum_{i=1}^{24} (x_i - f_{j,i})^2 \\ &s.t. \quad y \leq y_j \end{aligned} \tag{13.6}$$

We seek 10 training samples most similar with the test image under the condition that the sought training samples have higher indices than the test image and denote these similar images by $pl_1, pl_2, pl_3, \ldots, pl_M$. It should be pointed out that the scores of the sought 10 training samples must be 1 higher than that of the test image. Target control points $PD = [pd_1, pd_2, \ldots, pd_{101}]$ are obtained by

$$for\ each\ i\, pd_i = \frac{1}{N} \sum_{j=1}^{N} p_{j,i} \ where\ i \leq 101 \tag{13.7}$$

13.4.2.2 Facial Skin Beautification Model

For face skin beautification, we first determine the region to beautify, because we should apply face skin beautification to only the face skin region and should exclude regions of the eyes, mouth and nose. Based on facial landmark points

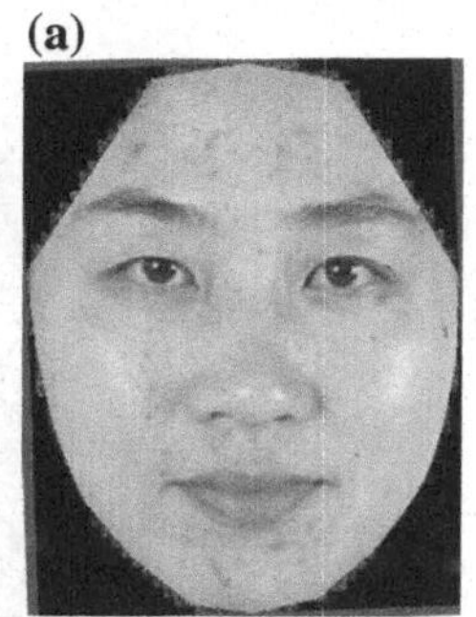

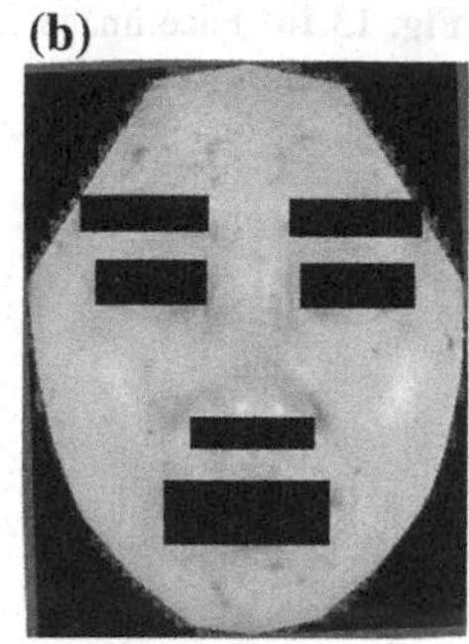

Fig. 13.9 Illustration of the face skin region. **a** Initialize face area. **b** Face skin beautification area

obtained by ASMs model we can easily determine the face skin region. The details are presented as follows.

Let F be the face region shown in Fig. 13.9a. Figure 13.9b shows the face skin region suitable for beautification (backs rectangular stand for the regions to exclude in face skin beautification). Then we realize face beauty for the face skin region shown in Fig. 13.9b by using an improved method of multi-level median filtering (Hu et al. 2009; Kuang et al. 2010). In our system, in order to get better results, we perform median filtering operation seven times for each face image.

13.4.2.3 Average Face Beautification Model

The average face is generated using some face images with the same size. A pixel in the average face is weighted sum of the pixels at the same position of these face images. When one produce the average face, the used face images should be well aligned and appropriate weights should be set. We align face images based on the position of the eyes. We resize the images for obtaining the same image size. In this chapter, a relatively simple ASMs based method for face mapping is proposed. First, a 'standard human face template' is adopted, and then the landmark points based on ASMs model are exploited to perform face triangulation. Taking into account the efficiency, this chapter obtains 42 triangles as shown in Fig. 13.10, where a number represents the No. of a triangle. In order to get our average face, we also carry out the above procedure for 100 images. Then we achieve face alignment by mapping these face images after face triangulation to new positions according to the 'standard human face template. Finally, the weighted sum of the aligned face images is viewed as average face. In the experiment we use the mean weighted method to generate the average face shown in Fig. 13.11.

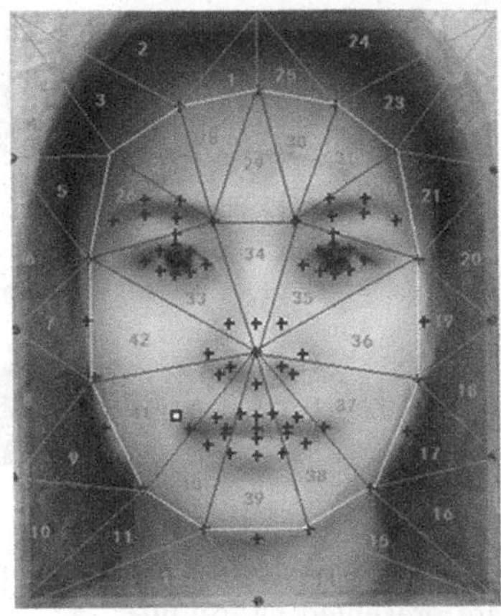

Fig. 13.10 Face image triangulation

Fig. 13.11 Average face

13.5 System Design for Facial Beauty Simulation

13.5.1 System Interface

This part mainly introduces the interface and function of the aesthetic system. Figure 13.12 is the main interface of the whole aesthetic system. Figure 13.12 shows that the main interface allows the image to be online or offline imported and allows landmark facial feature points to be depicted. It also provides the facial beauty index. We can also conveniently shift to the facial landmark point position adjustment interface and the functional interface of facial beautification to show facial shape beautification, facial skin beautification and average face beautification via the main interface. As shown in Fig. 13.12, the button of "Open Album" enables the test image to be imported from an album. We present the process to online import a facial image as follows. First, we should press button "Open Camera" to capture the video. Second, we can press button "Capture Image" to

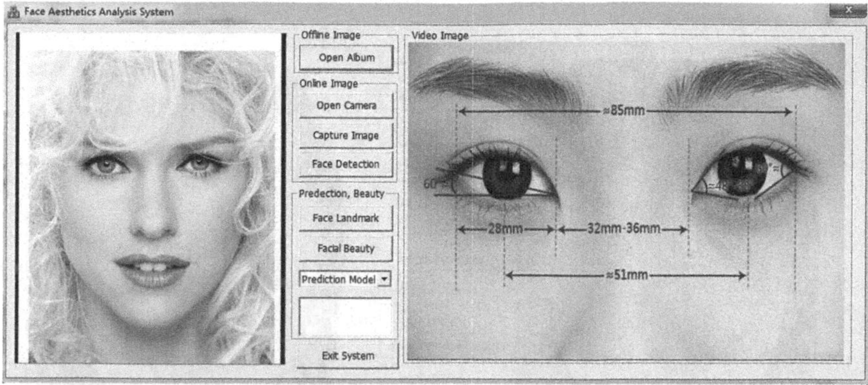

Fig. 13.12 The main interface of the whole aesthetic system

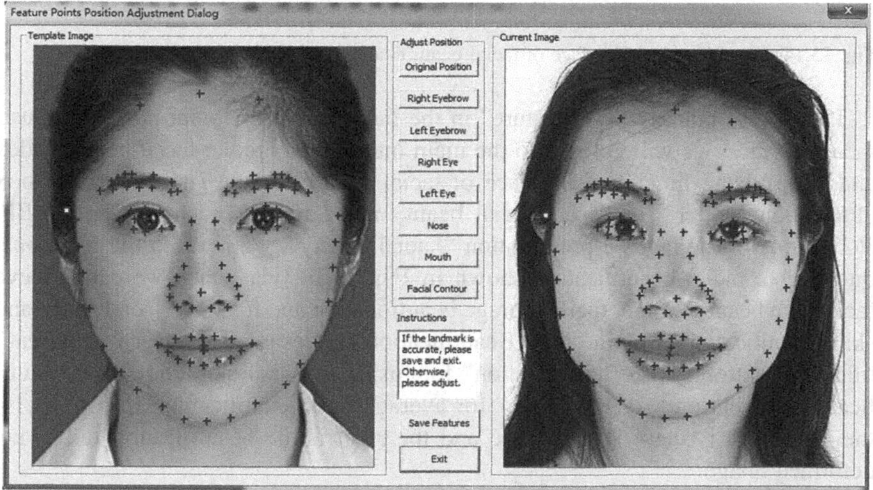

Fig. 13.13 Facial landmark points position adjustment interface

obtain current static picture. Finally, we should press button "Face Detect" to get the facial image. Then we should obtain face landmarks by pressing button "Face landmark". After we press button "Face Landmark", we turn to the facial landmark point position adjustment interface as shown in Fig. 13.13, which allows the landmark point position to be adjusted. We can choose points in different facial regions to adjust, such as the Right Eyebrow, Left Eyebrow, Left Eye and Nose. If button "original position" is pressed, the recovery of the original face landmark point position will be obtained. To press button "Save Feature" allows us to obtain the geometric and texture features.

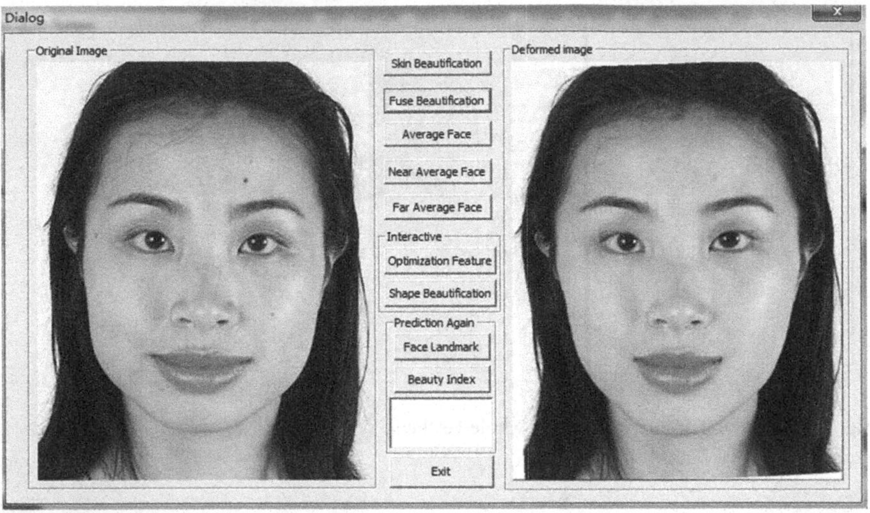

Fig. 13.14 The functional interface of facial beautification

If we press button "Save Feature" in the facial landmark point position adjustment interface, we will go back to the main interface to predict facial beauty index and jump to the functional interface of facial beautification. The drop-down box "Prediction Model" shows our facial beauty index models such as *Geo*, BLBP, *PCANet*, AFM. When we press button "Facial beauty", we jump to the functional interface of facial beautification shown in Fig. 13.14, via which we can achieve facial skin beautification, facial average beautification and fusion of facial shape and skin beautification. Button "Skin Beautification" is designed for facial skin beautification, button "Fuse Beautification" for fusion of facial skin and shape beautification and button "Average Face" for average face beautification. In Fig. 13.14, the left image is the original image and the right is the beautification result, i.e. deformed image.

13.5.2 Data Collection and Database

In order to test beautiful index of new facial images, we have collected images to create a human face beauty score library as a training set. We collect female face images of 790 individuals. Firstly, we seek 9 human raters and number them by 1–9. Then we use the mean score of these human raters as the final human score of an image. In this chapter, we divide our image database into 10 parts. We randomly select a part as the test sample set and use the others as the training sample set to conduct an experiment. We do so 10 times and regard the average of all results as the final result. Some face images in the created image gallery are shown in Fig. 13.15.

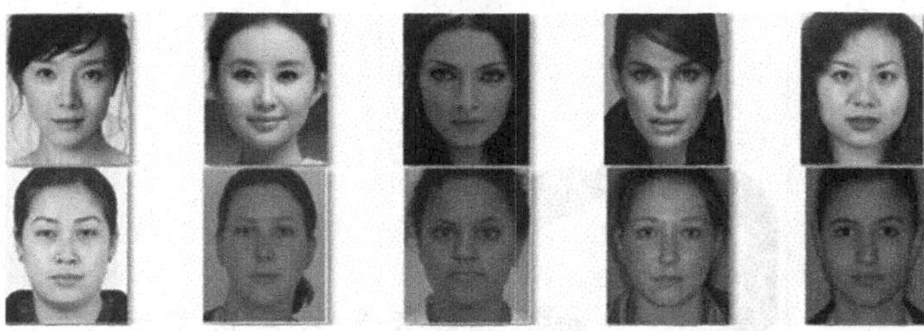

Fig. 13.15 Some face images in the created image gallery

13.5.3 Experimental Results

Our system is implemented by the C++ programming language and WIN7 OS platform. In this system we use the OpenCV as the image processing tools to read and save an image and to perform image scaling and face detection. According to Table 13.4, we should use the *Geo + PCANet* model to predict the facial beauty index owing to its best performance, and we also compare prediction results of the face beauty index obtained using different models such as *Geo*, BLBP, *PCANet*, AFM, GRM. Table 13.5 shows some prediction results of the face beauty index, where the higher the score the more beauty the face is. As shown in Table 13.5, we see that the AFM, GRM, TCFEM models do not perform well in predicting the facial beauty index and the BLBP, *PCANet*, *Geo + PCANet* etc. models can get good results.

Figure 13.16 shows the results of facial shape beautification, from which we know that the moving least squares method based on the control points is effective for face shape beautification. Figure 13.17 shows the results of facial skin beautification. It tells us that the improved multi-level median filtering is effective for face skin beautification. Figure 13.18 shows the fusion results of the face skin beautification and face shape beautification.

Figure 13.19 shows the results of the average face beautification. For each test image, we first perform face triangulation. Then we map the testing image to a new image by virtue of our template image. Finally, the weighted sum of the new image and our average face template image is the result of the average face beautification. In the experiments, we set different weights for obtaining different average face beautifications.

Finally, the reliability of this system is tested by experiments. The first test is performed for validating the reliability about facial beauty prediction. The second test is performed for validating the reliability about facial skin beautification. The third is performed for validating the reliability on facial shape beautification. At the same time, we also record the time spent on completing each function. For facial beauty prediction, the Pearson correlation of facial beauty prediction and human scoring results is used to evaluate the reliability, and according to Sect. 13.4.1, the result is 0.869. The running time of the system is evaluated according to the average time spent for prediction of each image. 100 face images are first selected to

Table 13.5 The results of prediction facial beauty

Origin image				
Prediction facial beauty				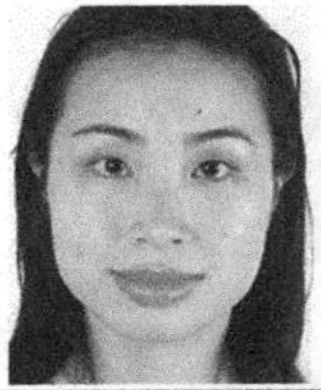
Geo	6.58	4.65	3.25	5.16
BLBP	6.07	7.55	2.22	4.24
PCANet	8.53	7.25	3.42	5.48
AFM	8.00	2.00	1.00	10.00
GRM	1.00	1.00	1.00	1.00
TCFEM	2.00	10.00	6.00	4.00
Geo + BLBP	6.22	6.68	2.53	4.52
Geo + PCANet	7.94	7.12	3.37	5.38
BLBP + PCANet	7.30	7.40	2.81	4.86

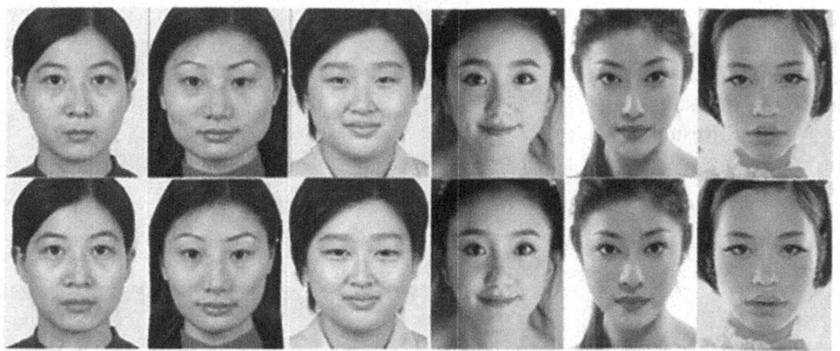

Fig. 13.16 Face shape beautification for mouth, contour and eyes, eyebrows, nose, mean face

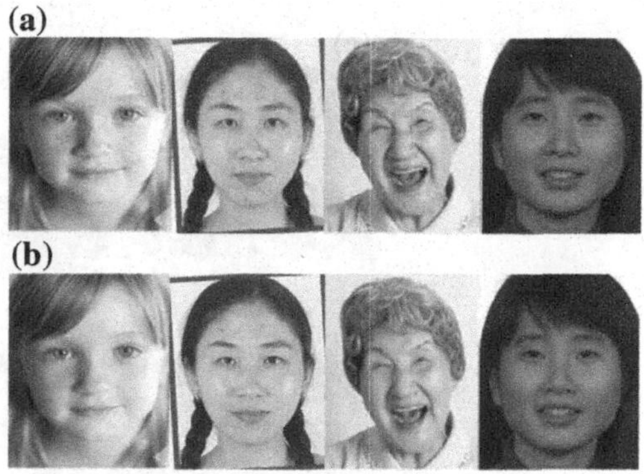

Fig. 13.17 Facial skin beautification. **a** Origin image. **b** Results

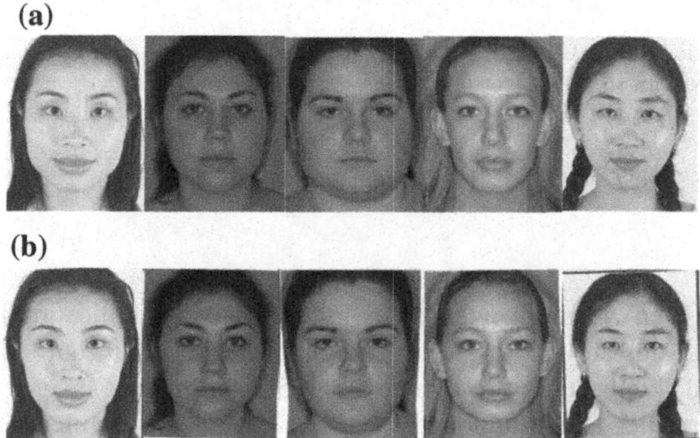

Fig. 13.18 Fusing face shape beautification with face shape beautification. **a** Origin image. **b** Results

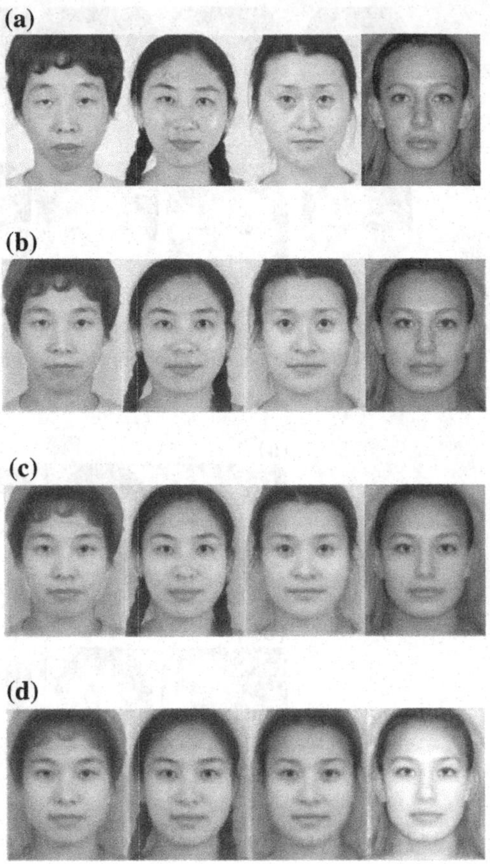

Fig. 13.19 Average face beautification. **a** Origin image. **b** Results (weight = 3:7). **c** Results (weight = 5:5). **d** Results (weight = 7:3)

Table 13.6 Reliability test results of the system

	Reliability (%)	Running time (s)
Facial beauty prediction	86.9	<3
Facial shape beautification	80.0	<3
Facial skin beautification	>95.0	<7

beautify, and then we get manual scores for the facial beautification images again. The manual scores are very useful for judging whether the beauty is improved or not. For facial skin beautification, more than 95 % of the face images obtain higher manual scores after face beautification, and the average beautification time is less than 7 s. For facial shape beautification, near 80 % of the face images obtain higher manual scores, and the average beautification time is less than 3 s. Table 13.6 shows the test results of the system reliability.

13.6 Summary

This chapter implements an ASM-based face beautification system. First, we realize face detection on the imported image based on OpenCV and obtain the face landmarks points based on ASMs. Then, we use the landmarks points to build the geometric features to represent the face beauty. Finally, the *Geo + PCANet* model is built to obtain the beautiful index of new images. The experiments show that our face beautification results are consistent with subjective evaluation of humans. As for the face shape beautification, we use the moving least squares method based on the control points to achieve face beautification, and the experiments show that this method is very effective. As for the face skin beautification, we use the multi-level median filtering to conduct experiments, and finally we obtain good results. We also propose a simple average face beautification model. There still exist some problems and the main one is the computational efficiency of face skin beautification is relatively low, so we should improve the method of multi-level median filtering for computational efficiency or find a new method for face skin beautification.

References

Aarabi P, Hughes D, Mohajer K, Emami M (2001) The automatic measurement of facial beauty. In: Proceedings of IEEE international conference on systems, man, and cybernetics, pp 2644–2647

Bradski G, Kaehler A (2008) Learning OpenCV: computer vision with the OpenCV library. O'Reilly Media Inc.

Chan T H, Jia K, Gao S, Lu J, Zeng Z, Ma Y (2014) PCANet: a simple deep learning baseline for image classification? arXiv preprint 1404.3606

Cormode G, Muthukrishnan S (2007) The string edit distance matching problem with moves. ACM Trans Algorithms 3(1):2

Eisenthal Y, Dror G, Ruppin E (2006) Facial attractiveness: beauty and the machine. Neural Comput 18(1):119–142

Gan J, Li L, Zhai Y, Liu Y (2014) Deep self-taught learning for facial beauty prediction. Neurocomputing 144:295–303

Golub GH, Heath M, Wahba G (1979) Generalized cross-validation as a method for choosing a good ridge parameter. Technometrics 21(2):215–223

Gray D, Yu K, Xu W, Gong Y (2010) Predicting facial beauty without landmarks. In: Proceedings of European conference on computer vision, pp 434–447

Gunes H, Piccardi M (2006) Assessing facial beauty through proportion analysis by image processing and supervised learning. Int J Hum Comput Stud 64:1184–1199

Han J (2010) Face beautification based on iterated multistage median filtering. Computer applications & software, 227–229

Hu Y, Ji H (2009) Research on image median filtering algorithm and its FPGA implementation. In: Proceedings of WRI global congress on intelligent systems, pp 226–230

Kagian A, Dror G, Leyvand T, Cohen-Or D, Ruppin E (2006) A humanlike predictor of facial attractiveness. In: Proceedings of advances in neural information processing systems, pp 649–656

Khalfe NM (2008) Support vector regression (SVR)

Kuang P, Sun L (2010) An improved two-dimensional multi-level median filtering algorithm. In: Proceedings of international conference on apperceiving computing and intelligence analysis, pp 359–362
Lee RJ, Nicewander WA (1988) Thirteen ways to look at the correlation coefficient. Am Stat 42:59–66
Leyvand T, Cohen-Or D, Dror G, Lischinski D (2008) Data-driven enhancement of facial attractiveness. ACM Trans Graph 27(3):38
Liang L, Jin L, Li X (2014) Facial skin beautification using adaptive region-aware masks. IEEE Trans Cybern 44(12):2600–2612
Ma S, Du T (2010) Improved Adaboost face detection. In: Proceedings of international conference on measuring technology and mechatronics automation, pp 434–437
Mao H, Chen Y, Jin L, Du M (2011) Evaluating facial attractiveness: an Gabor feature approach. J Commun Comput 8(8):674–679
Melacci S, Sarti L, Maggini M, Gori M (2010) A template-based approach to automatic face enhancement. Pattern Anal Appl 13(3):289–300
Pearson K (1920) Notes on the history of correlation. Biometrika 25–45
Schaefer S, McPhail T, Warren J (2006) Image deformation using moving least squares. ACM Trans Graph 25(3):533–540
Schmid K, Marx D, Samal A (2008) Computation of a face attractiveness index based on neoclassical canons, symmetry, and golden ratios. Pattern Recogn 41(8):2710–2717
Shen D (2007) Image registration by local histogram matching. Pattern Recogn 40(4):1161–1172
Song Y, Huang J, Zhou D, Zha H, Giles C L (2007) Iknn: Informative k-nearest neighbor pattern classification. Knowledge Discovery in Databases: PKDD, pp 248-264
Turkmen H, Kurt Z, Karsligil ME (2007) Global feature based female facial beauty decision system. In: Proceedings of EURASIP07, pp 1945–1949
Zhang C, Zhang Z (2014) Improving multiview face detection with multi-task deep convolutional neural networks. In: Proceedings of IEEE winter conference on applications of computer vision, pp 1036–1041
Zhang D, Zhao Q, Chen F (2011) Quantitative analysis of human facial beauty using geometric features. Pattern Recogn 44(4):940–950
Zhang J, Li J, Jiang S, Wei Z, Li J, Xu S, Wang S (2013) The research of face detection based on double skin model and Adaboost algorithm. In: Proceedings of IEEE conference anthology, pp 1–4
Zhou Y, Qureshi R, Sacan A (2012) Data simulation and regulatory network reconstruction from time-series microarray data using stepwise multiple linear regression. Netw Model Anal Health Inf Bioinform 1(1–2):3–17
Zhu X, Ramanan D (2012) Face detection, pose estimation, and landmark localization in the wild. In: Proceedings of IEEE conference on computer vision and pattern recognition, pp 2879–2886

Chapter 14
Book Review and Future Work

With the title "Computer Models for Facial Beauty Analysis" this book mainly focuses on building computation models for analysis and prediction of the face beauty. The book contains five parts. Part I presents a brief overview of the facial beauty analysis methods proposed in recent years. Part II introduces some features, such as geometric features and texture features, which are widely used for facial beauty analysis. Part III analyzes the hypotheses based beauty analysis method and proposes a new hypothesis for facial beauty perception. Part IV presents a computational model for facial beauty analysis. In this part, the facial model evaluation criterion is also offered. Part V gives a briefly introduction to the online and offline face beautification simulation system for automatic beauty analysis. In this chapter, we summarize the book and present future work for facial beauty analysis. Section 14.1 gives an overview of the previous chapters. In Sect. 14.2, we discuss the challenges in facial beauty analysis and future work.

14.1 Overview of the Book

Using the computation technology to perform facial beauty analysis has wide applications, especially in the field of aesthetic surgery and beauty evaluation. This book can be viewed as a guide to analysis of the facial beauty. The book is organized with five parts.

PART I introduces the background and some traditional methods of facial beauty analysis. In Chap. 1, we first introduce potential applications of computational-based facial beauty analysis to demonstrate its importance. Then we give a review on the development history of the facial beauty analysis. After that, from the computational aspect, the chapter summarizes some problems of the facial beauty study. The databases which are used in this book for facial beauty analysis are also introduced in detail. Chapter 2 gives a review of the typical facial beauty analysis methods such as the golden ratio rules, vertical thirds and horizontal fifths rules,

D. Zhang et al., *Computer Models for Facial Beauty Analysis*,
DOI 10.1007/978-3-319-32598-9_14

averageness hypothesis and symmetry hypothesis and discusses the advantages and limitations of them.

PART II mainly discusses and introduces features, such as geometric features, texture features, and representative features used in the application of facial beauty analysis. Chapter 3 presents the landmark model and its optimal model by extracting the key points (KPs) and inserted points (IPs) based on facial geometry features. Then in Chap. 4, the book presents an useful landmark model evaluation method for the assessment of different models. The proposed model evaluation method is also based on facial geometric features. Chapter 5 mainly assesses the putative ratio rules, including neoclassical canons, golden ratios, and horizontal fifths and vertical thirds by virtue of both whole dataset and individual clusters. Unlike other methods that extract and exploit only geometric features for facial beauty analysis, the method presented in Chap. 6 also extracts texture features, and combines texture features and geometric features to analyze facial beauty. The experiment shows that the combination of the two types of features obtains better performance than either of them. In order to obtain features best suitable for features for facial beauty analysis, Chap. 6 makes a comprehensive comparison of some well-known features including putative ratios, shape parameters, eigenface, active appearance models, Gabor, local binary patterns (LBP), PCANet features, and different combination of above features for facial attractiveness prediction. Chap. 7 shows that combining multiple types of features at the score level can significantly improve the performance of facial beauty prediction.

PART III mainly analyzes hypotheses based facial beauty prediction methods. In this part Chap. 8 presents the averageness hypothesis and proves the effectiveness of the averageness hypothesis on facial beauty prediction. Chapter 9 presents a new hypothesis on facial beauty perception. It also proposes a convex hull-based beautification method and compares it with state-of-the-art methods and analyzes their intrinsic relationships.

PART IV focuses on data-driven facial beauty modeling methods. In this part Chap. 10 presents an evolutionary cost-sensitive extreme learning machine for facial beauty analysis in detail. Chap. 11 proposes a causal effect criterion for model evaluation, which enables the facial models to be interpretable. Chap. 12 describes a general framework of data-driven facial beauty modeling and illustrates its applications.

PART V aims at introducing our designed online and offline facial beauty analysis system. This applicable system can implement face image processing, facial beauty analysis and prediction as well as face beautification.

14.2 Challenges and Future Work

Though a number of facial beauty models have been proposed for facial beauty analysis, there are still challenges and unsolved issues. For example, the first challenge is to extract proper features for beauty analysis from facial images with expressions such as gladness and enjoyness. Actually, facial features will be affected by expressions, so to obtain stable features for beauty analysis is crucial. The following means may be adopted by data-driven beauty analysis algorithms to alleviate the above influence. When collecting labels or beauty indices of faces given by human raters, we provide multiple images of the same face including images with various facial expressions. As a result, human raters can more clearly observe the face and are easier to find beautiful and unbeautiful factors. Moreover, human raters are required to give the same evaluation result for all images of the same face. Compared with conventional schemes in which facial images are evaluated one by one, the above scheme can effectively prevent human raters from being affected by exaggerated beautiful or unbeautiful factor from an individual facial image. With more 'accurate' evaluation on the facial images of human raters, a data-driven beauty analysis algorithm can be better trained by respectively using the facial images and corresponding manual evaluation e.g. labels or beauty indices as inputs and outputs. In other words, the algorithm will perform better in seeking more essential beauty hidden in the raw various images. Thus, the algorithm will be able to better perform beauty analysis on unseen facial images. Moreover, if multiple facial images of the subject to be assessed are also available, a more reliable analysis result may be obtained.

The second challenge is to compare facial beauty of faces with different expressions. It seems that usually some faces with similes are more charming. Moreover, even if one smiling facial image and one neutral facial image are captured from the same face, it is usually that the smiling facial image is more attractive. In other words, from the viewpoint of human perception, smiling facial images are usually more beautiful than neutral facial images. Thus, it is significant for a real-world system to eliminate the beauty gap between faces with different expressions for 'fair' comparison and analysis of beauty analysis and to obtain more objective evaluation on facial beauty, which is dominated by intrinsical features or factors and is almost not influenced by superficial and external factors. In our opinion, we may partially address the above challenge with the help of methodologies of other fields. For example, if we first exploit facial expression analysis algorithms to identify the expression of a facial image, we will be able to better evaluate its beauty index by applying a beauty analysis and taking into the influence of different expressions account. On the other hand, to properly eliminate the influence on beauty analysis of facial expressions seems not to be an easy work.

The third challenge is from the skin difference associated with races. An extreme case is that a general skin beauty analysis model or method may be not suitable for people with black skin. Therefore, it is necessary for the designed system to take into account this special case and to design an elaborated algorithm to perform beauty analysis and prediction. In order to achieve this, researchers also should try to collect face beauty evaluations of different races on the faces of their own races such as black people, by virtue of which supervised learning can be performed on the basis of available data. After being trained by massive facial images and labels or beauty indices, the obtained algorithm can perform well in analyzing the face beauty of a certain race. We think that to obtain race-associated skin beauty analysis model or method is also an interesting issue.

Another important problem is how to efficiently perform beauty analysis and prediction for 3D faces. What humane perceive are 3D faces rather than 2D faces, so automatic facial beauty analysis of 3D faces is of course closer to perception of humans. Extraction of stable and reliable 3D facial features is one important aspect of beauty analysis of 3D faces. Of course, 3D geometrical measurement of the face is the key to beauty analysis and prediction for 3D faces. It is also significant for extended applications of facial beauty analysis. For example, computer assisted plastic surgery is an important possible application of facial beautification, so the corresponding 3D face beautification had better give plastic surgery suggestions with 3D geometrical measurement of facial organs, which is helpful for the operation. Moreover, if the system implements the corresponding function, people can see the result of a tentative plastic surgery scheme. Of course, the plastic surgery scheme can be adjusted based on the assistance of the system.

Besides the above challenges should be addressed, it is very useful to obtain more supervisors and subjective evaluations for better training supervised learning methods on beauty analysis. A feasible scheme is to issue a large number of facial images and to allow people to evaluate them via the internet. We can obtain labels or beauty indices of these facial images by collecting the subjective evaluation results. In order to obtain commonly agreed evaluation, the subjective evaluation results may be processed before they are be used. We can choose only the facial images whose subjective evaluation results are not very homogeneously distributed. A homogeneous distribution means that evaluation on the facial image of people severely diverges. By using the chosen facial images and corresponding subjective evaluation results, we can get a very large scale face beauty database. As a result, it is also possible to use more complex and competent algorithms such as the deep learning algorithm with a very deep layer to model the database. As we know, 'big data' is a basic condition to apply complex algorithms.

As for the methodology of beauty analysis, a new feasible approach is to integrate beauty analysis of facial organs such as the eyes, nose and mouth with holistic face beauty analysis. Also, we can take beautification of facial organs into account when performing facial beautification. According to human experience, beautification and plastic surgery of facial organs plays an important role in enhancing attractiveness of faces. This requires us to design dedicated beautification for a certain facial organ.

Another interesting issue closely associated with face beautification is selection of the hair style. To our knowledge, the hair style can influence attractiveness of faces especially female faces. In other words, a proper hair style will improve attractiveness of the face and vice versa. Thus, if a real-world face beautification system also has the function of selecting a suitable hair style, it will be more useful and practical.

To extract sex-associated beauty features is also an open and challenging problem. Some previous studies show that femininity can enhance the attractiveness of female faces. This partially illustrates that beauty features of males and females are different. On the other hand, we also see that some beauty features of males and females have no obvious difference. For example, there is no clear difference in the face shapes of beautiful males and females. As a result, to determine distinctive beauty features for male and female faces is very valuable for real world applications. It is also beneficial to enhance the consistence between the beauty index obtained using the system and human perception on male and female faces. However, this seems to be a uneasy task and many efforts should be made.

In summary, we may say that up to now the secret of facial beauty has been partially revealed through the endeavors of numerous researchers. However, we are still faced with challenges which are not only hard but also interesting. In the facial beauty analysis field, people have found a number of ways but strange perhaps better ways are yet to be found and deserve our continuous efforts, which is also the attractiveness of scientific exploration.

Index

D. Zhang et al., *Computer Models for Facial Beauty Analysis*,
DOI 10.1007/978-3-319-32598-9

Printed in the United States
By Bookmasters